ENDORSED BY

CAMBRIDGE
International Examinations

ECONOMICS

for Cambridge International AS & A Level

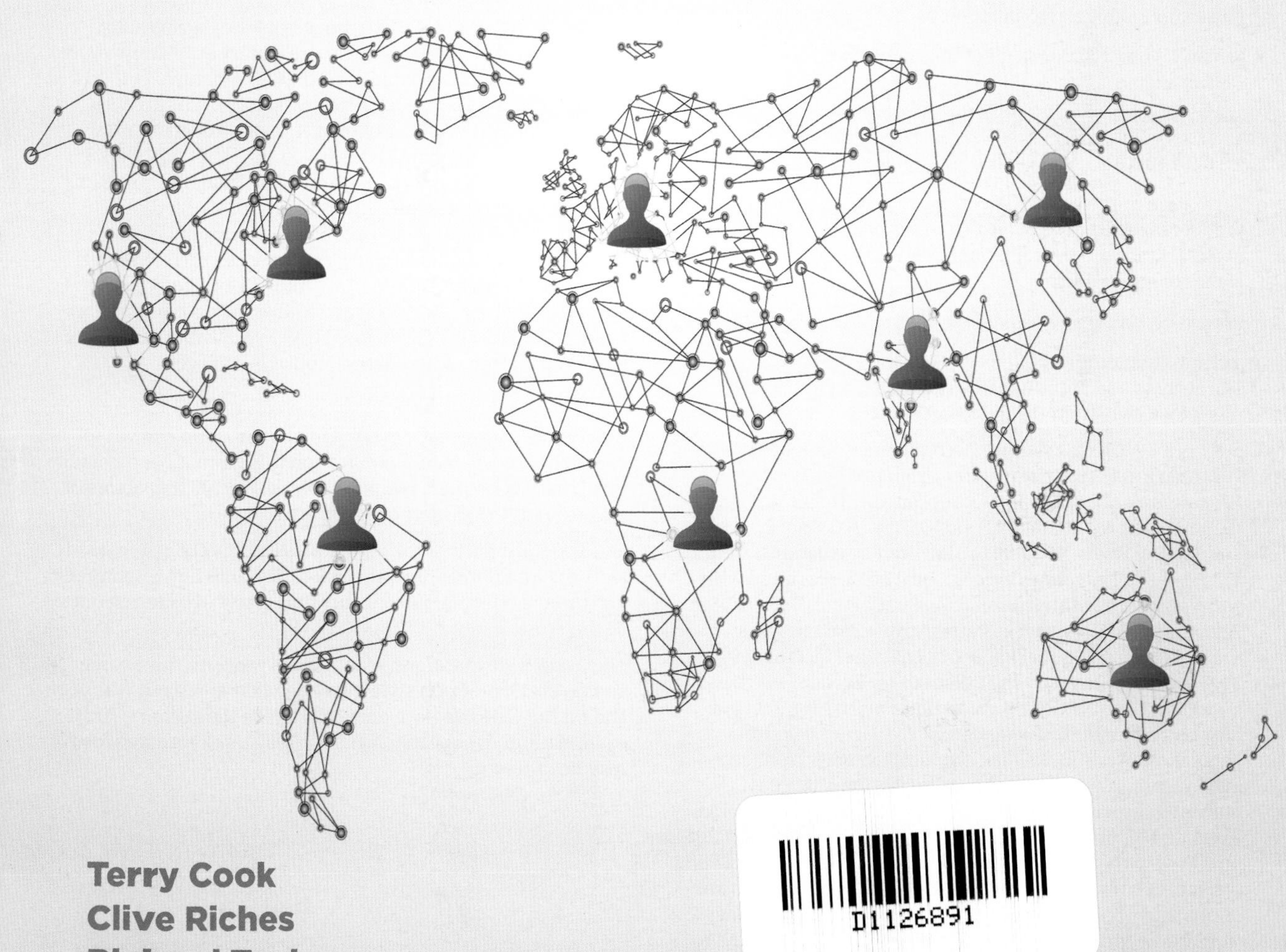

Terry Cook
Clive Riches
Richard Taylor

Oxford and Cambridge
leading education together

OXFORD
UNIVERSITY PRESS

OXFORD
UNIVERSITY PRESS

Great Clarendon Street, Oxford, OX2 6DP, United Kingdom

Oxford University Press is a department of the University of Oxford. It furthers the University's objective of excellence in research, scholarship, and education by publishing worldwide. Oxford is a registered trade mark of Oxford University Press in the UK and in certain other countries

First published in 2015

British Library Cataloguing in Publication Data
Data available

978-14-0-852711-5

1 3 5 7 9 10 8 6 4 2

MIX
Paper from responsible sources
FSC www.fsc.org FSC® C007785

Paper used in the production of this book is a natural, recyclable product made from wood grown in sustainable forests. The manufacturing process conforms to the environmental regulations of the country of origin.

Printed by Bell and Bain Ltd, Glasgow

Acknowledgements
The authors and publisher are grateful for permission to reprint extracts from the following copyright material:

p. 97 Figure 'China's Current Account and Components, 1971–2011' IMF staff calculations, from p. 43 of *World Economic Outlook*, April 2012, reprinted with permission of the International Monetary Fund (IMF). p. 105 Figure 'World Commodity Prices, 1970–2011', IMF staff calculations, from p. 125 of *World Economic Outlook*, April 2012, reprinted with permission of the International Monetary Fund (IMF). p. 256 Figure is based on/includes Statistics New Zealand's data (Figure 'Government debt and gross national income, 1994–2008') which is licensed by Statistics New Zealand for re-use under the Creative Commons Attribution 3.0 New Zealand licence, reprinted by permission. p. 261 Figure 'Mexico's population pyramid (age–sex diagram) for 2010' from geo-mexico.com, copyright Sombrero Books, Canada, 2011, reprinted by permission. p. 266 Figure 'Gross domestic product based on PPP' from *World Economic Outlook*, September 2011, reprinted with permission of the International Monetary Fund (IMF). p. 289 Bank of England, *The transmission mechanism of monetary policy*. p. 288 Figure 'Annual growth in money supply (M2)' from www.theglobaleconomy.com, reprinted by permission.

The publishers would like to thank the following for permissions to use their photographs:

Cover image: iconeer/iStock; p7: Aman Ahmed Khan/Shutterstock; p8: Hung Chung Chih/Shutterstock; p11 (B): RedTC/Shutterstock; p11 (T): c sa/Shutterstock; p17 (T): junrong/Shutterstock; p17 (BR): Paul Grover/Rex Features; p17 (BL): Adrian Sherratt/Rex Features; p19: Photographee.eu/Shutterstock; p21: Richard Thornton/Shutterstock; p25: Anthony Asael/Art in All of Us/Corbis; p28: Aman Ahmed Khan/Shutterstock; p31: American Spirit/Shutterstock; p33 (T): Thomas Cockrem/Alamy; p33 (B): Jeremy Horner/Alamy; p37: Owen Franken/Corbis; p38 (R): Jung Yeon Je/AFP/Getty Images; p38 (L): Pete Burana/Shutterstock; p61: urosr/Shutterstock; p65: Owen Franken/Corbis; p73: Paul Prescott/Shutterstock; p76: Paul Prescott/Shutterstock; p79: Christopher Pillitz/Getty Images; p82: Gallo Images/Getty Images; p86: View Pictures/Rex Features; p90: Steve Allen/Alamy; p96: View Pictures/Rex Features; p107: Bettmann/Corbis; p118: John Carnemolla/Corbis; p122: Robert Harding World Imagery/Getty Images; p124: S-F/Shutterstock; p126: Club4traveler/Shutterstock; p127: Robert Harding World Imagery/Getty Images; p133: Bettmann/Corbis; p136: Namas Bhojani/Bloomberg/Getty Images; p140 (T): Interfoto/Alamy; p140 (B): Monty Rakusen/Corbis; p146: Ross Land /Getty Images; p147: JEROME FAVRE/EPA/Corbis; p149: Namas Bhojani/Bloomberg/Getty Images; p151: Paul Kennedy/Alamy; p152: ERproductions Ltd/Blend Images/Corbis; p164: Simon Dack/Alamy; p165: Paul Kennedy/Alamy; p176: Egon Bomsch/Image Broker/Glow Images; p189: Degtyaryov Andrey/Shutterstock; p196: imagedb.com/Shutterstock; p198: BOB STRONG/AFP/Getty Images; p203: Owaki/Kulla/Corbis; p211: Robert Harding Picture Library Ltd/Alamy; p213: SS/Keystone USA/Rex Features; p215: VIEW Pictures Ltd/Alamy; p218: littlewormy/Shutterstock; p219: LAKRUWAN WANNIARACHCHI/AFP/Getty Images; p224: Robert Harding Picture Library Ltd/Alamy; p239 (R): Rune Hellestad/CORBIS; p239 (L): Beretta/Sims/Rex Features; p247: Imaginechina/Rex Features; p249 (T): junrong/Shutterstock; p249 (B): Global Warming Images/Rex Features; p253: Imaginechina/Rex Features; p265: Moment Open/Getty Images; p271: Hulton-Deutsch Collection/CORBIS; p287: Andy Dean Photography/Shutterstock; p289: Brooks Kraft/CORBIS; p297: Xinhua News Agency/Rex Features; p299: José Fuste Raga/Corbis; p306: José Fuste Raga/Corbis; p308: Harry Cabluck/AP Images.

Artwork by QBS Learning and OUP.

The exam-style questions, example answers, marks awarded and feedback on exam-style questions that appear in this book and on the CD-ROM have been written by the authors. In an examination, the questions and the way marks are awarded may be different.

Contents

Introduction

What is Economics?

There are many different definitions of Economics, but one of the best known is by Lionel Robbins (1898–1994) who stated that "Economics is the science which studies human behaviour as a relationship between ends and scarce means which have alternative uses". This definition stresses three important elements of the subject. First, it can be regarded as a science. Second, it is concerned with the concept of scarcity, both in terms of the possible consequences of scarcity and as ways in which it might be possible to try to deal with the problem of scarcity. Third, there are alternative ways in which scarce resources can be allocated, suggesting that choices will need to be made about how to utilise them in the most effective way.

The aims of the Cambridge 9708 syllabus

This book has been written specifically to meet the requirements of AS Level and A Level Economics for Cambridge. The Cambridge International AS and A Level syllabus has a number of distinct aims, enabling candidates to develop:

- an understanding of the factual knowledge of Economics
- a facility for self-expression, not only in writing but also in using additional aids, such as statistics and diagrams, where appropriate
- the habit of using works of reference as sources of data specific to Economics
- the habit of reading critically to gain information about the changing economy we live in
- an appreciation of the methods of study used by economics, and of the most effective ways economic data may be analysed, correlated, discussed and presented.

The content of the Cambridge 9708 syllabus

The Cambridge syllabus is divided into five topic areas:

1 Basic economic ideas and resource allocation

2 The price system and the micro economy

3 Government microeconomic intervention

4 The macro economy

5 Government macro intervention.

Each of the ten chapters in this book will focus on a particular curriculum topic area at either AS or A Level. Occasionally, A Level content is introduced in passing in AS Level chapters to help you contextualise the AS Level content you are learning. There is also a section at the end of the book focusing on preparing for an examination. Remember that AS + A = A Level.

How to use this book

This book is designed to cover information in a clear way that is easy to access. Its features include:

- **Learning objectives** to help you identify the main topics you will be covering in each chapter.
- **Key terms** and their definitions, which are identified throughout the book and also feature in a glossary.
- **Case studies** which identify up-to-date business practice from around the world. These also contain questions or activities to help you develop your understanding.
- **Getting it right** to help you identify common errors or misconceptions in examinations.
- **Progress questions** which will help you to remember what you have been learning in each chapter. Answers to some of these questions are featured on the CD-ROM.
- **Activities** which help you to look at the economic environment, often in your area or country. Many of these activities can be done individually, in pairs or in groups.
- **Links** to other chapters and content areas of the syllabus.
- **Key concepts** at the end of each chapter, which show how the key concepts from the syllabus are covered in each chapter (see key concepts section below).
- **Progress check** at the end of each chapter, to summarise what you should be able to do after completing the chapter.
- **Exam-style questions** to help you to reinforce what you have learnt in the chapter and to give you practice of the type of questions you can expect in an examination, although remember that there is no substitute for looking at questions from past papers.

The key concepts of the Cambridge 9708 syllabus

In addition to the five topic areas of the syllabus, there are also a number of key concepts. The key concepts are essential ideas, theories, principles or mental tools that will help you to develop a deeper understanding of the subject of Economics and make you better able to make links between the different topics in the syllabus.

The key concepts which run through the study of Economics are described below. These key concepts will be referred to throughout the course and can be used as helpful tools when considering both familiar and unfamiliar issues and contexts in Economics.

The key concepts of the Cambridge 9708 syllabus ▼

Key concept	Description
Scarcity and choice	The fundamental problem in Economics is that resources are scarce and wants are unlimited, so there is always a choice required between competing uses for the resources.
The margin and change	Decision-making by individuals, firms and governments is based on choices at the margin; that is, once behaviour has been optimised, any change will be detrimental as long as conditions remain the same.
Equilibrium and efficiency	Prices are set by markets, are always moving in and out of equilibrium, and can be both efficient and inefficient in different ways and over different time periods.
Regulation and equity	There is a trade-off between, on the one hand, freedom for firms and individuals in unregulated markets and, on the other hand, greater social equality and equity through the government regulation of individuals and markets.
Progress and development	Economics studies how societies can progress in measurable money terms and develop in a wider, more normative, sense.

CD-ROM

At the back of this book you will find a CD-ROM containing interactive resources to help you practice exam-style questions:

- **Test Yourself** multiple-choice questions, which reinforce learning for Papers 1 and 3.
- **On Your Marks,** which are worked exam-style questions that provide guidance on how to answer data response and essay questions for Papers 2 and 4.
- **A glossary,** which contains all the key terms you need to know for A Level Economics.
- **Ideas for answers** to odd-numbered progress questions, activities where it is possible to provide answers, and odd-numbered exam-style questions to help you review your progress and prepare for the examination.
- **Exam preparation,** which will help you prepare for success.

1 Basic economic ideas and resource allocation

In this chapter you will develop your knowledge and understanding of:

- scarcity, choice and opportunity cost
- positive and normative statements
- production possibility curves
- factors of production (land, labour, capital and enterprise)
- resource allocation in different economic systems and issues of transition
- money
- classification of goods and services.

Scarcity, choice and opportunity cost

The fundamental economic problem and the meaning of scarcity

The fundamental economic problem, which underlies all that is in this book, is that there are scarce resources to satisfy the unlimited wants and needs of people.

The resources are finite and yet the wants and needs of people are infinite. This is why scarcity is at the heart of economics. Skilled labour could be regarded as a scarce resource; there may be some unemployment in all economies, but highly skilled labour is always scarce in terms of the potential demand for it. If there was not a condition of scarcity, there would be no need to consider the different ways in which resources could be allocated. This is one of the key concepts on the Economics course.

Key terms

Economic problem: the situation of the relative scarcity of resources in relation to the unlimited wants and needs of people.
Scarcity: a condition where there are insufficient resources to satisfy all the needs and wants of people.

Getting it right

Do not confuse the existence of the economic problem, which underlies economics in all countries, with the existence of particular economic problems in specific countries, such as in relation to a high rate of inflation or a low rate of economic growth.

Economic goods and free goods

Strictly speaking, this basic condition of scarcity relates to economic goods (in this sense, goods can refer to both goods and services). An economic good is defined as a private good which has the feature of relative scarcity.

A free good, however, is one in which this situation of scarcity does not apply. There is a sufficient quantity of it to satisfy demand so that it is not necessary to involve an allocative mechanism. As free goods are not scarce, there is no cost involved in the consumption of them, unlike the consumption of an economic or private good. Examples of free goods include sunshine, air and sea water.

Of course, although air may be regarded as a good example of a free good, it may not necessarily be the case that fresh air is such a good example.

Key terms

Private or economic good: a private good that is relatively scarce and so will need to be allocated to a particular use in some way through an allocative mechanism.
Allocative mechanism: a method whereby scarce resources are distributed in an economy.
Free good: a good which is not scarce and so therefore does not need a mechanism to allocate it. The demand for the free good is equal to the supply of it at zero price.

The existence of pollution will affect the quality of air in a community ▲

Progress question

1 Discuss to what extent fresh air is a free good or an economic good.

The inevitability of choice

As a result of the economic problem, and particularly the existence of the condition of scarcity, decisions need to be made about the allocation of these scarce resources, i.e. a choice will need to be made between alternative possible uses of the scarce resources. Such choices will need to be made in relation to the variety of economic agents in an economy, such as individuals, firms and governments. Given the existence of limited resources and unlimited wants and needs, a choice is inevitable. This is why choice is one of the key concepts on this Economics course.

Needs and wants

The existence of needs and wants has already been referred to, but it is very important to distinguish between these two terms. A need is something of vital importance that is demanded, such as a need for food, shelter or clothing. A want is something of less crucial importance that is demanded, such as a new television or a new car.

Opportunity cost

The concept of opportunity cost enables the true cost of any choice that has to be made to be assessed. Opportunity cost is defined as the next best alternative that is foregone as a result of making a choice, i.e. when a decision is taken to produce one product with a given combination of resources, it is very clear what other products *cannot* be produced with those scarce resources. The concept can apply to both production decisions and consumption decisions.

Activities

Your own opportunity cost

1 You have to think about what you are going to do in a two-hour period of time this evening. Decide what you are going to do in that time and then make a list of the other things that you could have done in that time. Rank these in descending order of importance. The one that is at the top of the list of other possibilities is the opportunity cost of doing what you are going to do in the time, i.e. it is the *next best* alternative that you have decided to forego.

2 You have a certain amount of money that somebody has given you. Decide what you are going to do with that sum of money and then make a list of the other things that you could have bought with that money. Rank these in descending order of importance. The one that is at the top of the list of other things that you might have bought with the money is the opportunity cost of your decision to buy whatever you have decided to purchase, i.e. it is the *next best* alternative that you have decided to forego.

Activity

Scarcity

Working in groups, discuss which economic resources or factors of production are particularly scarce in your own country or in your region of the world.

Activity

Is air a free good?

Working in groups or as part of a class discussion, discuss whether or not fresh air in certain parts of the world really is an example of a free good.

Key terms

Choice: the need to make decisions about the possible alternative uses of scarce resources, given the existence of limited resources and unlimited wants and needs.

Needs: the demand for something that is essential, such as food or shelter.

Wants: the demand for something that is less important than the demand for a need, such as a new car, and which is not necessarily achieved by a consumer.

Opportunity cost: the cost of something in relation to a foregone opportunity, i.e. it indicates the benefits that could have been obtained by choosing the next best alternative.

Getting it right

Do not confuse a free good, such as air, with a good or service that is provided free by a government. For example, in some countries a visit to a hospital may be free in the sense that a patient does not pay a fee directly to the hospital, but it is still an economic good because the resources involved have alternative uses.

Link

Given the nature of the economic problem, the concept of opportunity cost can be related to many aspects of economics. For example, it is an important element in the theory of comparative advantage; see Chapter 4 pages 107–8.

Key term

Production possibility curve: a curve that joins together the different combinations of products that can be produced in an economy over a particular period of time given the existing resources and level of technology available. It can also be known as a **production possibility frontier**, a **production possibility boundary** or a **production transformation curve**.

Case Study

Opportunity cost

Governments in every country in the world need to take important economic decisions in terms of how they allocate scarce resources. A government will have a certain amount of money to spend on a variety of different areas and these could include education, health care, police, defence and national security, transport and infrastructure.

All of these areas of economic activity need vast amounts of money to be spent on them, but a country will only be able to budget for a certain amount of money to finance public expenditure. A government will need to take a number of difficult economic decisions, such as how much will be spent on health and how much on education.

For example, the UK government has decided to spend a great deal of money on the building of a new, high-speed rail service between London and Birmingham. This will then be continued on to more cities in the future. This will substantially reduce the journey time between these two cities, but if money is spent on this project, there is an opportunity cost in that the money cannot be spent on something else.

1 Explain how the decisions faced by governments indicate the concept of opportunity cost.
2 Discuss the implications of the UK government deciding to spend money on a high-speed rail link between London and Birmingham on other possible areas of public expenditure.

Production possibility curves

Opportunity cost and the production possibility curve

A production possibility curve (PPC) (it can also be called a production possibility frontier, a production possibility boundary or a production transformation curve) can be used to illustrate the idea of choice and the concept of opportunity cost. A PPC shows the maximum possible output or production that can be achieved in an economy given the use of a particular combination of resources and technology in a given time period.

If an economy is operating on its PPC, in order to increase the output of one type of product it will be necessary to reduce the output of the other. The two axes of the diagram can be labelled two different types of product and then a decision to move from one point on the PPC to another can be shown in terms of the changes in output of the two products.

Getting it right

You may be asked in a multiple-choice question to indicate that you understand the output that must be given up of one type of product, as a result of increasing the output of another.

Figure 1.1 shows the opportunity cost of moving from one point on a PPC to another.

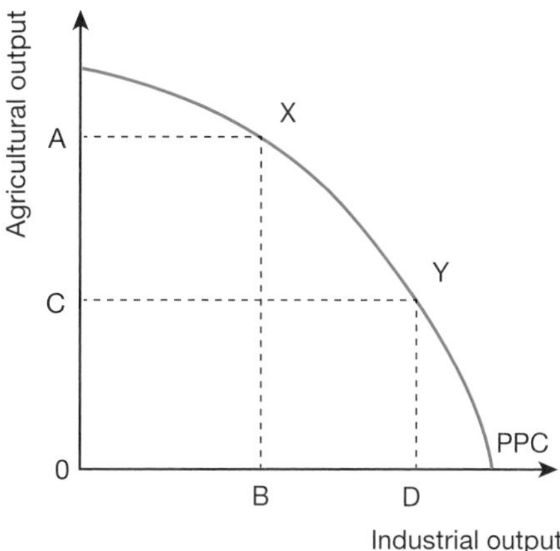

Figure 1.1 Opportunity cost and the production possibility curve ▲

An example of agricultural output ▲

An example of industrial output ▲

At point X, the economy is producing a combination of OA (in a diagram, the O indicates the origin) agricultural output and OB industrial output. If there is a movement down the PPC from point X to point Y, the new combination of production would be OC agricultural output and OD industrial output. In other words, as a result of this movement along the PPC, there has been a reduction of agricultural output by AC and an increase of industrial output by BD. This clearly shows that the opportunity cost of the decision to increase industrial output by BD is a loss in agricultural output of AC. The diagram therefore shows what the next best alternative would have been.

The choice between consumer goods and capital goods

Figure 1.2 shows the potential trade-off between allocating resources to the production of consumer goods and capital goods.

The allocation of resources to the production of consumer goods will be good for an economy in terms of current consumption today, but in the long run an economy will need to allocate resources to capital goods, a process known as investment.

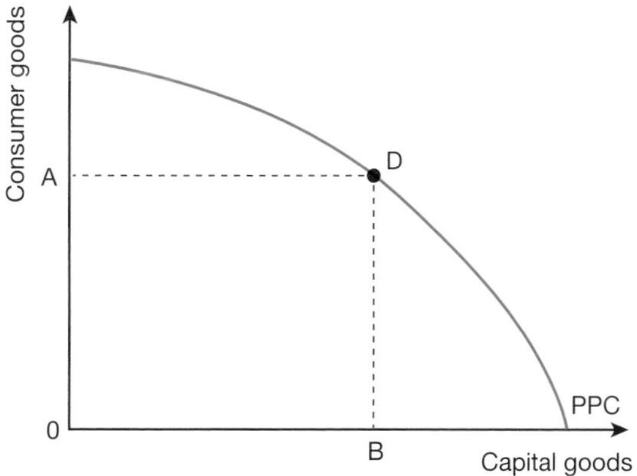

Figure 1.2 The choice between consumer goods and capital goods ▲

Key terms

Investment: the expenditure on capital goods or assets, not for current consumption but for future consumption. It broadly refers to spending now on an asset that should generate an income at some point in the future.
Fixed capital formation: investment in the form of buildings, plant, equipment, machinery and infrastructure.
Working capital: investment in the form of stocks of finished goods or semi-finished goods that will either soon be consumed or turned into finished consumer goods.

Link

The production possibility curve is a very helpful concept in the analysis of productive efficiency; see Chapter 6 pages 138–9.
The law of diminishing returns is explained in more detail in Chapter 7 page 169.

Key term

Increasing opportunity costs: this occurs when the extra production of one good involves ever-increasing sacrifices of another.

Investment is usually defined in terms of either fixed capital formation or working capital. Investment will lead to an improvement in a country's standard of living in the long run.

Microeconomics and macroeconomics

A production possibility curve can be used in relation to microeconomics and macroeconomics. For example, within microeconomics a PPC can be used to indicate the concept of opportunity cost or productive efficiency in a particular firm. Within macroeconomics a PPC can be used to show the extent of unemployment or the existence of economic growth in an economy.

The shape of a production possibility curve

As has already been indicated, a PPC shows the maximum combination of goods and services which can be produced in a particular time period given the existing resources and level of technology.

It might be thought that it could be drawn as a straight line, rather than as a curve, but this would only be the case if there were constant returns as economic resources were transferred from the production of one type of product to another, i.e. the amount of production sacrificed by one product and gained by the other are the same or constant.

In reality, this is unlikely to happen because of the law of diminishing returns. This means that as extra units of a resource are used in production, they will lead to successively smaller increases in output. This is why a PPC is drawn the way it is. This can be seen in Figure 1.1 on page 11. As resources are transferred from agricultural output to industrial output, the extra output of industrial production becomes successively smaller while the amount of agricultural production being sacrificed becomes successively larger. This is because not all factor inputs are equally suited to the production of different products.

Constant and increasing opportunity costs

As has been explained above, a production possibility curve is not drawn as a straight line. This is because of the distinction between constant and increasing opportunity costs. At some point along the curve, it would be possible to move from one point on the curve to another with an equal sacrifice of resources. This would indicate constant opportunity costs.

However, as a position is reached that is closer to the end of the production possibility curve, this is no longer the case. Ever increasing amounts of one will need to be sacrificed to produce more of the other. The reason for this is that different factors of production have different qualities. If a country concentrates more on the production of one good, it has to use an increasing amount of resources that are less suitable. The use of an increasing number of factors that are increasingly less suitable will lead to an increase in the marginal cost of production.

> **Links**
> Unemployment is discussed in Chapter 9 pages 268–76 and economic growth is considered in Chapter 9 pages 248–9.

> **Progress question**
> **2** Explain why a production possibility curve is not usually drawn as a straight line.

Shifts of a production possibility curve

Figure 1.1 (page 11) showed a movement from one point on a PPC to another, but it is also possible for there to be a shift of the whole PPC. This is shown in Figure 1.3, where there is a movement of the PPC to the right from PPC1 to PPC2. In this situation, an economy can produce more of both types of good.

> **Link**
> The law of diminishing returns is also covered at A Level, see Chapter 7 pages 169–70.

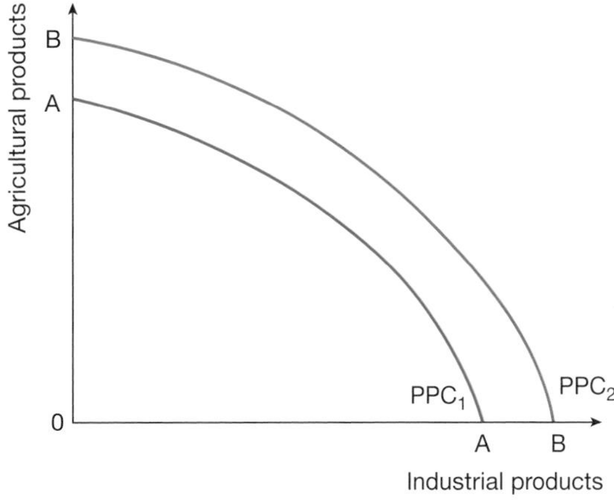

Figure 1.3 Capacity of an economy to produce agricultural and industrial products ▲

Table 1.1 indicates what can influence a shift of a PPC to the right.

Table 1.1 Causes of a shift of a PPC to the right ▼

Investment in improved technology	An improvement in technology could help to shift a country's PPC to the right. For example, if there was a move towards more intensive capital production, such as through making greater use of machinery, this should enable an economy to produce more. This improvement in technology should contribute to an increase in the productivity of labour. Such investment in capital equipment should increase an economy's future production potential or capacity.
Introduction of new resources	This could involve a new resource in terms of land, such as new mineral deposits. This would enhance the possibility of an economy to produce more.
Increase in the supply of labour	An increase in the size of a country's population would affect labour. For example, if the birth rate of a country substantially increased and/or there was a substantial increase in net migration into a country, this would increase the potential quantity of labour available for employment.
Improvements in human capital	It is not simply the quantity of labour that is important, but also the quality of labour. The skills of the labour force can be improved through education and training. This is sometimes referred to as an increase in human capital and this can also lead to an increase in the rate of productivity.
Improved management of resources	Changes in the system of production can lead to greater output. For example, if there is a greater degree of division of labour in the production process, the level of productivity should be improved.
Encouragement of an enterprise culture	A government could encourage the development of an enterprise culture by providing support to new firms, such as through financial support and/or the provision of appropriate information.

Of course, it is always possible that the PPC of an economy could shift to the left rather than to the right. For example, if there was net migration out of a country, reducing the labour supply, or if there was a reduction in the money provided by a government to education and training initiatives, possibly reducing the quality of the future labour force.

Progress question

3 Discuss the extent to which a country is able to shift its production possibility curve to the right.

A shift of a production possibility curve and economic growth

The shift of a country's PPC to the right, as shown in Figure 1.3 on page 13, can be used to illustrate the concept of economic growth. The shift from PPC1 to PPC2 shows that more of both goods can be produced, i.e. the productive capacity or potential of an economy has been increased.

Key term

Economic growth: an increase in the productive potential or real level of output of an economy. It is possible to distinguish between actual and potential growth in national output.

This increase in the productive capacity or potential of an economy can be linked to the key concepts of progress and development. Economic growth can lead to an increase in living standards and this will indicate the progress and development of a society.

Link

The concept of economic growth is examined more fully in Chapter 9 pages 248–9.

The meaning of the term "ceteris paribus"

One of the problems in regarding Economics as a science is that it would in practice be difficult to isolate certain behaviour from other possible influences. For example, in the case of the law of demand already referred to, it may be the case that there is a close correlation between changes in the price of a product and changes in the level of demand for the product, but there may well be other possible influences on the level of demand for the product other than changes in its price, such as changes in the income of people, changes in the prices of other products or the impact of an advertising campaign.

Economists, in dealing with this problem, isolate other possible influences so that it is possible to derive the law of demand. This gives rise to the idea of *ceteris paribus*. This Latin phrase translates as "all other things being equal". This means that to make it possible to derive economic laws or models of behaviour, certain variables should be isolated so that the link between them can be identified without other factors impacting on the relationship.

Key term

Ceteris paribus: literally "all other things being equal", i.e. the other factors which could influence a relationship between two variables are assumed to remain constant.

It has already been stated that it would be impossible to study economic behaviour in a laboratory, but the existence of *ceteris paribus* enables such behaviour to be studied with an element of control, similar to what does happen with scientific experiments in a laboratory.

Getting it right

The concept of *ceteris paribus* is extremely important in the study of Economics, especially in relation to the claim that it can adopt a scientific approach to study. Make sure that you fully grasp what the term means and that you can explain it.

Key terms

Margin: the point at which the last unit of a product is consumed or produced.
Short run: a period of time in which at least one factor of production is fixed in supply, and output can only be increased by using more of the variable factors.
Long run: a period of time when all factors are variable and output can be increased by using more of all factors.
Very long run: a time period when technical progress is taking place, affecting the ability of firms to supply. In the other two time periods, technical progress is held constant.
Positive statement: a statement that is based on factual evidence.

Getting it right

The concept of the margin is very important in Economics and you are likely to use this concept in a number of times. For example, the distinction between marginal utility and total utility is one which you will need to stress in any answer to a question on satisfaction.

Progress question

4 Can Economics be regarded as a science?

The margin and decision-making at the margin

Economists, when analysing decision-making, will tend to concentrate on decisions that are taken at the margin. This is the point at which the last unit of a product is consumed or produced. The discussion of constant and increasing opportunity costs pointed out that where increasing opportunity costs applied, the marginal cost of production would increase.

There are a number of examples of decision-making at the margin in Economics. For example, marginal cost refers to the additional cost of producing one more unit of a product. Marginal utility refers to the additional satisfaction gained from the consumption of one more unit of a product. The marginal efficiency of capital is the additional output produced by the last unit of capital investment that has been employed in the process of production.

It is for this reason that the margin was selected as one of the key concepts in this course. Decision-making by individuals, firms and governments is based on choices at the margin.

The short run, long run and the very long run

It is important to distinguish between three different time periods. The short run refers to a time period in which only some variables may change, i.e. some factors will be fixed and some will be variable.

The long run refers to a period of time when all factors of production may change.

The very long run is a time period when it is possible for supply to change as a result of technical progress. In the other two time periods, technical progress is said to be held constant.

Positive and normative statements

The distinction between facts and value judgements

Positive statement

A positive statement is one which is based on factual evidence, i.e. it will be objective rather than subjective. An emphasis on positive, rather than normative, statements reflects a broadly scientific approach to the study of Economics where facts can be discovered as a basis for producing theories of behaviour. This approach stresses the importance of the construction of appropriate models of behaviour in an attempt to predict future developments with a reasonable degree of accuracy.

Key terms

Normative statement: a statement that is based upon beliefs rather than on factual evidence.
Value judgement: a judgement that is a reflection of particular values or beliefs.

Activities

Positive or normative

Read the following statements and decide whether they are examples of positive or normative statements.

1. A government should intervene as much as possible in an economy.
2. A price index is used to measure the rate of inflation in a country.
3. A government ought to impose controls on all imports.
4. A national rail system ought to be controlled by the state.
5. Gross domestic product is the value of all that has been produced in an economy over a given period of time.
6. The external value of the country's currency should have been lowered last year.
7. More money should be spent on education than on health care.
8. Income tax is a direct tax.

Getting it right

Learners sometimes confuse normative and positive statements and the terms "subjective" and "objective". Make sure that you clearly understand the differences between them and can demonstrate this.

Normative statement

In contrast to a positive statement based on factual evidence, a normative statement is one which involves making a value judgement, i.e. an opinion that is based upon a belief rather than on factual evidence. This is usually referred to as a normative statement because the person expressing the judgement has based it on particular norms or values, i.e. it will be subjective rather than objective.

Factors of production

It has already been stressed that economic resources are scarce in relation to the infinite wants and needs of people in an economy. It is now necessary to establish exactly what is meant by economic resources. Economic resources can be divided into four factors of production.

The rewards to the factors of production

Land

This factor can also be referred to as the natural resources of an economy. It includes all that is on the surface of the earth, including forests, lakes and rivers. It also includes the mineral deposits of a country, such as coal or oil. It is sometimes referred to as the gifts of nature. The reward to land is rent.

Labour

This factor refers to the labour force of an economy, including both the physical and mental aspects of work. It therefore includes not only physical output but also the skills, knowledge and abilities (sometimes referred to as the intellectual capital) of the workforce. This factor is sometimes referred to as human capital and the size of it in any economy will depend on such influences as population size, the working age (i.e. the difference between the age at which people in a country can leave education and the age at which they retire) and the level of education and training of the workforce. It is important to note that the term "labour" includes not only those who are actually working in an economy, but also the potential workforce. The reward to labour is wages and salaries.

Key terms

Resources: the inputs used to produce goods and services.
Land: the factor of production that is concerned with the natural resources of an economy, such as farmland or mineral deposits.
Labour: the factor of production that is concerned with the workforce of an economy in terms of both the physical and mental effort involved in production.

Health workers are an example of the factor of production, labour ▲

Key terms

Capital: the factor of production that relates to the human-made aids to production.

Enterprise: the factor of production that takes a risk in organising the other three factors of production. The individual who takes this risk is known as an entrepreneur.

Getting it right

The term "capital", used in this sense as a factor of production, can often be confused with the capital or money that is used to purchase the aids to production. It is important to understand this difference in meaning.

Activity

Entrepreneurs

Select an entrepreneur, preferably from your own country or region of the world, and research what he or she has achieved and the skills used. You can then give a presentation to the class on what you have discovered about this person.

Capital

This factor can be referred to as the human-made aids to production, such as tools, machinery and equipment. It can also refer to buildings, such as factories. A distinction is sometimes made between fixed capital, such as machinery, and working capital, such as stocks of raw materials. The reward to capital is interest.

Enterprise

This factor refers to the role of the entrepreneur in combining, organising and coordinating the other three factors of production to enable production to take place and in doing so, takes a risk. This element of risk-taking is fundamental to the factor and distinguishes the entrepreneur from other workers. Enterprise is responsible for organising the other factors of production to promote efficiency and an increase in output. The reward to enterprise is profit.

Two entrepreneurs: James Dyson and Lakshmi Mittal ▲

The role of the factor enterprise in a modern economy

Enterprise plays a very significant role in a modern economy. Entrepreneurs are vital in organising the other factors of production and, in doing so, take a risk. This risk arises from the situation of uncertainty that will be associated with any initiative that they take.

Activity

Contributing to economic development

Research an entrepreneur in your own country and explain how this person has contributed to the economic development of your country. You can use the same entrepreneur that you used in the previous activity or choose a different one.

Case Study

The entrepreneur

Lakshmi Mittal is an Indian entrepreneur who founded the Mittal Steel Company in India. This is now part of Arcelor Mittal, a multinational company established in 2006. The company has steadily expanded and now produces in 14 countries worldwide. It has become a truly global steel company and produces about 10 per cent of the world's steel. It is by far the world's largest steel company, employing 239,000 workers in 2013. Mittal is the chief executive officer of the company and owns 40 per cent of the shares in the company. In 2012, he was ranked the 21st richest person in the world. He opened his first steel plant in India in 1976 at the age of 26. He was awarded the Entrepreneur of the Year Award by the *Wall Street Journal* in 2004, and in 2008 he received a Lifetime Achievement Award from *Forbes* magazine.

1 Discuss the role of Lakshmi Mittal in starting and expanding this business.

Key terms

Specialisation: the process by which individuals, firms, regions and whole economies concentrate on producing those products in which they have an advantage.

Division of labour: the process whereby workers specialise in, or concentrate on, particular tasks.

Specialisation and the division of labour

Specialisation

Specialisation can apply to an individual person, a particular firm, a specific district or region or, at the national level, to a whole country. It refers to the concentration on the provision of particular goods and services rather than other products. Specialisation allows, and indeed encourages, individuals, firms, regions or whole countries to concentrate on what they are best at producing; as a result of this specialisation, the production of such products will be increased.

The division of labour

One particular form of specialisation is the application of the principle to the work of particular individuals. Division of labour is the specialisation of economic activity by product or process.

A famous example of this was included in the book *An Inquiry into the Nature and Causes of the Wealth of Nations*, by the Scottish economist Adam Smith (1723–1790) in 1776. In this book, he applied the principle of the division of labour to production in a factory.

Activity

Specialisation

As an individual or in pairs, think of as many examples of specialisation as you can in your own country. These can be by individuals, firms, districts, regions or the whole country.

Link

The concept of specialisation is very important in international trade, especially in relation to the concept of comparative advantage. See Chapter 4 pages 106–18.

Case Study

Adam Smith

Adam Smith applied the concept of the division of labour to the production of pins in a factory. He argued that the production of pins could be broken down into 18 specific operations. If each worker concentrated on just one of these operations, rather than attempting to work on every one of the operations, production would rise significantly. Smith calculated that each worker would be able to produce about 5000 pins per day, a significant increase on the number that could be produced if each worker performed all 18 of the operations which he estimated might be only 20 pins a day.

In his book, *An Inquiry into the Nature and Causes of the Wealth of Nations*, Smith wrote: "The greatest improvement in the productive powers of labour, and the greater part of the skill, dexterity, and judgement with which it is anywhere directed, or applied, seem to have been the effects of the division of labour".

He went on: "One man draws out the wire, another straights it, a third cuts it, a fourth points it, a fifth grinds it at the top for receiving the head; to make the head requires two or three distinct operations; to put it on, is a peculiar business, to whiten the pins is another; it is even a trade by itself to put them into the paper."

1 Find out about a firm in your country that uses a production system based on the principle of division of labour.

Advantages and disadvantages of the division of labour

It has already been stated that one advantage of division of labour is that it enables production or output to be increased. It does, however, have a number of potential disadvantages. Table 1.2 indicates some of the various advantages and disadvantages of the division of labour.

Table 1.2 The advantages and disadvantages of the division of labour ▼

Advantages of the division of labour	Disadvantages of the division of labour
Saving of time: it can take a lot of time moving from one task to another in the production process. Division of labour helps to reduce this wastage of time and so can contribute to a reduction in costs.	Dependency on others: specialisation, through the division of labour, means that the process of production is divided into separate tasks, but there is a potential danger of one group of workers being held back by another group at a different part of the production process.
Application of technology is made easier: division of labour involves workers becoming specialists in particular tasks and this will make it easier to apply technology, such as machinery, to specific tasks.	Dependency on technology: although technology can be used to support workers, and enhance their skills, there is always the danger that the technology takes over and this may cause workers to become disaffected.
Increase in skill: division of labour enables workers to concentrate on particular tasks and this will enable the worker to become very skilled in these specific tasks. Repeated practice in the task will enhance efficiency and by concentrating on what they do best, workers will become highly motivated.	Frustration, boredom and alienation: by its very nature, division of labour involves workers in repetitive tasks and this may lead to a reduction in levels of motivation (some firms get round this by giving workers some degree of variety in what they do rather than getting them to do the same thing every day). If levels of motivation are reduced, this is likely to have a negative effect on the productivity of a worker.
Increased productivity: division of labour enables workers to specialise in particular tasks and, as a consequence, productivity, or the output per worker per time period, is likely to increase. If output is increased, this will lead to an improvement in the standards of living of economies.	Over-concentration on particular skills: division of labour is based on the idea that workers concentrate on using particular skills, but there is a danger that this focus on certain skills could be at the expense of other useful skills that are not being encouraged.
The potential to earn higher earnings: an individual worker who is highly skilled and well motivated is in a better position to try to secure higher earnings (this will, of course, depend on a number of other factors, such as the profitability of the firm).	Unemployment: specialisation, through division of labour, is useful as long as there is a demand for the particular skills of workers, but there is a danger that if the demand for such skills decreases, some workers may find themselves unemployed. This would be less of a problem if the workers soon found alternative employment (this would be frictional unemployment), but if the demand for such skills applies to a whole industry, it may be very difficult for the workers to find alternative employment (this would be structural unemployment).

Getting it right

There are both advantages and disadvantages of the division of labour and you should be prepared to answer a question on the topic from both points of view. It would also be helpful to consider the advantages and disadvantages from the perspective of the worker, the firm and the national economy.

Link

See Chapter 9 on the different types of unemployment on pages 272–3.

Progress question

5 Discuss the advantages and disadvantages of division of labour to (a) an individual worker, (b) an individual firm and (c) to the whole economy.

The three fundamental questions

The key elements of the economic problem have already been referred to in this chapter and it is now necessary to focus on the three basic questions that need to be asked in every economy.

What will be produced?

It is important to consider in every economy what is going to be produced and how much will be produced. There is therefore a process of selection involved in terms of what products will be produced in an economy. Figure 1.1 on page 11 has already indicated this in terms of decisions about how many agricultural products and industrial products to produce in an economy.

How will it be produced?

It has already been made clear that the production process involves the combination of four factors of production – land, labour, capital and enterprise. However, it is still necessary to consider how these four factors will be coordinated to produce what is required in an economy, i.e. which methods of production will be used.

For whom will it be produced?

The key feature of the economic problem is that it is impossible to satisfy all the wants and needs of all the people in a country in the same period of time. It is therefore necessary to consider who is going to receive what, i.e. decisions need to be taken in terms of priorities in the process of distribution.

Resource allocation in different economic systems and issues of transition

These three fundamental questions can be answered in different ways depending on the type of economic system in existence in a country. There are three main types of economic system in existence in the world and they each use different allocative mechanisms to decide on how the scarce resources should be used.

Key terms

Economic system: the way in which a particular country attempts to answer the basic economic problem.

Market: a means of bringing together buyers and sellers to exchange products. A market can exist in a physical sense, but it can also be used to refer to an exchange of goods and services through the internet or by telephone.

Decision-making in market economies

This type of economic system (also known as a free enterprise economy) is characterised by a very low level of state or government intervention in the economy. In theory, there will be no state intervention and everything will be controlled by the private sector. However, in reality, there are no countries in the world without some form of state intervention. The USA is sometimes regarded as a good example of a market economy, but even in that country the government will intervene in a number of ways. For example, the rail system Amtrak is state-owned.

Case Study

Amtrak

In many economies, there has been a move away from passenger rail transport being organised in the public sector towards a greater role for the private sector, a process generally known as privatisation.

In the USA, however, there has been an opposite trend. Rail passenger transport had generally been provided by private sector firms, but by the 1960s these firms found themselves in severe financial difficulties. In 1970, the Rail Passenger Service Act was passed and on 1 May 1971 Amtrak came into existence (the name Amtrak comes from the words "America" and "track").

Today, it employs 19,000 people and operates passenger services on 21,000 miles of track connecting 500 destinations in 46 states. In 2012, it had 30.2 million passengers.

1 Discuss the advantages and disadvantages of a national government running a rail passenger service.

Key term

Market economy: also known as a market system, this is the type of economic system where decisions about the allocation of resources are taken in the private sector by producers and consumers.

Price mechanism: the process by which changes in price (resulting from changes in demand and/or supply) bring about changes in the allocation of resources in a free market economy.

In market economies:

- decisions are made by individual sellers and buyers who can generally be expected to act in their own self-interest
- the producers' main aim is to maximise their profits
- the consumers' main aim is to maximise their satisfaction or utility, giving rise to the idea of consumer sovereignty
- the allocation of resources is determined by the market forces of demand and supply through what Adam Smith termed the "invisible hand" of the price mechanism
- there is no, or certainly very little, state or government intervention.

•International diplomacy

Table 1.3 shows the advantages and disadvantages of this type of economic system.

Table 1.3 The advantages and disadvantages of market economies ▼

Advantages of market economies	Disadvantages of market economies
Resources are allocated through market forces and the operation of the price mechanism; there is therefore no need for state or government intervention in the economy, and the state can then concentrate on areas such as international diplomacy.	Some goods, called public goods, would not be provided in a market economy. Examples of these would include the provision of police and defence forces.
In a market economy, the key objective of producers is profit maximisation and the profit motive can give an incentive to sellers; they will be encouraged to be more innovative and cost-effective than might otherwise have been the case.	Some goods, called merit goods, would be under-produced and under-consumed in a market economy. Examples of these would include the provision of education and health services.
If firms can be more cost-effective in such an economy, this should lead to lower prices for consumers. Consumers would also be likely to benefit from more choice.	Some goods, called demerit goods, would be over-produced and over-consumed in a market economy. Examples of these would include the production and consumption of alcohol (in some countries) and tobacco.
The market economy, based on the idea of free enterprise, will maximise both producer surplus and consumer surplus.	There could be negative externalities in a market economy. Examples of these would include noise and visual pollution.

Decision-making in planned or command economies

This type of economic system is characterised by a very high level of state or government intervention in the economy. In theory, there will be no private sector involvement and everything will be controlled by the public sector. However, in reality there are no countries in the world without some form of private sector involvement. North Korea is sometimes regarded as the country that comes nearest to this type of economic system.

In planned or command economies:

- economic decisions are primarily made by the state or government through some form of central planning agency, rather than through the operation of market forces
- the state or government will own all, or certainly most, of the economic resources
- the prices are generally determined by the state rather than the price mechanism
- the key aim of production is the maximisation of social welfare rather than profit.

Link

Public, merit and demerit goods are explained on pages 30–5. Externalities will be explained more fully in Chapter 6 on pages 141–6.

Key term

Planned or command economy: the type of economic system where decisions about the allocation of resources are taken by the state or by government agencies.

Table 1.4 shows the advantages and disadvantages of this type of economic system.

Table 1.4 The advantages and disadvantages of planned or command economies ▼

Advantages of planned or command economies	Disadvantages of planned or command economies
The state or government controls all, or at least most, of the economic resources and so economic decisions can be taken in the interests of the whole society. For example, it might be the policy of such a government to bring about a more equitable distribution of income and wealth in the society.	The economic system tends to be very bureaucratic because the government intervenes in so many areas. This can contribute to the system being very inflexible and unresponsive to changes in consumer demand.
The state or government can decide which goods are going to be produced and to whom they are going to be supplied. For example, it could decide to ban the production of products which it believes are against the public interest.	There is less of an incentive for firms to be innovative. The profit motive is not as important as in a market economy and, as a result, the variety of goods on offer is often rather restricted and sometimes the products are of poor quality.
	The majority of firms will be state owned and the lack of competition means that there is often a high level of inefficiency and a low level of productivity.

Decision-making in mixed economies

It should be clear that while both market and planned economies have a number of advantages, they also have considerable disadvantages. It is for this reason that the majority of economic systems in the world today are mixed economies, i.e. they combine elements of both a market economy and a planned economy. Both the private sector and the public sector are involved in the taking of economic decisions. The broad idea is that such an economy will maximise the advantages of both market and planned economies and minimise the disadvantages.

In mixed economies:

- ownership of the economy's resources is divided between the public sector and the private sector
- the private sector will be influenced by self-interest, with producers aiming to maximise profits and consumers aiming to maximise their welfare, whereas the public sector will have broader, community aims relating to the public interest
- there will (possibly) be competition within the private sector, whereas the public sector will intervene through such measures as taxation and regulation
- the allocation of resources in the private sector will be determined through the price mechanism, whereas in the public sector decisions will be taken by the government, with prices either free at the point of use or in the form of certain charges.

Key term

Mixed economy: the type of economic system where decisions about the allocation of resources are taken in both the private sector and the public sector.

Getting it right

Mixed economies are not static, i.e. the extent of the mixture changes over the years. Sometimes there is a trend towards more state intervention and sometimes a trend in the other direction. In 2008–9, a number of financial institutions in different countries experienced difficulties and many of these were supported by the governments of such countries, indicating a trend towards more state intervention in the economy.

Progress question

6 To what extent do you think a government should intervene if a firm in its country was facing financial difficulties and needed state support to avoid collapsing?

Case Study

Mauritius

Mauritius is a small island in the Indian Ocean with a population of just over 1 million people. Many important economic decisions are taken by both producers and consumers and in many ways it can be seen as an example of a market economy.

The government of Mauritius, however, has been prepared to intervene in the economy. For example, it has developed a strategy to encourage the economic development of the country. Sugar cane is grown on about 90 per cent of the cultivated land area, accounting for 15 per cent of export earnings, and the government has provided financial support to increase the area of fertile soil for growing the cane.

Another example is the decision of the government to put a maximum limit on water use at certain times of the year when there is a water shortage.

1 Research your own country and find out the extent to which the state intervenes in the economy.

Issues of transition when central planning in an economy is reduced

In a number of countries, there has been a move away from planned economies towards economies with a greater role for the market. This has particularly been the case in the former communist countries of Eastern Europe and it has also been a feature of economic developments in the People's Republic of China. The World Bank, an international organisation which aims to support developing economies, has encouraged such economic changes.

Key term

Transitional economy: an economy that is in the process of changing from a planned or command economy to more of a mixed economy where market forces have greater importance.

A transitional economy is one which is in the process of changing from a planned or command economy towards a more market-focused economy, but there have been problems associated with this process of transition. These are shown in Table 1.5.

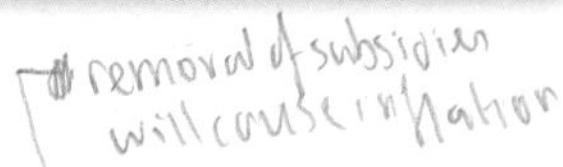

Table 1.5 The issues of transition ▼

Inflation	Planned economies tended to keep prices relatively low, but when the economy allowed a greater role for market forces, the state could no longer control prices in the way that it previously did. One possible effect of this is that the rate of inflation in a transitional economy could be higher than that experienced in a planned economy, although of course it is possible that the general level of prices in such an economy could fall, a situation known as deflation. Either way, a government will have less control than used to be the case in a planned economy.
Industrial unrest	Trade unions had largely limited powers in a planned economy, but once state control was reduced, the trade unions demanded wage rises to match the increases in prices and these demands were backed up by strike action. There is therefore the possibility of more working days being lost in a transitional economy than in a planned economy as a result of this industrial action.
International trade	The various planned economies had been in a trading bloc, but as they moved towards market economies they needed to establish new trading relationships with other countries. Transitional economies have a greater degree of freedom in terms of which countries they trade with, but this could possibly cause problems, such as an imbalance between exports and imports, leading to a deficit in the current account of the balance of payments.
Employment	In many of the former planned economies, there have been changes in the employment structure, such as a move from the secondary to the tertiary sector. Many workers were unable to move from one form of employment to another and so the rate of unemployment in many of the countries increased significantly, leading to a fall in incomes. The rate of unemployment in planned economies tended to be very low, but the rate is likely to be much higher in a transitional economy.
Output	When the economies had a great deal of state intervention, many firms were supported by the government, but when a greater degree of market forces were introduced, a number of these firms were unable to survive. There was therefore a consequent fall in output. The level of output in a transitional economy will depend on the demand for the various products and so it is quite possible that a number of firms will fail to survive.

Continued . . .

Reduction in welfare services	The planned economies had generally had a good level of welfare provision, such as in education, housing and health care, but as the economies moved towards a larger role for the market, some groups of people found that there was a fall in the quality of their standard of living.
Markets	When these countries had planned economies, the vast majority of decisions were taken by the state. Once the role of the state was reduced, and greater market forces introduced, it was recognised that specialised markets and services needed to be significantly improved, such as in banking and legal services. In many of the transitional economies, the quality of banking and legal services is still relatively poor.

Case Study

Change in Eastern Europe and China

Dismantlement of USSR

In Russia and eastern Europe, at the end of the 1980s and the beginning of the 1990s communism collapsed and the economic systems have gone through a process of transition away from a command or planned economy towards more of a market economy. There was less state intervention and control and more economic decisions were taken by producers and consumers. In some of these countries, such as Poland and Hungary, the move towards a greater role for market forces has led to greater efficiency and there have been significant increases in income and output. In some countries, however, such as Bulgaria and Ukraine, the process of transition has been more painful; the rate of unemployment, for example, is now significantly higher than it was at the end of the 1980s.

China has also experienced significant change since the late 1990s. It remains a communist country, in which the state still plays an important role, but there has been a process of transition allowing market forces to have a greater influence on economic decisions. The annual rate of economic growth averaged 10.5 per cent in the period between 2006 and 2011.

Entrepreneurs have been encouraged to set up businesses and there has been a great deal of investment in the economy, both from Chinese and foreign investors. The high rate of economic growth, however, has been associated with environmental concerns and there has also been a worry that the high rate of growth could lead to increases in the rate of inflation.

China overtook Japan in 2011 as the world's second-largest economy by gross domestic product ($bn):

1	USA	$15065
2	China	$ 7319
3	Japan	$ 5867
4	Germany	$ 3629
5	France	$ 2808
6	Brazil	$ 2518
7	UK	$ 2445
8	Italy	$ 2246
9	Russia	$ 1885
10	India	$ 1873

Source: The World Factbook (www.cia.gov/library/publications/the-world-factbook)

1 Discuss the possible advantages and disadvantages of an economy moving away from a planned or command structure towards more of a market economy.

Economic structure

The economic structure relates to the fact that any economy can be divided into a number of different sectors. There are three such sectors although one of them (the secondary sector) is often divided into two parts.

Key term

Primary sector: refers to all activities in an economy that are concerned with extraction, such as agriculture.

The primary sector

The primary sector is concerned with extractive activities and examples would include forestry, fishing, agriculture, mining, quarrying and oil extraction.

Key terms

Secondary sector: refers to all activities in an economy that are concerned with either manufacturing, such as the production of televisions, or construction, such as the building of an airport runway.

Tertiary sector: refers to all activities in an economy that are concerned with services, such as tourism.

Gross domestic product (GDP): the total value of all goods and services produced in a country over a given period of time, usually one year.

The secondary sector

The secondary sector can be divided into two parts. Firstly, it is concerned with manufacturing activities and examples would include car production, computers and textiles. Secondly, it is concerned with construction activities and examples would include the building of roads, houses and factories.

The tertiary sector

The tertiary sector is concerned with the various services that are provided in an economy, such as financial services, education and health.

Countries vary enormously in the division of their economy into these three distinct sectors. Table 1.6 shows the division of a range of countries into these three sectors on the basis of the contribution of the different sectors to the country's gross domestic product. Table 1.7 shows the division according to the proportion of the workforce that work in the different sectors.

Table 1.6 The economic structure of selected countries in terms of contribution to GDP ▼

Country	Primary sector	Secondary sector	Tertiary sector
Argentina	8%	32%	60%
Bangladesh	19%	29%	52%
Brazil	6%	25%	69%
China	10%	46%	44%
Egypt	14%	37%	49%
Indonesia	16%	49%	35%
Malaysia	10%	44%	46%
New Zealand	5%	24%	71%
Pakistan	22%	24%	54%
Singapore	0%	26%	74%

Source: The World Factbook (www.cia.gov/library/publications/the-world-factbook)

Table 1.7 The economic structure of selected countries in terms of the proportion of the workforce that work in the different sectors ▼

Country	Primary sector	Secondary sector	Tertiary sector
Argentina	1%	24%	75%
Bangladesh	52%	14%	34%
Brazil	19%	21%	60%
China	41%	25%	34%
Egypt	31%	22%	47%
Indonesia	41%	19%	40%
Malaysia	15%	29%	56%
New Zealand	7%	22%	71%
Pakistan	44%	21%	35%
Singapore	0%	23%	77%

Source: The World Factbook (www.cia.gov/library/publications/the-world-factbook)

Progress question

7 In some of these countries, the figures in the two tables are very similar, but in some of them, the figures are very different. Explain why this may be the case.

Activities

Three sectors

Research your own country and find out information about:

1 the size of the three sectors
2 the change in the size of the three sectors over the last hundred years.

The economic structure and the development of a country

The figures for the size of the primary, secondary and tertiary sectors in any particular country will not be static, but will change over a period of time as a country becomes more developed. It would be expected that the size of the primary sector would fall, the size of the secondary sector would first grow and then shrink and the size of the tertiary sector would continually grow.

Money

Barter and the development of money

Money can be defined as anything which is generally acceptable as a means of payment. Before the development of money, barter was used. This involves the direct exchange of goods and services without the use of any monetary mechanism.

Barter had a number of distinct disadvantages:

- it required a double coincidence of wants, i.e. one person offering a good or service needs to find someone who wants that good or service *and* that person also needs to be offering something in exchange that the seller wants
- it was often difficult to compare the value of different goods and services
- the products may be indivisible, e.g. in the case of animals
- the products may be difficult to store while a seller is looking for an appropriate buyer.

These various disadvantages of barter meant that economies moved towards the development of money which would avoid the direct exchange of goods and services.

Key terms

Money: usually defined as anything which is universally acceptable as a means of payment for goods and services and a settlement of debt. Not all coins in an economy, however, may be acceptable for all transactions; the term "legal tender" indicates if coins are only acceptable up to a specified amount.

Barter: the direct exchange of one good or service for another.

Double coincidence of wants: the situation where, in a barter system of exchange, a seller needs to find a buyer who not only wants what the seller is selling, but also has something that the buyer wants.

Progress question

8 Discuss why money is a more effective means of exchange in an economy than barter.

Getting it right

You need to be able to clearly explain why money is preferred to barter as a means of exchange.

Cash and bank deposits, cheques, near money and liquidity

Although money has largely replaced barter, it is still necessary to appreciate what is, and what is not, money.

The most obvious form of money is cash, whether in the form of notes or coins. Some money, however, may only be acceptable in transactions up to a certain amount and this is referred to as legal tender. This means that it must be accepted legally as a means of payment.

Much money, however, is in the form of bank deposits, i.e. money deposited in banks, building societies, credit unions and other financial institutions. These monetary deposits can be in current accounts or various forms of savings account.

Near money, or quasi money as it is sometimes called, refers to an asset that is immediately transferable into money and so can be used to settle some, but not all, debts. Near money, therefore, is able to fulfil some of the functions of money, but not all of them. For example, it cannot be used as a medium of exchange.

The ability to turn an asset into cash refers to its liquidity. Cash is the most liquid form of asset. The more liquid an asset, the easier it is to convert it into money.

It is important to know not only what money is, but also what it is not. For example, a cheque is sometimes believed to be a form of money, but this is incorrect as a cheque is simply a means of payment and is not actually a form of money.

The functions of money

Money is said to perform four essential functions in an economy and these are as follows:

- a medium of exchange
- a measure of value or unit of account
- a standard for deferred payment
- a store of value or wealth.

A medium of exchange

A very important function of money is that it operates effectively as a means of exchange. Money is generally accepted as a means of payment for goods and services. This is the great advantage of money over barter, i.e. it overcomes the problems associated with the need to have a double coincidence of wants between two people.

A measure of value or unit of account

This function of money can either be described as a measure of value or as a unit of account. This is the idea that money enables the value of different goods and services to be compared. The direct exchange of goods and services in a barter system made it very difficult to give a valuation of the different products being traded. This function of money makes it possible to compare the value of different goods and services.

Key terms

Bank deposits: money that is held in accounts with a financial institution, such as a bank, building society, credit union or friendly society.
Cash: the notes and coins in existence in an economy. This is the most liquid form of asset.
Near money: an asset that can easily and quickly be transferred into money, but is not actually money. Sometimes known as "quasi money".
Liquidity: a term used to indicate when a financial asset is turned into cash. Cash is 100 per cent liquid, but a three-year bond will be less liquid than a one-year bond because there is a longer period of time to its maturity, i.e. when it can be changed into cash.
Cheques: are often used as a method of payment, but a cheque is simply a written instruction to a financial institution to pay an amount of money from an account; a cheque is therefore not a form of money.

Money ▲

A standard for deferred payment

Money enables people to borrow money and pay it back at a later date. This encourages the provision of credit and so acts as an incentive to trade. Buyers are able to consume goods and services immediately, but the payment can be spread over a period of time. This was a major limitation of the barter system.

A store of value or wealth

A final function of money is that it enables wealth to be stored in the form of money. Compared to the barter system, money does not physically deteriorate and it is usually not expensive to store it, although this function of money does face the problem of a possible deterioration in its value if there is a situation of inflation in an economy as inflation erodes the value or purchasing power of a given sum of money over a period of time.

Link

See the discussion of inflation and its effects in Chapter 4 pages 90–3.

Money and economic progress

The development of money in terms of these four functions has contributed to economic progress over the centuries as it has allowed greater opportunities for specialisation and division of labour, leading to an increase in output and higher standards of living.

The characteristics of money

Money has a number of distinctive characteristics and these are outlined in Table 1.8.

Table 1.8 The characteristics of money ▼

Characteristic	Explanation
Acceptability	Money needs to be generally acceptable in an economy if it is going to be used to facilitate the exchange of goods and services.
Divisibility	Money in an economy needs to be divided into smaller units, especially so that cheaper items can be bought and sold. This division into smaller units is explained by the term "denominations". For example, in Mauritius, the Mauritian rupee is divided into 100 cents.
Portability	Any money needs to be portable if it is going to be convenient for the users of it.
Durability	Money needs to be relatively durable if it is going to be acceptable although, of course, bank notes will eventually need to be replaced by newly printed ones.
Scarcity	Money needs to be relatively scarce; if it literally did "grow on trees", it would soon become worthless.
Stability of supply	As well as being relatively scarce, there also needs to be a stability of supply over a long period of time.
Recognisability	Money needs to be easily recognisable in an economy and this contributes to confidence in it.
Uniformity	It is necessary that each particular coin or note being used in an economy is uniform, i.e. has exactly the same value.
Stability of value	It is important that money has a reasonable degree of stability of value over a period of time, although inflation will erode the value or purchasing power of money over time.

Getting it right

Make sure that you do not get the characteristics and the functions of money confused, although, of course, the characteristics are necessary for money to function effectively in an economy.

Classification of goods and services

The distinction between free goods and economic goods has already been covered earlier in this chapter. It is now necessary to consider other ways of classifying goods and services in an economy.

Private goods

A private good, or economic good, is a product which has two essential characteristics: it is both rival and excludable. Examples of a private good would include a bicycle, a car or an item of clothing.

> **Key terms**
>
> **Rival**: a rival good is one where if one person consumes a good, there is less available for others.
>
> **Excludable**: a situation that exists when a price is charged for a good. It will be excluded from those who are unable and/or unwilling to pay this price.
>
> **Public good**: a good which has the two characteristics of being "non-rival" and "non-excludable".

Rival

A good that is said to be rival means that when one person consumes a product, it reduces the quantity available to others.

Excludable

A good that is said to be excludable means that a producer can exclude consumers from using a particular product by charging a price for the product.

Public goods

A public good is the opposite of a private good. It also has two essential characteristics: non-rival and non-excludable. Examples of a public good would include the following:

- street lighting
- a lighthouse
- a flood control system

Non-rivalness or non-rival

Non-rivalness (or non-rival) means that if one person consumes a product, it does not reduce the extent of its availability to other people (the opposite of the case with a private good). As more people consume the product, it is impossible to stop all the other consumers from benefiting from it.

> **Key terms**
>
> **Non-rivalness or non-rival**: if one person consumes a product, it does not reduce the extent of its availability to other people.
>
> **Non-excludability or non-excludable**: if a public good is produced, it is not possible to exclude any person from its use.
>
> **Free rider**: a person who has no incentive to pay for the use of a public good because there can be consumption without any payment being made.

Non-excludability or non-excludable

Non-excludability means that if a public good is produced, it is *not* possible to exclude any person from its use (the opposite of the case with a private good), i.e. it is not possible to prevent other people from benefiting from the consumption of the good.

The free rider problem

As a result of the characteristic of non-excludability, the benefits gained from the production and consumption of public goods could not be limited to those who had paid for it if a price was charged for the product in a market, i.e. it would be impossible to exclude those who had not paid for the product. This is known as the free rider problem and it is a significant reason why a price cannot be charged for such a product.

Non-rejectability

Some economists have added a third characteristic of a public good to those of non-rivalness and non-excludability. This is the idea of non-rejectability, i.e. that certain public goods cannot be rejected. A police force would be an example of this; everybody in a society would benefit from the existence of a police force (except the criminals!) because it would help to deter crime. The armed forces of a country would be another such example as the existence of these would help to deter an attack on, or an invasion of, a country.

Key term

Non-rejectability: the idea that certain public goods cannot be rejected, such as the police force or the armed forces of a country.

Progress question

9 Explain the difference between a private good and a public good.

Activity

Private and public goods

Working in groups, think about the possible consequences of providing street lighting and a police force as a private, rather than as a public, good in an economy, i.e. by charging a market price for them.

Public goods and market failure

It should be clear that private goods can be provided through a market because a price is charged for its consumption. In the case of a public good, however, because of the characteristics of non-rivalness and non-excludability, it would not be possible to charge a price for it in a market and so it would not be produced in a market economy. This is why a country's police force and armed forces are usually provided by the state or government.

Activity

Quasi-public goods

Working in groups, think of three examples of quasi-public goods.

Quasi-public goods

It is possible to distinguish between private goods and public goods, but some goods are somewhere in-between the characteristics of the two types of goods. These goods are called quasi-public goods (the word "quasi" meaning near or almost).

Case Study

Nairobi National Park

Nairobi National Park is a national park in Kenya. It was the first national park in Kenya, established in 1946. It is located about 7 kilometres (4 miles) outside Nairobi, the capital city of Kenya. It covers an area of 117.21 square kilometres or 28,963 acres.

A national park that is open to all, without the requirement for any payment for entry, would be non-excludable. Given its large size, a national park could also be seen as non-rival because there is enough space for everybody to enjoy the park.

On the other hand, a national park could be regarded as excludable if a payment was required to enter it. It could also be regarded as rival in that if too many people entered the park at the same time, space would become increasingly limited and this could adversely effect the enjoyment of the people visiting the national park.

1. Describe the characteristics of a private good and a public good.
2. To what extent do you think a national park, such as the one near Nairobi, is an example of a quasi-public good?

Merit goods and demerit goods

Merit goods

A merit good is a product which, like a private good, has the characteristics of being rival and excludable, but if provided in a market economy, would be likely to be under-produced and under-consumed. The reason for this is because people may not be aware of the potential benefits of the product to themselves, or underestimate such benefits, and may also not be aware of the potential benefits of the consumption of such goods to the whole society, i.e. they fail to take into account the possible external benefits of the consumption of such goods. Merit goods are therefore the outcome of imperfect information held by consumers. Examples of a merit good would include education, public libraries, health care and museums.

> **Key terms**
>
> **Merit good**: a product which has positive externalities, but which would be under-produced and under-consumed in a market economy as a result of the imperfect information held by consumers.
>
> **Imperfect information**: a situation in which people, including both consumers and producers, do not have the full information needed to make rational decisions, reducing the extent of efficiency.

Providing a merit good

Governments may decide to subsidise, or provide free at the point of use, a product such as education so that consumption is not limited to those who have the ability to pay for it. This will involve government expenditure. Such a merit good is considered to provide external benefits, or positive externalities, whereby the social benefit of consumption is greater than the private benefit. For example, a more educated workforce in a country are not only likely to gain higher wages or salaries for themselves, but this is also likely to benefit the whole economy as the workforce will be more productive than would otherwise be the case.

> **Activity**
>
> **Museums**
>
> Working in pairs or groups, consider the possible advantages of being able to go to a museum, either for free or for a very low price, because of a government decision to use public money to make entry to museums either free or relatively cheap.

> **Getting it right**
>
> You need to demonstrate that you understand that a merit good is an example of a private good, not a public good.

Figure 1.4 shows how a merit good can be under-provided and under-consumed in a market.

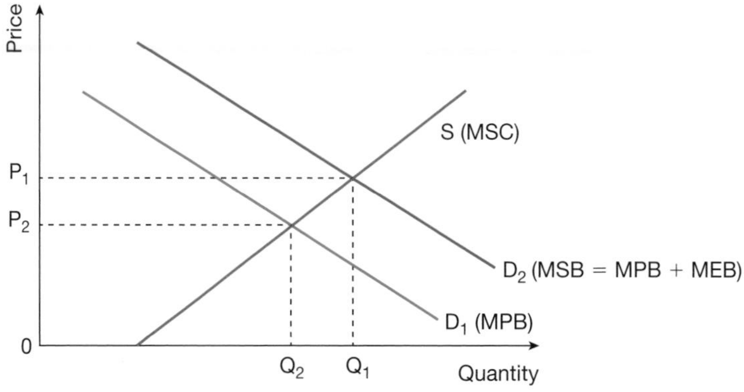

Figure 1.4 The under-production and under-consumption of a merit good in a market ▲

In Figure 1.4, the original market equilibrium is a price of P_2 and a quantity of Q_2. This is determined by the intersection of the demand curve D_1 (representing the marginal private benefit of consumption) and the supply curve S (representing the marginal social cost of production). In this situation, however, the consumers undervalue the potential benefits of the merit good, such as education. If the demand curve took into account the marginal external benefit as well as the marginal private benefit, the demand curve would shift to the right and now be D_2 (representing the marginal social benefit). This equilibrium would involve a price of P_1 and a quantity of Q_1. Without this recognition of the external benefits of a merit good, such as education, there would be both under-production and under-consumption of the good, shown in the diagram by the horizontal distance between Q_1 and Q_2. This is why governments intervene in many countries to encourage the consumption and the production of merit goods, such as education or health care.

Case Study

Education in Mauritius

After Mauritius became independent in 1968, the government announced that the quality of the education system was going to be one of its main objectives, recognising the importance of education to the development of the country.

There has been substantial investment in the education system by a succession of governments and

progress in the education system has been very impressive. Education through the primary and secondary sectors has been free since 1976 and through the post-secondary level since 1988.

1 Discuss why governments in Mauritius have been so keen to allocate resources to education.

Case Study

Public libraries in the Maldives

On 20 May 2010, there was a lecture at a meeting of the Maldives Library Association on the importance of public libraries and the role that they can play in a democracy.

In the lecture, it was stated that important aspects of a successful democracy, such as freedom of speech and the freedom to read, could be supported by public libraries.

It was also stated that an important aspect of democracy was that individuals should be allowed to achieve their fullest possible potential. In order to achieve this potential, individuals required knowledge and access to ideas. This is where public libraries could contribute to democracy in a country.

1 Explain why a public library can be regarded as an example of a merit good.

Case Study

Health care in Brunei

Brunei has been an independent country since 1984. It has the second highest Human Development Index in South East Asia, after Singapore, and is classified as a developed country. It is ranked fifth in the world by gross domestic product per capita at purchasing power parity.

The country has developed a very good health-care system, recognising the various benefits that this can bring. A comprehensive and efficient

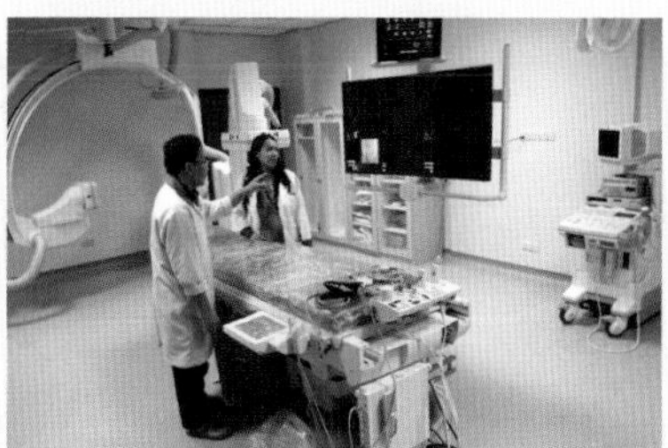

health–care system is available to all, and the Ministry of Health in Brunei ensures that the health-care service is accessible and reliable. It also concentrates on the improvement of the standard of health care in the country.

1 Explain why the Ministry of Health in Brunei is so keen to make a comprehensive and efficient health-care system available to all.

Merit goods and free goods

A merit good needs to be clearly distinguished from a free good. This confusion can arise from the fact that some merit goods are free at the point of consumption, such as education. A free good, however, is a product which can satisfy demand without a need for an allocative mechanism, i.e. the product is not scarce and does not require a market as demand and supply are equal at zero price. This not the same as the consumption of a merit good, such as education, which *does* involve the allocation of scarce resources.

Getting it right

You need to demonstrate that you understand that a merit good is *not* an example of a free good.

Demerit goods

A demerit good is the opposite of a merit good. It is a product which, like a private good, has the characteristics of being rival and excludable, but if provided in a market economy, would be likely to be over-produced and over-consumed. The reason for this is that individuals may not be aware of the potential damage to themselves and to the wider society of such over-consumption. A demerit good is therefore the outcome of imperfect information held by consumers. Examples of a demerit good would include products such as cigarettes and alcohol.

Key term

Demerit good: a product which has negative externalities and which would be over-produced and over-consumed in a market economy as a result of the imperfect information held by consumers.

Governments may decide to discourage the consumption of such products, such as by putting a very large tax on them to make them much more expensive than would otherwise be the case, leading to a reduction in the demand for them. For example, if the demand for cigarettes and alcohol could be reduced, this would not only be good for the individuals concerned, but would be good for the whole society, such as through less working days lost if the workforce was healthier. The effect of such a tax would clearly depend on the price elasticity of demand for them. The demand for many of these products is likely to be quite price inelastic and so consumers may not be able to significantly reduce their consumption because of addiction to the product.

Figure 1.5 shows how a demerit good can be over-provided and over-consumed in a market.

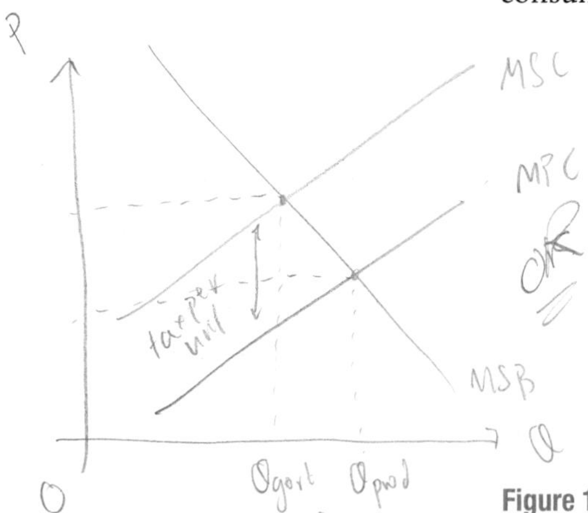

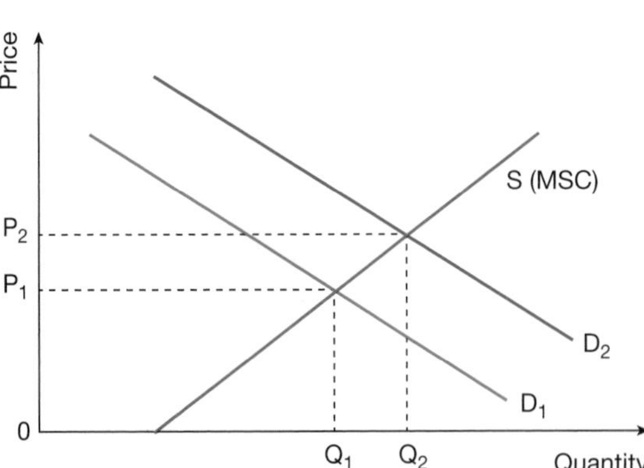

Figure 1.5 The over-production and over-consumption of a demerit good in a market ▲

The socially optimum level of demand, taking into account not only private benefits but external benefits as well, would be a price of P_1 and Q_1. This is where S (representing marginal social cost) is equal to D_2 (representing marginal social benefit). Consumers, however, are likely to over-consume and producers to over-produce in a market economy and this is shown in the diagram by a price of P_2 and a quantity of Q_2. This is where S is equal to D_1 (representing only private marginal benefit).

Progress question

10 Explain what is meant by a demerit good.

Information failure

A key element in both merit and demerit goods is the existence of information failure. Consumers may under-consume merit goods, such as education or health care, because they do not have enough information about the potential benefits of the consumption of such goods, both for themselves and for society as a whole.

Similarly, consumers may over-consume demerit goods such as cigarettes or alcohol, because they do not have enough information about the potential dangers of the consumption of such goods, both for themselves and for society as a whole.

This is why a government may decide to intervene in a market, either to encourage the consumption and production of merit goods or to discourage the production and consumption of demerit goods. This can be regarded as an imperfection of a market, especially in relation to having an understanding of the potential long-term benefits of the consumption of a merit good or of the potential long-term disadvantages of the consumption of a demerit good. Such an imperfection in a market means that a product will be produced and consumed, but not in the right quantities, i.e. the merit goods will be under-produced and under-consumed and the demerit goods will be over-produced and over-consumed. There is therefore a misallocation of resources in the market.

Key terms

Information failure: a situation where people do not have the full information needed to make informed decisions about their behaviour.

Imperfection: a situation where a market does not behave as it is expected to, leading to a misallocation of resources.

Getting it right

Make sure that you can clearly demonstrate an understanding of the link between information failure and the possible under-consumption of merit goods and over-consumption of demerit goods.

Key concepts

- **Scarcity and choice** are fundamental to the economic problem.
- **The margin and change** can be considered in the many decisions in Economics that are taken at the margin.
- **Progress and development** can be illustrated in the shift of the production possibility curve to the right which can be used to show economic growth and, as a result of such growth, standards of living can be raised, indicating growth and development in an economy.

Progress check

After completing this chapter you should be able to:

- understand the importance of scarcity, choice and opportunity cost in terms of the economic problem
- appreciate the distinction between positive and normative statements
- appreciate the importance of the production possibility curve in Economics
- understand the different factors of production
- understand the differences between the three different allocative mechanisms
- appreciate the problems of transition from one type of economic system to another
- understand how different economic structures can be compared
- understand the various advantages and disadvantages of the division of labour
- understand the functions and characteristics of money
- understand how goods and services can be classified.

Exam-style questions

Essay questions

1 Explain the role of the factor enterprise in a modern economy. [8 marks]

2 Discuss the issues involved as economies move towards the market economy and away from the planned economy. [12 marks]

3 Explain how resources are allocated in a market economy. [8 marks]

4 Explain the characteristics required by money if it is to carry out its functions effectively. [8 marks]

5 Discuss whether a market economy can solve the economic problem more effectively than a command economy. [12 marks]

6 Discuss why the mixed economy has become the most usual economic system. [12 marks]

Multiple-choice questions

7 Which of the following could cause an outward shift of a production possibility curve? [1 mark]

A A reduction in unemployment
B A more efficient use of existing resources
C An improvement in the level of technology
D An increase in net migration out of a country

8 Which of the following is a positive statement? [1 mark]

A Trade unions should be encouraged in an economy
B A government ought to discourage smoking in public places
C The rate of inflation is measured through a prices index
D Teachers ought to have significant increases in their salaries

2 The price system and the micro economy

In this chapter you will develop your knowledge and understanding of:

- demand and supply curves
- price elasticity, income elasticity and cross-elasticities of demand
- price elasticity of supply
- interaction of demand and supply
- market equilibrium and disequilibrium
- consumer and producer surplus.

Key term

Forex market: a short way of stating foreign exchange market.

The role of markets

As we saw in Chapter 1, the problem of scarcity means that societies have to make decisions about how to allocate resources within markets. In a free market economy these decisions are made through changes in prices. The role of a market is to provide a mechanism for bringing buyers and sellers together to establish a price for goods, services and factors of production. Markets can be located in a single physical place where buyers and sellers meet face to face such as a weekly fruit and vegetable market in a small town or village, Smithfield meat market in London or the Mercat de la Boqueria in Barcelona, or they can be global such as the foreign exchange market (FOREX) which encompasses virtually every financial institution in the world where the majority of trade is undertaken over the internet.

Local fruit and vegetable market ▲

Dealing on the forex ▲

The functions of prices

Within any market prices perform three basic functions:

- a signalling function indicating surpluses or shortages in the market
- a rationing function allocating resources among alternative uses
- an incentive function encouraging producers to supply more or less of a good or service.

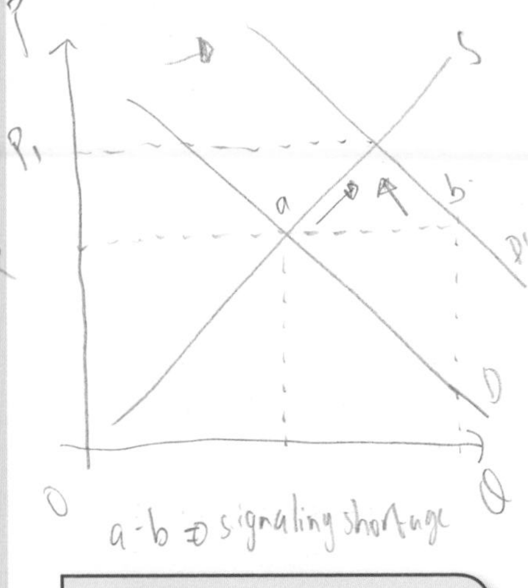

Let us take the example of the housing market in a particular area of a country. Assume that as a result of a significant influx of population into the area the demand for houses increases. As supply cannot be increased immediately the price of houses will rise signalling a shortage in the market. This rise in prices will mean that some individuals are no longer able to afford to purchase a house and so will ration or reduce their demand. The increase in prices of houses and the potential profits to be made will act as an incentive to building firms to increase the supply of houses, thereby removing the initial shortage. There will be similar changes in the market for factors of production, e.g. labour. In order to provide the increased supply of houses building firms will need to employ more workers. This will increase the demand for labour creating a shortage signalled by a rise in wages (the price of labour). The rise in wages will mean that some firms will no longer be able to afford to employ as many workers and will reduce (ration) the number

Activity

Operation of markets

In groups, explain how the signalling, rationing and incentive functions of prices would operate following a significant increase in the price of oil for a major oil importing country such as Japan.

they employ. The increase in wages will act as an incentive for existing building workers to move into the area and for more individuals to train to become building workers thereby removing the shortage of labour. Changes in prices have thus brought about a reallocation of resources in the product and factor markets.

Link

See Chapter 8 pages 233–44 for the determination of wages.

The determination of price

How are prices determined in a particular market? To begin with we will concentrate on the price of goods and services; the price of labour (the wage rate) is considered later.

The price of any good or service is determined by the interaction of quantity demanded (from buyers) and supply (from sellers). The equilibrium price (which is the price from which there is no tendency for change) will be that at which the quantity demanded = the quantity supplied.

We need, therefore, to look at the factors that affect the quantity demanded and supply of a particular product.

We will begin with demand.

Key terms

Equilibrium price: the market price from which there will be no tendency for change. This will be at the price where demand = supply.

Effective demand: the quantity of a good or service an individual is willing and able to purchase over a range of prices over a period of time.

Demand and supply curves

Individual and effective demand

An individual's demand for a good or service is the quantity they are willing and able to purchase over a range of prices over a period of time. It is important to distinguish an individual's demand for a product from the desire or need for a product. For example, an individual may desire a Ferrari motor car, but because they do not have the money to buy one, as far as economists are concerned, they do not have a demand for it. Economists often, therefore, refer to effective demand, which is the desire for a product backed up with the ability to pay for it.

Getting it right

Make sure you understand the difference between the *desire* for a good or service and the *effective demand* for it.

Determinants of demand

The relationship between individual demand and the price of a product

For most goods and services (but not all) the quantity demanded varies inversely with the price. This is sometimes referred to as the law of demand.

The relationship between demand and price is generally illustrated by either a demand schedule or a demand curve. The demand schedule (Table 2.1) and demand curve (Figure 2.1) show the quantity of rice demanded by an individual (Vikram) over a range of prices.

As can be seen from both the demand schedule and the demand curve, as the price of rice falls the demand rises and vice versa.

The demand curve is drawn on the assumption of *ceteris paribus*, that all other factors affecting Vikram's demand for rice remain unchanged. At this stage we only know how much rice Vikram is prepared to purchase at various prices. Until we combine the demand curve with a supply curve we cannot say exactly how much will be purchased and at what price.

Key terms

Law of demand: for most goods and services the quantity demanded varies inversely with its price.

Demand curve: a curve showing the relationship between quantity of a product individuals are willing and able to buy over a range of prices over a period of time, on the assumption that all other factors affecting demand are held constant.

Supply curve: a curve showing the relationship between the quantity of a product producers are willing and able to offer for sale over a range of prices over a period of time, on the assumption that all other factors affecting supply are held constant.

Table 2.1 Vikram's demand schedule for rice ▼

Price of rice per kilo (cents)	Quantity demanded (kilos per month)
5	60
10	50
15	40
20	30
25	20
30	10

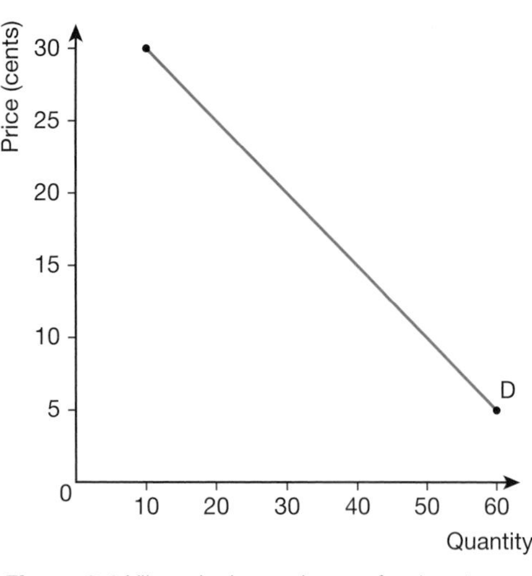

Figure 2.1 Vikram's demand curve for rice ▲

> **Link**
>
> See Chapter 1 page 14 for an explanation of *ceteris paribus*.

> **Key term**
>
> **Market demand**: the total demand for a particular product in the market.

Market demand

In addition to individual's demand for a product, Economists are often interested in the total or market demand for a product. This is found simply by adding together the quantity demanded of each individual, in this case for Vikram, Hamza and Bella, at any given price. This is shown in the demand schedule (Table 2.2) and demand curve (Figure 2.2).

Table 2.2 The market demand schedule for rice ▼

Price of rice per kilo (cents)	Quantity demanded (kilos per month) Vikram	Quantity demanded (kilos per month) Hamza	Quantity demanded (kilos per month) Bella	Market demand (kilos per month)
5	60	40	30	130
10	50	35	25	110
15	40	30	20	90
20	30	25	15	70
25	20	20	10	50
30	10	15	5	30

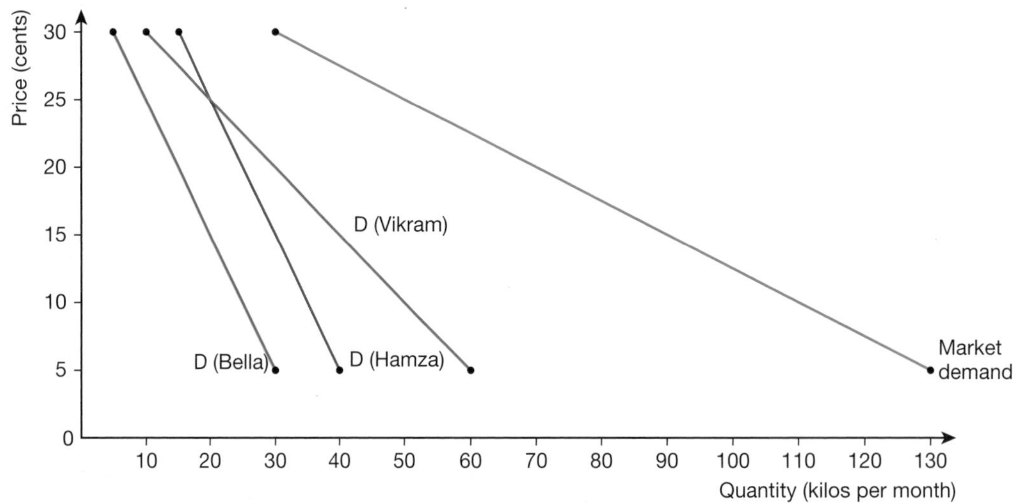

Figure 2.2 Market demand for rice ▲

Other influences on demand – the conditions of demand

There are a range of factors other than price which affect an individual's demand for a good or service. These conditions of demand affect how much an individual will demand at each price and as we shall see later will bring about a shift of the demand curve to the right or left.

Income

Here we need to distinguish between normal and inferior goods. A normal good is one for which the demand rises as income rises and falls as income falls. This applies to most goods and services. However, there are some exceptions to this. For example, during the recession in the UK in 2010–2011 as unemployment rose and consumers' incomes fell many supermarkets found their sales of low price "value" own brands increased.

> **Key terms**
>
> **Normal good**: a good whose demand rises as income rises and falls as income falls.
>
> **Inferior good**: a good whose demand falls as income rises and rises as income falls.

The price of other goods

Many goods are related to one another as substitutes or complements. Coffee and tea are, for many people, substitutes for one another. The demand for coffee will vary directly with the price of tea. If the price of tea rises individuals will reduce their demand for tea and switch to coffee. The demand for coffee will therefore increase. The opposite will happen if the price of tea falls.

> **Key terms**
>
> **Substitutes**: goods that are alternatives to one another.
>
> **Complements**: goods that are consumed together.

Fuel is a complement to a motor car. Consequently the demand for fuel is likely to be inversely related to the price of cars. If there is a significant rise in the price of cars it is likely that the demand will fall and consequently so will the demand for fuel.

Tastes

This relationship is relatively straightforward in that individuals are unlikely to buy goods they do not like. The more attractive individuals find a particular product the greater their demand for it is likely to be. However, it is important to remember that our tastes and preferences can be swayed and influenced by intensive advertising and promotion campaigns.

Expectations of future prices

Some products are purchased because of their investment potential. Individuals may buy these products in the hope that their price will rise and they can be sold at a profit in the future. Examples of such products are houses, shares and antiques. If individuals believe the price of such goods is likely to rise in the future this may lead to an increase in demand. Speculators hoarding sugar because they anticipated a rise in price following a poor crop yield is another example.

Size, age and gender distribution of the population

Generally the overall demand for most goods and services will rise and fall as the population rises and falls. Changes in the age and gender distribution of the population will influence the pattern of demand for particular goods and service, e.g. those purchased primarily by the young or elderly or by males or females.

Distribution of income

Generally if the income distribution in a country becomes more even, the demand for most normal goods increases. If the distribution becomes less even, the demand for basic necessities and luxury goods will be affected depending on the nature of the change in distribution. It is likely that the demand for both luxury and inferior goods would increase.

Shifts of the demand curve

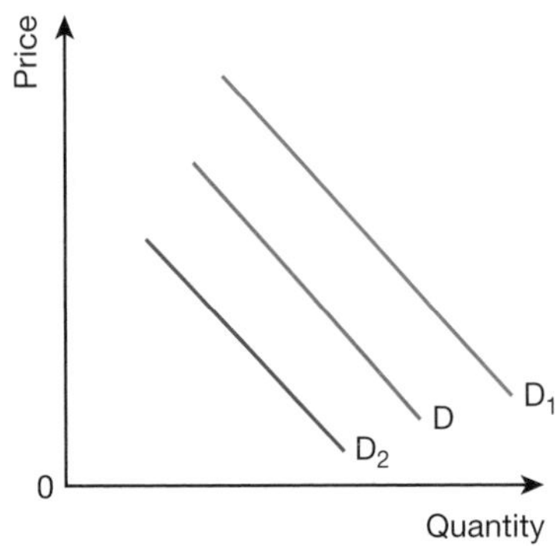

Figure 2.3 Shifts of the demand curve ▲

If any of the conditions of demand described above change then it means that individuals are able to purchase more or less at each and every price. This will cause the whole demand curve to shift. If the change enables individuals to buy more of the product the demand curve will shift to the right (D to D_1) and if they are able to purchase less it will shift the curve to the left (D to D_2) as illustrated in Figure 2.3.

Table 2.3 summarises the effect of changes in the conditions of demand on the demand curve for a product.

Table 2.3 The effect of changes in the conditions of demand on the demand curve for a product ▼

Shifts the demand curve to the right (an increase in demand)	Shifts the demand curve to the left (a decrease in demand)
A rise in income for a normal good	A fall in income for a normal good
A fall in income for an inferior good	A rise in income for an inferior good
A rise in the price of a substitute	A fall in the price of a substitute
A fall in the price of a complement	A rise in the price of a complement
A change in tastes in favour of a product	A change in tastes away from a product
The expectation of a future price rise	The expectation of a future price fall
An increase in population	A fall in population
A more even distribution of income	A less even distribution of income

Progress questions

1 Using diagrams, explain the effect of each of the following on the demand curve for privately owned housing in a particular area.
 - **a** Rising unemployment in the area
 - **b** A reduction in private rents in the area
 - **c** A rise in mortgage interest rates
 - **d** An increase in the number of single person households
 - **e** Expectations of significant increases in house prices over the coming year.

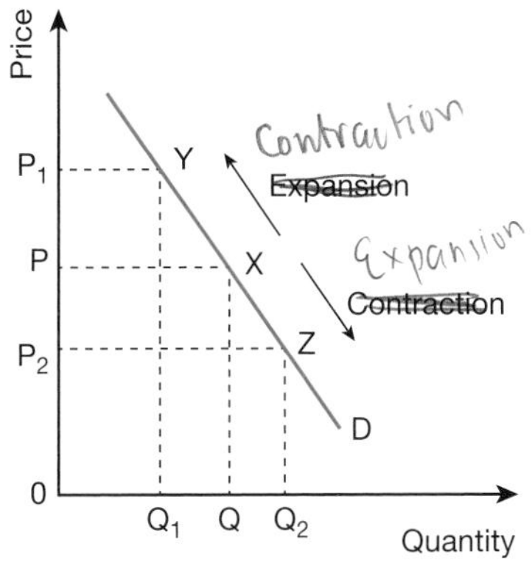

Figure 2.4 Changes in the quantity demanded resulting from price changes ▲

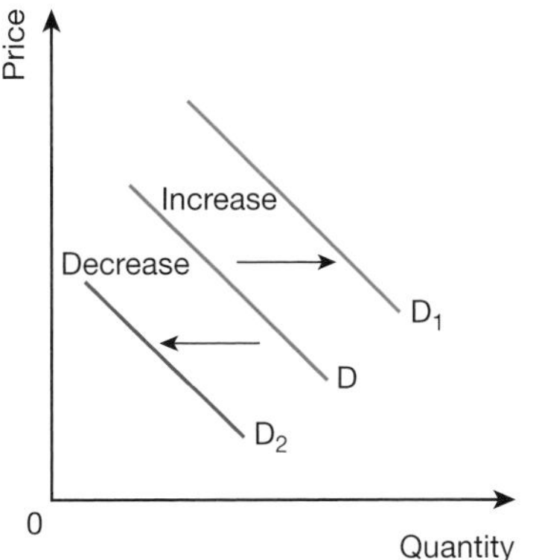

Figure 2.5 Changes in demand resulting from changes in the conditions of demand ▲

Getting it right

It is very important that you have a clear understanding of the distinction between movements along a demand curve (caused by price changes) and shifts of the whole demand curve (caused by a change in the conditions of demand).

Movements along the demand curve versus shifts of the demand curve

It is important to distinguish clearly between movements along a demand curve and shifts of the whole curve.

A market demand curve shows the relationship between changes in price and changes in the quantity purchased and so if the price of a product increases it will simply mean a movement from one price quantity combination to another. In Figure 2.4 an increase in price from P to P_1 will result in a movement up along the demand curve from X to Y resulting in a fall in demand from Q to Q_1. Correspondingly a decrease in price from P to P_2 will result in a movement down along the demand curve from X to Z resulting in an increase in demand from Q to Q_2.

If, however, any of the factors other than price, i.e. the conditions of demand, change resulting in more or less being demanded at each and every price then this will result in a shift in the whole curve; an increase in demand resulting in a shift of the curve to the right and a decrease a shift to the left. This is shown in Figure 2.5.

In order to distinguish between changes in demand resulting from movements along a demand curve from those resulting from shifts of the whole curve, we use the terminology shown in Table 2.4.

Table 2.4 Changes in demand ▼

Change in demand	Description
Increase in demand resulting from a fall in price (movement down along the demand curve)	Increase in the quantity demanded or expansion of demand
Decrease in demand resulting from a rise in price (movement up along the demand curve)	Decrease in the quantity demanded or contraction of demand
Increase in demand resulting from a shift of the demand curve to the right	Increase in demand
Decrease in demand resulting from a shift of the demand curve to the right	Decrease in demand

Activities

Demand curves

Using the figures in the table below, draw the demand curve for oil for a particular country.

Price per barrel ($)	80	90	100	110	120	130	140
Barrels consumed per day (millions)	20	18	16	14	12	10	8

Now the country's demand increases by 10 per cent at each price. Draw the new demand curve.

Supply

> **Key term**
> **Supply**: the quantity of a good a producer is willing and able to offer for sale over a range of prices over a given period of time.

As indicated at the beginning of this chapter, in order to establish the equilibrium price for a product we need to look at both the demand for and supply of it. The supply refers not simply to the quantity produced, but the quantity producers are prepared to offer for sale over a range of prices over a period of time.

Determinants of supply

The relationship between supply and the price of a product

In most cases as the price rises producers are willing to supply more because it is likely to be more profitable. It is also likely to be the case that costs of production will increase and so it will be necessary to increase price in order to maintain profit margins. The relationship between the supply of a product and its price is, as with demand, generally illustrated by either a schedule or a curve. Table 2.5 and Figure 2.6 show the supply schedule and supply curve for rice respectively.

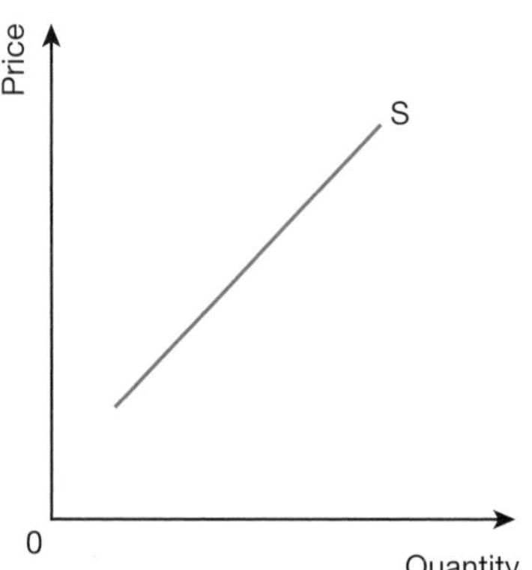

Figure 2.6 An individual producer's supply curve for rice ▲

Table 2.5 An individual producer's supply curve for rice ▼

Price of rice per kilo (cents)	Quantity supplied (kilos per month)
5	10
10	15
15	20
20	25
25	30
30	35

> **Key term**
> **Law of supply**: for most goods and services the quantity supplied will increase as pay rises and decrease as pay falls.

As can be seen from both the supply schedule and the supply curve, as the price of rice increases the supply increases and vice versa. This is known as the law of supply.

Like the demand curve, the supply curve is drawn on the assumption of *ceteris paribus*, that all other factors affecting the supply of rice remain unchanged. At this stage we only know how much rice the producer is prepared to purchase at various prices. Until we combine the supply curve with a demand curve we cannot say exactly how much will be supplied and at what price.

Market supply

In order to establish the market supply we simply add together the quantity offered by each producer at each price. Table 2.6 and Figure 2.7 show the market supply schedule and market supply curve for rice respectively.

Other influences on supply – the conditions of supply

There are a range of factors other than price which affect an individual's supply for a good or service. These are collectively known as the conditions of supply and will bring about shifts of the whole supply curve.

Table 2.6 Market supply of rice ▼

Price of rice per kilo (cents)	Quantity supplied (kilos per month) Producer A	Quantity supplied (kilos per month) Producer B	Quantity supplied (kilos per month) Producer C	Market supply (kilos per month)
5	10	5	15	30
10	15	25	20	60
15	20	45	25	90
20	25	65	30	120
25	30	85	35	150
30	35	105	40	180

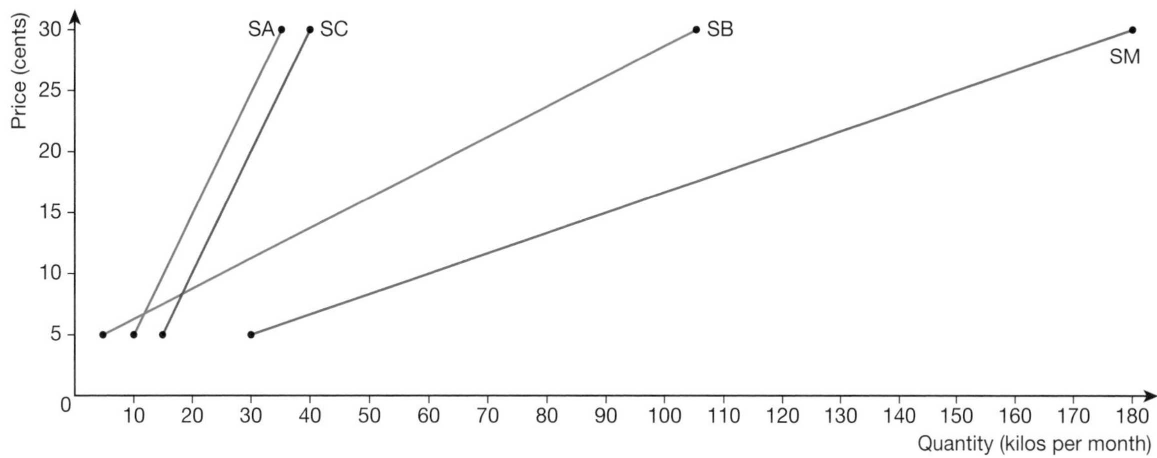

Figure 2.7 Market supply of rice ▲

Costs of production

Generally as the costs of production increase supply falls. If the cost of land for growing rice rises or there is an increase in wages of farm workers it means that producers are able to offer less for sale at each and every price.

Availability of resources

As more resources become available it is likely that more will be offered for sale. If, for example, more land becomes available then it will be possible for a farmer to grow more rice.

Climate

Clearly this factor will not affect all goods, but it is important in some, e.g. agriculture. Adverse weather conditions will obviously reduce the ability to produce and supply most crops. Weather conditions can also have an impact on the construction industry.

Technology

Technology can affect supply in a number of ways. It can lead to the creation of new products, e.g. the airline industry did not exist 100 years ago, or it can reduce costs of production enabling firms to produce more at each price. The introduction of new advanced machinery might significantly increase a farmer's ability to grow rice.

Government regulation

This looks mainly at health and safety, consumer protection, minimum standards legislation and employment legislation which affects employees' rights in such areas as equal pay and the minimum wage. These can all have an impact on a producer's costs and, therefore, the supply of a particular product.

Taxes and subsidies

Here we are looking at indirect taxes on expenditure such as Value Added Tax (VAT) and Goods and Services Tax (GST) which are initially paid by producers, but then may be passed on to consumers through higher prices. These taxes increase costs of production and, therefore, reduce supply. Subsidies, which are payments made by the government to producers, are designed to reduce firm's costs of production and enable them to supply more at lower prices.

Price of other goods the producer could supply

A farmer is in a position to grow a range of crops. If the farmer is currently concentrating on the production of wheat but the market price of barley rises significantly relative to wheat making its production more profitable, then the farmer would switch to growing barley and the supply of wheat would fall. The supply of a product, therefore, varies inversely with the price of alternative products the firm could produce.

Shifts of the supply curve

If any of the conditions of supply described above change then it means that producers are now able to offer more or less for sale at each and every price. This will cause the whole supply curve to shift. If the change enables producers to offer more for sale the supply curve will shift to the right (S to S_1) and if they are able to offer less for sale it will shift the curve to the left (S to S_2) as illustrated in Figure 2.8.

Table 2.7 The effect of changes in the conditions of supply on the supply curve for a product ▼

Shifts the supply curve to the right (an increase in supply)	Shifts the supply curve to the left (a decrease in supply)
Reduced costs of production	Increased costs of production
More resources become available	Fewer resources become available
Improved climate conditions (mainly agriculture)	Worsening climate conditions (mainly agriculture)
Improvements in technology	Setbacks in technology
Changes in government regulations in an industry reducing costs or making it easier to supply	Changes in government regulations in an industry increasing costs or making it more difficult to supply
Fall in expenditure taxes or granting of a subsidy	Increase in expenditure taxes
Reduction in the price of an alternative product the firm could produce	Increase in the price of an alternative product the firm could produce

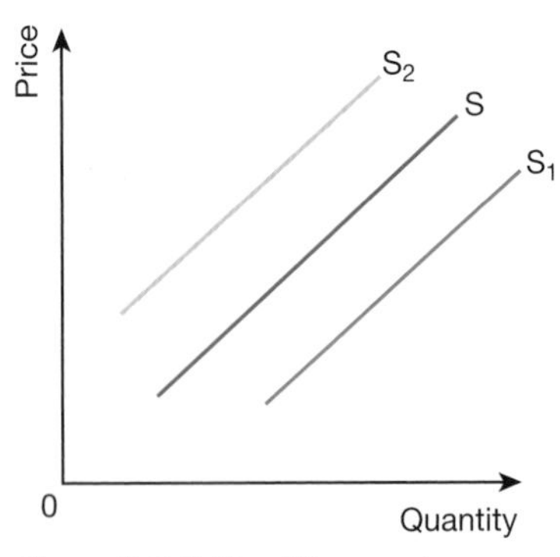

Figure 2.8 Shifts of the supply curve ▲

Progress questions

2 Using diagrams explain the effect of each of the following on the supply curve for privately owned housing in a particular area.

- **a** A decrease in the productivity of building workers
- **b** An increase in wages in the building industry
- **c** The government relaxes planning restrictions on building in the area
- **d** A rise in VAT or sales tax on building materials
- **e** A subsidy to builders of low-cost housing for first-time buyers
- **f** A major supplier of bricks in the area goes bankrupt.

Movements along the supply curve versus shifts of the supply curve

Just as in the case of demand it is important to distinguish between a movement along a particular supply curve and a shift of the whole curve. As the supply curve shows the relationship between the price of a good or service and the quantity supplied, a change in price will simply result in a movement along the curve. In Figure 2.9 the rise in price from P to P_1 results in a movement up along the supply curve from X to Y leading to an increase in supply from Q to Q_1 and a fall in price from P to P_2 results in a movement down along the curve from X to Z leading to a reduction in supply from Q to Q_2.

If, however, any of the factors other than price, i.e. the conditions of supply, change resulting in more or less being supplied at each and every price then this will result in a shift in the whole curve; an increase in supply resulting in a shift of the curve to the right and a decrease, resulting in a shift to the left. This is shown in Figure 2.10.

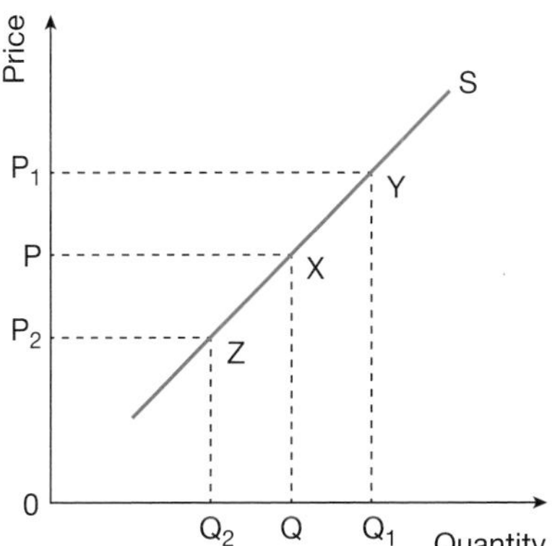

Figure 2.9 Changes in the quantity supplied resulting from price changes ▲

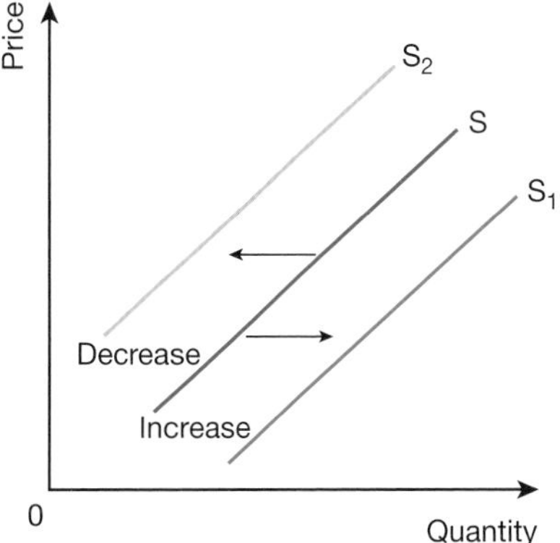

Figure 2.10 Changes in supply resulting from changes in the conditions of supply ▲

In order to distinguish between changes in supply resulting from movements along a supply curve from those resulting from shifts of the whole curve we use the terminology shown in Table 2.8.

Getting it right

It is very important that you have a clear understanding of the distinction between movements along a supply curve (caused by price changes) and shifts of the whole supply curve (caused by a change in the conditions of supply).

Table 2.8 Changes in supply ▼

Change in supply	Description
Increase in supply resulting from a fall in price (movement down along the supply curve)	Increase in the quantity supplied or expansion of supply
Decrease in supply resulting from a rise in price (movement up along the supply curve)	Decrease in the quantity supplied or contraction of supply
Increase in supply resulting from a shift of the supply curve to the right	Increase in supply
Decrease in supply resulting from a shift of the supply curve to the right	Decrease in supply

Activities

Supply curves

Using the figures in the table below, draw the supply curve for oil for a particular country.

Price per barrel (US $)	80	90	100	110	120	130	140
Barrels produced per day (millions)	10	15	20	25	30	35	40

Now the country demand increases the production of oil by 5 million barrels per day at each price. Draw the new supply curve.

Key terms

Market equilibrium: the price from which there will be no tendency for change given existing conditions of demand and supply – the price at which demand equals supply. Also known simply as "equilibrium".

Market disequilibrium: a situation in which demand does not equal supply, in which case there will be a tendency for price to change – to rise if demand is greater than supply and to fall if supply is greater than demand. Also known simply as "disequilibrium".

Market equilibrium and market disequilibrium

The determination of the equilibrium market price

In order to establish the market equilibrium price for a particular good or service, in this case rice, we bring together the market demand and supply schedules and curves for rice considered earlier.

Table 2.9 Market demand and supply schedules for rice ▼

Price of rice per kilo (cents)	Market demand (kilos per month)	Market supply (kilos per month)
5	130	30
10	110	60
15	90	90
20	70	120
25	50	150
30	30	180

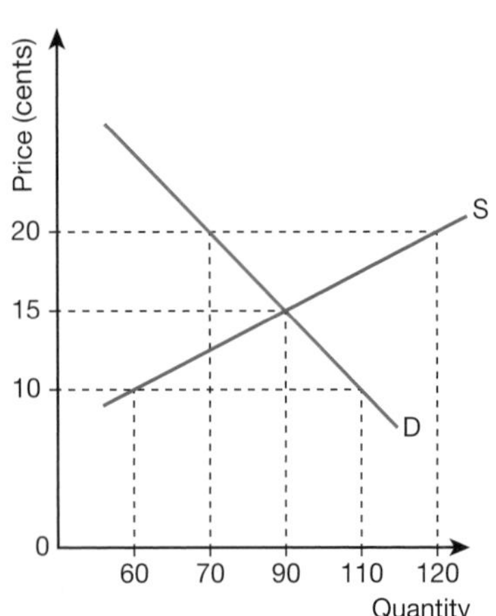

Figure 2.11 Market demand and supply curves for rice ▲

The equilibrium price and quantity demanded and supplied are given by the intersection of the demand and supply curve, giving, in this case, a price of 15 cents and an equilibrium quantity demanded and supplied of 90 kilos per month.

In order to see why this must be the equilibrium (the position from which there is no tendency for change) let us look at what happens if the price is above or below 15 cents.

> **Getting it right**
>
> It is important to remember that the equilibrium price and quantity demanded and supplied cannot change unless there is a change in the conditions of demand and/or supply.

> **Getting it right**
>
> The effect of an increase in demand is to increase both the equilibrium price and quantity demanded and supplied.

If we assume that the price is above the equilibrium at, say, 20 cents, then the quantity supplied is 120 kilos, but consumers wish only to consume 70 kilos. There is a surplus or excess supply of 50 kilos. Producers will rather receive something for their rice rather than let it go to waste and so will begin to reduce the price. As this takes place there will be a movement down along the supply curve as the quantity supplied falls, but at the same time the fact that the rice is now cheaper encourages some consumers into the market leading to an increase in the quantity demanded and a movement up along the demand curve. This process continues until there is no longer any surplus remaining – i.e. at the point where the demand and supply curves intersect.

No price above 15 cents can be an equilibrium because there will always be a surplus and, therefore, a tendency for the price to fall.

Similar logic applies if we look at any price below 15 cents, e.g. 10 cents. Here the quantity demanded exceeds the quantity supplied by 50 kilos. Competition for rice amongst consumers combined with producers seeing an opportunity to increase profits will result in the price beginning to rise. This rise in price will bring about a movement up along both the supply and demand curves as producers increase the quantity supplied and some consumers find they can no longer afford the rice, reducing the quantity demanded. Price will continue to rise until there is no longer any excess demand, i.e. where the demand and supply curves intersect.

No price below the point at which the quantity demanded equals the quantity supplied can be an equilibrium position because there will always be excess demand which will tend to drive up the price. Hence the equilibrium price and quantity demanded and supplied will be found at the point where the demand and supply curves intersect and there is no excess supply which would tend to drive the price down or excess demand which would tend to drive up the price.

The effect of shifts of the demand and supply curves on the equilibrium price and quantity demanded and supplied

Market equilibrium refers to the price and quantity demanded and supplied from which, once they have been achieved, there will be no tendency for change. As we shall see this will be at the point where the quantity demanded of a product equals the quantity supplied. Market disequilibrium will occur if the price is set above or below this level because there will be pressure for the price to change. If price is set above the level at which the quantity demanded equals the quantity supplied there will be surplus, which will exert downward pressure on price, and if price is set below this level there will be a shortage in the market, which will exert upward pressure on the price.

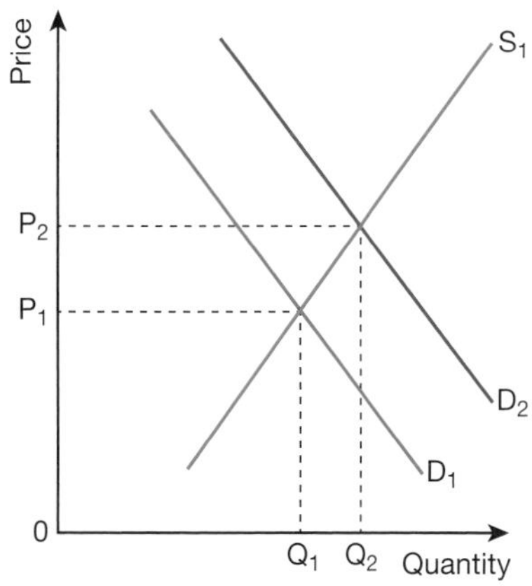

An increase in demand

Price
S_1
P_2
P_1
D_2
D_1
0
Q_1 Q_2 Quantity

Figure 2.12 The effect of an increase in demand ▲

In Figure 2.12 the original demand curve for rice is D_1 and the supply curve is S_1 giving an equilibrium price of P_1 and quantity demanded and supplied of Q_1. If now the conditions of demand change causing an increase in the demand for the good at each and every price the demand curve will shift outwards to the right. This leads to a new equilibrium price of P_2. Supply expands along the existing supply curve leading to a new equilibrium quantity demanded and supplied of Q_2. Note that there is no need for a new supply curve because all that has changed for the producer is the price; the conditions of supply have not altered.

A decrease in demand

In Figure 2.13 the original demand curve for rice is D_1 and the supply curve is S_1 giving an equilibrium price of P_1 and quantity demanded and supplied of Q_1. If now the conditions of demand change causing a decrease in the demand for the good at each and every price the demand curve will shift inwards to the left. This leads to a new equilibrium price of P_2. Supply contracts along the existing supply curve leading to a new equilibrium quantity demanded and supplied of Q_2. Note that there is no need for a new supply curve because all that has changed for the producer is the price; the conditions of supply have not altered.

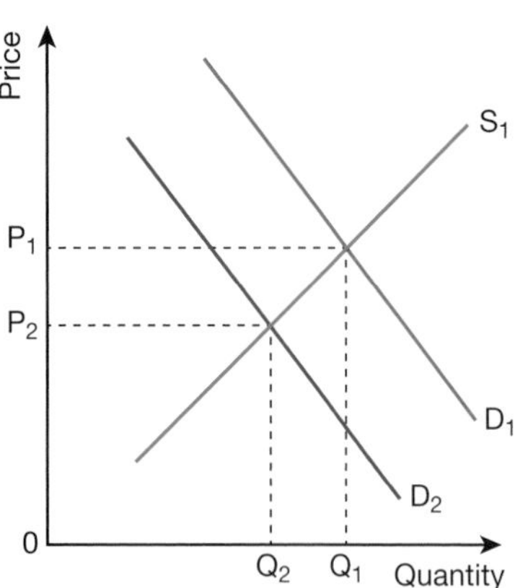

Figure 2.13 The effect of a decrease in demand ▲

Getting it right

The effect of a decrease in demand is to decrease both the equilibrium price and quantity demanded and supplied.

An increase in supply

In Figure 2.14 the original supply curve for rice is S_1 and the demand curve is D_1 giving an equilibrium price of P_1 and quantity demanded and supplied of Q_1. If now the conditions of supply change causing an increase in the supply of the good at each and every price the supply curve will shift outwards to the right. This leads to a new equilibrium price of P_2. Demand expands along the existing demand curve leading to a new equilibrium quantity demanded and supplied of Q_2. Note that there is no need for a new demand curve because all that has changed for consumers is the price; the conditions of demand have not altered.

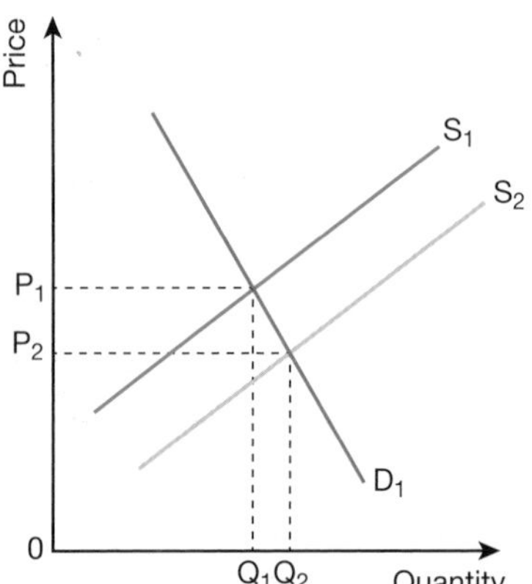

Figure 2.14 The effect of an increase in supply ▲

Getting it right

The effect of an increase in supply is to decrease the equilibrium price and increase quantity demanded and supplied.

A decrease in supply

In Figure 2.15 the original supply curve is S_1 and the demand curve is D_1 giving an equilibrium price of P_1 and quantity demanded and supplied of Q_1. If now the conditions of supply change causing a decrease in the supply of the good at each and every price the supply curve will shift inwards to the left. This leads to a new equilibrium price of P_2. Demand contracts along the existing demand curve leading to a new equilibrium quantity demanded and supplied of Q_2. Note that there is no need for a new demand curve because all that has changed for consumers is the price; the conditions of demand have not altered.

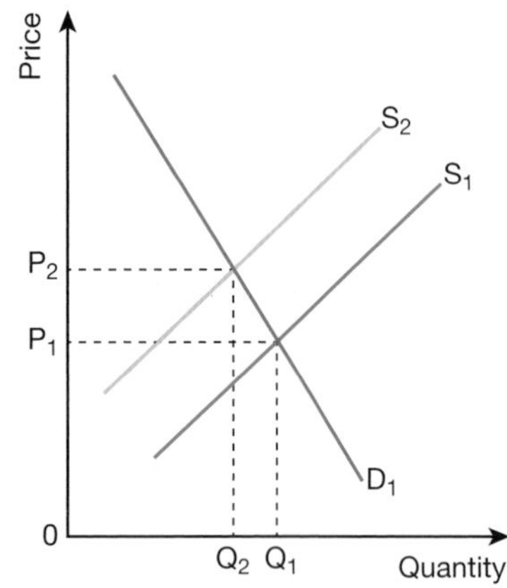

Figure 2.15 The effect of a decrease in supply ▲

Getting it right

The effect of a decrease in supply is to increase the equilibrium price and decrease quantity demanded and supplied.

Elasticity of demand and supply

In the previous section we saw that a change in the price of a product, caused by a shift of the supply curve, brought about a change in the quantity demanded. A rise in price will bring about a fall in the quantity demanded, and a fall in price will bring about an increase in the quantity demanded. We now need to look at the *extent* of these changes.

Price elasticity of demand (PED): the responsiveness of demand for a product to a change in its price.
Elasticity: the responsiveness of demand or supply to a change in one of its determinants.

Figures 2.16 and 2.17 show the demand curves for two different products. In both cases the price has fallen by the same amount, but the rise in the quantity demanded is significantly different. The reason for this is clearly the fact that the two demand curves have different slopes, which, in turn, is due to the fact that the two products have a different price elasticity of demand (PED). Price elasticity of demand is one of a number of types of elasticity which measure the extent of changes in demand or supply resulting from a change in one of their determinants.

We will be concerned with four types of elasticity, as listed below.

- Price elasticity of demand (PED) which measures the extent of the change in the quantity demanded of a product as a result of a change in its price.
- Income elasticity of demand (YED) which measures the extent of the change in the quantity demanded of a product as a result of a change in consumers' income.
- Cross price elasticity of demand or cross-elasticity of demand (XED) which measures the extent of the change in the quantity demanded of a product as a result of a change in the price of other products.
- Price elasticity of supply (PES) which measures the extent of the change in quantity supplied of a product as a result of a change in its price.

Price elasticity of demand (PED)

As Figures 2.16 and 2.17 indicate that the quantity demanded of product A is significantly more responsive to a change in its price than product B. However, the term "more responsive" is rather vague and so economists attempt to be more precise by calculating the actual magnitude of the price elasticity of demand.

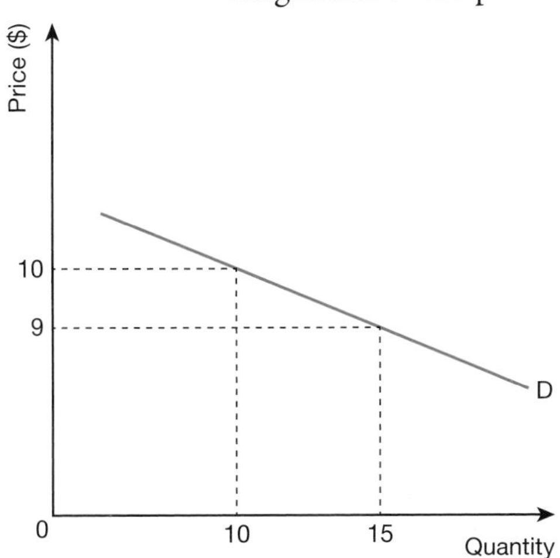

Figure 2.16 Demand curve for product A ▲

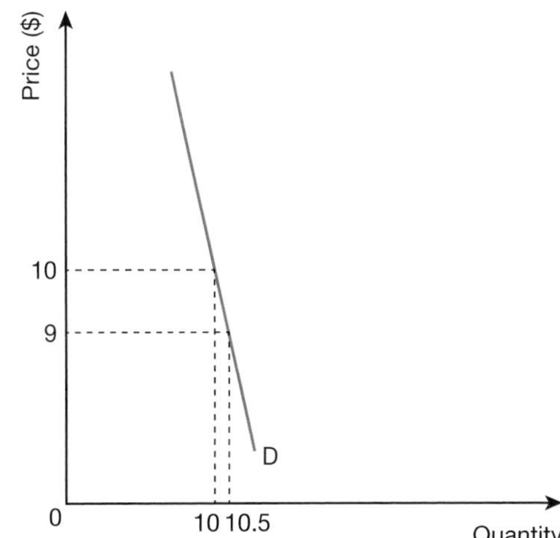

Figure 2.17 Demand curve for product B ▲

Calculation of the price elasticity of demand

The formula for the price elasticity of demand is:

$$\text{PED} = \frac{\text{The proportionate change in quantity demanded}}{\text{The proportionate change in price}}$$

$$\text{PED} = \frac{\text{New quantity demanded } (Q_1) - \text{Original quantity demanded } (Q)}{\text{Original quantity demanded } (Q)}$$

$$\div \frac{\text{New price } (P_1) - \text{Original price } (P)}{\text{Original price } (P)}$$

If we now apply the formula to product A in Figure 2.16, then:

New quantity demanded (Q_1) = 15

Original quantity demanded (Q) = 10

New price (P_1) = \$9

Original price (P) = \$10

$$\text{PED} = \frac{Q_1 - Q}{Q} \div \frac{P_1 - P}{P} = \frac{15 - 10}{10} \div \frac{9 - 10}{10}$$

$$= \frac{1}{2} \div \frac{-1}{10} = \frac{1}{2} \times \frac{-10}{2} = -5$$

Hence the price elasticity of demand for product A when the price falls from \$10 to \$9 is −5.

We could instead have used percentages in the calculation, in which case the formula is:

$$\text{PED} = \frac{\text{Percentage change in quantity demanded}}{\text{Percentage change in price}}$$

$$\text{PED} = \frac{\%\Delta Qd}{\%\Delta P}$$

In the case of product A this would now give us:

$$\text{PED} = \frac{50\%}{-10\%} = -5$$

> **Progress question**
>
> **3** Calculate the price elasticity of demand for product B when the price rises from \$9 to \$10 in Figure 2.16.

Interpreting the figure for the price elasticity of demand

We have calculated the price elasticity of demand for product A for a fall in price from \$10 to \$9 to be (−)5, but what does this figure actually mean?

Remember that we are interested in the extent to which the quantity demanded for a product changes. Because the quantity demanded of a product varies inversely with its price, the demand curve will have a negative slope, which means that the numerical value of the price

Getting it right

Although when interpreting the meaning of any value for the price elasticity of demand it is conventional to ignore the negative (minus) sign it is essential that in any calculation made it is included.

elasticity of demand will always be negative (−). However, we are only interested in whether the absolute value of the proportionate or percentage change in the quantity demanded is greater than, less than or equal to the proportionate or percentage change in price. Hence, although it is important that the negative sign is always included in any calculation, when we are interpreting any figure for the price elasticity of demand it is conventional to ignore this negative (−) sign so that the price elasticity of demand of 5 in this example means that the change in the quantity demanded is *five times* (5×) the change in price. As the answer is greater than 1, economists describe the demand for the product as elastic. If the answer had turned out to be less than 1 we would describe the demand for the product as being inelastic.

Key terms

Elastic demand: the proportionate (percentage) change in demand is greater than the proportionate (percentage) change in price.

Inelastic demand: the proportionate (percentage) change in demand is less than the proportionate (percentage) change in price.

The numerical value for the price elasticity of demand can vary between zero and infinity. Table 2.10 summarises the meaning of particular values for the price elasticity of demand.

Table 2.10 Meaning of values for price elasticity of demand ▼

Value of PED	Terminology	Meaning
0	Perfectly inelastic demand	A change in price leaves the quantity demanded unchanged
<1	Inelastic	Proportionate or percentage change in quantity demanded is less than the proportionate or percentage change in price
$=1$	Unitary elasticity of demand	Proportionate or percentage change in quantity demanded is equal to the proportionate or percentage change in price
>1	Elastic	Proportionate or percentage change in quantity demanded is greater than the proportionate or percentage change in price
Infinity	Perfectly elastic demand	A tiny change in price brings about an infinite change in the quantity demanded

Key terms

Arc price elasticity of demand: a measurement of the price elasticity of demand over a range of prices.

Point price elasticity of demand: a measurement of the price elasticity of demand at a particular price.

Point elasticity of demand

Up to now we have been considering the price elasticity of demand for a change in price. This is referred to as the arc price elasticity of demand. There are occasions, however, when economists are interested in the price elasticity of demand at a single price or point on the demand curve. This is known as point price elasticity of demand and is particularly useful when considering straight-line demand curves. This is illustrated in Figure 2.18 and Table 2.11.

In order to calculate the point price elasticity of demand at any particular price we take the corresponding point on the demand curve, X, and then divide the distance XZ by the distance XY. Clearly at the price corresponding to the midpoint of the demand curve XZ = XY and, therefore, the price elasticity of demand is equal to unity. In this case this corresponds to a price of $5.50 and a quantity demanded of 11. At prices below the midpoint of $5.50, XZ is less than XY and so the price elasticity of demand is less than 1 or inelastic. At point Z the price elasticity of demand is zero. At prices above $5.50, XY is greater than XZ and so the price elasticity of demand is greater than 1 or elastic. At point Y the price elasticity of demand is infinity.

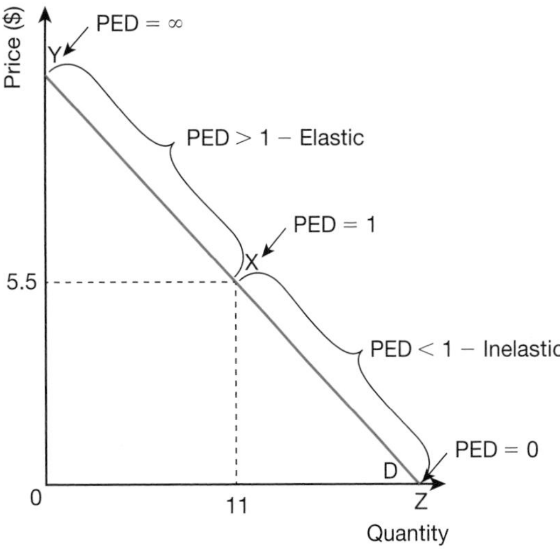

Figure 2.18 Demand curve for product ▲

Table 2.11 The demand schedule for a particular product ▼

Price ($)	Quantity demanded
1.00	20
2.00	18
3.00	16
4.00	14
5.00	12
5.50	11
6.00	10
7.00	8
8.00	6
9.00	4
10.00	2

From this discussion and that of arc elasticity it is clear that for a product with a normal downward-sloping demand curve the price elasticity of demand will vary along the length of the curve. For this reason, it is not possible to say that the demand for a product is elastic or inelastic; we can only say that demand is elastic or inelastic at a particular point on the curve (at a particular price) or over a range of prices. It also means that price elasticity of demand can only be meaningfully measured for small price changes.

However, there are three cases illustrated in Figure 2.19 where the price elasticity of demand is constant throughout the whole length of the curve.

- **Perfectly elastic** demand refers to a case in which even a tiny change in price brings about an infinite change in the quantity demanded so that the demand curve is a horizontal straight line.
- **Perfectly inelastic** demand refers to a case in which however great the change in price there is no change in the quantity demanded so that the demand curve is a vertical straight line.
- **Unitary elasticity of demand** at all prices means that the demand curve is a rectangular hyperbola, which means that any price/quantity combination will yield exactly the same total revenue.

Figure 2.19 Perfectly elastic demand, perfectly inelastic demand and unitary elasticity of demand ▶

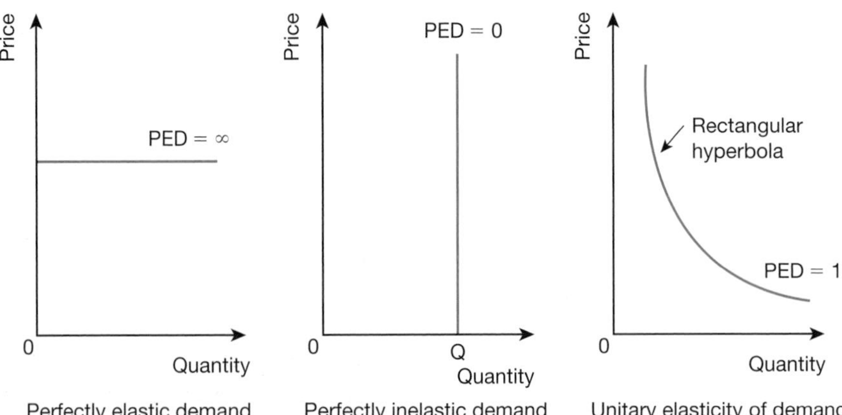

Factors affecting the price elasticity of demand

Time

Generally the longer the time period being considered, the more elastic the demand for a particular product is likely to be. There are a number of reasons for this. Firstly it may take time for individuals to become aware of price changes, particularly for products they may buy infrequently such as cookers or refrigerators. In addition it may take time to research and discover suitable substitutes.

The number of substitutes

This leads us into another factor affecting the price elasticity of demand for a product – the number and closeness of any substitutes it has. A product such a particular brand of chocolate bar will have a considerable number of close substitutes to which consumers could quickly switch if the price of this brand rose and so we would expect the demand for it to be relatively price elastic. If on the other hand a product has relatively few substitutes and we would expect the demand to be relatively price inelastic.

Link

See page 68 of this chapter for more on composite demand.

Linked to this factor is the number of uses to which a product may be put. Generally the more uses a product has, the more markets in which it can be sold and hence the more price elastic its demand is likely to be. Sugar, for example, has a range of possible domestic and business uses and so a change in price may have a significant impact on the overall market demand when prices change even though the effect in any individual market may be relatively small. Economists use the term "composite demand" to describe products that are demanded for more than one purpose.

The degree of necessity

The more essential an individual believes a product to be the more inelastic the demand for it is likely to be. Generally, therefore, necessities have an inelastic demand and luxuries an elastic demand. We should be aware, however, that what one individual or group may deem a necessity, others may see as a luxury. For example, a family living in a remote rural area may believe it is a necessity to have two or even three cars to enable them all to get to work and engage in their leisure activities, whereas a similar family living in a town with good public transport facilities might see owning more than one car as a luxury.

Durability and perishability

Some products by their very nature are durable, such as televisions, cars and cookers, which means they are consumed over a long period of time. It is possible to postpone the purchase of these products and repair them when prices are high or rising and bring forward the purchase of replacements when prices are falling. The more durable a product is the more price elastic the demand is likely to be. On the other hand products such as batteries for digital cameras have a relatively short lifespan and have to be replaced immediately when worn out. Such products have a more inelastic demand.

Proportion of income taken by the product

Another important factor in determining price elasticity of demand is the proportion of an individual's income taken up by a product. A product will account for a significant proportion of a family budget if its price is high or it is consumed regularly in large quantities. In such cases a given percentage change in price will have a significant impact on the family's budget. Rice, for example, takes up a high proportion of family expenditure in some countries and so a given percentage change is likely to have a much greater impact on the quantity of it demanded than the same percentage change in the price of say salt which accounts for a much lower proportion of income.

Table 2.12 Factors affecting the price elasticity of demand ▼

Factor	Impact on PED
Time period	The longer the time period the more price elastic the demand
Number of substitutes	The greater the number of substitutes the more price elastic the demand
Degree of necessity	The more necessary an individual believes a product to be the more inelastic the demand
Durability	Durable goods tend to have a more elastic demand than perishable goods
Proportion of income	The greater the proportion of a consumer's income taken up by a product the more elastic the demand

Activities

Elastic or inelastic

Which of the following products would you expect to have an elastic demand and which an inelastic demand? In each case explain why demand might be price elastic or price inelastic.

1 Bread
2 Unleaded petrol
3 Exotic foreign holidays
4 Visits to the cinema
5 Mobile phones
6 Designer jeans

Key term

Total revenue: the total amount received from the sale of a product.

TR = Price × Quantity sold

The importance of price elasticity of demand

Price elasticity of demand is particularly useful to producers in deciding on their pricing strategies and for the government in deciding on the likely impact of decisions taken about the level of expenditure taxes on goods and services.

In order to explain this we need to first introduce the concept of total revenue.

The total revenue (TR) received from the sale of a good or service is found by multiplying the price of the product by the quantity sold.

$TR = P \times Q$

Using the demand schedule in Table 2.11, we can now illustrate the relationship between, changes in the price of the product, the total revenue and the price elasticity of demand. This is shown in Table 2.13.

A knowledge of the price elasticity of demand for a firm's product will clearly influence its pricing strategy. It will aim to set a price of $5.50 because this will maximise the revenue from sales. If it is currently charging a price below this, then it knows that demand is price inelastic and so any increase in price will increase *total revenue*. If it is currently charging a price above $5.50, then demand is price elastic over this range and the firm knows that reducing price will increase *total revenue*.

Table 2.13 Price elasticity of demand and total revenue ▼

Price ($)	Quantity demanded	Total revenue	PED
1.00	20	20.00	Over this price range PED < 1
2.00	18	36.00	
3.00	16	48.00	
4.00	14	56.00	
5.00	12	60.00	
5.50	11	60.50	= 1
6.00	10	60.00	Over this price range PED > 1
7.00	8	56.00	
8.00	6	48.00	
9.00	4	36.00	
10.00	2	20.00	

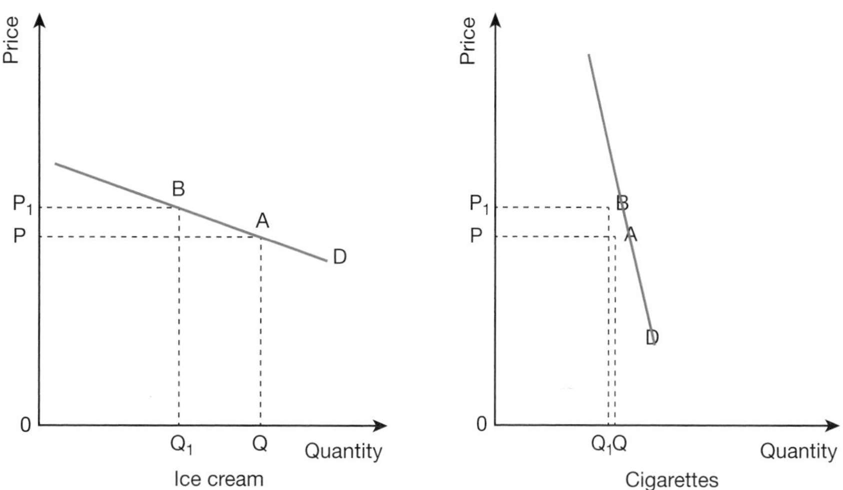

Figure 2.20 Demand curves for ice cream and cigarettes ▲

The same point can be illustrated diagrammatically. Figure 2.20 shows the demand curves for a particular brand of ice cream and cigarettes. Ice cream is likely to have a relatively more elastic demand curve than cigarettes and hence the demand curve has a shallower slope. In both cases the initial price is P giving a total revenue equal to the area of the rectangle equal to OPAQ. If both products have an equal percentage rise in price to P_1 then the total revenue becomes OP_1BQ_1. Clearly the total revenue has fallen in the case of ice cream and risen in the case of cigarettes. A fall in price will have the opposite effect on total revenue in each case.

Link

For more on indirect taxes see Chapter 3 page 76.

Key term

Indirect tax: a tax on expenditure which is levied on the producer, but may then be passed on to consumers through an increase in price.

Price elasticity of demand and indirect taxes

The price elasticity of demand is also important for the government in deciding on which goods to impose indirect taxes.

Indirect taxes on expenditure are either ad valorem or specific. An ad valorem (according to value) tax is a percentage tax such as VAT in the UK or state sales taxes in the USA. A specific tax such as UK excise duty levies a fixed amount per unit of a particular product. Figure 2.21 illustrates the effect of a specific tax on ice cream and on cigarettes.

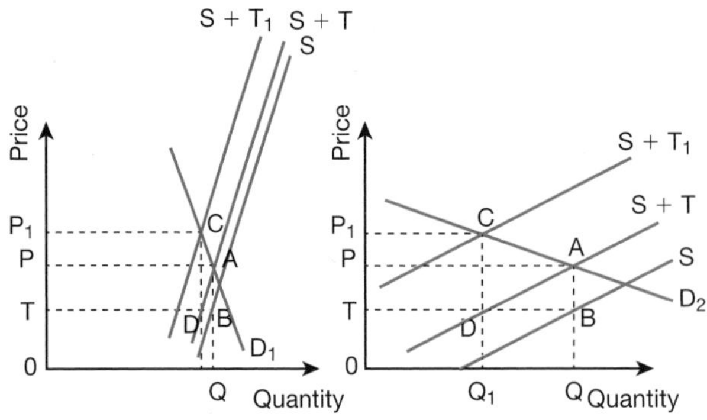

Figure 2.21 The effect of a specific tax on cigarettes and ice cream ▲

Figure 2.21 show the demand curves for cigarettes (D_1) and ice cream (D_2). In each case the government initially imposes a specific tax of TP per unit on the product generating a tax revenue in each case of TPAB (= tax per unit × quantity sold). If the government now increases the tax to TP_1 per unit the tax revenue is now TP_1CD in each case. It can clearly be seen that in the case of ice cream the tax revenue received by the government will fall as the increase in price has resulted in a more than proportionate decrease in the quantity demanded. In the case of cigarettes, however, the tax revenue has increased because the proportionate fall in the quantity demanded is less than the proportionate increase in price. This is the rationale behind governments imposing taxes on goods which have an inelastic demand such as fuel, tobacco and alcohol. However, governments need to be aware of the fact that some goods which have an inelastic demand are basic necessities, e.g. food, so that imposing taxes on them might cause hardship for those on low incomes.

Income elasticity of demand

> **Key term**
>
> Income elasticity of demand: the responsiveness of demand for a product to a change in consumers' income.

Economists are also interested in the extent to which the quantity demanded for a product varies with changes in consumers' real income, which is measured by the income elasticity of demand.

Calculation of the income elasticity of demand

The formula for the income elasticity of demand is:

$$\text{YED} = \frac{\text{The proportionate change in quantity demanded}}{\text{The proportionate change in income}}$$

$$\text{YED} = \frac{\text{New quantity demanded } (Q_1) - \text{Original quantity demanded } (Q)}{\text{Original quantity demanded } (Q)}$$

$$\div \frac{\text{New income } (Y_1) - \text{Original income } (Y)}{\text{Original income } (Y)}$$

We could instead have used percentages in the calculation, in which case the formula is:

$$\text{YED} = \frac{\text{Percentage change in quantity demanded}}{\text{Percentage change in income}}:$$

$$\text{YED} = \frac{\%\Delta Qd}{\%\Delta Y}$$

Unlike price elasticity of demand – which is always negative income – elasticity of demand can be either positive or negative. Table 2.14 summarises the meaning of particular values for the income elasticity of demand.

Table 2.14 Meaning of values for the income elasticity of demand ▼

Value of YED	Terminology	Meaning
> 1	Income elastic	Proportionate (or percentage) change in the quantity demanded greater than proportionate (or percentage) change in income
= 1	Unitary income elasticity	Proportionate (or percentage) change in the quantity demanded is equal to proportionate (or percentage) change in income
< 1	Income inelastic	Proportionate (or percentage) change in the quantity demanded less than proportionate (or percentage) change in income
0	Zero income elasticity	A change in income has no effect on demand
< 0	Negative income elasticity of demand	A change in income results in a change in demand in the opposite direction

Values above zero clearly indicate positive income elasticity which means that changes in the quantity demanded and changes in income move in the same direction, rising and falling together. This will be the case for normal goods. Inferior goods will have a negative income elasticity indicating that a rise in income will result in a fall in the quantity demanded for a product and vice versa.

Importance of income elasticity of demand

Knowledge of the income elasticity of demand for a firm's products, particularly whether it is positive or negative, is clearly important in informing its production and marketing strategies. For example, during the recession in the UK in 2009 and 2010, a number of large food retailers such as Sainsbury's and Tesco, found that the quantity demanded for their own-brand "value" labels, which might be regarded as inferior goods with a negative income elasticity, increased while the quantity demanded for more expensive branded goods with a positive income elasticity of demand declined. This would clearly be important in these companies' decisions on where to concentrate their production and marketing resources. In the same way, if an economy is experiencing full employment and rising incomes holiday firms may devote more resources to marketing expensive holidays overseas.

Cross price elasticity of demand

Cross price elasticity of demand, more commonly referred to as cross-elasticity of demand (XED), is a measure of the responsiveness of the quantity demanded for one good (X) to a change in the price of another good (Y).

Key term

Cross price elasticity of demand: the responsiveness of the quantity demanded for one product to a change in the price of another.

Calculation of the cross-elasticity of demand

The formula for the price elasticity of demand is:

$$\text{XED} = \frac{\text{The proportionate change in quantity demanded for product X}}{\text{The proportionate change in price of product Y}}$$

$$\text{XED} = \frac{\text{New quantity demanded X } (Q_{1x}) - \text{Original quantity demanded X } (Q_x)}{\text{Original quantity demanded X } (Q_x)} \div \frac{\text{New price Y } (P_y) - \text{Original price Y } (P_y)}{\text{Original price Y } (P_y)}$$

We could instead have used percentages in the calculation, in which case the formula is:

$$\text{XED} = \frac{\text{Percentage change in quantity demanded for product X}}{\text{Percentage change in price of product Y}}$$

$$\text{XED} = \frac{\%\Delta Q_d \text{ good}_x}{\%\Delta P \text{ good}_y}$$

When looking at cross-elasticity of demand economists are interested not only in its magnitude, but also whether the answer is positive or negative. If the answer is positive it means that a given change in the price of one good has led to a corresponding change in the quantity demanded for another in the same direction. For example, an increase in the price of tea will lead to a reduction in the quantity of tea demanded and an increase in the quantity of coffee demanded. Products with a positive cross-elasticity of demand are *substitutes* for one another. Products with a negative cross-elasticity of demand are *complements* to one another; an increase in, say, the price of cars is likely to lead to a reduction in the quantity of cars demanded and a consequent reduction in the quantity of fuel demanded.

Getting it right

The value of the cross-elasticity of demand will be positive for substitutes and negative for complements.

The greater the magnitude of the value of the cross-elasticity of demand for two products the closer is their relationship as substitutes or complements.

Importance of cross-elasticity of demand

As with income elasticity, cross-elasticity of demand is important to firms in relation to its production and marketing decisions. For example, a local bus company might know that its cross-elasticity of demand in relation to other bus companies, train services and taxi fares to local destinations has a high positive value. This will indicate that the services are close substitutes for one another and so the company would be wary of increasing its prices and instead embark on non-price competition such as more frequent services. If, however, it felt it would be able to cover its costs in such a move, it might decide to reduce its prices knowing it would be likely to increase its market share.

Case Study

Lamb prices soar

Over the year to March 2012 lamb prices in the UK shot up from an average of £7.33 per kilo to £8.51 leading to a decline in sales of 66,427 tonnes or nearly 20 per cent over this period. EBLEX, the organisation for the English beef and sheep industry, highlighted a number of factors causing the price rise. The most important was the change in farming practices in New Zealand, the source of much of the lamb sold in Britain.

Farmers there were increasingly shifting from sheep to cattle herds, which were far more profitable, with the result that New Zealand export production was at a near 50-year low.

This reduction in supply on international markets also drove up the demand for UK lamb on the export market, particularly from new and expanding markets in the Far East.

1 Calculate the price elasticity of demand for lamb.
2 With the aid of demand and supply diagrams, explain the increase in the price of lamb.
3 What is the likely nature of the cross-elasticity of demand between lamb and beef?
4 With the aid of demand and supply diagrams, explain how the increase in the price of lamb and the changing farming practices in New Zealand might affect the market for beef.

Price elasticity of supply (PES)

Key term

Price elasticity of supply: the responsiveness of the quantity supplied of a product to a change in price.

Figure 2.22 shows the supply curves for X and Y. In each case an increase in demand has brought about the same percentage increase in price providing producers with an incentive to increase quantity supplied. However, it is clear that there has been a significantly greater increase in the supply of X compared to Y – as in the case of demand. The reason for this is the differences in the slopes of the two curves which are determined by their different price elasticity of supply.

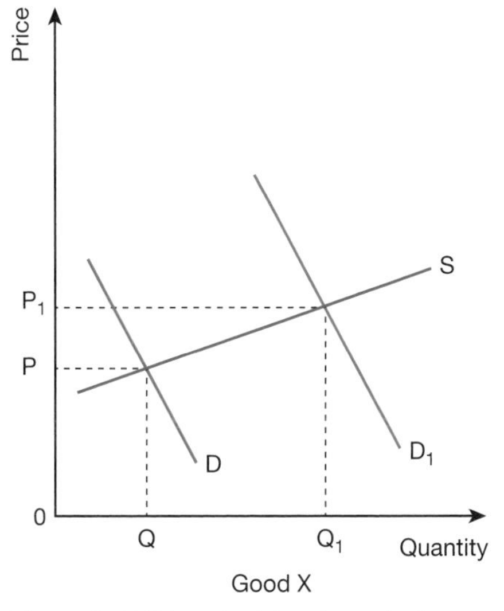

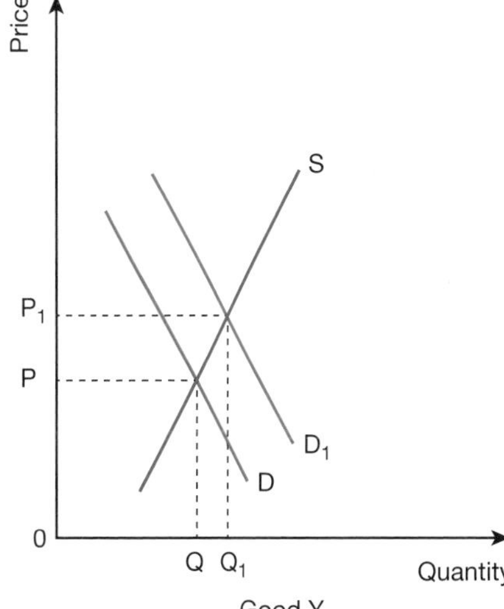

Figure 2.22 Price elasticity of supply ▲

Calculation of the price elasticity of supply

The formula for the price elasticity of supply is:

$$\text{PES} = \frac{\text{The proportionate change in quantity supplied}}{\text{The proportionate change in price}}$$

$$\text{PES} = \frac{\text{New quantity supplied } (Q_1) - \text{Original quantity supplied } (Q)}{\text{Original quantity supplied } (Q)}$$

$$\div \frac{\text{New price } (P_1) - \text{Original price } (P)}{\text{Original price } (P)}$$

If instead we use percentages in the calculation, the formula is:

$$\text{PES} = \frac{\text{Percentage change in quantity supplied}}{\text{Percentage change in price}}$$

Unlike demand the price elasticity of supply for a product will always be positive. The price elasticity of supply will vary in magnitude at different prices along a normal upward-sloping supply curve.

Table 2.15 Meaning of values for the price elasticity of supply ▼

Value of PES	Terminology	Meaning
0	Perfectly inelastic supply	A change in price leaves quantity supplied unchanged
< 1	Inelastic	Proportionate or percentage change in quantity supplied is less than the proportionate or percentage change in price
$= 1$	Unitary elasticity of supply	Proportionate or percentage change in quantity supplied is equal to the proportionate or percentage change in price
>1	Elastic	Proportionate or percentage change in quantity supplied is greater than the proportionate or percentage change in price
Infinity	Perfectly elastic supply	A tiny change in price brings about an infinite change in the quantity supplied

Although the elasticity of supply will vary along the length of a normal upward-sloping supply curve, in parallel with demand, there are three possible limiting cases where the elasticity of supply is the same at all points on the curve. These cases are illustrated in Figure 2.23.

Figure 2.23 Perfectly elastic supply, perfectly inelastic supply and unitary elasticity of supply ▶

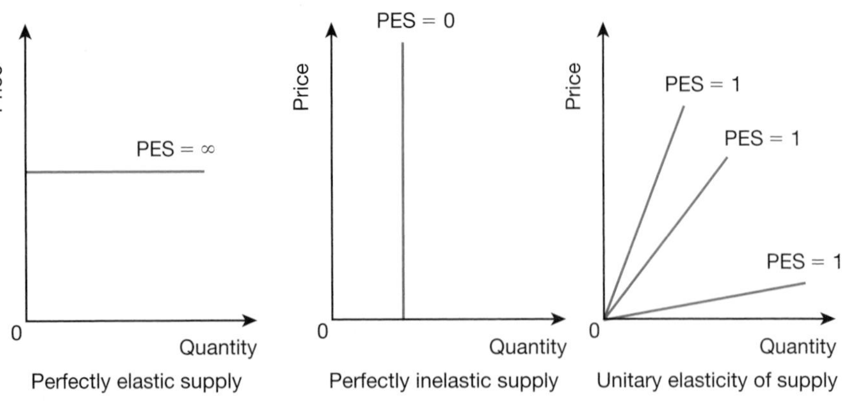

▶ **Perfectly elastic supply** refers to a case in which even a tiny change in price brings about an infinite change in the quantity supplied so that the supply curve is a horizontal straight line.

- **Perfectly inelastic supply** refers to a case in which however great the change in price there is no change in the quantity demanded so that the supply curve is a vertical straight line.
- **Unitary elasticity of supply at all prices** is illustrated by any straight-line supply curve passing through the origin.

Factors affecting the price elasticity of supply

Time

As with demand, time is an important factor determining the price elasticity of supply. Generally the longer the time period under consideration the more elastic the supply will be. Economists often distinguish between three time periods when considering the price elasticity of supply:

- **the immediate or market period** – in this period the quantity supplied is completely fixed
- **the short period** – in this period one or more factors of production are fixed and the quantity supplied can only be increased by making greater use of the variable factors
- **the long period** – in this period all factors of production are variable and the producer can increase the quantity supplied by increasing the scale of production.

Take the case of fresh fish. If there is a sudden significant increase in the demand for fresh fish, it will not be possible for fish companies to increase the quantity supplied to the market in the immediate period and so the supply will be perfectly inelastic. However, the increase in demand is likely to provide an incentive for companies to increase the quantity supplied by using more variable factors – recruiting more workers and making greater use of existing ships, plant and equipment – thereby, making supply more elastic in the short run. At this stage, though, companies will not be able to produce more ships. If fishing companies believe that the increase in demand is likely to be permanent, they can, in the long run, increase the entire scale of production, not only utilising existing resources more fully, but building new ships and investing in new technology and training more workers. In the long run, therefore, supply becomes yet more elastic. Because elasticity of supply can vary significantly over time, it cannot in fact be measured without specific reference to the time period involved.

Availability and nature of resources

Clearly the supply of a product will be more elastic if the resources required to produce it are plentifully available. The nature of the resources required is also important in that if highly specialised, expensive capital is needed or labour has to be highly qualified or requires long periods of training then supply is likely to be inelastic.

Extent of spare capacity in a firm

Supply is likely to be more elastic if a firm has spare capacity in terms of labour and capital. If all factors of production are being fully utilised it will not be possible for a firm to increase production quickly in response to an increase in demand, and supply will be inelastic.

Availability of stocks

If a firm has stocks of goods available or stocks can be obtained very quickly then supply is likely to be relatively elastic. Clearly it is easier to store and stockpile some products more easily than others. Manufactured goods and those that can be processed or frozen can be stored relatively easily whereas perishable goods like fresh vegetables cannot.

Number of firms in the market

Link

See contestable markets in Chapter 7 page 201.

The number of firms in a particular market is also an important factor. The greater the number of firms in a market the more elastic the supply is likely to be. Linked to this is the ease of entry to and exit from the market with more firms being able to enter if start-up costs are low and there are no sunk costs.

Possibility of switching factors of production between alternative uses

The range of products produced by a firm and the ease with which it can switch capital and labour between them is another important factor. The greater the range of products and the more flexible are the resources the more elastic supply is likely to be. For example, in a school or college, Economics teachers can switch quickly to teach Business Studies in response to a sudden change in demand.

Table 2.16 Factors affecting the price elasticity of supply ▼

Factor affecting PES	Impact on PES
Time period	Longer the time period the more elastic is supply
Availability of resources	The greater the number of resources and the less specialised they are the more elastic is supply
Spare capacity	The existence of spare capacity will make supply more elastic
Stocks	Supply will be more elastic if stocks are available or can easily be obtained
Number of firms in the market	The greater the number of firms in the market the more elastic is supply
Possibility of switching factors between uses	If factors can easily be switched between uses then supply will be more elastic

Case Study

Rising vanilla prices hit food and drinks manufacturers

During February and March 2012 the price of vanilla rose by nearly 20 per cent and was expected to rise even further. Vanilla used in food preparation, known as black vanilla, is grown in few countries and, as a consequence, is the second most expensive spice in the world. It is grown mainly in Indonesia, India, Mexico and Madagascar, which is the world's largest supplier. With the exception of Madagascar, producers saw poor harvests in 2012, with Mexico's production falling by 90 per cent.

Fears of a worldwide shortage and price rises fuelled large-scale purchases of black vanilla from Madagascar. Around 1000 tonnes or 40 per cent of the world's supply was purchased at the beginning of 2012 from Madagascar driving up the world price from $25 to nearly $40.This price rise will have an impact on the costs of food and drinks manufacturers and may impact on the market for synthetic vanilla.

1 What does the article suggest about the price elasticity of supply of black vanilla?
2 With the aid of demand and supply diagrams, explain the reasons for the change in the price of black vanilla.
3 With the aid of demand and supply diagrams, explain the likely impact of the change in price of black vanilla on the price of ice cream.
4 With the aid of a demand and supply diagram explain the likely impact of the change in price of black vanilla on the market for synthetic vanilla.

The impact and incidence of indirect taxes

Key terms

Impact of a tax: where the initial burden of paying the tax falls.

Incidence of a tax: where the final burden of paying a tax falls.

Link

See Chapter 3 page 76 for more on the impact and incidence of taxes.

Having considered both elasticity of demand and elasticity of supply we are now in a position to apply these concepts to the way in which the burden of indirect taxes on expenditure is distributed between consumers and producers. In looking at this economists refer to the impact and incidence of taxation.

The impact of taxation refers to the individual or group who bears the initial burden of any tax, i.e. who actually pays the money to the tax-gathering authority. The incidence of taxation refers who ultimately bears the burden of paying the tax. In the case of a direct tax, such as income tax in the UK, which is levied on a worker's weekly or monthly pay, the individual worker bears both the impact and incidence of the tax. The tax is paid directly by the individual to the revenue-collecting authority and the individual normally has no mechanism for passing the tax on to anyone else.

This is not, however, the case with indirect taxes on expenditure. Here, although the impact is born by the producer who initially makes payment of the tax, the producer will then attempt to pass the tax on to consumers in an attempt to ensure they bear all or part of the incidence of the tax by raising the price of the product. The proportion of the incidence of the tax that the producer is able to pass on to the consumer will depend upon the extent to which the producer is able to raise the price and this, in turn, will depend upon the relative magnitudes of the elasticity of demand and elasticity of supply for the product. This is illustrated in Figure 2.24.

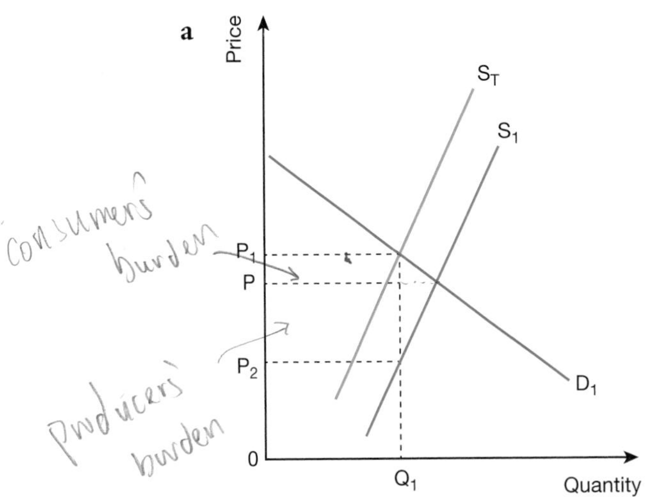

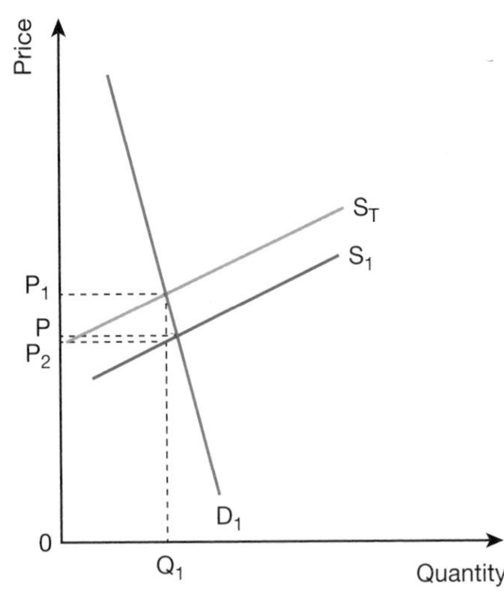

Figure 2.24 Incidence of indirect taxation ▲

In both cases the initial demand and supply curves are D_1 and S_1 giving an initial equilibrium price, P. The government now imposes a specific tax on the product which shifts the supply curve upwards to the right to S_T, increasing the price to P_1. The amount of the tax per unit is given by the vertical distance between the two supply curves, i.e. P_2P_1.

The proportion of the incidence which is borne by the consumer is given by the increase in price – PP_1 and the proportion borne by the producer is the remainder of the tax – P_2P.

Where demand is elastic relative to supply as in Figure 2.24a, the majority of the incidence of the tax is borne by the producer because it is not possible to raise the price without a much greater proportionate change in demand. In Figure 2.24b, however, demand is relatively inelastic compared to supply, which means that the producer is in a strong position to increase the price of the product and so the consumer bears the majority of the incidence of the tax.

Progress questions

4 How would the incidence of an indirect tax between producers and consumers in the following situations?

a Demand for the good is perfectly elastic or supply perfectly inelastic.

b Demand for the good is perfectly inelastic or supply perfectly elastic.

c The elasticity of demand for and elasticity of supply of the good are the same.

Interaction of demand and supply

Competitive demand (substitutes)

If two products are close substitutes for one another in that they serve more or less the same purpose to consumers, then an increase in the demand for one will bring about a corresponding fall in the demand for the other. Examples include butter and margarine, fish and meat, tea and coffee and – in the market for factors of production – in some

Key term

Competitive demand: a situation in which two goods are regarded as alternatives for one another.

processes, machines and labour. These are examples of competitive demand. In Figure 2.25 an increase in the demand for product A shifts the demand curve to the right and leads to an increase in the price and the quantity demanded and supplied. This will have the effect of reducing the demand for product B, shifting the demand curve to the left and bringing about a reduction in the price and the quantity demanded and supplied. The extent of the rise in price and quantity demanded and supplied will depend on the price elasticity of supply (the slope of the supply curve).

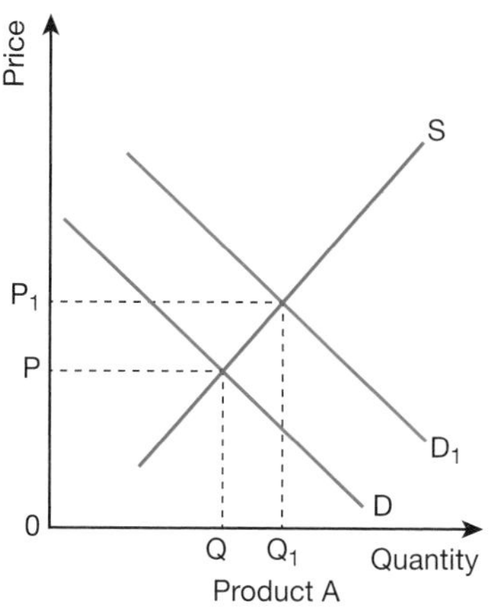

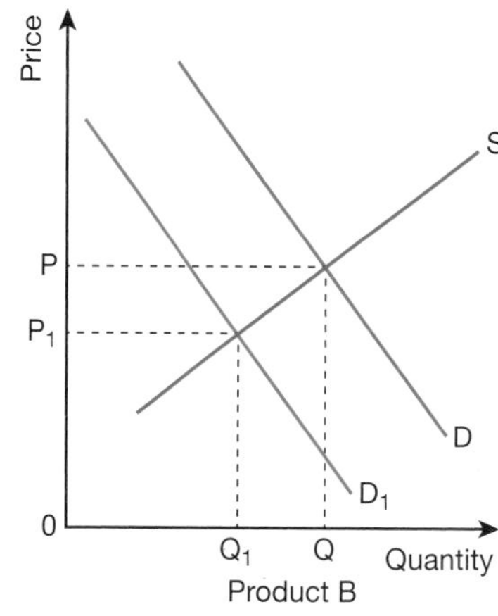

Figure 2.25 Competitive demand ▲

Joint or complementary demand

Key term

Joint or complementary demand (substitutes): a situation in which two goods are normally demanded together.

If two or more products are commonly consumed together, such as cars and fuel or bread and butter then an increase in demand for one will lead to an increase in the demand for another. Such products are in joint or complementary demand. Hence, in Figure 2.26, an increase in the demand for cars has led to a shift in the demand curve for cars to the right, and an increase in price and quantity demanded and supplied. As a consequence, there will be an increase in the demand for fuel shifting the demand curve for fuel to the right, and increasing its price and quantity demanded and supplied. The extent of the increases in price in each case will depend upon the elasticity of supply.

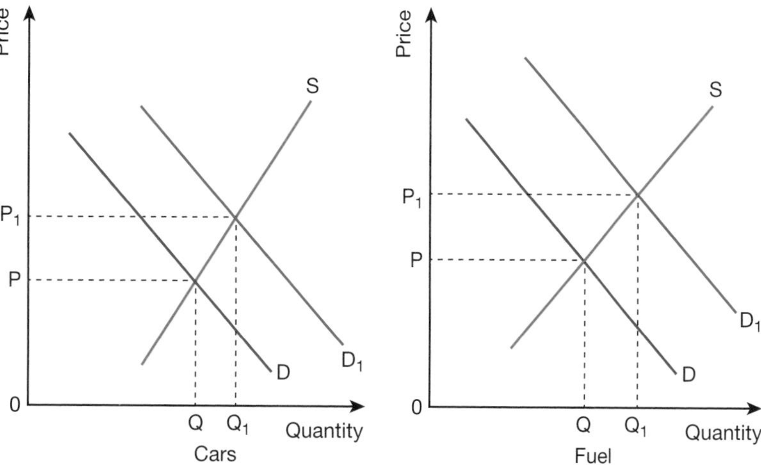

Figure 2.26 Joint demand ▲

Key term

Composite demand: the situation in which a good is demanded for more than one purpose.

Composite demand

Products which can be used for more than one purpose are said to have a composite demand. Bricks, for example, can be used to build schools, office blocks, houses or a garden wall. Wheat can be used as animal feed or increasingly to produce bio fuels. An increase in the demand for wheat to produce bio fuels will shift the demand curve to the right and raise the price, but in the short run, at least, the supply of wheat for animal feed will be reduced, shifting the supply curve to the left and raising the price in this use. This is illustrated in Figure 2.27.

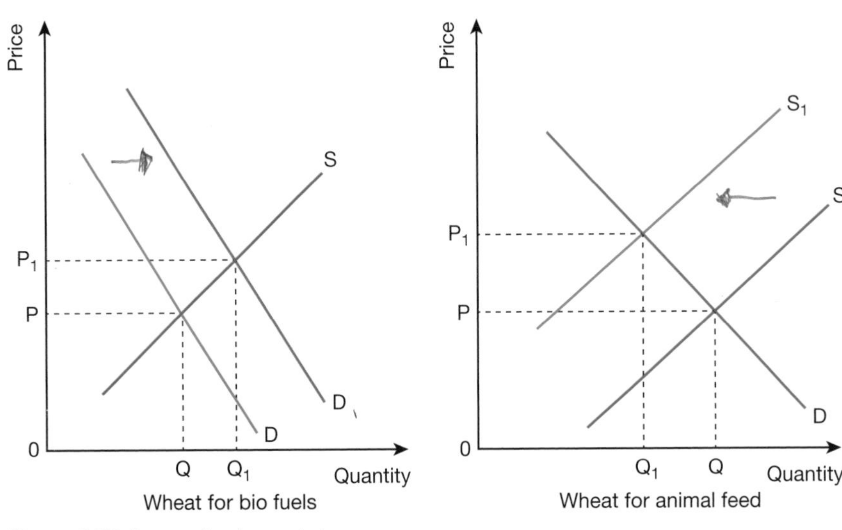

Figure 2.27 Composite demand ▲

Key term

Derived demand: a situation in which a product or service, such as labour, is not demanded for itself, but its demand is dependent on the demand for the product it helps to produce.

Derived demand

Factors of production such as labour are not demanded for themselves, but because they produce goods and services which people want. Hence the demand for labour is derived from the demand for the goods and services it provides. The demand for workers in a supermarket will, therefore, increase if the demand for the products sold by the supermarket increase.

Link

See more about the demand for labour in Chapter 8 page 227.

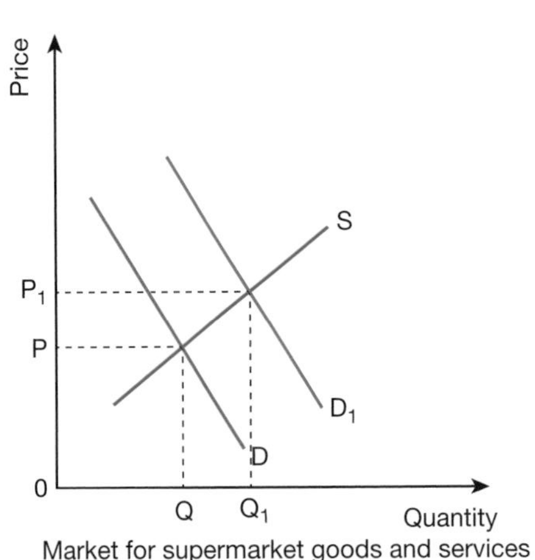

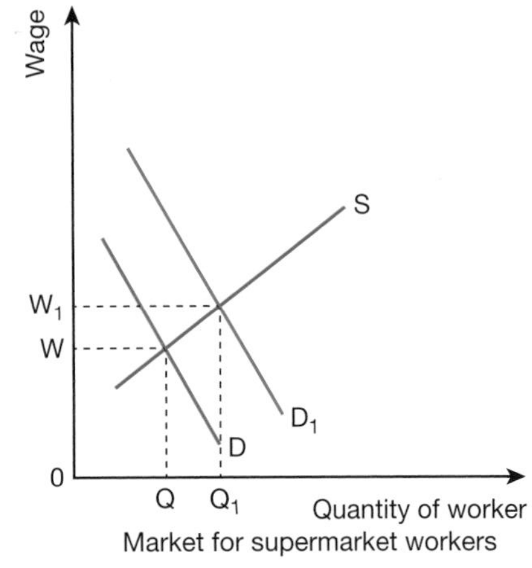

Figure 2.28 Derived demand ▲

Joint supply

> **Key term**
>
> **Joint supply**: the production of one good automatically brings about an increase in the supply of another.

Products such as beef and hides for making leather are in joint supply because an increase in the production of beef will lead to an increase in the supply of hides also. In Figure 2.29 an increase in the demand for beef has shifted the demand curve for beef to the right raising production and its price, but at the same time it has resulted in an increase in the supply of hides with a consequent fall in the price.

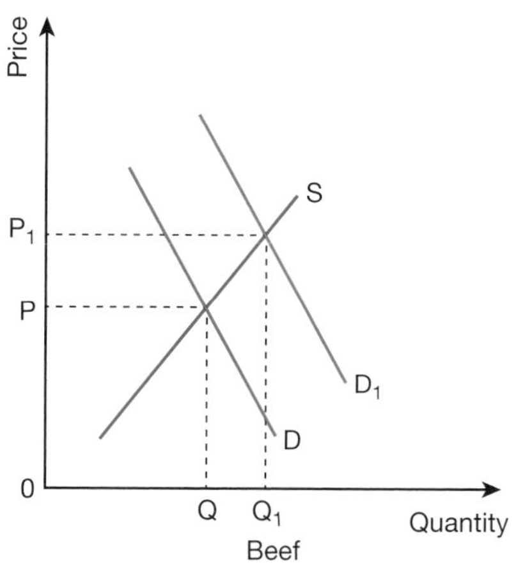

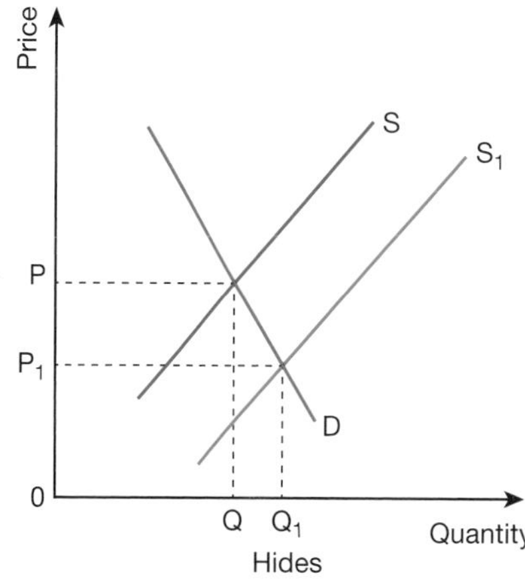

Figure 2.29 Joint supply ▲

Competitive supply

> **Key term**
>
> **Competitive supply**: an increase in the supply of one product will automatically lead to a reduction in the supply of another.

Given that the overall supply of land in a particular area is fixed, a decision to increase the quantity used for building houses will result in less being available for farming. In a fully employed economy, if more workers move into the tertiary sector clearly fewer will be available for the primary and manufacturing sectors. These are examples of competitive supply where an increase in the production of one product reduces the supply of another. In Figure 2.30 an increase in the supply of houses has led to a reduction in the supply of agricultural products and an increase in their price.

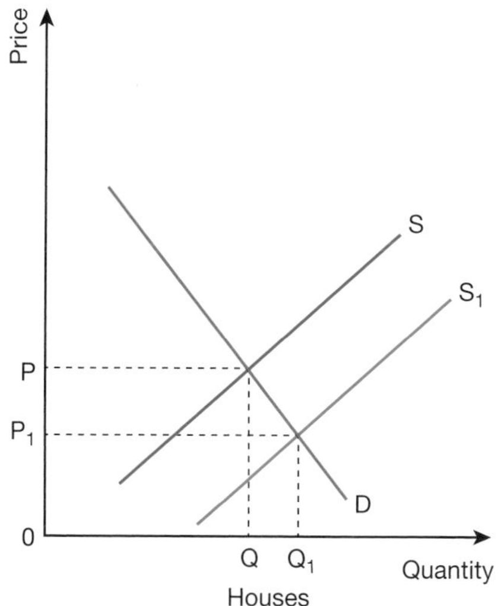

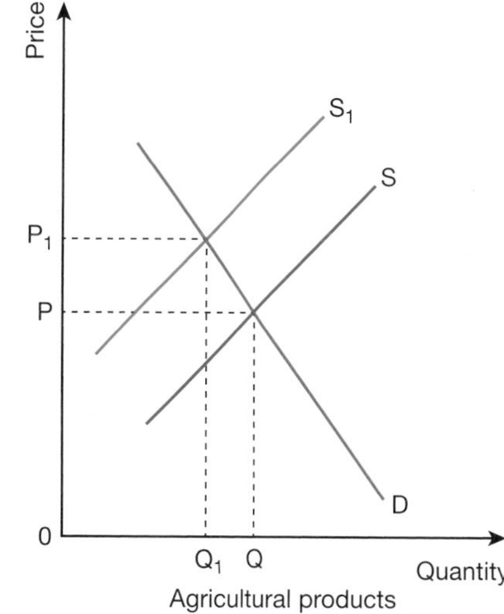

Figure 2.30 Competitive supply ▲

Consumer and producer surplus

> **Key term**
>
> **Consumer surplus:** the difference between the maximum price an individual is prepared to pay for a good and the price actually paid.

Figure 2.31 shows the demand and supply curves for a product for an individual. At the equilibrium price of $6, four units are demanded and supplied. However, the section of the demand curve AB shows that the individual derives so much satisfaction from consuming the product that he or she would be prepared to pay a higher price in order to consume it. The difference between the price an individual is prepared to pay for the product and the price actually paid is known as consumer surplus and in this case amounts to $8 ($3.50 for the first unit + $2.50 for the second + $1.50 for the third + $0.50 for the fourth). The total consumer surplus is shown by the green shaded area PAB (the area under the demand curve at the equilibrium output – the Total Revenue from the sale of this output).

> **Link**
>
> Consumer and producer surplus are important concepts in the analysis of utility, monopoly, and welfare and price discrimination. See Chapter 4.

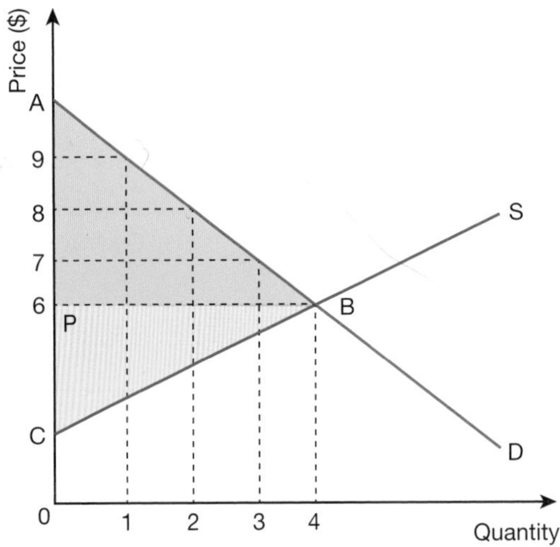

Figure 2.31 Consumer and producer surplus ▲

> **Key term**
>
> **Producer surplus:** the difference between the minimum price a supplier is prepared to accept for a good and the price actually received.

The supply curve indicates that the producer may also gain what is known as producer surplus. The producer would have been prepared to accept a lower price for the first three units than is actually received and this difference, producer surplus, is given by the pink shaded area CPB. The relative size of consumer and producer surplus at any given price will depend upon the slopes of the demand and supply curves which will in turn depend upon the price elasticities of demand and supply for the product. Shifts of the demand and supply curves will also have an impact on the amount of consumer and producer surplus.

> **Progress questions**
>
> **5** Explain with the aid of a diagram (one in each case) the impact on consumer and producer surplus in relation to a particular product of:
>
> **a** the demand for the product becoming more price elastic
>
> **b** the supply of the product becoming more price elastic
>
> **c** the demand curve for the product shifting to the right, supply remaining unchanged
>
> **d** the supply curve shifting to the right, demand remaining unchanged.

Key concepts

- **Scarcity and choice** is covered in the role of markets. Within markets, changes in price signal surpluses and shortages ration the available quantity of a good or service amongst consumers and provide incentives for producers to allocate scarce resources between competing uses.
- **Margin and change** is explored in the section on the determination of the equilibrium price and quantity demanded and supplied of a product. This shows that any movement away from this position will be detrimental as long as the conditions remain unchanged. This position will only be altered if individuals, firms and governments make decisions to optimise their behaviour in the face of changing demand and supply conditions.
- **Equilibrium and efficiency** is covered throughout the chapter. The equilibrium price and quantity demanded and supplied of a good or service is determined by the interaction of the demand for it from consumers and the supply of it from producers. Shifts in the demand and supply curves explain how the equilibrium position may change over time.

Progress check

After completing this chapter you should be able to:

- understand the nature and functions of markets
- understand the role of prices in allocating resources
- explain individual and market demand curves
- explain individual and market supply curves
- explain how the interaction of demand and supply bring about the equilibrium price and quantity demanded and supplied for a product
- explain how the equilibrium price and quantity demanded and supplied will be affected by shifts of the demand and supply curves
- explain the interaction of demand and supply and apply the analysis to real-world problems
- define, calculate and explain the factors affecting price, income, and cross-elasticity of demand and elasticity of supply
- understand and be able to apply to real-world problems the concepts of price, income-and cross-elasticity of demand and price elasticity of supply
- explain the nature of consumer and producer surplus.

Exam-style questions

Essay questions and data response

1 a Explain the factors that affect the price elasticity of demand for a product? [8 marks]

b Discuss the importance of a knowledge of the price elasticity of demand for:

i producers

ii a government. [12 marks]

2 a Explain the difference between the impact and incidence of an indirect tax. [8 marks]

b Explain the factors which affect the share of the incidence of an indirect tax born by producers and consumers. [12 marks]

3 a Explain what is meant by the cross price elasticity of demand. [8 marks]

b With reference to the concept of cross price elasticity of demand, discuss how the demand for one good will be affected by a change in the demand for another. [12 marks]

4 a Explain the factors which are likely to affect an individual's demand for a particular product. [8 marks]

b Discuss with the aid of diagrams the likely effects on the price of a particular brand of designer sportswear of:

i an increase in the wages of workers producing the sportswear

ii a substantial decrease in incomes of consumers

iii a major advertising campaign by the company. [12 marks]

5 a Explain the factors that affect the price elasticity of supply of a product. [8 marks]

b Discuss the likely impact of a significant increase in the demand for a good with:

i a price elasticity of supply of +0.2

ii a price elasticity of supply of +2.0. [12 marks]

6 a Explain what is meant by the price elasticity of supply. [8 marks]

b Discuss the factors which explain the difference in the price elasticity of supply for fresh and tinned tomatoes. [12 marks]

Multiple-choice questions

7 At a price of $50 a bookshop can sell 200 copies of a textbook each month. If it reduces the price to $45 it can increase its sales to 212. The price elasticity of demand for this textbook for a fall in price from $50 to $45 is: [1 mark]

A −0.42

B −1.67

C −0.60

D −2.40

8 Which of the following will cause a movement down along the demand curve for apples? [1 mark]

A A decrease in consumer incomes

B A major advertising campaign emphasising the health hazards of eating apples

C An increase in the demand for a substitute, oranges

D A fall in the wages of workers producing apples

3 Government microeconomic intervention

In this chapter you will develop your knowledge and understanding of:

- maximum and minimum prices
- taxes (direct and indirect)
- subsidies
- transfer payments
- direct provision of goods and services
- nationalisation and privatisation.

Key term

Maximum price control: a situation where a maximum price or price ceiling is established in a market below what would have been the equilibrium price without government intervention.

Getting it right

Make sure that you know how to stress that if a maximum price control was established in a market, this would need to be below what would normally be the equilibrium price.

Activity

Maximum price

Carry out research in your own country to find out if there are any examples of a maximum price in operation. Work in pairs or groups and find out how well it seems to be working in terms of its objectives.

Maximum and minimum prices

Meaning and effect on the market

A government could intervene in a market by establishing a maximum price control, but this would only be the case if the maximum price imposed is below what would normally be the equilibrium price in the market as determined by demand and supply. If the maximum price set was above the equilibrium price in a market, it would have no effect.

The effect of establishing a maximum price control in a market can be seen in Figure 3.1.

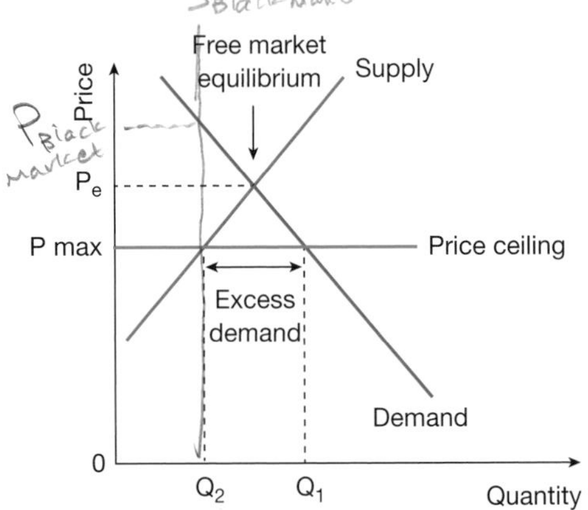

Figure 3.1 Maximum price control in a market ▲

There are clearly both advantages and disadvantages of a maximum price being imposed in a market by a government, as Table 3.1 indicates.

Table 3.1 The advantages and disadvantages of a maximum price control in a market ▼

Advantages of a maximum price control in a market	Disadvantages of a maximum price control in a market
The price of essential products, such as important items of food, can be limited, making such items more affordable to people.	The maximum price control will lead to excess demand in the market and this will create some form of queue or waiting list.
In the housing market, the rent of certain types of accommodation could be prevented from becoming too expensive.	The existence of a queue or waiting list may lead to bribery and corruption of those who are responsible for regulating the queue or waiting list.
In the transport market, fares could be restricted from going above a certain price.	It is possible that a secondary or informal market, or black market, may emerge where the supply is increased through illegal methods outside of the market. In such a situation, the price is likely to be well above the maximum price in the formal market.

Progress question

1 Discuss the advantages and disadvantages of using a maximum price control in a market.

Minimum price controls

As well as imposing maximum price controls in an economy, a government could also decide to impose minimum price controls. Minimum prices work in the same way as price ceilings, but instead of having a maximum price, prices are not allowed to fall below a minimum price or price floor.

Such a situation can occur when a government intervenes in an agricultural market to ensure that the incomes of farmers do not fall below a certain level.

The effect of establishing a minimum price control in a market can be seen in Figure 3.2.

Price
Excess supply
Supply
P_{min}
Price floor (guaranteed)
P_e
Demand
0
Q_3 Q_2 Q_1
Quantity of output

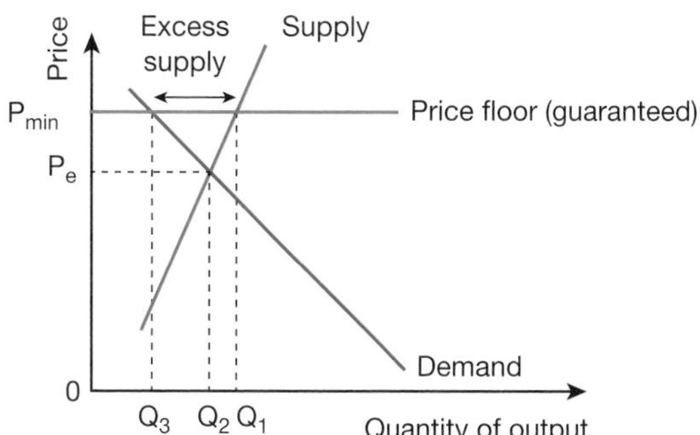

Figure 3.2 Minimum price control in a market

The normal equilibrium position, without government intervention, would be at P_e and Q_2 where demand is equal to supply. However, if a government decided to prevent the price falling below a particular level, indicated by P_{min}, then the price would not be allowed to fall beneath this. In such a situation, the supply would be Q_1 and the demand Q_3, creating an excess supply shown by the distance between Q_3 and Q_1. If the minimum price set was below the equilibrium price in a market, it would have no effect.

Key term

Minimum price controls: a situation where a minimum price or price floor is established in a market above what would have been the equilibrium price without government intervention.

Taxes

Another way in which a government can intervene in a market is through taxation. This would particularly be the case if a firm or an individual was responsible for a negative externality or an external cost. The effect of this is that the external cost would be internalised through the price mechanism.

Link

See Chapter 6 page 141 for more on externalities.

The effect of imposing a tax in a market can be seen in Figure 3.3.

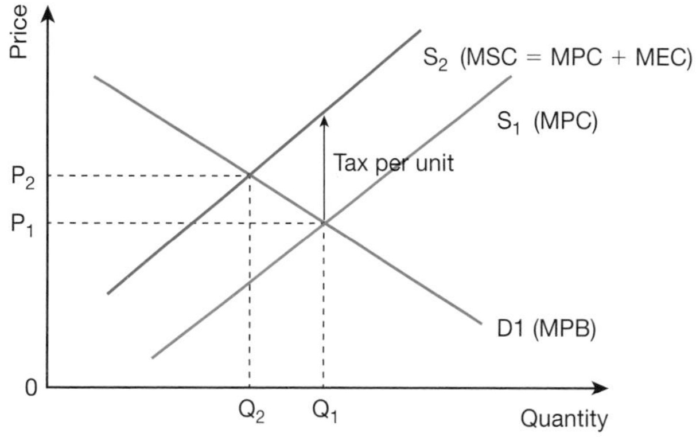

Price
S_2 (MSC = MPC + MEC)
S_1 (MPC)
Tax per unit
P_2
P_1
D1 (MPB)
0
Q_2 Q_1
Quantity

Figure 3.3 The effect of imposing an indirect tax in a market

Direct and indirect taxes

It is important to distinguish between direct and indirect taxes.

A direct tax is one which is levied on the incomes of individuals and firms. Direct taxes also include taxes on inherited wealth. Examples include: income tax, corporation tax and inheritance tax.

An indirect tax is one that is levied when goods and services are bought. Indirect taxes are, therefore, taxes on expenditure. Examples include value added tax (VAT) and goods and services tax (GST).

> **Key terms**
>
> Direct tax: a tax levied on incomes and wealth.
>
> Indirect tax: a tax levied on expenditure.

> **Activity**
>
> **Direct and indirect taxes**
>
> Carry out research in your own country to discover the main examples of direct and indirect taxes.

The impact and incidence of taxes

It is important to distinguish between the impact and the incidence of taxes. The impact of a tax refers to the person or company on which a tax is levied, i.e. someone will be legally responsible for handing over the levy to the tax authorities.

The incidence of a tax, however, refers to the eventual burden of a tax. For example, a tax on a retailer, or at least part of the tax, could be passed on to the consumer. With a specific sales tax, the incidence will depend on the elasticity of the demand and supply curves. The more inelastic is the demand, and the more elastic is the supply, the greater the burden will be on the consumer.

Specific and ad valorem *taxes*

Indirect taxes can take different forms. One of these is excise duties. This is a tax imposed on a product, such as petrol, alcohol or tobacco. An excise duty is usually a specific tax placed on a particular product, i.e. a specific amount is required to be paid.

◀ Tax on petrol is a specific tax.

As opposed to a specific tax which imposes a fixed amount, an *ad valorem* tax is one which places a percentage rate on a good or service, e.g. a sales tax might charge a 20 per cent rate. This is the case with a tax such as value added tax.

Average and marginal rates of taxation

Average rates of taxation refer to the average percentage of total income which is paid in taxes. The average rate of tax can also be known as the effective rate of tax or the average propensity to pay tax.

Marginal rates of taxation refer to the proportion of an increase in income which is taken in tax.

> **Key terms**
>
> Specific tax: this is where a specific amount of money has to be paid in taxation.
>
> *Ad valorem* tax: this is where the tax on the consumption of products is a percentage of the value of the product rather than a fixed amount.
>
> Average rate of tax: the average percentage of total income that is paid in taxes.
>
> Marginal rate: the proportion of additional income that is taken in tax.

Key terms

Marginal rate of tax (MRT): the addition to tax paid out of a change in income.

Progressive tax: where the proportion of income paid in tax increases as income increases.

Regressive tax: where the proportion paid in tax falls as income increases.

Proportional, or flat, tax: where the proportion of income paid in tax remains constant regardless of the level of income.

Getting it right

You need to understand that a progressive tax does not just mean that a person pays more tax as their income increases, they pay an increasing proportion of their income.

Activity

Income tax

Carry out research in your own country to discover what the rates of income tax are. This will enable you to judge how progressive income tax is in your country.

Link

See Chapter 8 page 223.

Key term

Canons of taxation: the five principles of taxation by which a particular tax should be judged.

Progressive, regressive and proportional taxes

Changes in taxes can have different effects depending on the marginal rate of tax (MRT).

Progressive taxes

If as people's income rises a higher proportion of the increase is taken in tax, MRT increases, then the tax is said to be progressive. In many countries, the proportion of income taken in tax rises when the income goes above certain levels or thresholds. For example, income tax might start at 20 per cent and then increase to 30 per cent, 40 per cent and 50 per cent as income levels rise.

Regressive taxes

On the other hand, if MRT falls as income increases, then it is regressive. This will apply to any *ad valorem* tax, such as value added tax, because this tax will be at a fixed percentage whatever a person's income.

Proportional taxes

Finally, proportional, or flat, taxes have a constant MRT whatever the income level. In this situation, the marginal and the average rate of tax is the same.

Progress question

2 Discuss whether changing your country's tax system to one based on a flat tax would be beneficial.

The relationships of the three types of tax to income are shown in Figure 3.4.

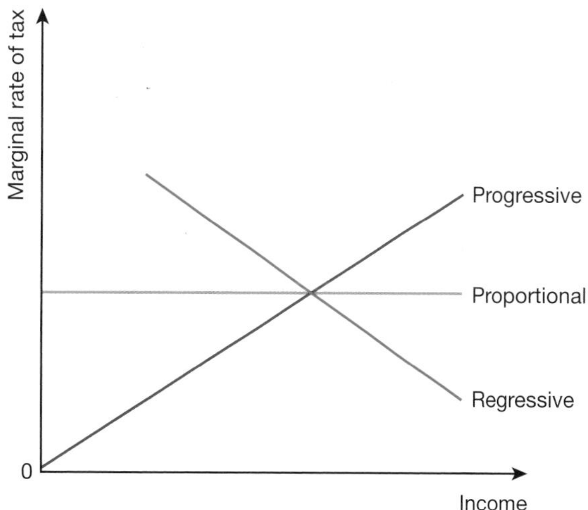

Figure 3.4 Progressive, proportional and regressive taxation ▲

The canons of taxation

There are a number of principles or canons of taxation and these are shown in Table 3.2.

Table 3.2 The canons of taxation ▼

Canon or principle	Explanation
Equity or fairness	The burden of taxation should take into account the ability of people or organisations to pay the tax.
Certainty or transparency	Information about taxation needs to be made available in such a way that it is seen as clear and transparent.
Convenience	The payment and collection of taxes need to be as convenient as possible, e.g. they should be collected at a time and in a way that is convenient for the taxpayer.
Cost	The cost of administering and collecting taxes needs to be as low as possible; taxes should not be expensive to collect and should not discourage business.
Efficiency	Taxation should not lead to any disincentives, such as in relation to work disincentives.

Key terms

Poverty trap: a situation where a person can become worse off as a result of an increase in wages because they will lose their entitlement to certain benefits which are means tested. This can occur where there is a low tax threshold and means-tested benefits up to a particular level of income.

Work disincentive: a situation where the existence of benefits acts as a disincentive for a person to go out to work.

In relation to the fifth canon or principle of taxation, one problem caused by taxation is the poverty trap. If people receive benefits from governments if they have low incomes, e.g. are unemployed, then if they take low-paid work they may find that this brings them above the tax threshold. As a result they start to pay tax and at the same time lose their benefits. This may leave them basically no better off financially than before. A person may actually be worse off working than living on means-tested benefits because the marginal rate of taxation and the rate at which benefits are lost, when taken together, can mean that any incentive effect of working will disappear. The reason for this is that there are often low tax thresholds, i.e. the level of income when tax has to be paid, combined with the fact that means-tested benefits fall rapidly as incomes rise. In countries that have an extensive benefits system, this can be a work disincentive. It has been calculated that the MRT for these people can be as high as 95 per cent.

Discouraging goods or services

Governments in many countries tax certain goods or services to deliberately try to discourage their consumption. The actual effect of any such government intervention may well be limited by the extent of the price elasticity of demand for such products. For example, the consumption of cigarettes and alcohol can be very addictive and so the imposition of taxes on such products may not change the level of demand

Case Study

South Africa is planning to ban all alcohol advertising

Many countries try to reduce the consumption of alcohol. Alcohol consumption in South Africa is high by comparison with other countries. For example, the World Health Organization has produced figures which show that per person, alcohol consumption in South Africa is twice as high as that in either France or the USA.

The government in South Africa has estimated that about 75 per cent of knife murders and 40 per cent of gun murders are committed by people under the influence of alcohol. It also estimates that about 50 per cent of the 14,000 road deaths in the country each year are due to the influence of alcohol.

The South African government, therefore, is planning to introduce a ban on all alcohol advertising in the country.

1 Discuss whether a ban on alcohol advertising would be likely to have an impact on the demand for the product.

for them by very much. It is for this reason that a government may decide to make the smoking of cigarettes or the drinking of alcohol illegal.

Key term

Subsidies: an amount of money paid by a government to a producer so that the price to the customer will be lower than it otherwise would have been.

Subsidies

Whereas a tax is imposed in a situation of negative externalities, the opposite happens when there is a situation of positive externalities or external benefits.

The effect of imposing a subsidy in a market can be seen in Figure 3.5.

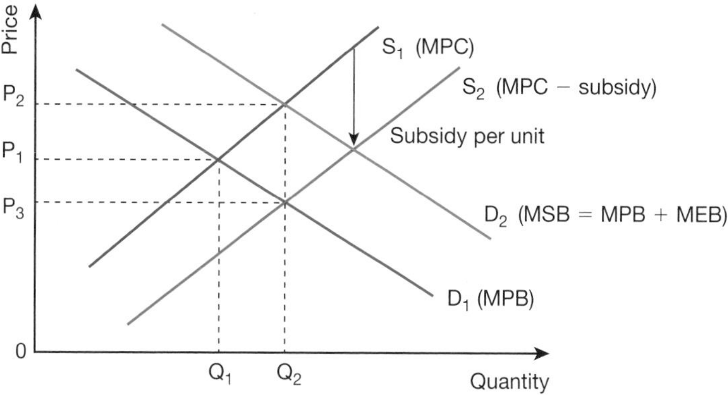

Figure 3.5 The effect of providing a subsidy in a market ▲

The market equilibrium would be price P_1 and quantity Q_1. At this point, the demand curve D_1 (representing the marginal private benefit) intersects with the supply curve S_1 (representing the marginal private cost). This equilibrium position, however, only includes the private benefits and the private costs. If external benefits have been created as a result of the production process, the consumption needs to be increased. If a government decides to subsidise the production of such a product, the supply will shift to the right, from S_1 to S_2. The subsidy can be seen by the vertical distance between the two supply curves. The effect of the external benefit can be seen in the demand curve D_2 which represents the marginal social benefit of consumption, including both the marginal private benefit and the marginal external benefit. The optimum position in the market is therefore price P_3 and quantity Q_2; it is clear that there is a greater quantity in the market at a lower price.

Case Study

Electricity subsidies in Pakistan

In Pakistan, subsidies are provided to people to keep down the price of electricity so that all of the population, whether rich or poor, are able to benefit from the electricity.

One problem arising from the provision of the subsidies to people, however, is that they are expensive for the government to finance. Economists have pointed out that they contributed to the large budget deficit in the 2011–2012 financial year.

A further problem is that the subsidies have led to an increase in the demand for electricity, so that the demand exceeds supply. One effect of this is that there are frequent electricity blackouts, some of which can last as long as ten hours.

1 Discuss the advantages and disadvantages of a country, such as Pakistan, providing electricity subsidies to its population.

Progress question

3 Contrast the effect of a tax and a subsidy in a market.

The impact and incidence of subsidies

The distinction between impact and incidence has already been referred to in relation to taxes, but impact and incidence can also be applied to subsidies. The different effects of a subsidy reflect differences in demand for, and the supply of, a product. For example, if the demand for a product is elastic, the provision of a subsidy would lead to a relatively small reduction in price, but a relatively large increase in consumption.

If, on the other hand, the demand for a product is inelastic, the provision of a subsidy would lead to a relatively large reduction in price, but a relatively small increase in consumption. The incidence of a subsidy, therefore, clearly depends on the demand and supply conditions in a market for a particular product.

Transfer payments

Key term

Transfer payments: where revenue is received from one part of society, such as taxpayers, and paid to another part of society, such as pensioners.

A government could decide to intervene in a market through the provision of transfer payments. This is where revenue received from taxation is used to provide financial support to people, such as in the form of pensions and social security payments.

The effect of transfer payments on the market

Transfer payments can be given out in various forms of income support to assist those who are less well off. These payments can be in the form of pensions and social security payments. One type of transfer payment is unemployment benefit, which is money paid out to those who are unable to find employment. It has been argued by some economists that these payments are too high; it may have a distorting effect on the labour market, making some people unwilling to make themselves available for employment.

Activity

Transfer payments

Carry out research in your own country to discover examples of transfer payments.

Case Study

Unemployment benefits in the USA

In the USA, unemployment benefits – or unemployment compensation, as it is more usually called – are paid to workers who have become unemployed through no fault of their own. This is an example of a social welfare benefit and is usually paid by the state government.

This benefit is only paid for a certain period of time, usually six months. Once that period of time has elapsed, the unemployed worker will no longer receive this benefit.

1 Discuss the advantages and disadvantages of a country, such as the USA, providing unemployment benefit to its population for a limited period of time.

> **Key terms**
>
> **Direct provision of goods and services**: this is where a government decides to provide particular goods and/or services itself.
>
> **Nationalisation**: a process whereby private sector firms become part of the public sector of the economy, with the government or state involved in the direct provision of particular goods and/or services.

Direct provision of goods and services

Another way in which a government can intervene in a market is through the direct provision of goods and services.

Instead of intervening to discourage certain activities, such as through the use of indirect taxation, or to encourage other activities, such as through the use of subsidies, a government could decide to directly provide certain goods and services. Where a government decides to take over the provision of goods and/or services directly, it is called nationalisation.

The effect of the direct provision of goods and services on the market

As Table 3.3 indicates, there are clearly some advantages to the nationalisation of certain industries in an economy, but it is also the case that such direct provision can have an effect on the market, particularly in terms of the reduced role of the private sector. Critics of such direct provision of goods and services argue that without the existence of competition, and without the drive of the profit motive, the provision of such goods and services may be less efficient compared to what would be the case if provision was through competing firms in the private sector.

Nationalisation and privatisation

Nationalisation

Nationalisation refers to the process whereby private sector firms are transferred into public ownership and are owned and controlled in some way by the government.

The advantages and disadvantages of nationalisation are indicated in Table 3.3.

Table 3.3 The advantages and disadvantages of nationalisation

Advantages of nationalisation	Disadvantages of nationalisation
A nationalised industry can benefit from economies of scale, lowering cost and possibly price.	A nationalised industry may lack the incentive to be efficient, compared to the situation in the private sector.
If an industry is state owned, it can avoid a wasteful duplication of resources.	Nationalised industries may lack competitive pressure, such as the pressure to be innovative.
With state ownership, it is easier to control the negative externalities and encourage the positive externalities.	It is possible that some decisions taken by a nationalised industry could be taken primarily for political rather than economic reasons.
A nationalised industry will prevent monopoly power being held by a private firm.	A state owned firm may still be in a position to abuse its monopoly power.

Case Study

Mineral resources in Namibia and South Africa

African countries have a vast wealth of mineral resources. The dilemma for many of the countries, however, is whether to allow private sector companies to be responsible for the development of the resources or whether to bring this under greater state control.

In Namibia, it was decided to transfer all new mining and exploration to a state-owned company, the Epangelo Mining Company. The mineral resources would include uranium, copper, gold, zinc and coal. In 2011, mining contributed to about 15 per cent of the country's gross domestic product and its export earnings contributed to more than half of Namibia's total revenue from exports. The government of Namibia announced that the state-owned company would ensure that its people would reap the benefits from the country's rich endowment of mineral resources.

In South Africa, however, which has a great deal of mineral wealth, the government has decided against such state ownership of mineral resources. It believes, instead, that it would be better to encourage private sector companies to be responsible for the exploration and mining of the resources and then to put a significant tax on the profits made by the companies. One idea is to impose a 50 per cent windfall tax on the "super profits" made by the mining companies.

1 Discuss the advantages and disadvantages of bringing companies, such as those responsible for mining, under state ownership.

Of course, a government could establish the direct provision of goods and services alongside the private sector, rather than instead of it. This would especially be the case with certain merit goods. For example, in many countries education is provided through both the public and the private sector. In many countries, the provision of health care is also provided through both the public and the private sector.

Case Study

Joint venture in Mongolia

The government of Mongolia is very keen to develop the country's infrastructure, but it has decided to co-operate in joint ventures with private sector companies in certain projects rather than provide them as a purely state-owned operation.

For example, responsibility for the building of one of the world's biggest copper mines in the middle of the desert is in the hands of a joint venture between the Mongolian government, which is providing 34 per cent of the finance, and Ivanhoe Mines of Canada, which is providing the other 66 per cent of the money.

The Mongolian government has decided to be involved in this joint venture with a private sector company because the mine will eventually become one of the five biggest copper mines in the world, producing 450 000 tonnes of copper a year.

1 Discuss the arguments for and against a government co-operating with a private sector company in a joint venture.

In the case of public goods, however, such as police and national defence, it has already been made clear that a government would need to provide these directly because they would otherwise not be provided at all.

Privatisation

Whereas nationalisation is the process of transferring the ownership of assets from the private sector to the public sector, privatisation refers to the transfer of ownership in the opposite direction, from the public sector to the private sector. It can also be called denationalisation.

> **Key term**
>
> Privatisation: a process whereby public sector firms become part of the private sector of the economy, with the government or state no longer involved in the direct provision of particular goods and/or services.

As was indicated in Table 3.3, a nationalised or state-owned firm may not be as efficient as a firm operating in the private sector, and so a decision may be taken by a government to privatise a firm or industry by transferring ownership from the public sector to the private sector.

The advantages and disadvantages of privatisation are indicated in Table 3.4.

Table 3.4 The advantages and disadvantages of privatisation ▼

The advantages of privatisation	The disadvantages of privatisation
The reduction of government or state intervention in an economy so as to allow greater scope for the private sector to take key economic decisions. This view is based on the idea that there is a greater likelihood of economic efficiency occurring in a market that is not controlled by a government.	In some cases, a public sector monopoly could simply be replaced by a private sector monopoly. The impact of privatisation may therefore not be as great as had been predicted with one monopoly being replaced by another.
The sale of assets from the public sector to the private sector would have the effect of widening the extent of share ownership in an economy. The effect of this would be to encourage people to feel that they were part of the economic system.	Sometimes, it might be better to leave an industry in the public sector when there is a situation of natural monopoly. If a natural monopoly was privatised, the result could be a duplication of resources that is wasteful and inefficient.
A firm operating in the private sector would be more likely to be efficient and this would be likely to lead to an increase in quantity provided in the market and a lowering of cost. This lowering of cost could be passed on to consumers in the form of lower prices.	The greater efficiency of a private sector firm could come at a cost to the community if the number of employees was substantially reduced. This could be regarded as a negative externality resulting from the change of ownership from the public to the private sector.
The sale of assets would bring in a substantial amount of money and such revenue could play a key role in a government's fiscal policy.	The income that is brought in from the sale of shares in a former public sector company is a "one-off" source of income and not one that will bring in revenue on a regular basis in the future.
A private sector company, being more efficient, would be able to raise capital to fund future growth rather than relying on the state to finance such expenditure.	The establishment of a private sector monopoly is likely to lead to the need to introduce a number of regulations so as to control it and ensure that consumers are not being exploited. The establishment of such regulations could severely limit the ability of the privatised firm to operate as it wishes.

> **Activity**
>
> **Nationalisation or privatisation**
>
> Carry out research in your own country to find out if there are any examples of nationalisation or privatisation. Find out as much as you can about these examples.

The term "privatisation" can actually refer to a number of different government initiatives, beyond simply transferring ownership from the public to the private sector through the issuing of shares and the creation of a public limited company. These other methods can include deregulation and contracting out.

Deregulation

Deregulation refers to a situation where the number of regulations, rules and laws in an industry are reduced in an attempt to create greater flexibility and competition in the market. It is generally thought that greater competition will lead to greater efficiency.

Contracting out

Another form of privatisation is the process of contracting out when responsibility for the provision of a particular service is transferred from the public to the private sector. This may happen in such services as education, health care and waste disposal.

The effect on the market

As has already been argued, critics of nationalisation point out that without competition between a number of private sector firms, efficiency may be less than would otherwise be the case. This is why the process of privatisation has become so popular, with competition in a market leading to greater efficiency. However, despite its advantages, privatisation can also be criticised because it can lead to an increase in unemployment in an economy.

Key terms

Deregulation: the removal of legal restrictions and controls on economic activity, usually to allow a greater degree of competition in a market.

Contracting out: the transfer of responsibility for providing a particular service from the public to the private sector. This can also be known as outsourcing.

Link

See Chapter 8 page 214 for more on privatisation.

Key concepts

- **Margin and change** can be seen when applying the concept of the margin to taxation, such as when comparing the average and the marginal level of taxation in an economy.
- **Equilibrium and efficiency:** an equilibrium price will be determined in a market through the forces of demand and supply, but when a maximum or a minimum price is used, price will be determined at a point that is above or below what would otherwise be the equilibrium price.
- **Regulation and equity** can be seen through the use of progressive taxation, which can be used in an attempt to bring about a greater degree of equity in the distribution of income and wealth in an economy. Subsidies could also be used to keep down the price of essential goods in an economy, making such goods more affordable to the less well off.
- **Progress and development** can be viewed when a country could benefit if the state decided to take over a firm or industry, especially where such a firm in the private sector was abusing its position. This could enable the country to benefit from progress and development.

Progress check

After completing this chapter you should be able to:

- appreciate why maximum and minimum prices might be established in an economy
- understand the reasons for direct and indirect taxes in an economy
- understand why subsidies may be provided in an economy
- appreciate why transfer payments may be provided in an economy
- understand why a government may decide to directly provide particular goods and services
- explain the reasons for nationalisation and privatisation in an economy.

Exam-style questions

Essay questions

1 Discuss the advantages and disadvantages of using indirect taxes to deal with negative externalities. [12 marks]

2 Discuss why certain goods and services may be supplied directly by a government rather than through the market. [12 marks]

3 Discuss the case for and against the use of government subsidies for the production of milk. [12 marks]

4 Explain the case for microeconomic intervention by a government. [8 marks]

5 Discuss how the market system might be influenced by government intervention to provide certain goods and services. [12 marks]

6 Discuss the advantages and disadvantages of a government nationalising a particular industry. [12 marks]

Multiple-choice questions

7 What effect will a minimum price have on a market? [1 mark]

A A minimum price will be above the equilibrium price in a free market
B A minimum price will be equal to the equilibrium price in a free market
C A minimum price will be below the equilibrium price in a free market
D A minimum price will be likely to create a situation of excess demand

8 An income tax will usually be an example of a: [1 mark]

A proportional tax
B regressive tax
C progressive tax
D flat tax

4 The macro economy

In this chapter you will develop your knowledge and understanding of:

- aggregate demand (AD) and aggregate supply (AS) analysis
- inflation
- balance of payments
- exchange rates
- the terms of trade
- principles of absolute and comparative advantage
- protectionism.

Key terms

Aggregate demand: the total value of demand in the economy consisting of consumption (C), investment (I), government expenditure (G) and net exports (X–M).

Aggregate supply: the total value of goods and services produced in the economy.

Activity

Your country's aggregate demand

Try to find out what the values of C, I, G and X–M are for your country. How important is each for the whole?

Aggregate demand and aggregate supply

Aggregate demand (AD) is the total amount of goods and services demanded or total expenditure on goods and services in an economy. Aggregate supply (AS) is the total production of goods and services in an economy.

Shape and determinants of aggregate demand

Figure 4.1 shows that the AD curve slopes downwards so that if inflation rises (p_1 to p_2) real output falls (Y_1 to Y_2). This downward slope is due to rising price levels causing:

- nominal interest rates to rise leading to a fall in demand for goods and services (fall in C)
- reduction in the purchasing power of cash held as wealth (fall in C and I)
- domestic goods to be more expensive leading to a fall in exports and an increase in imports (fall in X−M).

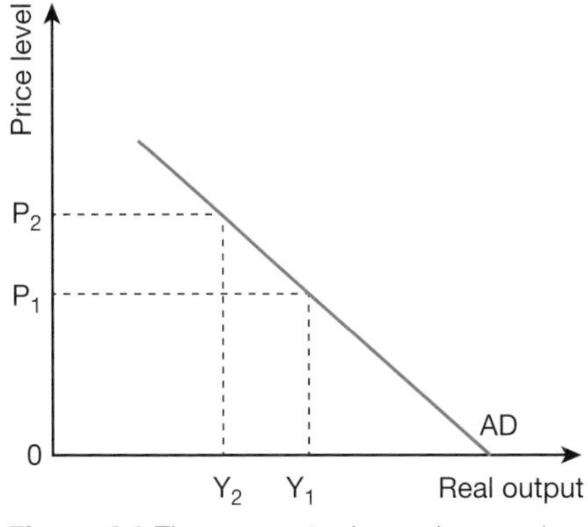

Figure 4.1 The aggregate demand curve ▲

All of this is because AD = C + I + G + (X−M). A change in any one of these components of AD will lead to a shift in the curve.

Figure 4.2 shows that as prices increase more will be supplied (Y_1 to Y_2). This is because although costs will rise, e.g. the need to pay workers overtime to produce more, the rise in prices will more than cover this. Indeed in some cases unemployment is so high that more can be produced without any increase in costs as there is considerable unused capacity so that the AS curve is completely horizontal. All of this depends on there being some excess capacity.

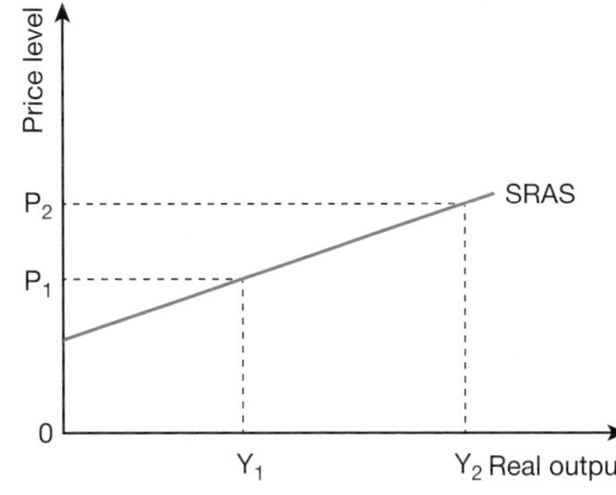

Figure 4.2 The short run aggregate supply curve ▲

The position of the short run aggregate supply (SRAS) curve is affected by anything which would increase the costs of firms. This would include changes in: wage rates, interest rates, raw material prices, taxes, etc.

Figure 4.3 shows that when AS reaches full capacity, i.e. all resources are fully employed (full employment), there is no ability to increase output so that any increase in demand can only be met by a rise in prices. The

Links

See also supply-side policies in Chapter 5 on page 127.

For labour productivity see Chapter 9 page 268.

long run aggregate supply (LRAS) curve can be shifted to the right, from LRAS to $LRAS_1$, by: improved education and training; increase in capital equipment; changes in technology; improved productivity etc. This shift will lead to an increase in output and employment and a fall in the price level.

The idea that as the full employment point is approached the AS curve becomes increasingly more vertical can be seen below.

The LRAS can only be shifted if the productive capacity of the economy is increased. This is equivalent to shifting the production possibility curve to the right.

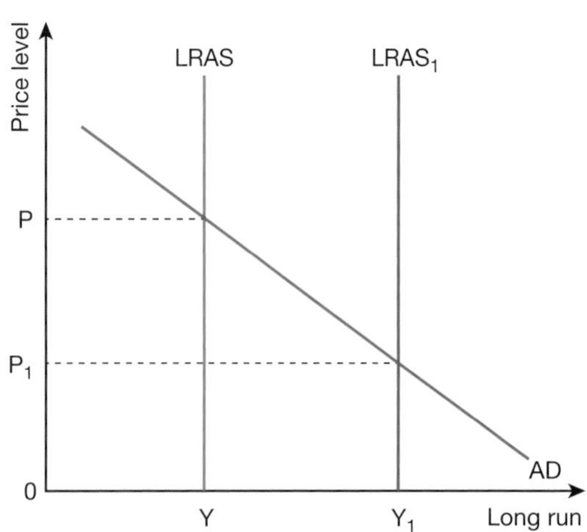

Figure 4.3 The long run aggregate supply curve ▲

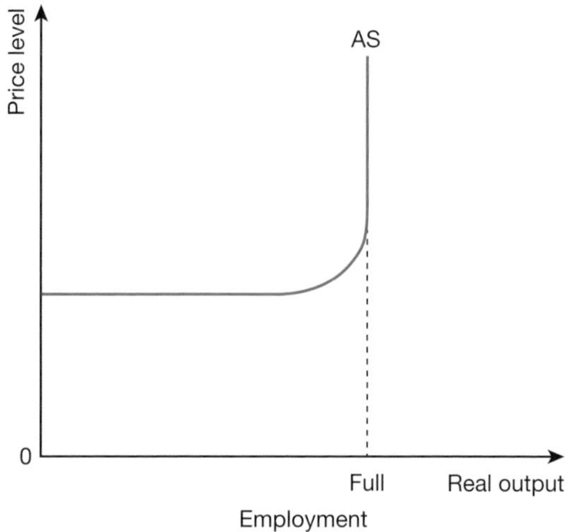

Figure 4.4 The aggregate supply curve ▲

Link

For more on the production possibility curve see Chapter 1 page 10.

The distinction between a movement along and a shift in AD and AS

A movement along the AD curve is caused by a shift of the AS curve. Similarly a movement along the AS curve is caused by a shift of the AD curve. These are shown in Figures 4.5 and 4.6.

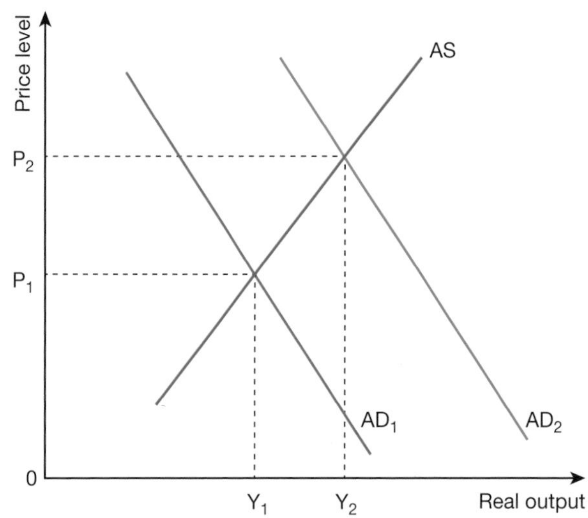

Figure 4.5 A movement along the AS curve/shift in AD ▲

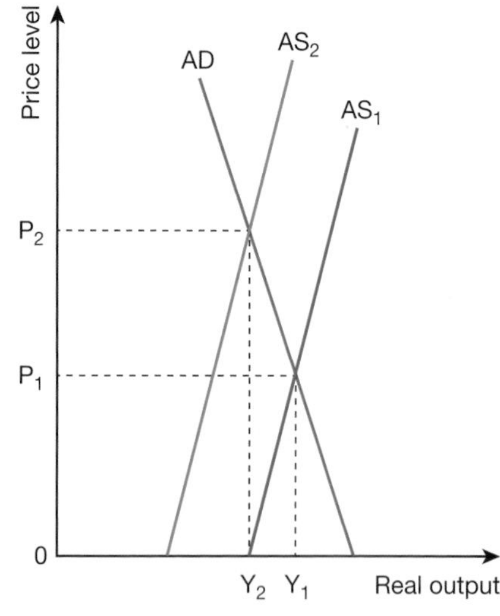

Figure 4.6 A movement along the AD curve/shift in AS ▲

> **Link**
>
> For more on the movement of the supply and demand curves see Chapter 1 page 32.

> **Link**
>
> For more on demand-pull inflation see page 93.

> **Getting it right**
>
> Remember the price level shows the rate of inflation. A fall in the price level, therefore, is a fall in the rate of inflation *not* a fall in price.

In both diagrams the movement is shown by the shift from p_1 to p_2 or Y_1 to Y_2.

Determination of the level of output, prices and employment

Real output, the price level and employment are all determined by the interaction of AD and AS. In Figure 4.8 the increase in AD from AD to AD_1 leads to a rise in output and thus employment, both shown by the move from Y_1 to Y_2. At the same time the price level has risen from P_1 to P_2. This rise in the price level shows demand pull inflation.

In Figure 4.7 the increase in the LRAS from $LRAS_1$ to $LRAS_2$ results in an increase in output and employment (Y_1 to Y_2), but a fall in the price level (P_1 to P_2).

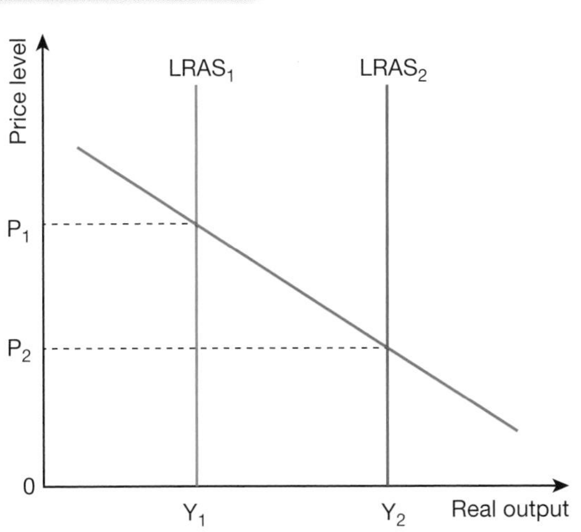

Figure 4.7 Increase in LRAS ▲

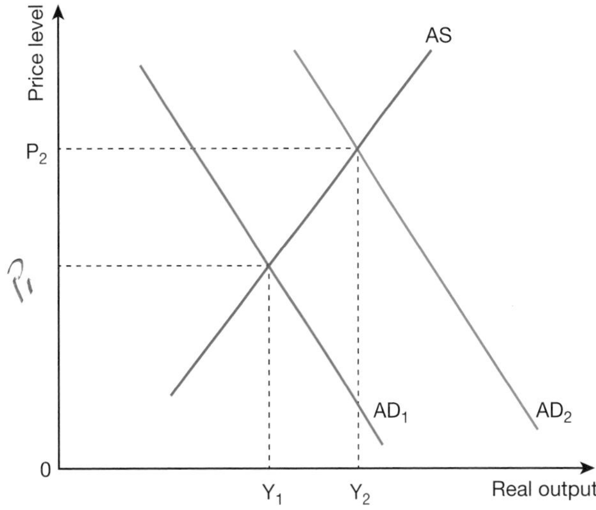

Figure 4.8 A movement along the AS curve/shift in AD ▲

Activities

Output, prices and employment

1. Copy the diagram.
2. Draw a new AD line to the right of AD and label AD_1.
3. Draw AD_2 to the right of AD_1.
4. Draw AD_3 and AD_4 to the left of AD.
5. For each of the shifts in AD state what has happened to output, employment and prices.

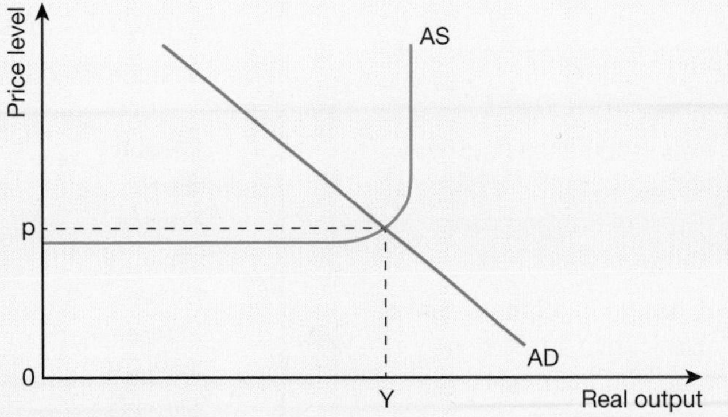

Inflation

The definition of inflation

Inflation can be said to occur when prices rise and what you can buy with your money falls. This is known as money value. If, to start with, you had one unit of your currency and could buy five oranges with it, but then found that you could only buy four oranges, you would be facing inflation.

In general, inflation is when most prices rise so that the cost of living increases, i.e. it costs people more to buy the same goods and services. It is possible for some prices to fall even though prices in general have risen. The rate of inflation is the rate at which the general level of prices is rising over time and it is usually expressed as an annual rate.

Key term

Inflation: a fall in the value of money shown by a persistent rise in the general price level. Alternatively, inflation is a persistant rise in the general price level leading to a fall in the value of money.

Money value: this is what money can buy, *see also* purchasing power parity. The value of money is dependent on the rate of inflation.

Degrees of inflation

The rate of inflation can range from nearly zero to hundreds of per cent. In this case inflation can get out of control. This is called hyperinflation. In 2008 inflation in Zimbabwe reached 11.2 million per cent. This led to the collapse of the currency in 2009.

At the other extreme, mild inflation is when the rate is less than 5 per cent. While this can be good for an economy in terms of increasing its competitiveness it can also indicate that the economy lacks growth. In the period 2008–2013 many of the Western industrial countries were in recession and had mild inflation.

In between are degrees of severity, e.g. inflation above 5 per cent is usually seen as a sign of too high growth leading to a sharp fall in competitiveness. Double-digit inflation is likely to lead to confidence in the currency falling, high interest rates and high wage demands leading to an upward spiral of prices.

Key term

Hyperinflation: inflation at a very high rate leading to money becoming worthless.

Bank notes from Zimbabwe ▲

Getting it right

Many countries now have inflation targets, e.g. the Bank of England has a target of 2 per cent.

Does your country's central bank have an inflation target? Make sure you know what it is.

Activities

Inflation

1 Find out what has happened to inflation in your country in the last five years.
2 Find out what happened to inflation in one of the countries below.
3 Then, compare the country with yours and explain it to the class focusing on whether inflation is:
   a higher or lower and to what extent
   b rising faster or slower and to what extent.

Inflation rates 2011–2014 consumer prices index

	2011	2012	2013	2014
Belgium	3.49	2.23	0.97	0.89
Brazil	6.50	5.84	5.91	6.15
Canada	2.30	0.83	1.24	1.14
Chile	4.44	1.49	3.02	3.86
China	4.06	2.41	2.51	1.90
Indonesia	3.79	4.30	8.38	6.65
Japan	−0.20	−0.10	1.61	1.51
Slovenia	2.00	2.67	0.68	0.11
South Africa	6.41	5.71	5.30	5.93
Turkey	10.45	6.16	7.40	8.39

Source: www.inflation.eu

Getting it right

Take care when looking at inflation figures. If the inflation rate in Year 1 is 5.4 per cent and in Year 2 is 3.2 per cent this does *not* mean that inflation or prices have fallen. What it shows is that prices have risen at a lower rate.

With percentage figures the value has to be negative before there is a real fall, e.g. in 2009 the inflation rate in Angola was −7.4 per cent.

Measurement of inflation

While the retail prices index (RPI) is the most commonly used method of measuring changes in the inflation rate, the UK and many other countries also use the consumer prices index (CPI). This is often referred to as the harmonised consumer prices index and is widely used for international comparisons.

Price indices are usually a weighted average of prices for goods and services. To construct an index a base year is chosen and the average price level for that year given the value of 100. This allows price changes to be expressed as a percentage change. A weighted index is used because the weights express the relative importance of each item in the index. For example, a change in the price of food is likely to have more effect on household expenditure than a change in the price of cinema tickets. These indices are used to measure the rate of inflation.

Key terms

Retail prices index: a measure of the weighted average of prices of a basket of goods and services purchased by households. In the UK it includes the costs of housing.

Consumer prices index: similar to the RPI, but in the UK it excludes the costs of housing, vehicle licence and TV licence duty, while including the cost of some financial transactions.

Base year: the year which is chosen as the point of reference for a comparison of prices in other years.

Weights: are values given to items in an index to show their relative importance.

Household expenditure: the total expenditure by consumers resident in a country whether at home or abroad minus expenditure by visitors on goods and services.

This can be calculated by: $\dfrac{\text{Index for Year 2} \times 100}{\text{Index for Year 1}}$

Both indices are constructed by:

1 choosing a base year against which price changes are measured – this is given the value of 100

2 selecting the items bought by an average family, the basket of goods

3 giving each item a weight showing its relative importance in the average family budget

4 obtaining new prices for each item from a wide variety of different sources across the country

5 taking this new price for each item and multiplying by its weight to give the weighted price relative

6 taking the sum of the weighted price relatives and dividing by the sum of the weights to give the change in price index.

Activities

Price Index

1 Find out which goods and services are included in your country's retail prices index, and consumer prices index if this is measured.

2 Using your country, or possibly the UK, how do the RPI and the CPI differ? Find figures for both and compare.

3 What goods and services would you and your friends have in a basket? How would this differ from that of your parents or grandparents?

There are a number of problems with these indices:

- the base year needs to be one in which there are not unusual fluctuations in prices, otherwise future calculations will be misleading
- the basket of goods may not be representative of all groups (e.g. pensioners); different groups of people have different baskets of goods and services – they may, therefore, have a different cost of living
- unless the basket is regularly updated the goods and services included may not represent current expenditure patterns
- change in quality/type of good, e.g. mobile phones have many more features than they had ten years ago
- the importance of goods and services may change, i.e. weights need to change
- there are different measures, e.g. RPI and CPI.

Key term

Cost of living: the cost of maintaining your present standard of living.

Activities

Inflation and deflation

1 find out when there have been more recent periods of deflation If possible, in your country or you could use another country or countries.
2 What happened in your chosen country during deflation?
3 Does the central bank of your country have an inflation rate target?
4 As a group discuss what you think is an acceptable level of inflation.

Case Study

Consumer prices index in Ghana

January 2012 = 100

Month	Consumer prices index
January 2012	100.0
January 2013	106.5
January 2014	121.2

Source: www.statsghana.gov.gh/cpi.html

1 What has happened to prices in Ghana between the following dates?
  a January 2012 and January 2013
  b January 2013 and January 2014.

(Tip: Calculating the rate of inflation for each year will help you.)

Deflation and disinflation

Deflation is the opposite of inflation. It occurs when the general price level falls, i.e. negative inflation. It is usually associated with a recession. As an economy declines and unemployment rises then demand falls, which can lead to a fall in prices.

Disinflation is not the same as deflation. It occurs when the rate of increase of prices slows down, e.g. in 2012 Belgium had a rate of inflation of 2.23 per cent whereas in 2013 it was only 0.97 per cent.

Key terms

Deflation: a fall in the general price level.

Disinflation: when the general price level rises at a slower rate.

As can be seen in Table 4.1, many countries suffered from deflation in 2009.

Table 4.1 Inflation rates 2009 ▼

Country	Rate of inflation (%)
Chile	−2.58
Estonia	−1.68
Ireland	−5.00
Japan	−1.67
Portugal	−0.05

Source: www.inflation.eu/inflation-rates/cpi-inflation-2009.aspx

The distinction between money values and real data

> **Key terms**
>
> **Money data (money values)**: where figures are expressed in current prices.
>
> **Real data**: where figures are adjusted for the change in the value of money (rate of inflation).

Prices, and other figures measured in money, can be quoted either as money data (money values), or nominal prices or as real data prices. The difference is that money wages, for example, are the actual wage that people get, while real wages represent what that money can buy. The difference is the rate of inflation or the change in the RPI. If the RPI has risen by 5 per cent then a 6 per cent wage rise means that the real wage has gone up by 1 per cent, the difference between the wage rise and the rate of inflation.

This is an important distinction and you will meet it in many situations in economics, e.g. gross domestic product.

Causes of inflation

Demand-pull and cost-push inflation

> **Key terms**
>
> **Demand-pull inflation**: occurs when the total (aggregate) demand in the economy exceeds the total (aggregate) supply.
>
> **Cost-push inflation**: occurs when the cost of supplying goods and services is increased causing a rise in the cost of final prices.

Many economists argue that inflation is the result of either an increase in total demand which pulls up prices (demand-pull inflation) or an increase in the costs of production which pushes prices up (cost-push inflation).

Demand-pull inflation usually happens when the economy is near its full employment level. In this situation resources are unable to supply sufficient goods (scarcity of resources) to meet demand. This results in prices being bid or forced upwards in order to bring aggregate supply and aggregate demand into equilibrium.

Cost-push inflation is caused by three different factors.

> **Links**
>
> The following are examined in more detail on the pages indicated:
>
> Costs of production Chapter 2 page 44.
>
> Trade unions Chapter 8 page 235.
>
> Monopoly Chapter 7 page 183.

- The most common factor today is the rise in the cost of raw materials forcing up the costs of production. This is seen, in particular, by the rise in the price of energy sources especially oil. Many other raw materials as they become scarcer relative to demand have risen steeply in price.
- Where trade unions are powerful they can push up wages in excess of productivity gains. This means that costs of production rise so that producers raise their prices so as to maintain profit levels. This was common in countries such as the UK in the 1960s and 1970s.
- Monopolies can raise prices due to the lack of competition. This is often linked to the rise in wages with producers using the wage rise to justify even higher price increases.

The latter two give rise to a wage–price spiral as rising wages push up prices leading to more wage demands.

> **Key term**
>
> **Money supply**: the total amount of money in an economy. This can be taken as: notes; coins and easily accessible accounts, e.g. current accounts.

Monetarists, such as Milton Friedman, have argued, however, that the sole cause of inflation is an excess in the money supply and the velocity of its circulation. This stems from the Quantity Theory of Money. They would maintain that demand-pull and cost-push are then a result of this. If governments, or central banks, increase the money in circulation by more than the increase in real output then the excess is "soaked up" by a rise in prices.

Link

Quantity theory of money and money supply are explored in Chapter 9 page 285.

Activity

Hyperinflation

Working in small groups find out about at least two other examples of hyperinflation. Try to identify some of the causes of these hyperinflations. You could then share your information with others in the class.

A good source for this is: www.sjsu.edu/faculty/watkins/hyper.htm

Getting it right

When a question asks you to discuss whether something is the only cause, you are expected to look at other causes and then come to a conclusion.

Consequences of inflation

It is important to realise that inflation is the historical norm and that it is high levels of inflation that are potentially problematic. Deflation for any period of time leads to huge problems such as those which affected the world economy in the 1920s and 1930s. The questions are "what level of inflation is acceptable" and "why are higher rates problematical".

Many countries have now adopted policies requiring them to keep inflation at low levels. The Bank of England has a target of 2 per cent while the People's Bank of China has a target of 4 per cent. The target is never zero as a low positive one allows for greater flexibility such as allowing relative prices to adjust.

Table 4.2 The types of consequences of inflation and their effects ▼

Income distribution problems	Borrowers gain because they are paying back less in terms of the value of money, but lenders and savers lose as their money becomes worth less. Those on fixed incomes lose as the income can buy less, but members of strong trade unions etc. can get wage increases in excess of inflation.
Labour market problems	If inflation is 5 per cent then workers will demand more than this to maintain their living standard. Employers faced with falling sales due to higher prices will not want to pay leading potentially to strikes etc.
International competitiveness	Higher inflation causes goods and services to be expensive compared to other countries' goods. This results in less sales and exports being less than imports.
Unemployment	If sales fall workers are likely to be made unemployed. This gives rise to stagflation.
Investment	Inflation creates uncertainty about the future which is likely to lead firms to invest less thus leading to lower future economic growth.
Unanticipated inflation	This is where the rate of inflation cannot be predicted. This is likely to lead to uncertainty. The opposite is anticipated inflation.
Shoe leather costs	If prices are rising then consumers and businesses will waste time trying to find the cheapest price.
Menu costs	If prices change frequently then the administrative costs for firms rise in having to adjust price lists etc. and to change vending machines.
Fiscal drag	As inflation rises people demand higher incomes. If tax thresholds do not change then people can be dragged into higher tax bands thus paying more tax.

Key terms

Balance of payments: the systematic record of all economic transactions between a particular country and the rest of the world. It consists of the current account, capital account and financial account.

Exchange rate: the rate at which one currency can be exchanged for another. See nominal, real, trade weighted, fixed and floating exchange rates.

The balance of payments

The balance of payments is one of the key indicators of a country's economic performance. A country's balance of payments position is an indication of its competitiveness in world trade and can have a major impact on other economic indicators such as the exchange rate and unemployment levels.

The components of the balance of payments accounts

The International Monetary Fund (IMF) has a recommended method for the presentation of nations' balance of payments accounts to enable international comparisons to be made.

In order to explain the main components of a country's balance of payments accounts reference will be made to the UK accounts for 2012. These are summarised in Table 4.3.

Table 4.3 Summary of UK balance of payments accounts for 2012 ▼

Category	Credits	Debits	Balance
Current account			
Trade in goods	299 457	407 350	−107 893
Trade in services	193 353	119 361	73 992
Net trade in goods and services			−33 901
Income	161 980	164 234	−2 254
Current transfers	17 519	40 574	−23 055
Total current account	672 309	731 519	−59 210
Capital account	6 140	2 352	3 788
Financial account	−26 970	−75 183	48 213
Reserve assets	–	–	7 642
Total current, capital and financial account	651 479	658 688	
Net errors and omissions			7 209

All figures in £ million

Source: http://www.ons.gov.uk/ons/rel/top/united-kingdom-balance-of-payments

Key terms

Capital account: a record of the transfers of ownership of fixed assets and of non-financial assets.

Financial account: a record of the movement of money in the form of investments by the residents of a country overseas and the inward flow of investment.

The balance of payments account is a systematic record of all economic transactions between a particular country and the rest of the world.

The balance of payments accounts are divided into three sections:

- current account
- capital account
- financial account.

In all cases credit items bringing money into the UK are represented by a plus (+) sign and debit items taking money out of the country by a negative (−) sign.

Key term

Balancing item: a figure introduced into the balance of payments accounts to enable them to balance.

In addition, because the balance of payments is an account it must balance, i.e. the inflows of money must equal the outflows. As the figures are collected by many different government departments the account often does not balance. To correct the problem a balancing item is included.

The current account

The current account of the balance of payments comprises trade in goods, trade in services, income and current transfers.

Trade in goods is sometimes referred to as visible trade and is the difference between exports and imports of goods. The visible balance is also known as the *balance of trade.*

This visible account consists of exports and imports of goods such as oil, agricultural products, computers, white goods and clothing. Historically, the UK has run a substantial and increasing deficit in the balance of payments (income from merchandise exports less than the amount spent on merchandise imports) in contrast to countries such as China and Germany who run a substantial surplus (income from merchandise exports greater than money spent on merchandise imports) on this section of the accounts.

Key terms

Current account: a record of transactions in terms of trade in goods and services, income and current transfers.
Exports: the sale of goods and services abroad. Exports bring money into a country.
Imports: the purchase of goods and services from abroad. Imports take money away from a country.
Visible balance: also known as the *balance of trade* this is the difference between income from goods exported and imported.
Deficit in the balance of payments: an imbalance in a country's balance of payments, where payments made by the country exceed payments received by the country.
Surplus: this occurs on the balance of payments when the amount of money received from the sale of exports is greater than that paid for the purchase of imports.
Invisible balance: the difference between income from services exported and imported.

Invisible balance

Exports and imports of services such as international tourism, travel, financial services and insurance are referred to as invisible trade and lead to an invisible balance. The London 2012 Olympic Games brought thousands of tourists to the UK. In order to pay for goods and services while in the UK, these overseas tourists had to change their own currency into sterling, bringing money into the UK. This expenditure by overseas tourists represents an invisible export for the UK.

If on the other hand a UK producer uses a foreign shipping company to transport its goods this would represent an invisible import for the UK because it is taking money out of the UK.

◀ The London 2012 Olympic Games brought thousands of tourists to the UK

The UK invisible balance usually is in surplus, but it is not sufficient to offset the deficit on the visible balance.

Income balance

The income balance consists of income received in the forms of interest, profits and dividends from investments.

Key term

Net investment income: income received from investment abroad minus income from investment made abroad.

Key term

Current transfers: payments or receipts where there is no corresponding exchange of goods or services.

The net investment income balance is the difference between income received from direct or portfolio investment in your country's assets located abroad minus investment income from foreign-owned assets located in your country.

Compensation of individuals comprises the net balances of income earned by individuals from economies in which they are not resident.

Net current transfers

For the UK current transfers is made up largely of foreign aid and UK obligations as a member of the EU.

Overall the current account for the UK runs at a deficit because of the impact of the very large deficit on visible trade.

Progress question

1 Explain how the various sections of Brazil's balance of payments accounts are likely to have been affected by it hosting the soccer FIFA World Cup in June 2014.

Activities

Balance of payments (B of P)

Individually or in groups conduct an investigation into your own country's balance of payments and then answer the following questions.

1 How does your country present its B of P accounts?
2 Identify the size of your country's surplus or deficit in the trade in goods and services section of the current account.
3 Is your country's surplus or deficit in this section of the current account increasing or decreasing?
4 Explain the effects this surplus or deficit in this section of the current account has on your economy.

Case Study

China's current account balance

The IMF's *World Economic Outlook for 2012* indicated that China's current account surplus for 2012 declined from 10.1 per cent of GDP in 2007 to 2.8 per cent as indicated in the accompanying graph. This trend is predicted to reverse, but only slightly, to 4–4.5 per cent of GDP by 2017.

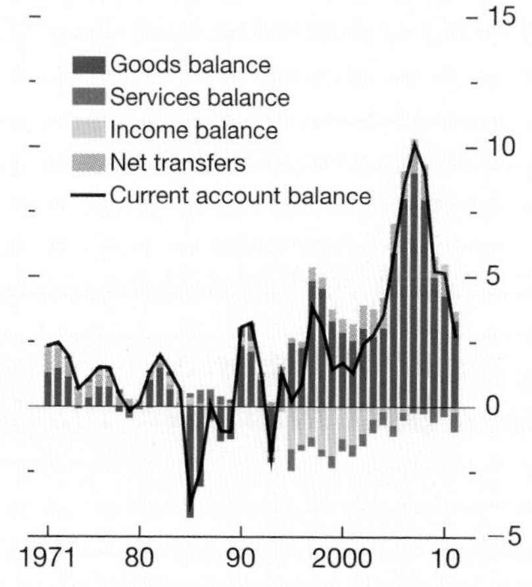

Source: IMF staff calculations, from p. 43 of *World Economic Outlook*, April 2012

A variety of factors have contributed to the decline in the goods balance:

- The recession in the EU and USA which together account for 40 per cent of China's exports.
- Investment in housing construction and for expansion of the manufacturing sector in China has required imports of commodities and minerals.
- China's terms of trade have deteriorated 10.5 per cent combined with the fact that China's exports tend to be price elastic while its imports are price inelastic.

1 Explain with examples what is meant by:
   a goods balance
   b services balance
   c income balance
   d net transfers
   e current account balance.
2 From the graph identify which of the elements of the current account (a)–(d) have contributed most to China's current account deficit.
3 Explain how the factors in the bulleted list explain the reduction in China's current account surplus.

Key term

Foreign direct investment: finance to provide for the building or purchase of productive assets in a country by the residents of a different country.

Financial account: a record of the movement of money in the form of investments by the residents of a country overseas and the inward flow of investment.

Activities

Current and financial accounts

Individually or in groups conduct an investigation into your own country's current and financial accounts in the balance of payments and then answer the following questions:

1. What is the size of these accounts?
2. How does this compare with your country's current account total?
3. How have the current and financial accounts changed over the last ten years?
4. Why have these changes taken place?

Link

IMF is covered in Chapter 9 page 293.

Link

Exchange rates are covered on page 99.

The capital account

This is the part of the balance of payments which shows the changes in a country's asset ownership as a result of both public and private investment inflows and outflows. Capital transfers are those involving transfers of ownership of fixed assets, except land, and transfers of funds linked to the acquisition or disposal of fixed assets or cancellation of liabilities by creditors.

The financial account

The financial account records an economy's transaction in external financial assets and liabilities, e.g. investment owned assets such as foreign reserves, gold, etc. Assets owned by foreigners, those private and official, are also recorded in the financial account. These assets are both fixed (e.g. the opening of mines or pharmaceutical production plants in Indonesia), often referred to as foreign direct investment, and portfolio investments such as shares as well as non-financial (e.g. the buying or selling of land).

The capital and financial accounts are closely linked and are often referred to together. Most entries in the capital and financial accounts should be made on a net basis; that is, each component should be shown as a credit or debit.

Meaning of balance of payments equilibrium and disequilibrium

Balance of payments equilibrium occurs when the inflow of money in the balance of payments is over a period of time equal to the outflows without requiring government intervention such as drawing on reserves or borrowing from the IMF.

Balance of payments disequilibrium occurs when the inflow of money is continually greater or less than the outflow of money over a period of time thus requiring government intervention. In this case the exchange rate is either overvalued, leading to a deficit, or undervalued, leading to a surplus.

Key terms

Balance of payments equilibrium: where the inflow of money into the country is equal to the outflow of money over a period of years and there is no need for government intervention.

Balance of payments disequilibrium: where the inflow of money is continually greater or less than the outflow of money over a period of time thus requiring government intervention.

Causes of balance of payments disequilibrium in each part of the account

As far as the current account is concerned, a disequilibrium is likely to occur when:

- There is limited domestic production so that a country relies on imports, or because of high standards of living residents demand a wider range of goods. It may be the case that the terms of trade are unfavourable so that developing countries, in particular, find that they need to export more and more goods just to maintain the same

> **Links**
>
> Terms of trade are covered on page 103.
>
> The euro is covered on page 109.
>
> For more on economic growth see Chapter 9 page 248.
>
> For more on government deficit see Chapter 9 page 255.

> **Links**
>
> For government policies see Chapter 5 page 123.
>
> Protectionism is covered on page 113.

> **Links**
>
> Marshall–Lerner is covered on page 102.
>
> J-curve is covered on page 102.

> **Activity**
>
> **Balance of payments disequilibrium**
>
> Individually or in groups investigate the causes and consequences of disequilibrium in your country or another country.

> **Key terms**
>
> **Nominal exchange rate**: the rate at which one currency exchanges for another. It is sometimes just called the foreign exchange rate.
>
> **Real exchange rate**: the value of a currency in terms of what it can actually buy.
>
> **Trade weighted exchange rate**: an index calculated using weights showing the relative importance of trade between the country and its trade partners.

export revenue. This would lead to a deficit. A surplus could arise because a country has a reputation for excellence in particular areas of production, e.g. Germany for engineering products or because of cheap labour leading to lower prices, e.g. China.

- Countries may lack competitiveness due to an overvalued currency (e.g. Portugal and Greece as members of the euro could not devalue in the period 2008–2011) and/or the rate of inflation may be greater than that of their competitors so that exports fall but imports rise. Equally, China not only had cheap labour, but also an undervalued currency allowing it to undercut other producers.
- Economic growth requires the import of capital goods, leading to a persistent deficit. It may also lead to consumers being better off and thus demanding more imports.
- There is lack of confidence in an economy. This may be because of economic factors such as persistent current account deficits or large increases in the government deficit. Equally, investors may fear political change or lack of a stable government. The opposite will be true for a country with a surplus.

Consequences of balance of payments disequilibrium on domestic and external economy

The consequences for the domestic economy include the following.

- The government may need to tighten fiscal and monetary policies to reduce domestic demand and to introduce supply-side policies to improve productive capability.
- Consumers will have less access to imported goods as the government imposes protectionist policies.
- There will be a fall in foreign investment as confidence declines. This is likely to result in lower economic growth, higher unemployment, etc.

The consequences for the external economy include:

- Governments will be under pressure to introduce or increase protectionist measures.
- Devaluation of the exchange rate so that the currency becomes worth less than it was. This will lead to higher import prices and lower export prices. Whether this works may depend on Marshall-Lerner and the extent of the J-curve. Devaluation may lead, however, to further loss of confidence.

As can be seen, the domestic and external consequences of a negative disequilibrium are closely connected.

Exchange rates

Definitions and measurement of exchange rates

Exchange rates can be measured in terms of nominal value, real value and trade weighted value.

The nominal exchange rate is the one which is usually quoted, e.g. if you go to a bank or look at the rate on the internet then you will see

Key terms

Purchasing power parity: a way of showing the exchange rate in terms of how much a typical basket of goods cost in one country compared to another country.

Floating exchange rate: where the value of a country's currency is determined solely by market forces.

this rate. The real exchange rate is what the currency will buy in terms of other currencies. This is often referred to as purchasing power parity. The trade weighted exchange rate is the measurement, in terms of an index, of changes in a country's currency against a basket of other currencies. These are weighted to reflect the relative importance of trade for the country of the currencies in the basket. If, for example, the UK does five times more trade with the EU than it does with Japan then the euro will be given five times more weight than the yen.

The determination of exchange rates

Floating exchange rate

If the exchange rate between two countries is determined by market forces then it is called a floating exchange rate.

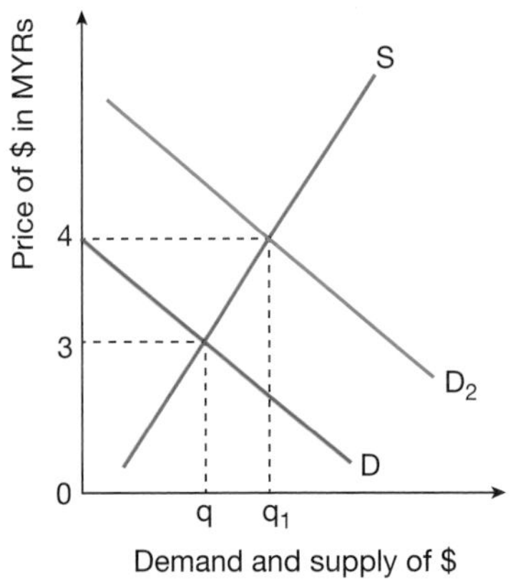

Figure 4.9 Demand and supply of $ in Malaysian Ringgits ▲

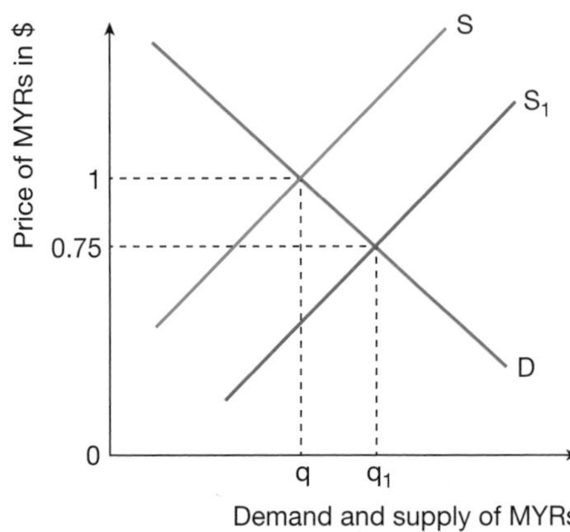

Figure 4.10 Demand and supply of MYRs ▲

Activity

Value of your exchange rate

Find out the value of your exchange rate against five different currencies. If you were to visit these countries and to take with you 100 units of your currency how much of these foreign currencies would you get for your 100 units?

The equilibrium price of the US dollar in terms the Malaysian ringgit is $1 to MYR3. If the demand for dollars increases, the demand curve shifts to the right D to D_1 and the price of the dollar rises from MYR3 to MYR4. It has *appreciated* in terms of the ringgit while the latter has *depreciated* in terms of the dollar. Figure 4.10 shows the effects on the ringgit. To buy more dollars more ringgits have to be supplied, causing the price to fall from $1 to $0.75.

Fixed exchange rate

A fixed exchange rate is one where little or no change is possible from the agreed rate. In practice, a small variation of around 2 per cent is usually allowed, but the central bank of the country is committed to maintaining the value by buying its own currency, to prevent the price falling, or to selling its currency to stop it rising. In practice, countries often have to either *revalue or devalue* their rates from time to time to allow for differences in economic growth.

Key terms

Fixed exchange rate: where the value of a country's exchange rate is determined by its government which is committed to maintain the value.

Managed float: where a government intervenes in the foreign exchange market to try and prevent wild movements of its currency.

Managed float and dirty float

Governments can try to manage their currency by intervening in the market to influence its price. This is called a managed float. The purpose

Key terms

Speculation: where one or more people gamble on a currency rising, by buying it, or falling, by selling it.
Dirty float: where a country deliberately sets its exchange rate at a low level to gain a trade advantage.

Links

For more on depreciation and appreciation see page 102.

For devaluation and revaluation see page 102.

Activity

Value of your currency's exchange rate

Find out what has happened to the value of your country's exchange rate over the last two years. Try to discover what factor(s) have affected its value.

is to try to prevent wild fluctuations in the value of the currency, one cause of which is speculation. Where governments use this idea to deliberately set their currency at a lower rate than the market would under a floating system in order to gain a trading advantage, this is called a dirty float. Japan was accused of this in the 1960s and 1970s while China has more recently faced similar accusations.

The factors underlying changes in exchange rates

Factors that cause the value of an exchange rate to change can include:

- Balance of payments disequilibrium. If a country runs a deficit then it is supplying more of its currency leading to a fall in its price. If it continues then foreign money will start to leave so it does not lose value. This again increases the supply of the currency.
- High inflation. A country with an inflation rate higher than that of other countries will find that people lose confidence in holding its currency.
- Interest rates. International money seeks the highest return. If a country raises its rate of interest this will attract inflows of money thus increasing the exchange rate.
- Foreign direct investment. Inflows of money to build factories etc. will increase the exchange rate.
- Speculation. If people expect the exchange rate of a country to fall, or rise, they will either sell or buy the currency to make a profit by buying it back at a lower price or selling it at a higher price.

The effects of changing exchange rates on the domestic and external economy

Table 4.4 shows some of the effects of changing exchange rates.

Table 4.4 Effects of changing exchange rates on the economy ▼

Exchange rate

Effect	How this affects the economy
Inflation	If the exchange rate falls imports will be more expensive. This will push up prices especially if the demand for imports is price inelastic.
Unemployment	If the exchange rate rises, the exports are more expensive leading to a fall in demand, especially if demand for exports is elastic.
Economic growth	A fall in the exchange rate will make exports cheaper. If the Marshall–Lerner condition holds then exports will increase and imports will reduce, thus increasing the country's aggregate demand leading to more growth and employment.
Capital flows	A change in an exchange rate will have different effects depending on expectations about the economy. If the economy is expected to benefit then money will flow in.
"Hot money"	This is money which seeks the best interest rate or looks for a rise in currency. If an exchange rate falls and people expect it to fall further then this money will leave the country resulting in this further fall. This could result in the Marshall–Lerner condition not holding, leading to further balance of payments problems.

Falls.

Rises

Falls

Key term

Marshall–Lerner condition: states that the sum of the price elasticities of demand for exports and imports must be greater than one if a devaluation is to lead to an improvement in the current account.

Getting it right

When thinking about the effects of exchange rate changes on the balance of payments and the economy always ask: "In which direction will money flow?" An inflow is positive, or is shown as a rise in exports, while outflows are negative, or shown by a rise in imports.

As exports and imports are part of AD = C + I + G + X−M any change in the exchange rate will affect both exports and imports, often called net exports, leading to a change in AD. If a country's exchange rate rises so that exports are more expensive and imports are cheaper then, if the Marshall–Lerner condition holds, the volume and value of exports will fall while the volume and value of imports will rise. This means that AD falls, to AD_1 at Y_1 and fewer people are employed as seen in Figure 4.11.

While a fall in the value of a country's exchange rate will, assuming the Marshall–Lerner condition holds, lead to an improvement in the current account as exports rise and imports fall, this may not happen immediately. Contracts have been signed at the old value and cannot be changed. It also takes time for exporters and importers to react to the change. This gives rise to the J-curve effect. Figure 4.12 shows that devaluation leads to an immediate worsening of the current account with this only benefiting from the devaluation in the longer run.

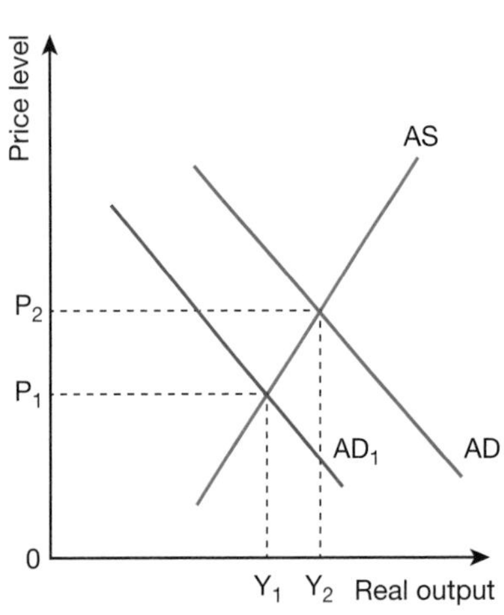

Figure 4.11 Using AD/AS analysis to show the effect of an appreciation ▲

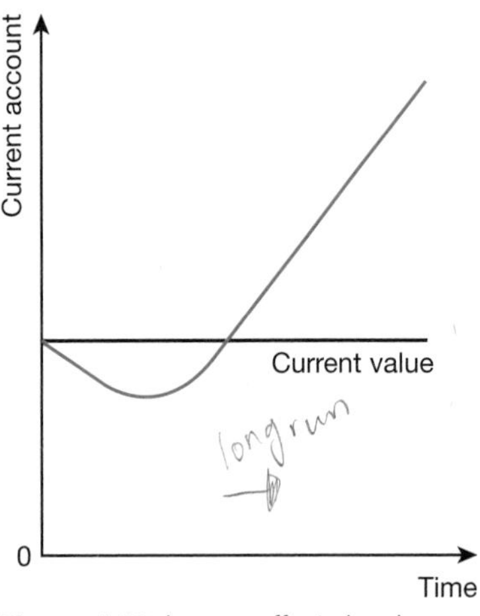

Figure 4.12 J-curve effect showing initial fall and then rise in the value of the current account ▲

Depreciation and appreciation

Floating exchange rates can either depreciate, i.e. fall in value, or appreciate, i.e. rise in value. As can be seen in Figure 4.13, an increase in demand for the currency, from DD to D_1D_1, leads to a rise in the currency's value, an appreciation, whereas a fall in demand leads to the opposite effect, a devaluation.

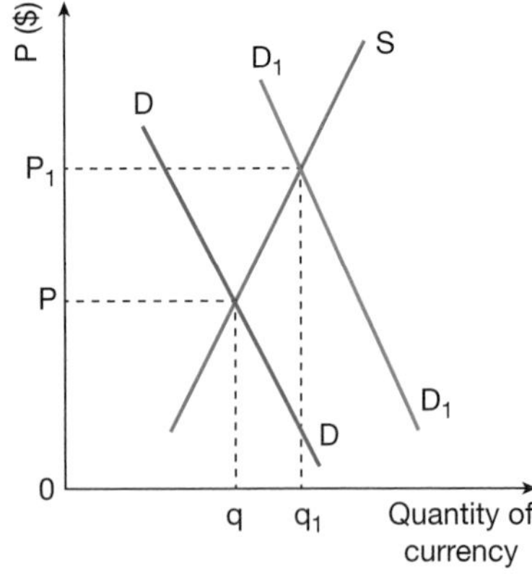

Figure 4.13 Depreciation and appreciation ▲

Devaluation and revaluation

Unlike floating exchange rates, fixed exchange rates can only change their value if the government decides that this is necessary. A lowering of the exchange rate, i.e. a fall in the value,

Key terms

J-curve: the short-term response of the current account to a significant fall in the exchange rate.

Appreciation: when a floating exchange rate increases in value.

Depreciation: when a floating exchange rate decreases in value.

is a devaluation, while a raising of the exchange rate, i.e. it goes up in value, is a revaluation.

Key terms

Devaluation: when the value of a fixed exchange rate is decreased to a new lower rate.
Revaluation: when the value of a fixed exchange rate is increased to a new higher rate.

Case Study

Latin American exchange rates in the 1990s

Countries in Latin America have attempted a number of ways of managing their exchange rates.

Fixed rates in Latin American countries led to inflation being controlled but the real effective rate of exchange to rise. This was due to the fixed rates attracting capital inflows as the risk of losing the value of investments was greatly reduced. In the longer term, however, this led to higher debt, higher interest rates and less competitive exports.

1 Why might a fixed exchange rate help to control inflation?
2 Explain why a fixed exchange rate might lead to current account disequilibrium.
3 Discuss whether fixed or floating exchange rates are better for developing countries.

The terms of trade

The measurement of the terms of trade

Key term

Terms of trade: ratio of export prices to import prices.

The terms of trade of a country are defined as the ratio of its export prices to import prices. They are calculated as follows:

$$\text{Terms of trade} = \frac{\text{Index of export prices} \times 100}{\text{Index of import prices}}$$

An increase in the index indicates that more imports can be purchased with a given quantity of exports and so the *terms of trade* are said to have improved or to have become more favourable. Conversely a reduction in the index indicates that fewer imports than previously can be purchased with a given quantity of exports and so the terms of trade are said to have deteriorated or worsened.

Activities

Terms of trade

Assume that between 2013 and 2014 a country's index of export prices falls from 100 to 95 and its index of import prices rises from 100 to 110.

1 Calculate the terms of trade for 2014.
2 Explain the likely effect of this change in the terms of trade on the trade balance of the country if the demand for both its exports and imports is (a) elastic (b) inelastic.

Causes of changes in the terms of trade

The terms of trade of any country will change over the years as can be seen in Table 4.5.

Table 4.5 Terms of trade for selected countries 2009–2012 (2000 = 100) ▼

Country	2009	2010	2011	2012
Australia	163.0	178.9	200.4	184.8
Bangladesh	65.2	60.8	55.8	59.2
Barbados	124.0	115.8	109.2	107.6
France	95.9	92.6	89.6	88.8
Nepal	78.5	77.8	79.7	77.7
Nigeria	152.7	181.6	216.3	221.8
Tanzania	129.7	141.9	150.8	145.2
Vietnam	99.4	99.7	99.9	100.5

Source: http://data.worldbank.org/indicator/TT.PRI.MRCH.XD.WD

Globalisation

Major factors in recent years have been globalisation and economic development. The fall in the price of manufactured goods due to globalisation has tended to cause the terms of trade of countries such as France to worsen. The increased demand for natural resources, however, has pushed up prices thus benefiting the terms of trade of exporting countries such as Australia and Nigeria.

> **Key term**
>
> **Globalisation**: the expansion of world trade in goods and services, together with capital flows, leading to greater international interdependence.

Table 4.6 Some factors affecting the terms of trade ▼

Factors influencing the terms of trade	Explanation
Price elasticity of demand	If a country's exports become more inelastic than its imports then the terms of trade will move in its favour as the price of its exports will be higher than the price of its imports.
Economic development	If this causes an increase in demand for imports then the terms of trade will worsen. On the other hand, if there is an increase in supply of substitutes for imports or more goods for export then the terms of trade will move favourably.
Exchange rate	If the exchange rate depreciates or devalues then the terms of trade will worsen as export prices have fallen and import prices have risen.
Protectionist measures, e.g. tariffs	If protectionist measures are taken then import prices are likely to rise leading to a deterioration in the terms of trade.
Population growth	A rapidly growing population will demand more goods and thus imports, leading to a worsening in the terms of trade.
Competition	If a country has a monopoly in the production of a good then it can raise prices causing an improvement in its terms of trade.
Globalisation	This has increased competition, leading prices of some countries' exports to fall, worsening the terms of trade. For other countries the ability to gain trade has resulted in more exports and an improvement in the terms of trade.

> **Activities**
>
> **Terms of trade**
>
> 1 Using the World Bank's website, see Table 4.5, find out what has happened to your country's terms of trade.
>
> 2 Compare the data to one or more of the countries listed in Table 4.5.
>
> 3 Why do you think the two terms of trade have changed?

> **Links**
>
> The following are examined in more detail on the pages indicated:
>
> Price elasticity of demand see page 51.
>
> Monopoly see page 183.
>
> Exchange rates see page 99.
>
> Protectionist measures see page 130.

The impact of changes in the terms of trade

The impact of changes in the terms of trade on a nation's economy will depend on the price elasticities of demand for imports and exports. If, for example, a nation's terms of trade improve because export prices have risen and import prices have fallen, and the price elasticities of demand for both exports and imports are greater than unity (price elastic), then the total income from exports will fall because there has been a more than proportionate fall in the demand for them, and the total expenditure on imports will rise because there has been a more than proportionate increase in the demand for them. The effect will be a worsening of the country's trade balance and possible adverse effects on unemployment.

If, however, the elasticities of demand for imports and exports are less than unity (inelastic) the improvement in the terms of trade will result in an improvement in the country's trade balance.

Getting it right

Make sure that you can explain the factors that affect a country's terms of trade and that you can explain the difference between an improvement and a deterioration in a country's terms of trade.

Over time it appears that the terms of trade have moved against less economically developed countries (LEDCs) in favour of developed countries (DCs) largely because of their reliance on primary products such as agriculture. During the past 10 years, however, commodity prices have risen steadily, peaking in 2011 resulting in an improvement in the terms of trade for producing nations. This is particularly true for oil exporting nations. Current IMF forecasts are for commodity prices to fall in the future, with the possible exception of oil in the short term.

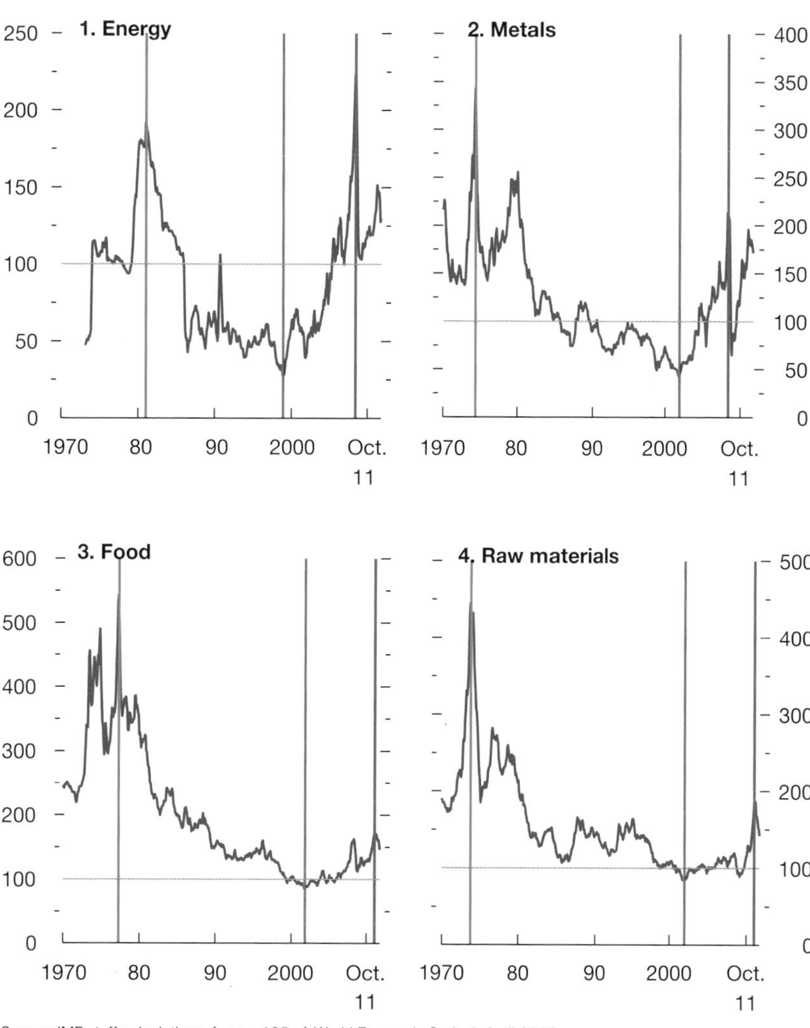

Source: IMF staff calculations, from p.125 of *World Economic Outlook*, April 2012

Figure 4.14 World commodity prices, 1970–2011 (in real terms) ▲

Principles of absolute and comparative advantage

The distinction between absolute and comparative advantage

Key term

Absolute advantage: the ability to produce more of a product than another country that has the same amount of resources can produce.

Absolute advantage occurs when one country, with the same amount of resources as another country, can produce more of a good than that other country.

The amount of each good that each country, Japan and Sweden, is able to produce with the same quantity of resources is shown in Table 4.7.

If we assume that only one person is available and that person shares their time and other resources equally between cars and toys then we could represent absolute advantage as shown in Table 4.7.

Table 4.7 Output, example 1 ▼

Country	Cars	Toys
Sweden	2	8
Japan	8	2

In this situation the opportunity costs are Sweden 1:4 and Japan 4:1. These production possibilities are shown in Figure 4.15.

Getting it right

In an exam keep it simple by using numbers that are easy to manipulate.

Remember this is an economics exam not a maths exam so there is no credit for complicated examples, only for correct ones.

Link

See Chapter 1 page 10 to review your understanding of production possibility curves.

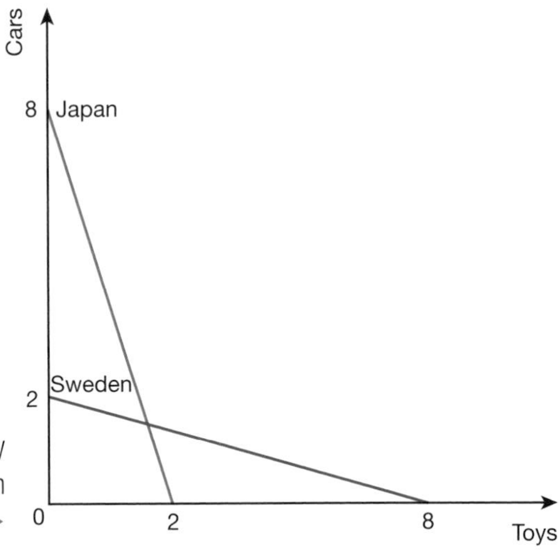

Figure 4.15 Production possibility curves for Sweden and Japan showing absolute advantage ▶

It is clear that Sweden can produce more toys than Japan and Japan can produce more cars. Sweden has, therefore, an absolute advantage in toys, while Japan has an absolute advantage in cars. In order to increase total output both countries should specialise in the good in which they have the absolute advantage.

Assuming that the output above represents what one person can produce in a day then the person in Sweden will now only produce toys and the person in Japan will produce only cars. The result is shown in Table 4.8.

Table 4.8 Output, example 2 ▼

Country	Cars	Toys
Sweden	0	16
Japan	16	0

The two countries can now trade so long as they stay within their opportunity costs (1:4; 4:1).

A possible exchange rate favourable to both is 1:1. If Sweden gives up six toys it will get back six cars resulting in the situation shown in Table 4.9.

Table 4.9 Output, example 3 ▼

Country	Cars	Toys
Sweden	6	10
Japan	10	6

David Ricardo ▲

Key term

Comparative advantage: the ability to produce a product at a lower opportunity cost.

Getting it right

Remember to keep the numbers simple.

Link

See Chapter 1 page 9 to review your understanding of opportunity.

As can be seen, Sweden has gained four cars and two toys, while the Japan has gained two cars and four toys. The result of specialisation and trade is that both countries have more cars and toys than they did previously.

Comparative advantage

The principle of comparative advantage was originally developed by David Ricardo in his book *On the Principles of Political Economy and Taxation* (1817), which demonstrates that it is possible for all countries to benefit from trade even in a situation in which one of the countries involved is more efficient at producing all products, i.e. has an absolute advantage in the production of all goods.

In this case, Indonesia can produce more cars and more toys so it has an absolute advantage in both (Table 4.10). The opportunity cost of production in the two countries is quite different.

Table 4.10 Output, example 1 ▼

Country	Cars	Toys
Indonesia	10	50
Botswana	8	8
Total output	18	58

In Indonesia five toys have to be given up to obtain one car (10 : 50 = 1 : 5), while in Botswana only one toy needs to be given up to get a car (8 : 8 = 1 : 1). The opportunity cost of a car is lower in Botswana than in Indonesia. In this case Botswana has a comparative advantage in the production of cars, while Indonesia has the advantage in toys: Botswana gives up one car for one toy, but Indonesia only gives up one-fifth of a car for a toy.

A country has a comparative advantage in the production of a product if it has a lower opportunity cost ratio than other countries in its production.

As Indonesia had an absolute advantage in both it will need to continue to produce both, but will move 50 per cent of the resources used on cars into producing toys. Botswana, however, will specialise just in cars.

Table 4.11 Output, example 2 ▼

Country	Cars	Toys
Indonesia	5	75
Botswana	16	0
Total output	21	75

As can be seen, output of cars has increased by three while output of cars has risen by 25. The countries could then trade at a ratio somewhere between their two opportunity costs. If we assume that they choose 1 : 3 then the final outcome could be as in Table 4.12 with both countries having more cars and toys.

It is important to note that specialisation and trade will only take place if the opportunity cost ratios are different as otherwise no advantage would be gained.

> **Link**
> See Chapter 7 page 173 for a detailed explanation of returns to scale.

Table 4.12 Output, example 3 ▼

Country	Cars	Toys
Indonesia	11	57
Botswana	10	18
Total output	21	75

To explain how countries can benefit from trade in these circumstances the following assumptions have to be made:

- there are only two commodities involved, toys and cars
- perfect competition in factor and product markets
- no transport costs
- no capital movements which would affect the exchange rate
- production is subject to constant returns to scale which means that all units are produced at the same cost
- no restrictions on trade.

Activities

Absolute and comparative advantage

Indonesia using all its resources to the full can produce 2000 tonnes of rubber or 1200 tonnes of rice.

Thailand using all its resources to the full can produce 1400 tonnes of rubber or 1000 tonnes of rice.

1 Draw the production possibility curves for rubber and rice for Indonesia and Thailand.
2 Identify which country has an absolute advantage in the production of rubber and which in rice.
3 Identify which country has a comparative advantage in the production of rubber and which in rice.
4 Choose an appropriate exchange rate for the two commodities and demonstrate that both Indonesia and Thailand can benefit from specialisation and trade in accordance with the principle of comparative advantage.

Progress question

2 Explain why trade between two countries on the basis of comparative advantage will only be beneficial if the opportunity cost ratios for two goods are different in the two countries.

Free trade area

In recent years a number of trading blocs, each of which practises free trade between members, have been formed.

Table 4.13 Some examples of trading blocs ▼

Trading bloc	Membership
European Union (EU)	28 members, 18 of whom are members of the single currency (euro)
Association of South East Asian Nations (ASEAN)	10 members
North American Free Trade Association (NAFTA)	Canada, Mexico and the USA
Union of South American Nations (USAM)	12 members (including Mercosur, the Andean Community of Nations, Chile, Guyana and Surinam)

A free trade area consists of countries which have removed barriers to trade between themselves, but maintain their own individual barriers against non-member countries. Free trade areas include: the European Free Trade Area – EFTA, NAFTA and South Asian Free Trade Area – SAFTA.

Customs union

In contrast, a customs union has free trade between its members, but common external tariff barriers against all non-members. An example of a customs union is the Caribbean Community (CARICOM).

Key terms

Free trade area: a group of countries that have few or no price controls in the form of tariffs or quotas between each other.

Customs union: a group of countries that have free trade between members, but common external barriers.

> **Link**
> For more on protection see page 130.

> **Key term**
> **Monetary union**: a group of countries with a single currency, or different currencies having a fixed mutual exchange rate monitored and controlled by one central bank.

> **Link**
> For more on monetary policy see Chapter 5 page 124.

> **Key term**
> **Full economic union**: a customs union which also co-ordinates a range of other economic policies, including social, fiscal and monetary policies, among its members.

> **Key terms**
> **Trade creation**: transfer of consumption from high- to low-cost producers.
> **Trade diversion**: transfer of consumption from low- to high-cost producers.

Monetary union

In the case of a monetary union the members adopt the same currency. This implies a common central bank which controls the quantity of money and the rate of interest, and by so doing seeks to influence the rate of inflation in the member countries.

Eighteen member countries of the European Union (EU) have formed a monetary union with the euro (€) as its currency. It is called the Eurozone. Although each member has kept its own central bank, the Eurozone is managed by the European Central Bank which sets monetary policy.

Full economic union

Full economic union is the highest form of integration encompassing the features of a common market, but going further to develop some harmonisation of economic policies. The EU for example has developed a range of policies in such areas as competition, agriculture and social policies. The Common Agricultural Policy (CAP) is one such example. CARICOM has also moved in this direction by creating the CARICOM Single Market and Economy (CMSE).

CMSE members have adopted measures to converge and coordinate their macroeconomic policies, harmonise foreign investment decisions and facilitate technology transfer. In monetary and fiscal policy there are measures to coordinate exchange rate and interest rate policy as well as to coordinate indirect taxes and national budget deficits.

In some ways economic integration into regional trading blocs can be regarded as a "second best solution" in that it enables members to enjoy the benefits of comparative advantage, but it involves protectionist policies against non-members and consequently stops short of allowing all nations in the world to benefit from free trade.

Trade creation and trade diversion

A feature of customs unions and higher forms of economic integration is that member nations experience both trade creation and trade diversion.

As a result of trade barriers being removed when a country enters a customs union it can buy goods at a lower price, by buying goods from a lower-cost and more efficient producer. If, for example, Thailand and Myanmar formed a customs union then Myanmar would remove tariffs from Thai imports so that trade will switch to the more efficient Thai producers. This shifting of consumption from high- to low-cost produce is known as trade creation.

Membership of a customs union however, may lead to trade diversion. For example, before joining the EU the UK could buy cheap food from Australia and New Zealand. However, now that the UK is a member of the EU it is required to impose the EU Common External Tariff on goods from non-EU members. As a result this food from Australia and New Zealand has become more expensive than the same food products produced by other members of the EU. So, although UK consumers may be purchasing from the cheapest nation in the EU, they are paying more than previously as they may be buying from a less efficient producer. This is trade diversion, the transfer of consumption from low- to high-cost producers.

Trade creation

Trade creation occurs when the removal of tariff barriers results in an increase in consumer welfare. In Figure 4.16 D_H and S_H represent the domestic demand for and supply of tomatoes in the UK assuming that the:

- UK imports tomatoes from Spain
- supply of tomatoes from Spain is perfectly elastic, so that the supply curve is Sw
- UK imposes a tariff on Spanish tomatoes equal to P_2P_1.

The effective supply curve for tomatoes from Spain is, therefore, Sw + Tariff.

Originally, the quantity of tomatoes in the UK will be Q_1 of which OQ_2 is produced in the UK and Q_2Q_1 is imported. The price will be P_1.

If the UK and Spain enter into a customs union the tariff will be removed and the price of Spanish tomatoes will fall to P_2. Consumption of tomatoes in the UK increases to OQ_3 of which OQ_4 is supplied by UK producers and Q_4Q_3 is imported. Trade creation has resulted as there has been a movement away from high-cost production to low-cost production. The UK consumer surplus has now been increased by 1 + 2 + 3 + 4. The overall welfare gain is, however, only areas 2 + 4 since area 1 represents a redistribution of producer surplus to consumers and area 3 a redistribution from the government to consumers (lost tariff revenue).

In this case there has been a net gain in welfare for the UK.

Link

For more on consumer and producer surplus see Chapter 2 page 70.

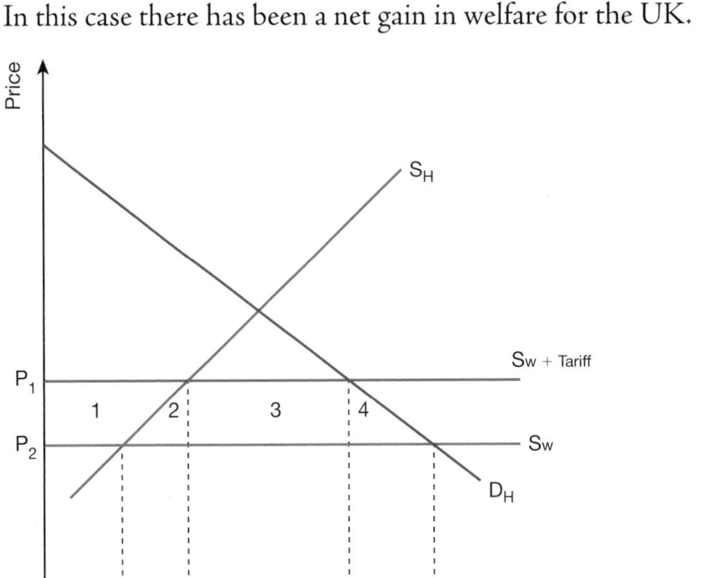

Figure 4.16 Trade creation ▲

Trade diversion

Trade diversion is when a tariff is imposed so that consumers can no longer benefit from low-cost supply. Assume that before the creation of the customs union the UK is importing tomatoes from the cheapest world producers. In Figure 4.17 D_H and S_H again represent the UK domestic demand for and supply of tomatoes and S_w represents the world supply curve. Before the customs union there were no tariffs on tomatoes. OQ_3 tomatoes would be consumed with OQ_4 produced in the UK and Q_3Q_4 imported.

If now the UK and Spain become part of a customs union then a tariff is imposed on imported tomatoes from outside the customs union meaning it is cheaper for the UK to purchase tomatoes from less-efficient producers such as Spain. The price rises to S_w+tariff. The demand falls to Q_1, but UK production increases to Q_2 with Q_2Q_1 being imported from Spain. The results will be:

- Consumer welfare falls by 1 + 2 + 3 + 4
- Government revenue rises by 3
- Producer surplus rises by 1
- Deadweight loss (lost by consumers, but not gained by government/producer) 2 + 4.

Activities

Economic integration

Conduct a class investigation to discover:

1. Whether your country is a member of a regional trading bloc and, if so, which one.
2. The type of trading bloc.
3. The other members of the trading bloc.
4. The advantages and disadvantages to your country of being a member of this trading bloc.
5. Whether membership of the trading bloc has resulted in trade creation or trade diversion and if so give examples.

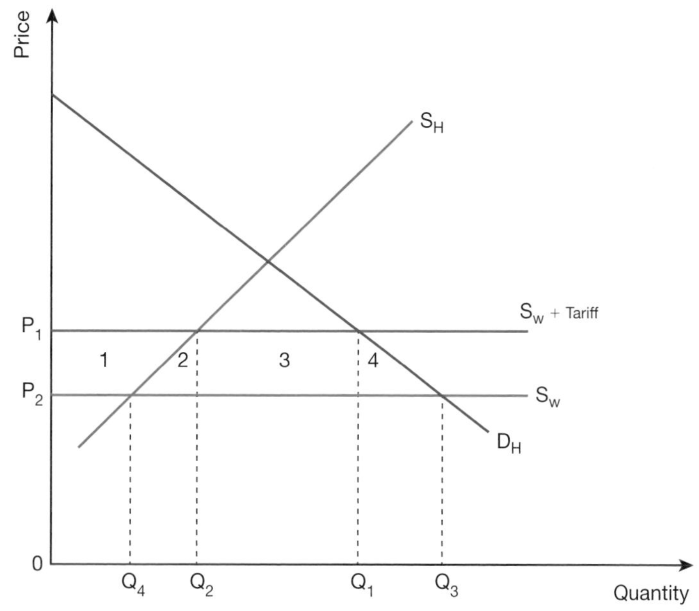

Figure 4.17 Trade diversion ▲

Progress question

3 What factors are likely to determine whether joining a customs union will lead to trade creation or trade diversion for a country?

The benefits of free trade

Not only does increasing world trade increase individuals' standard of living in terms of the quantity, quality and variety of goods and services available, but it represents an engine for growth and development particularly for the LEDCs. Exports are a component of aggregate demand and as such increases in the value of a country's exports can have a significant impact on GDP in a country. Certainly the high levels of economic growth experienced by countries such as China, South Korea and Taiwan have in no small measure been based on substantial export growth.

Currently exports from the LEDCs are rising faster than those from the DCs. LEDCs' export growth was 5.4 per cent in 2011 as opposed to 4.7 per cent in the DCs. In 2012 the figures for the growth of merchandise exports were 4 per cent for developing countries, but DCs reported a fall of 3 per cent. This growth in exports in the LEDCs may ultimately benefit the DCs as incomes in the LEDCs increase leading to an increase in the demand for consumer goods. Over the period 2005–2012 world merchandise exports grew on average by 3.5 per cent and GDP grew by 2.5 per cent.

The benefits of for free trade, based on the principle of comparative advantage, include:

- increased quantities of all goods for all nations
- increased variety of goods and services available for all countries
- increased productive and allocative efficiency as a result of specialisation by the producer with the lowest opportunity cost
- possibility of economies of scale resulting from increased output through specialisation
- lower prices resulting from increased efficiency and economies of scale.

Trading possibility curve

One way of showing the gains from free trade is to use trading possibilities curves. These show the maximum possible quantities of each good each country could consume at the prevailing terms of trade following specialisation.

Previously in looking at comparative advantage we used an example where the opportunity cost ratios in Indonesia and Botswana were one car for five toys in Indonesia and one car for one toy in Botswana and trade took place at one car for three toys.

Using 1 : 3 Indonesia could buy 33.3 cars if it specialised in toys and sold all of them to Botswana. Botswana could buy 48 toys if it specialised in cars and sold all of them to Indonesia. In both cases the countries are trading outside their production possibility curves (ppc) on their trading possibility curves (tpc). Although Botswana can only produce 16 cars, it is still clear that trading possibilities exist which are greater than the domestic production possibilities.

Links

The following are examined in more detail on the pages indicated:

Exports see page 96.

Standard of living see Chapter 9 page 255.

Economic growth see Chapter 9 page 248.

GDP see Chapter 9 page 254.

Link

For more on economies of scale see Chapter 7 page 173.

Activity

Trade

In groups discuss what advantages your country could gain from free trade. Report back and agree a list.

Which goods/services would you expect to have an absolute or comparative advantage in?

Key term

Trading possibilities curve: the consumption possibilities available for nations following specialisation and trade at any given terms of trade.

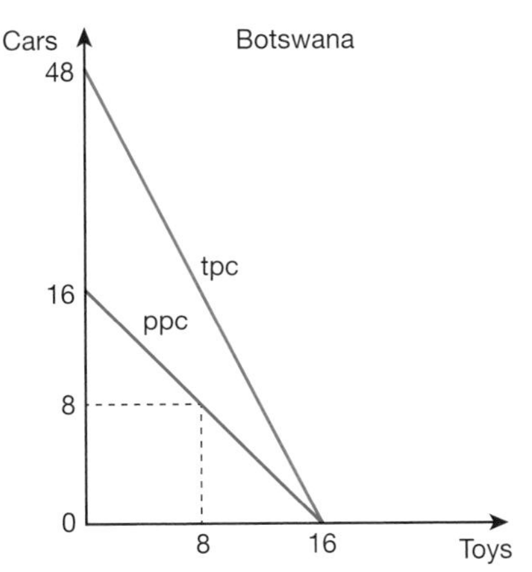

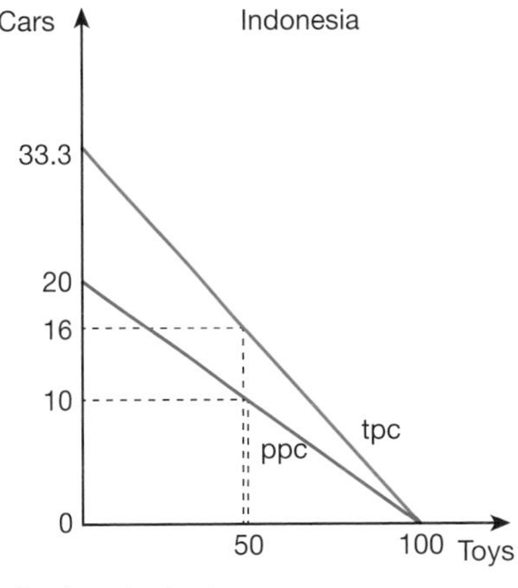

Figure 4.18 The trading possibility curves showing the gains from trade ▲

Protectionism

The meaning of protectionism in the context of international trade

> **Key term**
>
> **Protectionism**: an action designed to reduce international trade.

Protectionism is the opposite to free trade. It comes about because countries fear that without trade barriers their industries may not be able to compete with those of other countries.

Different methods of protection and their impact

> **Key term**
>
> **Tariff**: a tax on a product imported into a country. Tariffs can be specific or *ad valorem*.

Tariff

A tariff is a tax on a particular product as it is imported. It can be either specific or *ad valorem*.

In either case the effect is to shift the supply curve for the imported product to the left raising the price and reducing the quantity demanded of the imported product. The extent of the fall in the quantity demanded will depend upon the price elasticity of demand for the product. This increase in price clearly enables the domestic industry that was previously unable to compete with the foreign imports to increase its sales. However, the tariff has a significant impact on consumer welfare.

> **Links**
>
> For more on specific and *ad valorem* taxes see Chapter 3 page 76.
>
> For more on price elasticity of demand see Chapter 2 page 51.

The effects of a specific tax on an imported good are shown in Figure 4.19 with domestic output increasing from Q_1 to Q_2 and imports declining from Q_1Q_4 to Q_2Q_3, but demand falling from Q_4 to Q_3. This leads to a rise in price P_1 to P_2 where supply (S_w + tariff) is equal to D.

The other effects of the tariff are summarised below.

> **Link**
>
> See above page 109 for trade diversion.

Domestic production

The quantity of the product produced domestically has increased from Q_1 to Q_2. Previously no more than Q_1 could be supplied by domestic producers because their marginal costs of production, represented by the domestic supply curve (S_h), exceeded the world price. The tariff has allowed domestic production to rise to Q_2.

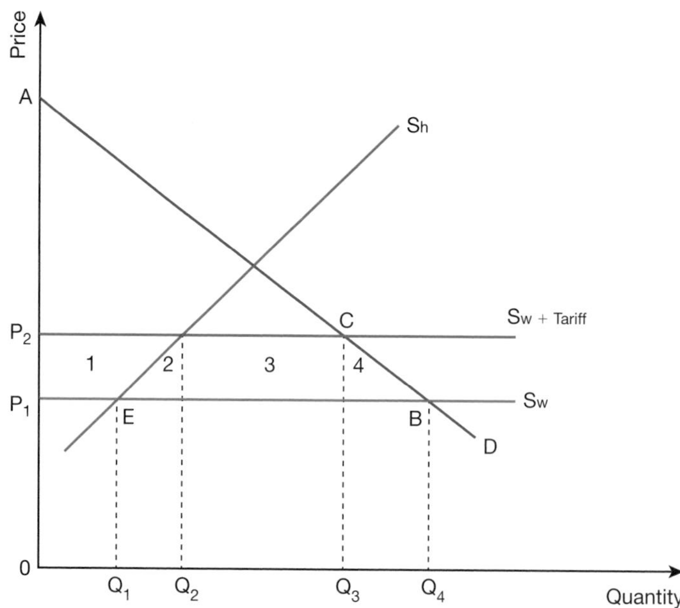

Figure 4.19 Effects of a tariff ▲

Imports

The tariff has resulted in the quantity of imports into the country being reduced from Q_1Q_4 to Q_2Q_3.

Consumer surplus

One of the most important welfare effects concerns the impact of the tariff on consumer surplus. Before the tariff was imposed the consumer surplus was represented by the area P_1 AB. After the imposition of the tariff the consumer surplus has fallen to P_2AC, a loss of P_1CB P_2 or the areas 1 + 2 + 3 + 4. Some of this has been lost to producers in the form of increased producer surplus and some to the government as revenue from the tariff.

Producer surplus

Originally the producer surplus equalled P_1EQ_10. The effect of the tariff is to increase it by area 1. This was previously part of consumer surplus and so the tariff has resulted in welfare redistribution from consumers to producers.

Link

See Chapter 2 page 70 to refresh your memory about consumer and producer surplus.

Revenue effect

The tariff will generate revenue for the government equal to the amount of the tariff per unit multiplied by the quantity of imports. This gives the area 3, which was previously part of the consumer surplus. Again, welfare has been redistributed away from consumers, in this case to the government.

Key term

Quota: a legal limit on the quantity of a product that can be imported into a country.

Quota

A second common method of protection is a quota which is a limit to the quantity imported. The limit can be in terms of an actual number or percentage share of the market. For example the USA currently imposes a quota on the import of sugar. Quotas normally involve the issuing of licences to companies allowing them to import the product up to a particular limit.

Like tariffs, quotas, involve society, particularly consumers, in a welfare loss, but arguably quotas may involve a greater overall welfare loss to society than tariffs because they generate no tax revenue for the government.

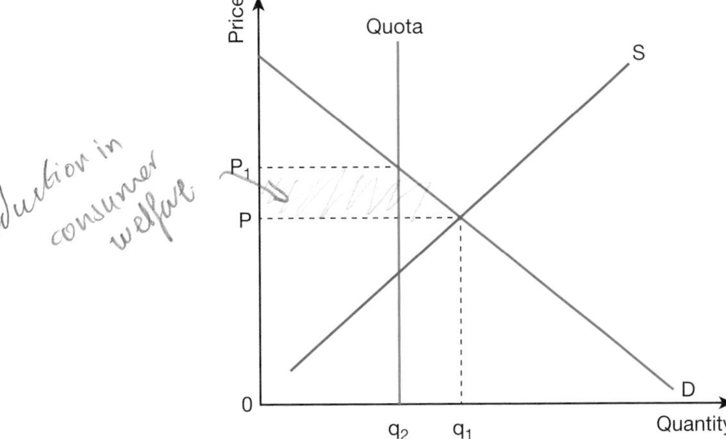

Figure 4.20 The effects of a quota ▲

As can be seen in Figure 4.20, the imposition of a quota raises the price from P to P_1 and reduces quantity from Q_1 to Q_2 again reducing consumer surplus.

Subsidies

Governments can also give subsidies either to home producers or to exporters. The first is to enable domestic producers to compete with imports from overseas by reducing their production costs. This will shift the supply curve to the right enabling domestic suppliers to reduce their price. The export subsidy allows businesses whose price would be too high abroad to sell in foreign countries at the world price thus increasing their competitiveness. Although subsidies will increase sales and thus output and employment, they may also increase inefficient allocation of resources. The government could have used the money to focus on goods in which the country had potential comparative advantage. In this case long-term economic growth may be reduced.

> **Link**
> See Chapter 3 page 79 and Chapter 8 page 212 for more on subsidies.

> **Key term**
> **Export subsidy**: money given to an exporter so the price of the product can be reduced to make it more competitive.

Exchange controls

Exchange controls are limits set by a government on the amount of domestic currency which is allowed to leave the country. Such controls have been abandoned by major industrial nations, but they are still adopted by some countries such as Malaysia and Zimbabwe. Clearly if there is a limit on the amount of a currency that is allowed to leave the country this will limit the quantity of a product that can be imported. The actual quantity of the product that can be imported will depend on the price of the product in question. While this preserves foreign currency it reduces consumer welfare similarly to the imposition of quotas.

> **Key term**
> **Exchange controls**: the imposition of limits on the amount of foreign currency available for importers.

Embargoes

> **Key term**
> **Embargo**: a complete ban on products from a particular country.

Embargoes involve a complete ban on the import of a particular product. Such bans are normally imposed for political reasons involving disputes between nations or during times of war. There may also be embargoes on products that are deemed to be dangerous or harmful such as drugs. The longest-standing embargo is that of the USA on foreign trade with Cuba.

Administrative burdens

> **Key terms**
> **Administrative burdens**: excessive red tape imposed on importers to make importing more difficult.
> **Red tape**: see administrative burdens.

Countries may seek to limit the quantity of imports of particular products into a country by imposing excessive administrative burdens, so-called "red tape", for importers to go through. These may include having to meet country-specific health or production standards, having to produce detailed documentation or having to bring all imports through only one entry point; procedures and documentation processes. The impact is to benefit domestic producers, but to reduce consumer welfare as foreign products are no longer available or are available only in small quantities thus reducing competition.

Voluntary export restraints

> **Key term**
> **Voluntary export restraints (VERs)**: where a country agrees to restrict its exports into a market to a particular limit, usually a percentage of the total market.

On certain occasions countries may impose voluntary export restraints (VERs) on themselves, restricting their share of an overseas market to a mutually agreed level. Such agreements are usually adopted on a bilateral basis and are normally in response to the threat or perceived threat of protectionist action being undertaken by the importing country. Japan For example between 1981 and 1998 entered into a bilateral agreement with the UK to limit its share of the UK car market to 9–11 per cent.

The arguments in favour of protectionism

A number of arguments to justify the imposition of protectionist policies have been put forward not all of which can be justified on purely economic grounds.

> **Key terms**
> **Infant industry**: an industry which is expected to have a comparative advantage, but at the moment is small and unable to compete with established industries elsewhere in the world.
> **Sunrise industry**: new or relatively new industries which are rapidly growing and are believed to have the potential to be market leaders in the future.

The infant industries argument is usually seen as the strongest case for protectionist measures. An infant industry is one which is expected to have a comparative advantage in production in the future, but at present is too small and lacks the economies of scale to enable it to compete with well-established firms in the market. A similar case can be made for sunrise industries.

Protection is designed to enable the infant industry to establish its comparative advantage and compete in its own right. Consumers will experience higher prices in the short run, but lower prices in the future. This particular argument has been used by a number of developing countries.

The major issues with this argument are first of all accurately identifying infant and sunrise industries and secondly establishing when they are able to compete without protection.

This argument is often linked with that of diversification. If a country is highly specialised in the production of a single good such as a primary product, then it is highly susceptible to fluctuations in the demand and price of this product. Protection can be used as a way of diversifying the economy to reduce dependence on a single product. It may also be suggested as part of a balanced growth strategy. This idea is often put forward by developing countries to justify trade barriers.

Again, however, it is difficult to justify on purely economic grounds. It goes against the principle of comparative advantage and, in addition, there are other ways of achieving diversification, for example the use of subsidies.

Case Study

Food processing in India – a sunrise industry

India is one of the world's leading food producers, producing over 600 million tonnes of grain each year. It is the largest producer of cereal in the world, the second-largest producer of fruit and vegetables and the second-largest exporter of rice.

However, despite this, food processing in India is relatively small with only 2 per cent of fruit and vegetables and 15 per cent of milk being processed domestically.

Food processing is regarded as a "sunrise industry" for India with great potential to generate economic growth with consequent implications for employment, export earnings and the attraction of FDI.

1. Explain what is meant by a "sunrise industry".
2. Discuss the advantages and disadvantages for India and for the rest of the world of the Indian government deciding to use tariff barriers to enable it to develop its sunrise food processing industry.

Unfair competition

Unfair competition has been a particularly popular argument put forward to justify imposing protectionist policies against products imported from countries with vast supplies of low-cost labour. These low labour costs mean that countries like China and India, and others in Asia, can sell at prices with which industrial countries cannot compete. Such arguments can appear even more compelling if it can be proved that the low wages of labour are the result of exploitation of labour.

This argument, however, cannot really be justified. The principle of comparative advantage shows that countries benefit from trade when differences in opportunity cost exist, whatever the reason for them. Consequently industrial nations should not be attempting to compete in these areas. Rather, they should be specialising in products in which they have a comparative advantage.

In addition, labour costs are not the only factor in determining the selling price. It is possible, therefore, that products manufactured by relatively high-cost labour, but using high-quality capital and sophisticated mass production methods might be able to produce at competitive prices.

People queue for work during the Great Depression ▲

In response, countries may claim that they are justified in employing tariffs and other restrictions on trade in order to retaliate against the protectionist policies of other countries. Although it is possible that the threat of retaliation might discourage another nation from imposing a tariff in the first place, actually imposing retaliatory tariffs cannot be justified. If countries continually raise tariffs in retaliation to one another the ultimate effect will be a significant reduction in world trade and a consequent reduction in consumer welfare in all countries. In 1930 the USA's decision to increase tariffs on some 20,000 imported products led to retaliation from its major trading nations which significantly reduced the volume of world trade and was probably instrumental in prolonging the Great Depression.

Employment

The idea here is that protecting home industries from foreign imports will enable domestic industries to compete and, therefore, preserve or increase employment in the country. This is sometimes used alongside either the infant industry or sunset industry arguments.

This, however, does not stand up to close scrutiny from an economics perspective. Instead, one should ask why these home industries cannot compete in the first place. If it is because they have higher costs than overseas producers and therefore lack comparative advantage, then they should not be competing in these markets, but in those where they have a comparative advantage.

There are also other ways of dealing with the problem of unemployment such as monetary, fiscal and supply-side policies.

Link

See Chapter 5 for more detail on the relevant monetary, fiscal and supply-side policies.

Sunset industries

Sunset industries are those long-established industries which are declining due to losing their comparative advantage. Often, factors of production are immobile and so cannot shift quickly to other expanding areas.

Key term

Sunset industries: industries which have lost their comparative advantage.

Whilst there might be a case for temporary protection for a short transitional period of time to enable factors to move into other areas and prevent significant structural unemployment, there is no case for long-term protection as this will be supporting inefficiency and reducing consumer welfare.

Dumping

Dumping refers to the practice whereby a product is sold in a foreign market at a price below its marginal cost of production and below the price received by producers in the importing country. Economists often distinguish between *persistent* and *predatory* dumping.

Key term

Dumping: the sale of a product in a foreign market at a price below its marginal cost of production.

Persistent dumping may continue indefinitely as a result of the exporting firm being a monopoly, able to practise price discrimination by exploiting different elasticities of demand in the home and overseas markets.

Although it may not always be easy to distinguish in reality between the two, persistent dumping may reflect the fact that the exporting country has a comparative advantage in the production of the product in question and as such it is difficult to justify protection on economic grounds as it provides consumers in the importing country with consistently lower prices and welfare gains.

Predatory dumping is undertaken with the specific intention of destroying foreign competition and normally involves predatory pricing. Although consumers in the importing country may experience temporary benefits, the destruction of the domestic industry and the consequent loss of competition may mean that in the long term consumers may suffer as a result of the creation of an overseas monopoly. In these circumstances protection against dumping is generally regarded as being justified.

Links

See Chapter 7 page 185 for a discussion of price discrimination under monopoly.

See Chapter 7 page 202 for a discussion of predatory pricing.

Getting it right

Make sure that you can clearly explain which arguments for protection can be justified on economic grounds and which cannot.

Activity

Free trade versus protection

Depending on the size of your class you could:

- have a debate on whether your country should adopt free trade or protection as its main trade policy and/or
- find out how your country justifies protection and whether there are any genuine infant industries that could grow and achieve comparative advantage.

Case Study

Sugar export subsidies – a case of "dumping"?

Australia, Brazil and Thailand have asked the WTO to investigate possible "dumping" of sugar onto world markets by the EU who authorised the export of 700 000 tonnes of sugar in 2011–2012 in addition to the 650 000 tonnes exported earlier in the year.

The three countries argue that this is the result of EU subsidies to producers and is likely to significantly reduce the price of sugar on world markets making it difficult for their own producers who do not receive subsidies to compete.

The EU on the other hand argues that it has abided by its international commitments on export subsidies for sugar.

1 Explain what is meant by the term "dumping".
2 With the aid of a diagram, explain the likely effects of the EU export subsidy on sugar.
3 With the aid of a diagram discuss the likely economic effects of the WTO authorising nations to use tariffs against imports of sugar from the EU if they wish.

Key concepts

- **Scarcity and choice** can be seen throughout this chapter, in particular in the balance of payments and absolute and comparative advantage.
- **Margin and change** can be seen in terms of terms of trade and absolute and comparative advantage.
- **Equilibrium and efficiency** can be seen in: AD and AS, exchange rates, trade creation and diversion, and in protection.
- **Regulation and equity** is briefly touched on under trade diversion and protection.
- **Progress and development** are referred to under free trade and protection and under absolute and comparative advantage.

Progress check

After completing this chapter you should be able to:

- understand and explain aggregate demand and supply analysis and be able to confidently use the diagrams
- define and measure inflation
- explain the causes and consequences of inflation
- identify the main components of a country's balance of payments
- explain the causes and consequences of a balance of payments disequilibrium
- explain how exchange rates can be determined and changed
- explain the effects of changes in the exchange rate on the domestic and external economies
- explain and evaluate the benefits and drawbacks for individual nations of being members of free trade areas, customs unions, monetary and full economic unions
- explain trade creation and trade diversion
- define what is meant by a nation's terms of trade and how they are measured
- explain how the principles of absolute and comparative advantage based on differences in opportunity cost explain why countries trade with one another
- explain the advantages of free trade based on comparative advantage
- explain the forms of protection used by nations
- evaluate the validity in economic terms of the arguments put forward to justify protection.

Exam-style questions

Essay and data response questions

1	a	Distinguish between a movement along and a shift in AD and AS.	[8 marks]
	b	Discuss whether an increase in AD will always lead to a rise in output and employment.	[12 marks]
2	a	Explain what is meant by cost-push and demand-pull inflation.	[8 marks]
	b	Discuss whether demand-pull is the most important cause of inflation in your country.	[12 marks]
3	a	Clearly explain how a retail prices index is constructed.	[8 marks]
	b	Discuss the view that inflation is always a major problem for an economy.	[12 marks]
4	a	Explain the factors that might bring about a deterioration in a country's terms of trade.	[8 marks]
	b	Evaluate the likely impact of deterioration in a country's terms of trade on its macroeconomic performance.	[12 marks]

5 a Explain the main components of the current account of a nation's balance of payments. [8 marks]
  b To what extent should a nation be concerned about a significant increase in the size of its deficit on the current account of the balance of payments? [12 marks]

6 a Explain the factors which determine a nation's exchange rate. [8 marks]
  b Evaluate the likely economic consequences of a substantial depreciation in a nation's exchange rate. [12 marks]

Multiple-choice questions

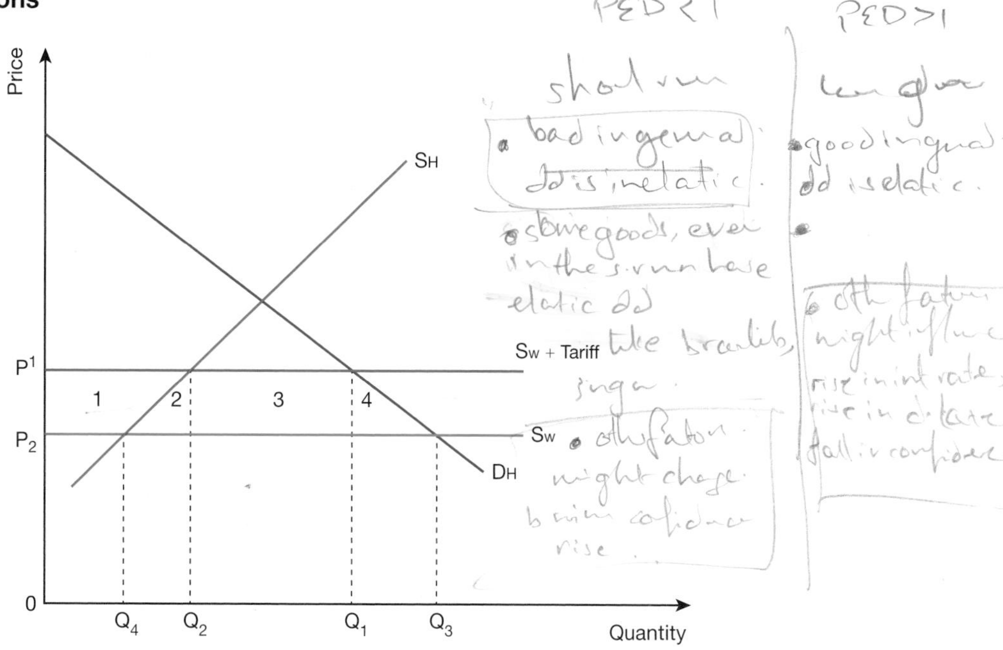

7 In the diagram above, which area(s) represent(s) the deadweight loss resulting from trade diversion? [1 mark]

A 1 only
B 3 only
C 2 and 4
D 1, 2, 3 and 4

8 Which of the following is a definition of the "real exchange rate"? [1 mark]

A An index showing the relative value of the exchange rate with other currencies
B How much a typical basket of goods costs in one country compared to another
C The rate at which one currency exchanges for another in the market
D The value of the currency in terms of what it can actually purchase

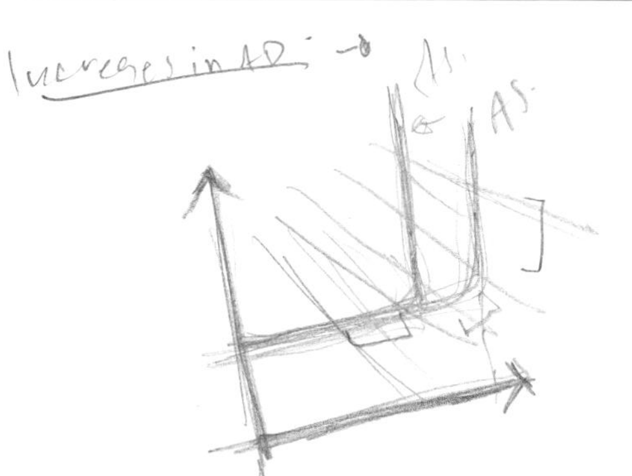

5 Government macro intervention

In this chapter you will develop your knowledge and understanding of:

- types of policy: fiscal, monetary and supply side
- policies to correct balance of payments disequilibrium
- policies to correct inflation and deflation.

Link

For more on Keynesian and monetarists schools see Chapter 9 page 289.

Key term

Fiscal policy: the use of government revenue and expenditure to control the economy.

Link

AD and AS analysis is explained in Chapter 4 page 87.

Links

For more on budgets see Chapter 9 page 255.

For more on injections and withdrawals see Chapter 9 page 276.

For more on public sector debt see Chapter 9 page 256.

Types of policy

This section will not only explore the different economic policies used by governments to try and achieve the macroeconomic objectives, but, where appropriate, it will place them in the context of the Keynesian and monetarist debate.

Fiscal policy

Fiscal policy is the use of government revenue and expenditure to control the economy. This also includes government borrowing. Expansionary fiscal policy involves increasing aggregate demand resulting in economic growth and more employment, but also higher inflation and possibly a deficit in the balance of payments. The opposite is deflationary fiscal policy.

Fiscal policy can also be used as a supply-side measure. This is covered under supply-side policies later on in this chapter.

Aims of fiscal policy

The aims of fiscal policy are:

- macroeconomic stability thus avoiding wild fluctuations in the trade cycle
- the achievement of the macroeconomic economic objectives
- funding of government expenditure without a damaging rise in government debt
- equity: to ensure that government expenditure and taxation is equitable to both the present and future generations.

Instruments of fiscal policy

The main instruments of fiscal policy are:

- Government spending on areas such as education, health, defence, social services. An increase in spending will increase aggregate demand (AD) as government expenditure (G) is a component of AD. Conversely, a fall in G will lead to a fall in AD.
- Borrowing: governments can run deficit budgets to stimulate the economy and cover the gap between revenue and expenditure by borrowing. This implies that expenditure is greater than tax revenue so once more there is an injection of money into the economy via G leading to an increase in AD. This will increase public sector debt.
- An increase in taxation reduces the amount of money in circulation. It is a withdrawal of money from the economy. This will result in a fall in AD. Conversely, a fall in tax rates will stimulate the economy and lead to a rise in AD.

The operation of fiscal policy is shown in Figure 5.1.

An increase in government expenditure (G) or cut in tax rates (T) will lead to an increase in AD from AD to AD_1. This will lead to actual growth and more employment, but it will also raise the price level.

Monetarists argue that fiscal policy only works in the short term as in the long run the aggregate supply curve is vertical so that any injection leads solely to inflation. Fiscal policy can also lead to crowding out due to governments using resources which are not then available to private sector investment.

Key term

Crowding out: where public sector spending is at the expense of private sector investment.

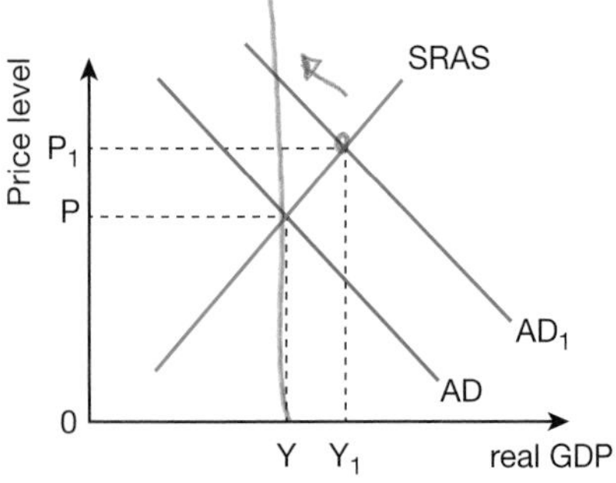

Figure 5.1 Expansionary fiscal policy ▲

Case Study

Fiscal policy in UAE

The United Arab Emirates consists of seven emirates of which the two largest economies are Abu Dhabi and Dubai.

Ignoring oil revenues the UAE has consistently run an expansionary fiscal policy based on a budget deficit. This has focused on stabilising prices, keeping unemployment low, and high and sustained economic growth.

In the period 2004–2009 the average growth rate was 8.98 per cent. This expansion led to higher inflation, reaching 12 per cent in 2009. This high growth and rising inflation was the direct result of a fiscal policy fuelled by oil revenues.

Since 2009 both growth and inflation have fallen, but unemployment has risen from 3.7 per cent to 4.3 per cent.

Some economists are concerned that the public sector dominated growth may affect private sector innovation. Others argue that public debt is greatly understated and has risen to 54.8 per cent of GDP in Abu Dhabi and over 100 per cent in Dubai.

1. Explain how expansionary fiscal policy could lead to higher economic growth and inflation.
2. Discuss whether a high public sector share of investment is likely to crowd out private sector innovation and invention.
3. Evaluate the possible effects of high public sector debt on the UAE economy.

Monetary policy

Monetary policy has consisted of:

- targeting the money supply
- controlling interest rates
- maintaining the exchange rate – see below.

Controlling the money supply has proved to be very difficult and has been largely abandoned in favour of controlling interest rates, although money supply is still measured as one aspect to consider when deciding policy.

Monetary policy therefore has meant, in many countries, controlling the rate of interest in order to control inflation. This is in line with monetarist thinking. In the recession of 2009 onwards, low interest

Links

For more on money supply see Chapter 9 page 285.

For more on quantity theory see Chapter 9 page 285.

Key term

Monetary policy: the use of the rate of interest or money supply or exchange rates to control the economy.

Getting it right

Remember that changes in the rate of interest affect the opportunity cost of spending as against saving.

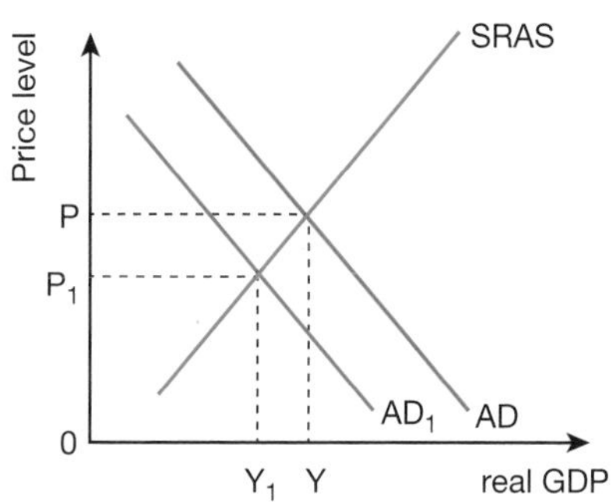

Figure 5.2 The effect of a rise in interest rates ▲

rates were also used as a means of trying to stimulate consumption and investment and thus economic growth. A cut in interest rates would lead to an expansion in aggregate demand. This is shown in Figure 5.2 by a shift from AD_1 to AD leading to a rise in GDP from Y_1 to Y and an increase in the price level from P_1 to P.

Equally, a rise in interest rates means that it is more expensive to borrow either new money or money already borrowed. This means that:

- consumers can afford to borrow less money, leading to their consumption being restricted
- consumers with existing loans have to pay more interest so they can afford to spend less on other goods and services
- firms are less likely to invest as it costs more to borrow or some projects are no longer economically viable as the return on them is less than the rate of interest.

As can be seen in Figure 5.2, a rise in interest rates will lead to a fall in aggregate demand from AD to AD_1 resulting in a fall in real GDP from Y to Y_1 and a decline in inflation. The overall result is likely to be: a fall in inflation and an improvement in the balance of payments, less imports are bought, but a decline in economic growth and a rise in unemployment.

Key terms

Open market operations: the buying and selling of government bonds to either increase or decrease the money supply.

Quantitative easing: where a central bank buys financial assets from banks and other private sector businesses with new electronically created money.

Open market operations

Monetary policy in many countries is controlled by the central bank. Two other ways in which the central bank can influence the money supply and thus interest rates, see Figure 5.3, is by the use of open market operations or through quantitative easing.

Open market operations involve the central bank in the selling or buying of government bonds. If the central bank wants to reduce the money supply it sells bonds. Banks, other financial institutions and individuals buy these bonds and the money goes to the central bank, which does not reissue it, thus reducing the supply of money in circulation. This selling of bonds will reduce their price, increasing their yield and thus the rate of interest, thus helping to control inflation. The reverse will be true if the central bank buys government bonds.

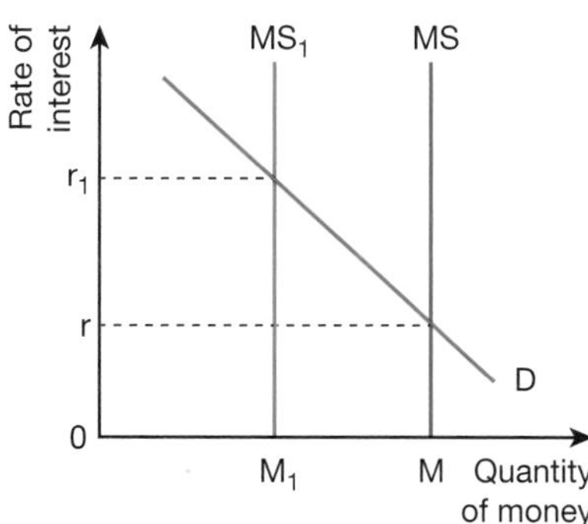

Figure 5.3 The effect of a decrease in the money supply ▲

As can be seen on Figure 5.3 a fall in the money supply from MS to MS_1 caused by the central bank selling government bonds, leads to a rise in interest rates from r to r_1.

Quantitative easing

Quantitative easing (QE) has only become popular since the recession of 2009, although the Bank of Japan claims to have first used it in 2001. Central banks use it when the rate of interest is close to zero to keep interest rates low and to reduce the yield on assets so as to encourage both consumers and firms, respectively, to spend and invest.

Table 5.1 Countries with interest rates at or below 1 per cent ▼

Country	Rate of interest mid-April, 2014 %
Bulgaria	0.04
Canada	1.00
Czech Republic	0.05
Denmark	0.20
Eurozone	0.25
Hong Kong	0.50
Isreal	0.75
Japan	0.10
Singapore	0.21
Sweden	0.75
Switzerland	0.00
United Arab Emirates	1.00
UK	0.50
USA	0.25

As can be seen in Table 5.1, 13 countries and one monetary union had a rate of interest of 1 per cent or less.

Central banks do this by creating new electronic money, i.e. not notes and coins, thus increasing the credit available to itself. With this it buys a wide range of assets, including government bonds, thus forcing their price up and the yield or interest rate down. With cheaper borrowing this should encourage greater spending, putting additional demand into the economy and pulling it out of recession. As the money ends up in bank deposits, banks should also find their funding position improved and this will make them more willing to lend.

A major issue with QE is that no one knows what amount is required for it to be effective and what amount would be too much, causing inflation. The latter is a major risk as is a potential loss of confidence in the currency together with the central bank making losses on its purchase of assets.

Both fiscal and monetary policies are demand-side policies affecting aggregate demand. Generally, they are used together, e.g. raise interest rates and taxes, although countries with large public sector debts such as the UK have kept interest rates low and used QE while at the same time pursuing a tight fiscal policy.

The difference is that while Keynesians would give priority to fiscal policy, monetarists would emphasise the primacy of monetary policy.

Activities

Monetary policy

1 What are the current interest rates of the countries shown in Table 5.1? Have any of the rates changed significantly?
2 What is the rate of interest in your country? How has it changed since April 2014?
3 Discuss the reasons for any of the changes you have found.

Progress question

1 Discuss whether fiscal or monetary policy would be more effective for controlling your country's economy.

Key term

Exchange rate policy: the use of exchange rates to control the economy.

Exchange rate policy

Exchange rate policy is a form of monetary policy and is often associated with fixing the currency to another currency such as the $, the euro or the yen. In 2013, 36 countries had currencies pegged to the US $ (13), the euro (19), the South African Rand (3) or the Indian Rupee (1).

In general, it is a way of controlling the economy by adjusting the exchange rate to meet its macroeconomic objectives. Between 1985 and 1992, the UK government maintained a high exchange rate to control inflation and to try to force firms to become more productively efficient in order to reduce costs and be more competitive. This ended in failure and has not been repeated.

Hong Kong dollars ▲

Exchange rate policy operates by either changing the rate of interest, e.g. lowering the rate of interest will lead to a fall in the exchange rate

Link

For more on balance of payments and exchange rates see Chapter 4 page 94.

as "hot money" leaves, or by the government/central bank buying or selling its currency. One problem is that changing the exchange rate may be offset by other factors. A good example is the price elasticity of demand for exports and imports.

One country which has pursued an exchange rate policy is Singapore. To do so, it had to give up control of domestic interest rates and the money supply. Its effectiveness for Singapore may be because of the very open nature of the Singapore economy.

Case Study

Singapore's exchange rate policy

The monetary policy of the Monetary Authority of Singapore (MAS) is based on managing the exchange rate with the primary objective of promoting price stability to achieve sustainable economic growth.

This has involved:

- a trade-weighted exchange rate being allowed to float between undisclosed bands
- intervention in the foreign exchange market to buy or sell the currency if it goes outside these bands
- regular reviews of the bands to ensure that the exchange rate is still allowing Singapore to achieve its economic objectives
- willingness to give up control of domestic interest rates so that the latter are determined by foreign interest rates and expectations about the value of the currency.

1. What is meant by a trade-weighted exchange rate?
2. Using diagram(s) show how the MAS could intervene if the currency went outside the bands.
3. Discuss whether a managed exchange rate policy would be suitable for your country.

Key term

Supply-side policy: any policy that helps to improve a country's productive potential.

Supply-side policies

Unlike the policies discussed above, supply-side policies are aimed at affecting the aggregate supply as can be seen in Figure 5.4. The aim is to shift the long run supply curve to the right in order to increase (potential) growth, and thus employment, without increasing inflation.

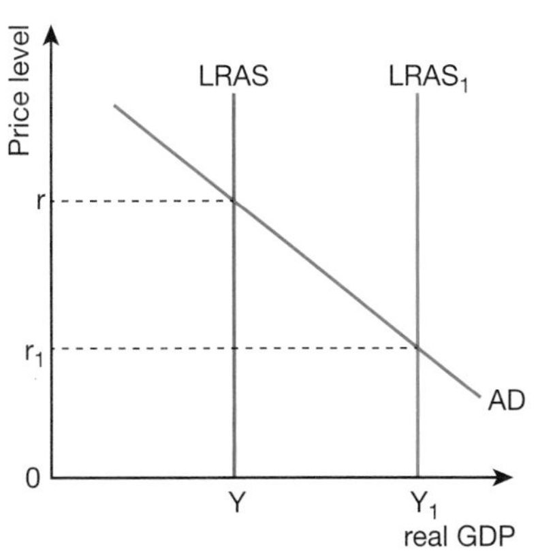

Figure 5.4 Supply-side policy ▲

These policies are often grouped under two headings: labour market measures and product market measures. As can be seen from this, they are essentially microeconomic measures used to influence the macro economy.

Labour market measures include:

- ▶ Ensuring that trade unions do not restrict the working of the labour market by making it more rigid. This has been controversial as it is difficult to decide between protecting the rights of workers and freeing up the market so it responds to the needs of the economy.
- ▶ Education and training: government spending on education and training improves workers' human capital. They become better-quality workers. Their productivity improves and so the LRAS curve shifts to the right.

- Tax and benefits: it is argued that high rates of direct tax act as a disincentive for people to work and firms to make profits. Lower rates would encourage more people to work especially if these were linked to lower unemployment benefits thus providing a real incentive to find jobs. Equally, lower taxes on firms would lead to them trying to be more efficient as they would keep more of their profits and could use these for investment. This idea is associated with Arthur Laffer. Lower income tax will act as an incentive for unemployed workers to join the labour market, or for existing workers to work harder. Lower corporation tax provides an incentive for entrepreneurs to start businesses and so increase national output.

Link

For more on the Laffer curve see Chapter 10 page 308.

- Local versus national pay agreements: national pay rates often fail to reflect differences within a country of the supply and demand for labour thus preventing people in areas of high supply from finding work.

Product market policies include:

- Privatisation and deregulation, wich are ways of introducing competition into the market thus increasing efficiency and greater productivity.
- Government help to improve supply-side performance by giving assistance to firms to encourage them to use new technology, and innovate. This can be done through grants or through the tax system. This will also encourage a more entrepreneurial culture.
- Reduction in bureaucratic systems which hinder the ability of businesses to either establish themselves or to make changes. This "red tape" hinders enterprise.

Links

For more on privatisation and deregulation see Chapter 3 page 83 and Chapter 8 page 212.

Case Study

Supply-side policies and India

In many ways India has been an economic success. Thanks to an entrepreneurial attitude, industry has grown and Bangalore has established itself as a world leader in IT. In addition agricultural productivity has steadily improved. All of this has led to rapid economic growth.

Some economists consider that the increase could be even greater if the infrastructure was better. Overall, supply constraints not only hinder growth, but also increase inflation. In addition, whereas the low wage costs have been a benefit for India, the increasing skills shortage means that wages will rise making it less attractive for foreign investment. The shortage of places at universities means that many Indian students have to seek places abroad from which they may not return to work.

Others have pointed out that raising interest rates to prevent inflation fails to tackle the real problem of supply-side blockages. Instead there needs to be more deregulation and lower taxes to facilitate greater enterprise.

1 Explain two ways in which India has achieved economic success.
2 Explain how improving the infrastructure could lead to greater economic growth.
3 Discuss whether monetary or supply-side policies are better at controlling inflation.

Getting it right

Make sure you can fully distinguish between both of the different policies associated with fiscal, monetary and supply side and how they affect AD/AS.

Activity

Policy committee

Either in pairs or as a group decide how you would improve the current account deficit on your country's balance of payments. Try to come up with several policies. Refer to Chapter 4.

When you have decided on your preferred policy share it with the others if in pairs, or defend your choice against those of the rest of the group.

Now read the material which follows. At the end repeat the exercise and see if you have changed your ideas.

Link

For causes of balance of payments disequilibrium see Chapter 4 page 98.

Links

See Chapter 4 page 93 for cost push inflation.

See Chapter 4 page 94 for exchange rates.

Supply-side policies are long-term ones. Improving education and training to increase aggregate supply can only be effective as these people enter the workforce. They are not, therefore, in opposition to fiscal and monetary policies. The great advantage of supply-side policies is that they avoid the trade-off between policies as economic growth, low inflation, low unemployment and a more favourable balance of payments can all be achieved at the same time.

Policies to correct balance of payments disequilibrium

Policies include:

- assessment of the effectiveness of fiscal, monetary and supply-side policies to correct a balance of payments disequilibrium
- expenditure reducing and expenditure switching.

Expenditure dampening/reducing policy

One approach is to consider the causes of the disequilibrium. If it is caused by excess demand in the economy then an interest rate policy such as raising interest rates could be used. This is an example of an expenditure-reducing policy. Interest rates would be raised so it was more expensive to borrow money for either consumption (C) or investment (I) purposes leading to a fall in demand for imports. The problem is that a rise in interest rates could lead to an inflow of money attracted by the higher interest, leading to a rise in exchange rates and thus cheaper imports and dearer exports, causing a more severe problem.

In addition, if the disequilibrium is due to your country's prices being too high a reduction in interest rates would lead to an outflow of money, hot money flows, thus reducing the value of the exchange rate making the price of the country's exports cheaper and imports dearer. This could lead to cost-push inflation.

Key terms

Interest rate policy: the use of interest rates to influence demand by both consumers and businesses.
Expenditure-reducing policies: used to correct a balance of payments disequilibrium by reducing consumer purchasing power. This is likely to involve monetary (interest rates) and fiscal policies (taxes).
Hot money: short-term capital flows in the foreign exchange market due to changes in interest rates.

This would only work so long as some form of floating exchange rate was being used.

Progress question

2 Discuss whether raising interest rates would result in a correction to disequilibrium in the balance of payments.

Another way to reduce demand would be the use of fiscal policy such as increasing income tax. In this case an increase in income tax would reduce consumers' income leading to a fall in demand for imports. This, in turn, could cause the exchange rate to rise.

Expenditure-switching policies

> **Key term**
>
> **Expenditure-switching policy**: policies which lead to a fall in imports and an increase in consumption of domestically produced goods and services.

An alternative to expenditure-dampening policies is expenditure-switching policies. These aim to shift expenditure from imported to domestically produced goods. This can be done in three ways.

Protectionist methods

The use of protectionist methods, such as tariffs and quotas, makes imports more expensive or more difficult to get hold of thus leading to more demand for domestically produced goods. This could lead to a rise in the value of the exchange rate. The use of protectionist measures, except in exceptional circumstances and for very short periods of time, is against the rules of the WTO. In addition members of customs unions, such as the EU, cannot use these methods against other members.

> **Links**
>
> The following are examined in more detail on the pages indicated:
>
> Protection see Chapter 4 page 113.
>
> WTO see Chapter 9 page 294.
>
> European Union see Chapter 4 page 108.

Devaluing or depreciating

Devaluation of a currency takes place in a fixed rate exchange system, whereas depreciation takes place in a floating rate exchange system. In this way imports will be dearer leading to a substitution of cheaper domestic goods for the more expensive foreign ones.

The effectiveness of these measures depends on the Marshall–Lerner condition.

> **Link**
>
> Marshall–Lerner condition is explained in Chapter 4 page 102.

Exchange controls

Using exchange controls means that the flow of money both into and out of a country is regulated by the central bank. These can be used both to reduce imports and as a means of preventing capital outflows where people fear a fall in the country's exchange rate or fall in the value of their money. This use of exchange controls could lead to a rise in the exchange rate assuming that imports fell and exports remained the same.

> **Case Study**
>
> **Exchange controls**
>
> On the 31 October 2011, the Argentine government imposed new restrictions on the purchase of US dollars in an attempt to reduce capital outflows and tax evasion.
>
> Billions of dollars worth of capital flowed out of the country as wealthy Argentines sought to protect their money from inflation and a possible devaluation of the peso.
>
> 1. Explain what is meant by "exchange controls".
> 2. Explain the advantages of imposing exchange control on a currency.
> 3. Explain the disadvantages of imposing exchange controls on a currency.

Short-term and long-term solutions

Both expenditure-dampening and expenditure-switching policies are essentially short-term solutions. As protection is not an option for members of the WTO, countries will sometimes try to combine some form of deflation, by reducing demand, with either depreciation or devaluation. If the disequilibrium is caused by high inflation then deflationary policies such as raising the interest rate will be needed to control this and improve competitiveness.

Link

For more on import control methods see Chapter 4.

Finally, countries can use exchange controls to reduce the ability of domestic businesses to import goods.

In the longer term, countries can try to increase their competitiveness by improving their labour productivity through more investment and/or better education and training. This can lead to a fall in the cost of domestically produced goods, and thus exports, and may be accompanied by better-quality products. Both will lead to more exports and, possibly, fewer imports.

Link

For more on labour productivity see Chapter 9 page 253.

Throughout this section it has been assumed that the disequilibrium is negative. Some countries run large balance of payments surpluses, e.g. China, Germany, Japan and Nepal. This is not always the blessing it first appears to be as net exports are part of aggregate demand (AD). An increase in AD can lead to inflation.

Link

Aggregate demand is covered in Chapter 4 page 87.

Overall the effectiveness of any policy to control a balance of payments disequilibrium will depend on the following features.

- The cause(s), e.g. lack of competitiveness, could be tackled by increasing government expenditure (G) on research and development so as to gain a comparative advantage.
- Responsiveness of the markets to the policies – increasing G might attract more foreign investment and thus an increase in production at lower costs. On the other hand, it might scare off investors if it increased government debt and thus make the situation worse.
- The price elasticity of demand for exports and imports, including Marshall–Lerner. Changes in interest rates/exchange rates must take this into account in order to avoid the wrong decision.
- The time span involved – see the J-curve effect. In addition, a short-term deficit may be corrected by raising interest rates to attract hot money and reduce internal demand.

Link

For more on J-curve effect see Chapter 4 page 102.

Case Study

Exchange control in South Africa

The Reserve Bank of South Africa controls and oversees all capital inflows and outflows. The main points of the exchange controls are:

- it applies to all transactions whatever the size
- no resident or organisation may make a transaction without prior approval
- only dealers approved by the Reserve Bank may make a currency transfer
- outward payments may only be made for permissible reasons and under conditions approved by the Reserve Bank

- all payments made to foreign individuals and organisations must be reported to the Reserve Bank
- personal transfers, in the form of personal allowances, must adhere to the allowed set amounts.

1 Explain *two* different reasons why the South African Government might have decided to impose exchange controls.

2 What effects will these exchange controls have on the South African balance of payments? Give reasons for your answers.

Policies to correct inflation and deflation

Assessment of the effectiveness of fiscal, monetary and supply-side policies to correct inflation and deflation

Governments normally pursue a mixture of fiscal, monetary and supply-side policies. Although supply-side policies can avoid the conflicts in policy objectives which fiscal and monetary policies face, the time span in which they operate means that they cannot be used to deal with immediate problems.

Fiscal policy

To reduce inflation a government should reduce government expenditure (G) and increase taxation (T). This will result in a fall in aggregate demand (AD).

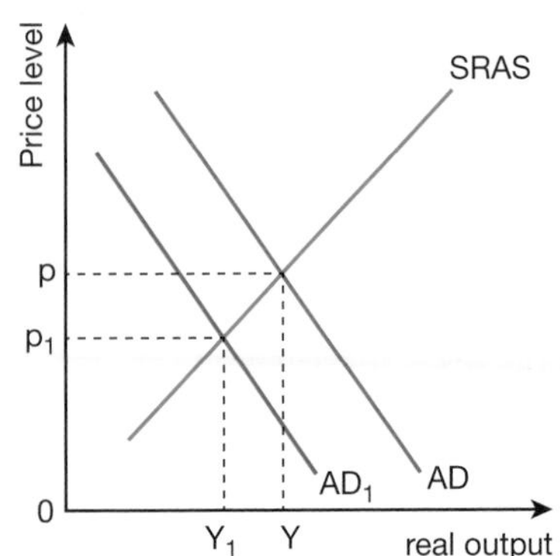

Figure 5.5 Operation of fiscal policy – control of inflation ▲

Figure 5.5 shows that if AD falls to AD^1 then inflation will fall from p to p_1. The problem is that except under extreme difficulties, such as Greece in 2013, it is very difficult to just cut G as against cutting future G so it takes time to implement. Equally, tax changes take time to work their way from announcement to implementation to having an effect.

There also appears to be a trade-off between inflation and employment. In Figure 5.5 the fall in the price level is accompanied by a fall in real output, and thus employment, from Y to Y_1.

In the case of deflation AD can be increased by cutting T and increasing G. In Figure 5.6 this would lead to AD shifting from AD_1 to AD and real output rising from Y_1 to Y while the price level rose, being negative at P_1 to being positive at P.

Links

The following are examined in more detail on the pages indicated:

Inflation see Chapter 4 page 90.

Deflation see Chapter 4 page 92.

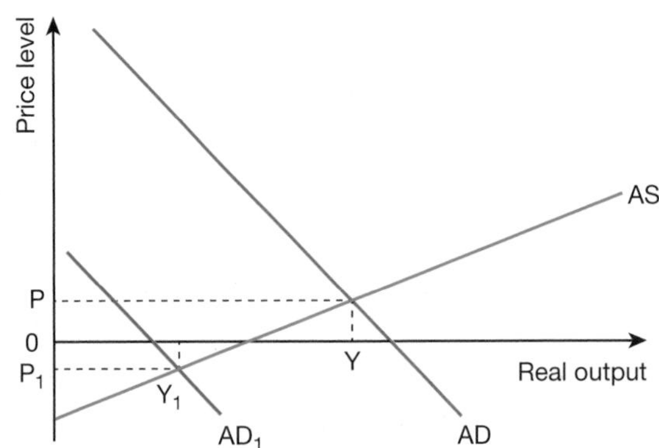

Figure 5.6 Operation of fiscal policy – dealing with deflation ▲

John Maynard Keynes ▲

John Maynard Keynes said that governments should be prepared to borrow money and spend it in order to get people back into work and to stimulate the economy. The problem is that this will result in a large increase in government debt. Since December 2012 Shinzo Abe, Prime Minister of Japan, has been using fiscal policy, along with monetary policy, to try to stimulate the economy. This has been called "Abenomics".

> **Activity**
>
> **Abenomics**
>
> Find out how successful Abenomics has been for Japan.
>
> What economic factors have affected its success? Would such a policy be suitable for your country's economy. If not, why not?

> **Link**
>
> For more on government debt see Chapter 9 page 255.

> **Links**
>
> The following are examined in more detail on the pages indicated:
>
> Friedman see Chapter 9 page 289.
>
> Unemployment see Chapter 10 page 301.
>
> Economic growth see Chapter 10 page 301.
>
> Balance of payments see Chapter 4 page 95.

Monetary policy

In that monetary policy operates on the demand side of the economy it has similar effects to fiscal policy, see Figure 5.5. The main difference is that control of inflation is the major emphasis stemming from Milton Friedman's view that only by controlling inflation can sustainable economic growth, low unemployment and a more favourable balance of payments be achieved.

By bringing down inflation interest rates can be lowered. This leads directly to more investment, assuming that investment is interest elastic. Higher investment generates more growth and employment as well as making goods and services more competitive through innovation and invention. Up until 2008 there was some evidence that this was happening, as many central banks brought inflation down while stimulating growth and employment. Governments have also set central banks inflation targets (see Table 5.2), which they can only achieve by using their policies which are all monetary.

Table 5.2 Selected central bank inflation targets for 2014 ▼

Country	Inflation target %
China	3
Eurozone	<2
Kenya	5, ±2
Mexico	3, ±1
Pakistan	8
UK	2

Changes in interest rates

Changes in interest rates also affect exchange rates. A fall in interest rates will lead to an outflow of hot money and a fall in the exchange rate. If the Marshall–Lerner effect holds then this would improve the balance of payments. Monetary policy, like fiscal policy, needs time to work its way through the economy. The Bank of England estimates that a change in interest rates takes between 18 months and two years to fully work its way through the economy.

Using monetary policy to combat unemployment would involve lowering interest rates and the use of quantitative easing (QE). In theory cutting interest rates to low levels should stimulate both consumers and business to spend and invest, thus generating demand

Link

For more on quantitative easing see Chapter 9 page 287.

and employment, leading to an increase in AD. The bank rate in Japan has been at or very near 0 per cent since 1999, but this has done little to stimulate demand due to underlying economic problems. Under Abenomics the Bank of Japan has used QE.

Supply-side policy

As previously stated, supply-side policies can avoid the trade-off between policies which tends to occur with both fiscal and monetary policies. They also reduce long-term inflation as aggregate supply increases to meet expansion in aggregate demand and provides sustainable growth as these policies increase a country's competitiveness and employment. In Figure 5.7 an increase in AD leading to inflation, p to p_1, can be offset by an increase in aggregate supply (AS) from AS to AS_1 leading to inflation being controlled while real output increases from Y to Y_1.

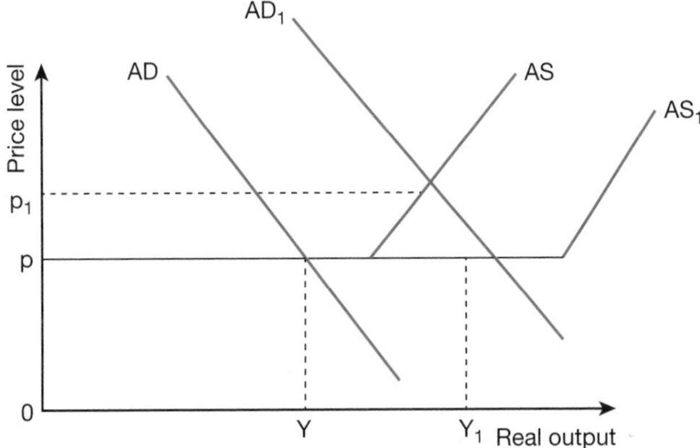

Figure 5.7 Operation of supply-side policy ▲

On the other hand, while fiscal and monetary policies can start to affect the economy relatively quickly, supply-side policies take a considerable time and are often expensive to implement, e.g. the cost of education and training, while others, e.g. labour market policies, may face resistance from interest groups.

Supply-side policies cannot immediately help with deflation, but by using public and private sector investment to generate more growth and employment by shifting the supply line from AS to AS_1 (see Figure 5.7) supply-side policy can reinforce the short-term effects of fiscal and monetary policies.

Since 1980 governments have favoured using fiscal and/or monetary policies to control inflation in the short term while implementing supply-side policies to achieve lower long-term inflation. In recent years both fiscal and monetary policies have been used by governments facing deflation, but supply-side policies can be effective in dealing with the underlying structural problems such as monopoly power, lack of innovation.

Activities

Economic policies

1 What policies has your country used during the last ten years?
2 How successful have these been?

This could be done in pairs and then reported back to the whole class.

Key concepts

- **Scarcity and choice**: choice and opportunity cost are covered in the section on absolute and comparative advantage.
- **Equilibrium and efficiency** are related to exchange rates and the setting of the currency value, and AD and AS in terms of equilibrium.
- **Regulation and equity**: regulation is covered in fixed exchange rates and protection.

Progress check

After completing this chapter you should be able to:

- explain the different macroeconomic policies
- assess the effectiveness of fiscal, monetary and supply-side policies to deal with a balance of payments disequilibrium
- assess the effectiveness of fiscal, monetary and supply-side policies to correct inflation and deflation.

Exam-style questions

Essay and data response questions

1 a Explain how fiscal policy works. [8 marks]
  b Discuss the policies a government could use to control inflation. [12 marks]
2 a Explain how supply-side policy works. [8 marks]
  b Discuss whether supply-side policies would be the most effective way of correcting a balance of payments disequilibrium. [12 marks]
3 a Explain the difference between inflation and deflation. [8 marks]
  b Evaluate the policies that could be used by a country facing deflation. [12 marks]
4 a Compare a free trade area and a customs union. [8 marks]
  b Discuss whether or not countries should use protectionist measures. [12 marks]

Multiple-choice questions

5 Which of the following changes in AD and AS will most likely lead to a fall in the rate of inflation? [1 mark]
  A Aggregate demand and supply both increase
  B Aggregate demand stays constant and productivity increases
  C Aggregate supply falls while aggregate demand remains constant
  D Aggregate supply remains constant and aggregate demand increases
6 Which of the following is likely to lead to an improvement in a country's terms of trade? [1 mark]
  A There is a rise in the value of the country's exchange rate
  B The average price of imports rises and the average price of exports falls
  C The average price of exports falls more rapidly than the average price of imports
  D The country decides to lower its tariff barriers

6 Basic economic ideas and resource allocation

In this chapter you will develop your knowledge and understanding of:

- efficient or optimum resource allocation
- externalities and market failure
- social costs and social benefits
- the use of cost-benefit analysis.

Efficient or optimum resource allocation

Economic efficiency refers to a situation where scarce resources are used in the "best" or most effective possible way to achieve the maximum output possible.

Another way of describing efficiency is in relation to the concept of optimality. Optimality (or optimum) can be defined as the best situation or outcome possible in a particular situation. It is a very important concept in Economics given the existence of scarcity that underpins the basic economic problem.

> **Key terms**
>
> **Economic efficiency**: the optimal use of scarce inputs to produce the largest possible output.
>
> **Optimality or optimum**: the best situation that can be attained in particular circumstances.
>
> **Productive efficiency**: the most efficient use of scarce resources whereby the maximum output is produced with the minimum of resources.
>
> **Technical efficiency**: the situation in a firm where production is at the lowest point on the average total cost curve.

Productive and allocative efficiency

Economic efficiency, or an optimal allocation of scarce resources, can only exist when there is *both* productive efficiency and allocative efficiency.

Productive efficiency

Productive efficiency occurs when products are made with the least possible use of scarce resources.

Productive efficiency in a firm

This can be shown in a diagram which illustrates the average total cost curves of a firm because productive efficiency will occur when products are produced at the lowest possible cost of production.

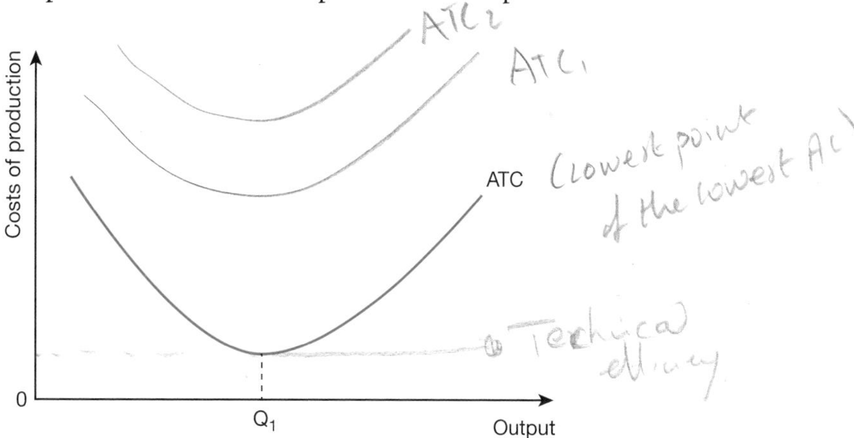

Figure 6.1 Productive efficiency in a firm ▲

Productive efficiency for a firm occurs where the firm's output is produced at the minimum point of the average total cost curve; in Figure 6.1, this is an output of Q1. There are actually two elements to this situation. Firstly, a firm may have a number of average total cost curves; productive efficiency takes place on the lowest possible average total cost curve. Secondly, production needs to be at the lowest point on the lowest average total cost curve (as shown in Figure 6.1). This second element is known as technical efficiency.

> **Link**
>
> Efficiency is generally concerned with how well resources are used to produce an output. It would therefore be useful to look back at the discussion of the three fundamental questions in page 20 of Chapter 1: what will be produced, how will it be produced and for whom will it be produced?

Link

See the discussion of scarcity in page 8 of Chapter 1.

Case Study

Jones and Tudor

The Jones and Tudor company operates in the fashion industry, where there is a great deal of intense competition. In the last few years, a number of companies in the industry have gone out of business, mainly because they were unable to get their costs down enough.

The Jones and Tudor company has been in existence for over 50 years and it is determined that it is not going to go out of business if it can possibly avoid it. The company has produced a plan which aims to reduce the costs of production by a third over the next two years.

1 You have been brought in as a management consultant to advise the company on what it will need to do to reduce costs by a third over the next two years. Produce a report that summarises your suggestions to the company.

Progress question

1 Explain how productive efficiency in a firm consists of two elements.

Productive efficiency in an economy

Productive efficiency can also be shown in relation to a whole economy rather than just a particular firm.

The production possibility curve can be used to show the existence of productive efficiency in an economy. Figure 6.2 assumes that there is a two-product economy where scarce resources are allocated to the production of either good A, shown on the horizontal axis, or to good B, shown on the vertical axis. The production possibility curve shows the possible combinations of production of these two goods. Point X, inside the production possibility curve, indicates that there are unused resources in the economy that could be used to produce either good A, good B or a combination of the two goods. Any point along the production possibility curve, however, such as point Y, indicates that all possible resources are being used to produce a particular combination of the two goods, i.e. productive efficiency is being maximised.

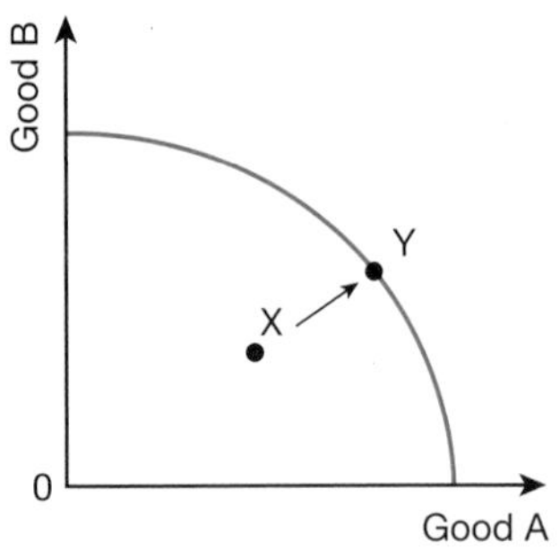

Figure 6.2 Productive efficiency in an economy ▲

Links

The production possibility curve was introduced on page 10 of Chapter 1. The concept of productive efficiency can also be seen in page 188 of Chapter 7 in relation to the characteristics of different market structures.

Progress question

2 Distinguish between productive efficiency in a firm and productive efficiency in an economy.

> **Key term**
>
> **Allocative efficiency**: the quantity of output produced with scarce resources that leads to the best satisfaction for consumers.

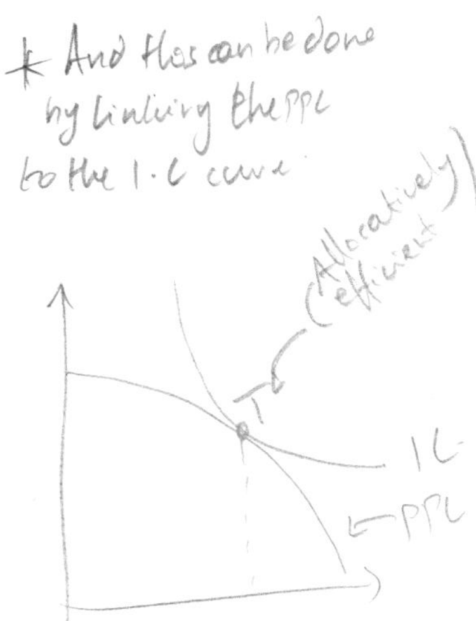

Allocative efficiency

Whereas the concept of productive efficiency placed the emphasis on production at the lowest possible cost, allocative efficiency emphasises that it is necessary that the right products are produced in an economy. This is related to the satisfaction or utility that consumers get from the consumption of particular products.

This is best shown in terms of the relationship between the marginal cost of production and the price of a product. The marginal cost of production refers to the cost of producing one more product; when this is equal to the price charged for the product, allocative efficiency is said to exist. The explanation for this is that the value put on the resources by the producer is exactly equal to the value put on the product produced by the resources by the consumer. If any more or any less was produced, price and marginal cost would no longer be in equilibrium.

> ### Activity
>
> **Allocative efficiency**
>
> Look at the following figures. State and explain which level of output would be allocatively efficient.

Quantity	25	50	75	100	125	150	175
Price ($)	12	12	12	12	12	12	12
Marginal cost ($)	4	6	8	10	12	14	16

> **Getting it right**
>
> Make sure you understand that a production possibility curve is usually used to illustrate the concept of productive efficiency, although if consumer preferences are known it could be used to show the concept of allocative efficiency.

It has already been explained that a production possibility curve can be used to illustrate the concept of productive efficiency in an economy (see Figure 6.2). A production possibility curve can also be used to show the concept of allocative efficiency, but only if the particular preferences of consumers are known. Any point along the production possibility frontier could possibly show the existence of allocative efficiency; the exact point on the curve would depend on the particular preferences of consumers.

For allocative efficiency to exist throughout an economy, this must operate in all markets in the economy.

Pareto optimality

> **Key term**
>
> **Pareto optimality**: this situation exists when it is not possible to make one person better off without making someone else worse off as a result of reallocating resources.

One particular type of optimality is associated with the Italian economist Vilfredo Pareto (1848–1923). Pareto optimality (or Pareto efficiency) refers to a situation where it is not possible to reallocate scarce resources to make someone better off without making someone else worse off. For this situation to be achieved, there needs to be *both* productive and allocative efficiency. This optimal allocation of resources means that inputs into the production process are used in the most efficient way (productive efficiency) and that the output produced yields the maximum possible utility or satisfaction to consumers (allocative efficiency).

Vilfredo Pareto ▲

Pareto first put forward this condition in 1909. If an allocation of resources is Pareto inefficient, this means that it would be possible to make at least one person better off without making anybody worse off.

Dynamic efficiency

Dynamic efficiency results from improvements in technical or productive efficiency over a period of time. For example, new products may appear in markets as a result of research and development, invention and innovation. New methods of production could be introduced, incorporating the latest technology. There could also be the introduction of radically different methods of management, resulting from investment in human capital.

Progress question

3 Explain the difference between invention and innovation.

Key term

Dynamic efficiency: the greater efficiency that results from improvements in technical or productive efficiency over a period of time.

Both productive and allocative efficiency can be regarded as examples of static efficiency, i.e. they are concerned with the allocation of scarce resources at a particular moment in time. Dynamic efficiency, in contrast, is concerned with the allocation of scarce resources over a period of time.

Progress question

4 Discuss how (a) new methods of production and (b) new methods of management might lead to the more efficient use of resources in an economy.

Activity

New products

Working in groups, think of examples of five new products that were not in existence 20 years ago.

Advances in technology can bring about dynamic efficiency ▲

Case Study

Allocation of resources

Some countries are more likely to be dynamic, such as in relation to the impact of technological change, than others and so it might be expected that the use of scarce resources might become more efficient in such countries over a period of time. The following tables give some indication of which countries these might be.

The Innovation Index

This index measures the use of new technology in economies. The higher the number, the greater the application of new technology in a particular economy. A figure of 5.00 or more is seen as very good.

Country	Innovation Index
USA	5.65
Switzerland	5.60
Finland	5.56
Japan	5.52
Sweden	5.45
Israel	5.30
Taiwan	5.23
Germany	5.19
Singapore	5.04
Denmark	4.89

The Technological Readiness Index

This index measures the ability of economies to adopt new technology. In this case, a figure of 6.00 or more is considered to be very good in terms of the ability of economies to adopt new technology.

Country	Technological Readiness Index
Sweden	6.12
Luxembourg	6.11
Iceland	5.99
The Netherlands	5.99
Hong Kong	5.96
Denmark	5.62
Switzerland	5.60
UK	5.58
Norway	5.56
Germany	5.36

Total expenditure on research and development (% of GDP)

Country	% of GDP
Israel	4.86
Sweden	3.75
Finland	3.50
Japan	3.44
South Korea	3.21
Switzerland	2.90
Taiwan	2.77
USA	2.76
Denmark	2.72
Singapore	2.68

1 Discuss how research and development and technological change could be used to improve the efficiency of the allocation of resources in an economy.

Activity

Dynamic efficiency

Use the Internet to discover how the Innovation Index and the Technological Readiness Index are compiled.

Externalities and market failure

Reasons for market failure

Public goods, merit goods, demerit goods and information failure have already been covered in Chapter 1 and the existence of externalities will be covered in this chapter. There are other examples of market failure, such as the existence of imperfect competition which will be covered in Chapter 7, inequality in the distribution of income and wealth which will be covered in Chapter 10, and government failure which will also be covered in Chapter 10.

It will therefore be useful at this point to provide a summary of the main reasons for market failure.

Links

For more on market failure see Chapter 1 page 31 and Chapter 10 page 307.

Table 6.1 Reasons for market failure ▼

Type of market failure	Explanation
Public goods	These are goods which would not be provided in a market economy because it would be impossible to charge a price for them because of the "free rider" problem.
Merit goods	These are goods or services which are regarded as being socially desirable and which would be under-consumed and under-produced in a market economy.
Demerit goods	These are goods which are regarded as being socially undesirable and which would be over-consumed and over-produced in a market economy.
Information failure	This is where there is a lack of full information and so the allocation of resources is less efficient than it would otherwise be. This information failure is a major reason why consumers make the wrong decisions in relation to the consumption of merit and demerit goods.

Type of market failure	Explanation
Government failure	A government can attempt to intervene in a market economy to try to overcome the existence of a market failure, but there is the possibility that such intervention might create further distortions in the market.
Externalities	Externalities are costs or benefits which can affect third parties and are sometimes referred to as "spill-over" effects. There can be both positive and negative externalities and these can be related to both production and consumption.
Imperfect competition	There are different forms of imperfect competition that can exist in an economy and one of these would be the existence of a monopoly where one firm controls a market. If a firm has monopoly power in a market, it will operate very differently from a firm in perfect competition. For example, the price is likely to be higher and the output lower than would be the case in perfect competition. Also, abnormal or supernormal profits can exist in the long run as well as the short run.
Inequality in the distribution of income and wealth	A market economy may lead to a very unequal distribution of income and wealth, and this will have the effect of giving some people more influence than others in the economy.
Price instability	Price acts as a signal in a market economy and it has sometimes been described as an "invisible hand", responsible for the allocation and reallocation of resources in an economy. However, in some situations, there can be a great deal of price instability in a market economy where prices can change quite rapidly in a relatively short period of time. This can, for example, be a feature of agricultural markets.
Factor immobility	The factors of production should be able to move easily from one sector to another in a market economy, but this is not always the case because of the existence of geographical and occupational immobility of labour.

Inefficient resource allocation

It should be clear from what has already been said that the existence of market failure gives rise to the inefficient allocation of scarce resources in an economy. For example, the existence of information failure is a significant reason why there can be inefficient resource allocation. If everybody understood the value of education or health care, not only to themselves but to society as a whole, people would be more willing to consume the service. However, as a result of information failure, the decisions that consumers take can lead to an under-production and under-consumption of such services.

On the other hand, the existence of information failure is a significant reason why there can be inefficient resource allocation in terms of the over-production and over-consumption of demerit goods. If consumers of such products as alcohol and tobacco really had all the information that is available, they would understand the risks that excessive consumption of such products can cause, and this would be likely to lead to a significant reduction in the demand for these products. However, because consumers do not have all the available information, they are unable to take the most sensible decisions and, as a result, more resources are allocated to the production of goods and services than ought to be the case. This leads to an inefficient resource allocation, not only in relation to the individual consumers themselves, but to the wider society as well. For example, the cost of dealing with health problems caused by the consumption of alcohol and/or tobacco is a major burden on the health services of a country.

Key term

Externality: an action that results in either external benefits or external costs in relation to either production or consumption.

Positive and negative externalities for both consumers and firms

An externality can be either a cost or a benefit of production or consumption which has effects that are not paid for by either the producer or the consumer. They are called external costs or external benefits because they are external to a market. They are said to have spillover or third party-effects. A third party refers to someone who is not directly involved, but who will be affected by the actions of others.

Table 6.2 gives some examples of different types of externality.

Table 6.2 External costs and benefits of production and consumption ▼

Type of externality	Example
External cost of production	A firm dumps waste into a river, causing pollution and killing the fish.
External benefit of production	A firm trains its workers, some of whom go on to work somewhere else and this reduces the costs of training for this other firm.
External cost of consumption	A person driving a motor vehicle produces car exhaust fumes and this increases the level of pollution.
External benefit of consumption	Well-maintained gardens can help to improve the environment of a particular neighbourhood.

Key terms

External cost: a cost which arises from any activity which is not paid for by the firm or the consumer carrying out the activity.

External benefit: a benefit to a third-party which arises from an activity carried out by a firm or a consumer.

Getting it right

Remember in the examination that an externality can refer to either production or consumption costs or benefits or to both.

Progress question

5 Explain the differences between external costs and external benefits.

Activity

External costs and benefits of production and consumption

Table 6.2 gives one example of each type of external cost and external benefit. Working in groups, think of three more examples of each of the different types of external cost and external benefit.

Negative externalities and positive externalities

Negative externalities

The external costs of production or consumption, i.e. the costs imposed on a third party not involved in the production or consumption of a product, can be referred to as negative externalities.

Positive externalities

The external benefits of production or consumption, i.e. the benefits to a third party not involved in the production or consumption of product, can be referred to as positive externalities.

Externalities have already been explained in terms of third-party effects from the production or consumption of products for which no payment is made. This is why they can be regarded as an example of market failure, because the price mechanism does not take into account the wider costs and benefits to the whole society as a result of the production or consumption that has taken place. In essence, the market fails to produce an allocation of scarce resources that is efficient.

Key terms

Negative externalities: a third-party effect resulting from production or consumption that imposes a cost on the society which is not paid for by either the producer or the consumer.

Positive externalities: a third-party effect resulting from production or consumption that creates a benefit to society.

Negative externalities and market failure

The existence of negative externalities in production or consumption creates a separation or divergence between the private costs and the social costs. In this situation, social costs are greater than private costs.

This can be seen in Figure 6.3. This shows demand and supply in a market, but it takes into account that decisions are generally said to be taken "at the margin". The marginal cost or marginal benefit refers to the additional cost or benefit as a result of producing or consuming one more unit.

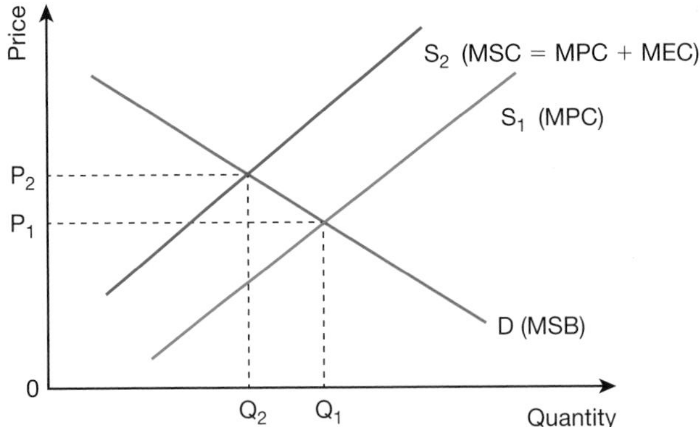

Figure 6.3 Over-production leading to a negative externality ▲

> **Key term**
>
> Marginal social cost: the addition of marginal private cost and marginal external cost.

Social costs are equal to the sum of private costs and external costs, but if the concept of marginal analysis is introduced, this can be rewritten as marginal social cost = marginal private cost + marginal external cost.

> **Getting it right**
>
> You need to be careful that you do not suggest that the pollution will no longer exist in such a situation. You need to emphasise, however, that the market has taken such external costs into account.

The equilibrium position in the market is where the demand curve D (representing marginal social benefit) crosses the supply curve S_1 (representing marginal private cost), producing a price of P_1 and a quantity of Q_1. However, if the production has involved an element of pollution, this equilibrium will not indicate the true cost of the resources used. If negative externalities exist, these need to be shown in a separate supply curve, S_2. This supply curve takes into account the external costs to society, i.e. the marginal social cost. The supply curve S_2 represents the addition of marginal private cost and marginal external cost. The new equilibrium position is now with a higher price of P_2 and a lower quantity of Q_2. The external costs have now been taken into account and this new equilibrium is therefore the socially efficient equilibrium. The pollution has not been eliminated, but it has been reduced and included in the equilibrium market price.

Case Study

Pollution from a factory in Bangladesh

An example of a negative externality is pollution from a factory in Dhaka, the capital city of Bangladesh. In the course of the production process, the factory gives off smoke which can be seen, and smelled, by all of the people in the neighbourhood. This pollution will make the neighbourhood a dirtier place to live in and some people with breathing problems may be particularly badly affected. The factory itself is likely to be an eyesore and there will certainly be greater traffic congestion with lorries going to and from the factory.

The owners of the factory will take into account the private costs of production, such as the wages and salaries that are paid to the workforce, but will not take into account the cost to the community. This external cost will have a spillover effect on third parties, i.e. people in the neighbourhood who have not been directly responsible for the pollution.

1. Describe what is meant by a spillover or third-party effect on a community.
2. Explain, with the aid of a diagram, how the amount of pollution in the community, caused by the factory, could be reduced.

Positive externalities and market failure

> **Key term**
> **Marginal social benefit**: the addition of marginal private benefit and marginal external benefit.

The concept of externalities does not apply only to negative externalities; it can also apply to positive externalities. The existence of positive externalities in production or consumption creates a separation or divergence between the private benefits and the social benefits. In this situation, social benefits are greater than private benefits.

This can be seen in Figure 6.4. The importance of decisions taken "at the margin" has already been stressed. Marginal social benefit can therefore be expressed as equal to marginal private benefit + marginal external benefit.

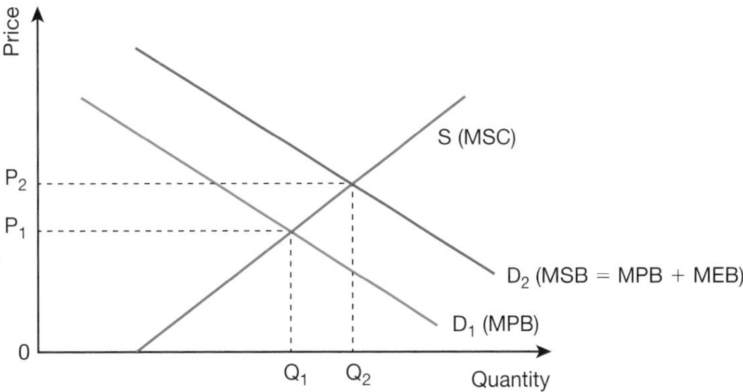

Figure 6.4 Under-production leading to a positive externality

The equilibrium position in the market is where the demand curve D_1 (representing marginal private benefit) crosses the supply curve S (representing marginal social cost), producing a price of P_1 and an output of Q_1. However, if all the benefits to society were taken into account, and not just the private ones, the demand curve would shift to the right with D_2 representing the marginal social benefit, consisting of both marginal private benefit and marginal external benefit. In a free market, there would under-production and under-consumption; if the positive externalities were taken into account, however, there would be a socially optimal equilibrium with a price of P_2 and a quantity of Q_2.

Case Study

The benefits of vaccination to a community in New Zealand

A good example of a positive externality is when people in a community are vaccinated against particular diseases. Individuals are only likely to consider the benefits to themselves of being vaccinated, i.e. they are less likely to contract the disease and so less likely to be ill. In New Zealand, for example, there is vaccination against diphtheria, tetanus, whooping cough and polio.

There is, however, a wider aspect that needs to be taken into account. There will be wider benefits to the whole community if a greater proportion of people in a community are vaccinated against particular diseases in that if the vast majority of the population, or indeed everybody, is vaccinated, there is much less likelihood of people in the neighbourhood catching the disease. Everybody therefore will be able to live a healthier life.

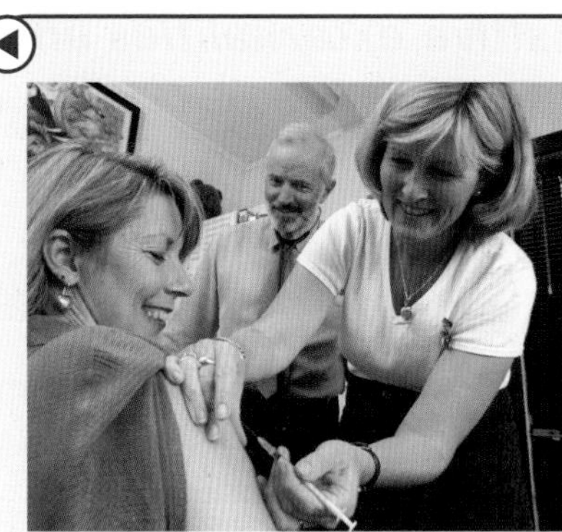

1 Describe what is meant by a positive externality.
2 Explain, with the aid of a diagram, how vaccination could be encouraged in a community.

Social costs and social benefits

Social costs

A social cost is defined as the sum of private costs and external costs. External costs have already been considered in this chapter. Private costs refer to those costs that are incurred by a firm in the process of production, excluding any external costs. They can also be called internal costs and could include such costs as wages and salaries, component parts and raw materials and interest payments. They also refer to the costs to a consumer of buying a product.

When all of the internal and external costs of production are added together, this represents the total costs to society of that production and these total costs are therefore known as social costs.

> **Key terms**
> **Social cost**: the total cost of producing a product which takes into account the private costs to the firm and any external costs to society resulting from that production.
> **Private cost**: the internal cost to a firm of producing a product, such as the cost of wages and salaries, or the cost of a product to a consumer.

Social benefits

A social benefit is defined as the sum of private benefits and external benefits. Private benefits refer to those benefits that are gained by a firm in the process of production, excluding any external benefits. They can also be called internal benefits and include such benefits as the revenue and profit received from sales of a product. They also refer to the benefits to a consumer of buying a product, such as the satisfaction gained.

When all of the internal and external benefits of production are added together, this represents the total benefit to society of that production and these total benefits are therefore known as social benefits.

> **Key terms**
> **Social benefit**: the total benefit of producing a product which takes into account the private benefits to the firm and any external benefits to society resulting from that production.
> **Private benefit**: the satisfaction or utility obtained by an individual when consuming a product, or the benefit to a firm of producing a product.

> **Progress question**
> 6 Explain the difference between external benefits and social benefits.

> **Getting it right**
> Make sure that you do not confuse external costs and social costs. External costs are only one part of social costs, along with private costs.

Cost-benefit analysis

The use of cost-benefit analysis in decision-making

One of the problems with external costs and benefits is that they can be very difficult to measure with any degree of accuracy. For example, it might be the case that a factory causes pollution in a neighbourhood, but how do you actually put a price or value on such pollution? Of

Getting it right

Make sure that you do not confuse external benefits and social benefits. External benefits are only one part of social benefits, along with private benefits.

Key term

Cost-benefit analysis: a method used to evaluate large-scale investment projects which takes into account all possible costs and benefits.

course, there may be ways of putting a figure on the consequences of pollution, such as the fall in value of properties nearby. It would be much more difficult, however, to put a monetary figure on a person who was finding it more difficult to breathe although if the person had to take a number of days off work as a result of the breathing problems, it would be possible to calculate the wages lost as a result of the absence of work.

One method which economists have used to aid the decision-making process when externalities are involved is cost-benefit analysis. It is an attempt to put figures on, or quantify, the externalities that can exist in a neighbourhood. It could be used, for example, to analyse a particular investment project and it would take a wide view of the impact of such a project by taking into account all of the costs and benefits involved in such a project and not just private ones. The advantage of cost-benefit analysis is that it can be used to thoroughly calculate and compare the costs and benefits of an investment project to determine whether it is a sound and worthwhile decision. As a result of this, it is possible to discover if the benefits outweigh the costs and, if so, by how much. The concept of cost-benefit analysis dates back to 1848 and was advocated particularly by the economist Alfred Marshall. Examples of such investment projects that have been analysed through cost-benefit analysis include the following:

- Hong Kong–Zhuhai–Macau Bridge
- US waterway infrastructure and flood control
- US public higher education
- Major transport projects in Canada.

Case Study

The Hong Kong–Zhuhai–Macau Bridge

The Hong Kong–Zhuhai–Macau Bridge is an example of a major infrastructure project that used cost-benefit analysis before a decision was taken to go ahead with the building of the bridge. It consists of a series of bridges and tunnels that will connect Hong Kong, Macau and Zhuhai, three major cities in East Asia. The link is 50 km (31 miles) in length. It is expected to cost $10.7 billion. Construction began in 2009 and the bridge is due to open in 2016.

1 Justify, with reasons, why you would or would not support the building of this bridge.

The stages of a cost-benefit analysis

Table 6.3 shows the four main stages that are usually involved in a cost-benefit analysis of an investment project.

Table 6.3 The four stages of a cost-benefit analysis ▼

	Stage	Description
1	The identification of all the relevant costs and benefits involved in the project	This first stage of the process involves identifying all relevant costs and benefits, i.e. the private costs, the private benefits, the external costs and the external benefits.
2	The decision about the monetary value of all of the relevant costs and benefits involved in the project	The second stage of the process involves putting a monetary value on all of these costs and benefits, including those where a market price can be established and those where a market price is not easily established, such as placing a value on time.
3	The forecasting of the future costs and benefits involved in the project	The third stage of the process involves forecasting the future costs and benefits of an investment project into the future; this forecasting will be based on estimates of future costs and benefits.
4	The interpretation of the results of the cost-benefit analysis so that an appropriate decision can be taken	The fourth stage of the process involves the compilation of all of the data obtained as a result of the cost-benefit analysis and this can then be used to ensure that the decision-making process is an informed one.

Advantages and disadvantages of cost-benefit analysis

It should be clear, from what has been said, that the process of cost-benefit analysis has both advantages and disadvantages. These are shown in Table 6.4.

Table 6.4 The advantages and disadvantages of cost-benefit analysis ▼

The advantages of cost-benefit analysis	The disadvantages of cost-benefit analysis
It takes into account all of the various costs and benefits resulting from a proposed investment project.	It may be difficult to identify all of the relevant external costs and external benefits. For example, how wide will the spillover or third-party effects be? It may therefore not be easy to decide on which costs and benefits to include in the analysis.
Many of the various costs and benefits will have market prices attached to them, making it relatively easy to calculate monetary values.	Some of the costs and benefits will not have market prices attached to them and this will make it much more difficult to calculate their monetary value. To overcome this problem, shadow prices can be used to estimate such values, but these shadow prices may be very difficult to estimate.
The process can analyse costs and benefits today, but also well into the future. This has the advantage that the cost benefit analysis can take a long-term view of the possible consequences of an investment project.	The estimation of costs and benefits well into the future can be very difficult. There are forecasting techniques which can be used, but it is very difficult to estimate the costs and benefits of a project 10 or 15 years into the future. This raises the issue of the time value of money, i.e. where the value of the costs and benefits today will be different from their value in 10 or 15 years' time; this will therefore involve a process of discounting these future values.
All of the information obtained as a result of the cost-benefit analysis can be used to ensure that the correct decision is taken. It is therefore a very significant aid to the decision-making process.	Cost-benefit analysis is normally used to assess investment projects in the public sector and so even if the analysis suggests that an investment project would yield a net benefit to a community, there may be political reasons why it does not actually go ahead.

The advantages of cost-benefit analysis	The disadvantages of cost-benefit analysis
It provides a framework that is particularly useful for investment projects in the public sector. For example, it may be that as a result of the analysis, it is shown that the private costs are greater than the private benefits, but it may still go ahead if the total benefits of the project are greater than its total costs, taking all of the costs and benefits into account and not just the private ones. The analysis may therefore lead to a better allocation of resources in the economy.	It may be that if the external costs and benefits are taken into account, a decision to go ahead with a project may be taken, but this could involve public expenditure, the money for which will need to be obtained from somewhere.

Progress question

7 Explain the advantages and disadvantages of using cost-benefit analysis.

Case Study

Bangalore Airport

In 2012 it was the fourth-busiest airport in India, handling over 11 million passengers a year, and by 2014 it is expected to be dealing with 18 million passengers a year. It has been built on 4,000 acres (1,600 hectares) about 40 kilometres (25 miles) from the centre of the city of Bangalore.

There are 21 international airlines and 10 domestic airlines operating out of the airport, connecting the city to over 50 destinations in India and the rest of the world.

It can handle 720 aircraft movements a day. There is, however, only one runway. It is planned to build a second runway when the number of passengers reaches 18 million.

1 Produce a cost-benefit analysis of the proposed second runway at Bangalore Airport.
2 Justify, with reasons, why you would or would not support the building of this second runway.

Key concepts

- **Scarcity and choice** is demonstrated by showing that resources are scarce and so a cost-benefit analysis could help to inform decisions about the choice of how scarce resources should be allocated in an economy.
- **The margin and change** can be seen through the concept that marginal cost is very important in relation to allocative efficiency.
- **Equilibrium and efficiency** is illustrated through economic efficiency, which comes about when there is both productive and allocative efficiency.
- **Progress and development** can come about in an economy as a result of a major infrastructure project, if this is supported by a cost-benefit analysis.

Progress check

After completing this chapter you should be able to:

- ▶ understand what is meant by an efficient or optimum resource allocation
- ▶ understand the meaning of productive efficiency
- ▶ understand what is meant by allocative efficiency
- ▶ appreciate the main differences between productive and allocative efficiency
- ▶ understand Pareto efficiency
- ▶ understand dynamic efficiency
- ▶ appreciate the reasons for market failure
- ▶ have an understanding of inefficient resource allocation
- ▶ understand the reasons for positive and negative externalities for both consumers and firms
- ▶ understand social costs as the sum of private costs and external costs
- ▶ understand social benefits as the sum of private benefits and external benefits
- ▶ appreciate the use of cost-benefit analysis in decision-making.

Exam-style questions

Essay questions

1 Explain what is meant by the terms "productive efficiency" and "allocative efficiency". [12 marks]
2 Discuss the costs and benefits of an increased demand for air travel. [13 marks]
3 Discuss to what extent national defence can be regarded as an example of a public good. [13 marks]
4 Discuss whether health care can and should be provided by the free market. [25 marks]
5 Discuss whether the use of cost-benefit analysis helps to improve economic decision-making. [13 marks]
6 Explain the difficulties of carrying out a cost-benefit analysis. [12 marks]

Multiple-choice questions

7 Which of the following indicates allocative efficiency? [1 mark]
- **A** Marginal cost is equal to price
- **B** Production is at the lowest point of average cost
- **C** Marginal cost is equal to marginal revenue
- **D** Production is technically efficient

8 Which of the following indicates marginal social cost? [1 mark]
- **A** Marginal private cost minus marginal external benefit
- **B** Marginal private cost and marginal private benefit
- **C** Marginal private cost minus marginal external cost
- **D** Marginal private cost and marginal external cost

7 The price system and the micro economy

In this chapter you will develop your knowledge and understanding of:

- the law of diminishing marginal utility
- indifference curves and budget lines
- types of cost, revenue and profit
- short-run production
- long-run production
- different market structures
- growth and survival of firms
- differing objectives of firms.

Marginal utility theory

We saw in Chapter 2 that the individual and market demand curves for a product normally slope downwards from left to right, indicating that as the price falls the quantity demanded increases and vice versa. We will now look in more detail at why this is the case using marginal utility theory.

In order to develop this theory we need to introduce three important concepts: utility, total utility and marginal utility. By utility we simply mean the satisfaction that an individual obtains from the consumption of a product at a particular moment in time. It is important to note that utility does not imply usefulness, in that products which are bad for us such as cigarettes may still yield satisfaction. It is also important to emphasise the time aspect of utility. An individual who has just played a strenuous game of tennis in hot weather will be likely to gain far more utility from a bottle of cold orange juice than another who may simply have been sitting watching and may, therefore, derive little or no satisfaction from the drink.

Key terms

Marginal utility: the satisfaction gained from the last unit of a product consumed over a particular time period.
Utility: the satisfaction gained from a product.
Total utility: the satisfaction gained from the consumption of all units of a product over a particular time period.

How much satisfaction? ▲

Clearly utility is subjective and very difficult to measure. However, Economists use the term "utils" to describe units of satisfaction, and in practice, as we shall see later, it is not necessary for the development of the theory for us to be able to give an absolute value to a unit of satisfaction.

If we return to the individual who has just played a strenuous game of tennis, it is quite likely that it will be necessary for them to consume a number of drinks to fully quench their thirst. Table 7.1 shows the amount of total and marginal utility an individual gains from consuming each of six drinks. The overall satisfaction that they obtain from consuming all six drinks is known as the total utility. The satisfaction obtained from the last unit consumed – the sixth – is known as the marginal utility.

Table 7.1 and Figure 7.1 illustrate the relationship between total and marginal utility.

Table 7.1 Total and marginal utility ▼

Quantity of drinks consumed	Total Utility (TU) utils	Marginal Uutility (MU) utils
0	0	–
1	40	40
2	65	25
3	85	20
4	100	15
5	108	8
6	102	−6

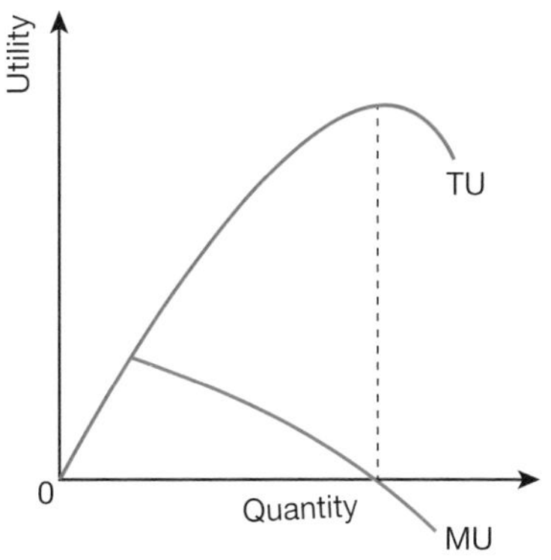

Figure 7.1 Total and marginal utility ▲

As shown in Table 7.1 total utility increases as more drinks are consumed up to five drinks, but at a decreasing rate, i.e. the marginal utility from consuming an additional drink is decreasing. Figure 7.1 shows the relationship between total and marginal utility graphically. As can be seen from the diagram, at the point at which total utility is at a maximum the marginal utility is equal to zero and when total utility begins to decline marginal utility becomes negative.

Progress question

1 Complete the following table:

Quantity	1	2	3	4	5	6	7	8
Total utility	100	190	250					
Marginal utility				50	40	10	7	3

Getting it right

Make sure you clearly understand the distinction between total and marginal utility.

The law of diminishing marginal utility

In taking the analysis further, if we look again at Table 7.1, it is clear that the amount of additional utility (marginal utility) the tennis player gains from each additional drink declines. The utility from the first drink following the tennis match is extremely high as the individual is extremely thirsty. A second drink may also be welcomed, but is unlikely to generate as much satisfaction as the first. The same is true of each subsequent drink, in that whilst each may add to the individual's overall satisfaction, the amount of additional utility added is likely to be less. This is known as the law of diminishing marginal utility. The individual having fully quenched their thirst by the fifth drink may find that further drinks actually reduce the overall level of satisfaction so that total utility declines and marginal utility becomes negative.

Key term

Law of diminishing marginal utility: as the quantity consumed of a product by an individual increases, the additional satisfaction gained from each unit (marginal utility) will eventually decline.

Derivation of an individual demand schedule

We are now in a position to derive the demand curve for a product. In order to do so we assume that the marginal utility of a product can be measured by the amount of money (the price) the individual is prepared to pay for it. In this case an individual's demand curve for a product will be the same as their marginal utility curve as shown in Figure 7.2.

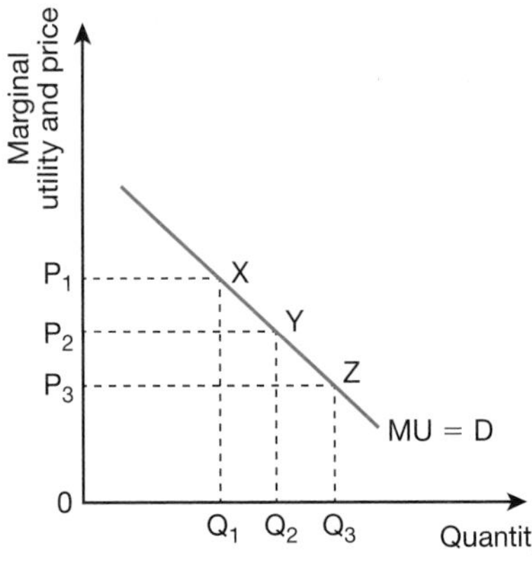

Figure 7.2 Individual marginal utility and demand curve ▲

A rational individual will wish to maximise their total utility from the consumption of a product and so will not purchase a product if the marginal utility obtained from it is perceived to be less than the price. Consequently an individual will consume a product up to the point where the price equals the marginal utility.

In Figure 7.2 if the price is at P_1 the individual will purchase quantity Q_1, corresponding to point X on the marginal utility curve because the extra satisfaction gained exactly equals the price paid. If now the price falls to P_2 and then P_3 the individual will increase purchases of the product to Q_2 and Q_3 corresponding to points Y and Z on the marginal utility curve. Clearly points X, Y and Z relate the quantity demanded by the individual and the price of the product and so are points on the individual's demand curve. Hence, as long as the individual continues to purchase up to the point where P = MU, the individual's demand curve will be the same as the marginal utility curve.

Getting it right

Consumers will purchase a product up to the point where P = MU.

The principle of equi-marginal returns

The analysis so far has been of the impact of a change in price on one product. However, a rise in the price of one good will affect the amount of income left over to purchase all other products and will, therefore, have an impact on the consumer's demand for its substitutes and complements.

Key term

Equi-marginal principle: this states that a rational individual wishing to maximise total utility will allocate their expenditure amongst different products so as to ensure that the satisfaction (utility) gained from the last unit of money spent on each product is the same, i.e. MUx/Px = MUy/Py

We can use marginal utility theory to explain the way in which a rational consumer will allocate their expenditure across all products. This is explained by the equi-marginal principle.

This maintains that a rational consumer wishing to maximise utility will allocate expenditure in such a way that the amount of satisfaction (utility) gained from the last unit of money (Great British pound, Hong Kong dollar, euro or rupee) spent on each product consumed is the same.

Mathematically this can be written for two products as:

$$MUx/Px = MUy/Py$$

Where:

MUx = marginal utility of product X

MUy = marginal utility of product Y

Px = price of product X

Py = price of product Y

Getting it right

The demand curve for an individual for a product is the individual's MU curve.

If now the price of product X falls, the equality above becomes:

$$MUx/Px > MUy/Py$$

This means that the extra satisfaction gained from the last unit of money spent on product X gives greater satisfaction than that spent on Y. A rational consumer will, therefore, increase consumption of X. Because of the law of diminishing marginal utility this will have the effect of decreasing the marginal utility of X. The individual will continue increasing purchases of X until the equality is restored.

Hence, as the price of a product falls the quantity of it demanded increases and vice versa.

Limitations of marginal utility theory

There are a number of limitations of marginal utility theory particularly in relation to the law of diminishing marginal utility.

Unit of measurement

As has already been indicated, it is difficult to find an appropriate unit of measurement of utility.

Habit and impulse

Some purchases may be habit forming or made on impulse with the consumer not really considering the marginal utility.

Enjoyment may increase as consumption increases

In some cases the amount of satisfaction gained from additional units of consumption of a product might increase as the number consumed increases. This may well be the case with collectors. A collector wishing to have the largest collection in the world of Beatles memorabilia will obtain greater satisfaction from each additional item purchased and may be prepared to pay increasingly higher prices to obtain them.

Quality and consistency of successive units of a good consumed

We are assuming throughout that all units of a product consumed are identical. If the quality of successive chocolate bars is not the same then the amount of satisfaction obtained from additional bars may be more or less than previous ones.

Link

A developing branch of Economics "Behavioural Economics" attempts to address some of these concerns – see page 162 of this chapter.

Other things remain constant

The theory assumes that all other factors affecting individuals' satisfaction remain the same. However, over time, there may be changes in income and the quality of other products as well as the development of new products and changes in individuals' tastes and attitudes, all of which may have an impact on consumers' satisfaction.

Having said all this, proponents of marginal utility theory argue that at any moment in time, once a particular pattern of expenditure has been established, the law of diminishing marginal utility is valid.

Key term

Indifference curve analysis: a theory of consumer behaviour based on the analysis of individuals' preferences.

Indifference curves and budget lines

Indifference curves

An alternative explanation of consumer behaviour which attempts to overcome some of the difficulties involved with marginal utility theory is that of indifference curve analysis.

Indifference curve analysis is based on the assumption that although it is not possible to measure exactly how much satisfaction (utility) an individual obtains from a product or combination of products, it is possible to conclude whether an individual obtains *more or less* satisfaction from one product than another or one combination of products as opposed to another.

Table 7.2 An individual's indifference set for apples and pears ▼

Apples	Pears
40	1
30	2
22	3
17	4
13	5
11	6
10	7

Indifference curve analysis argues that the behaviour of rational consumers in their expenditure decisions can be used to establish a scale of preferences. If a ticket for a soccer match has the same price as one for a rugby match and the individual chooses to go to the soccer match it is reasonable to assume that the individual prefers to go to the soccer match rather than the rugby match. The analysis goes on to argue that it is possible to identify different combinations of two goods between which an individual has no preference at all, i.e. the individual is indifferent as to which of the combinations they consume. Table 7.2 shows an individual's indifference set for apples and pears. The individual is willing to accept any of the combinations.

Key term

Indifference curve: a curve showing all possible combinations of two products between which an individual consumer is indifferent.

From this indifference set it is possible to construct an indifference curve which shows all possible combinations of apples and pears between which the consumer will be indifferent. This is shown in Figure 7.3.

Although we have assumed that there is only one indifference curve for each person, in fact there will be an infinite number, each one associated with a particular level of total utility. These indifference curves make up an indifference map such as the one illustrated in Figure 7.4.

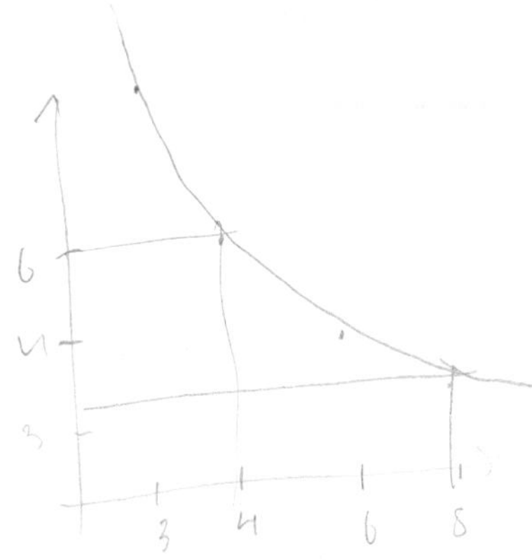

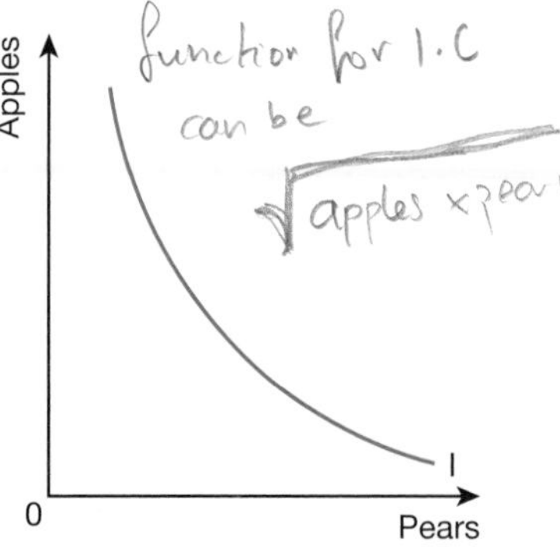

Figure 7.3 Indifference curve ▲

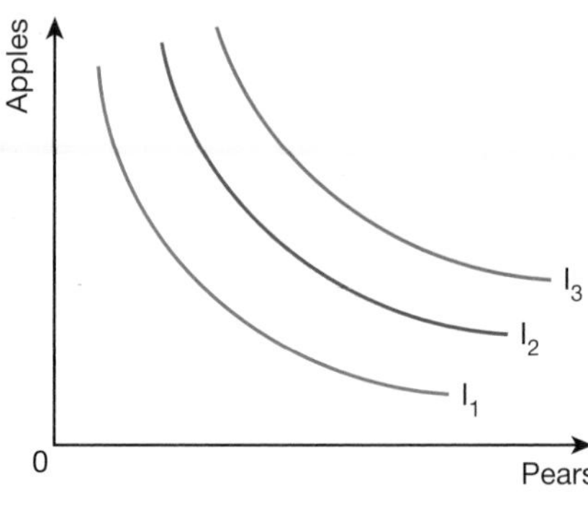

Figure 7.4 Indifference map ▲

Indifference curves further from the origin represent higher levels of total utility as they permit individuals to have increased quantities of at least one of the two goods, apples and pears.

Key term

Marginal rate of substitution: the quantity of one good an individual is prepared to give up in order to obtain an additional unit of another while leaving the individual at the same level of utility.

Properties of indifference curves

For rational consumers indifference curves have the following properties.

Indifference curves slope downwards from left to right and are convex to the origin. The slope of the indifference curve indicates the marginal rate of substitution, in this case of apples for pears. It shows the number of apples an individual is prepared to give up in order to

> **Key term**
>
> **Diminishing marginal rate of substitution:** as more and more units of one good, A, are obtained an individual will be prepared to give up fewer and fewer units of another, B, in order to obtain an additional unit of A.

obtain an additional pear while remaining at the same level of total utility. The indifference curve becomes shallower as we move down the curve from left to right reflecting the individual's diminishing marginal rate of substitution of one good for another. As an individual obtains more and more of one good, pears, they will be prepared to sacrifice fewer and fewer units of the other, apples, in order to obtain another pear. As Table 7.2 shows, when an individual has only 1 pear they will be prepared to give up 10 apples in order to obtain a second, but once the individual has 5 pears they will be prepared to sacrifice only 2 apples in order to obtain an additional pear.

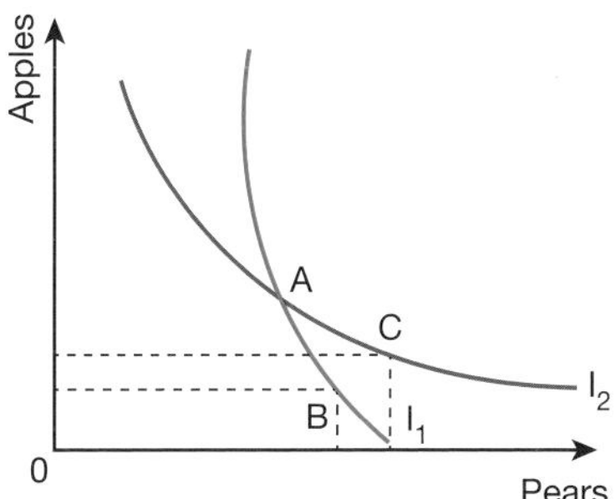

Figure 7.5 Indifference curves cannot intersect ▲

Indifference curves can never intersect one another. Figure 7.5 explains this.

Points A and B represent two combinations which must give an individual equal satisfaction since they are on the same indifference curve. Similarly, points A and C represent combinations that give the same satisfaction since they are on the same, albeit, different indifference curve. If combinations A and B and A and C give the same levels of satisfaction, then logically combinations A and C must also give the same satisfaction. However, this is not possible as inspection of the diagram shows that point C gives the individual more of both goods and must, therefore, give greater satisfaction than the combination at point B. Hence indifference curves cannot intersect.

Budget lines

Another aspect of the analysis of consumers' expenditure is the budget line. Budget lines show the combinations of two goods that an individual is able to consume at particular prices with a given level of income.

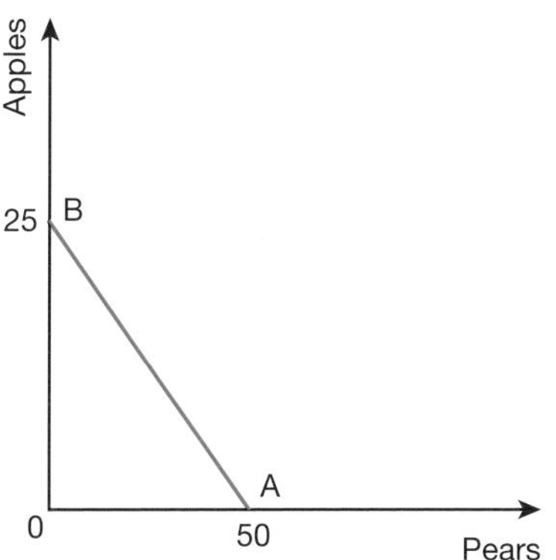

Figure 7.6 Budget line ▲

> **Key term**
>
> **Budget lines:** show all possible combinations of two products that an individual is able to purchase with a given level of income.

Figure 7.6 shows an individual's budget line for two products, apples and pears. Let us assume that the individual has an income of $100 to spend and that the price of apples is $4 per kilo and pears $2 per kilo. If all the income is spent on apples then it is possible to buy 25 kilos, but no pears. If all the income is spent on pears, then it is possible to buy a maximum of 50 kilos of pears, but no apples. The budget line is AB. Any combination of apples and pears inside or on the budget line can be consumed, but the individual cannot consume beyond it.

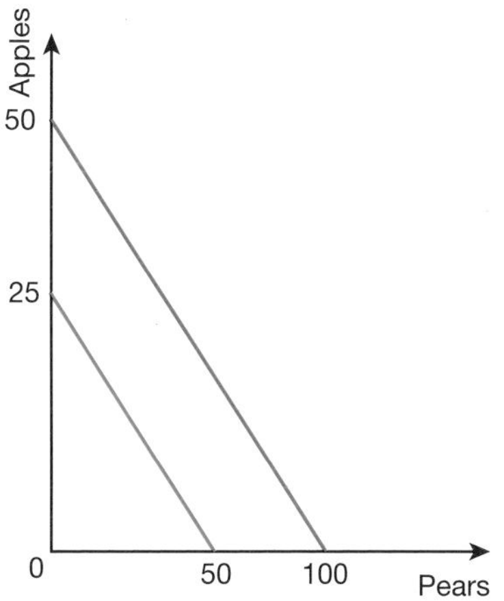

Figure 7.7 Effect on the budget line of a change in income ▲

Budget line and changes in income

Changes in an individual's income will clearly mean that more or less can be consumed of each product. If we assume that the individual's income increases to $200, then it is now possible for the individual to be able to buy 50 kilos of apples and 100 kilos of pears, which will shift the budget line upwards to the right parallel to the original budget line as indicated in Figure 7.7. Similarly any reduction in the individual's income will shift the budget line inwards towards the origin.

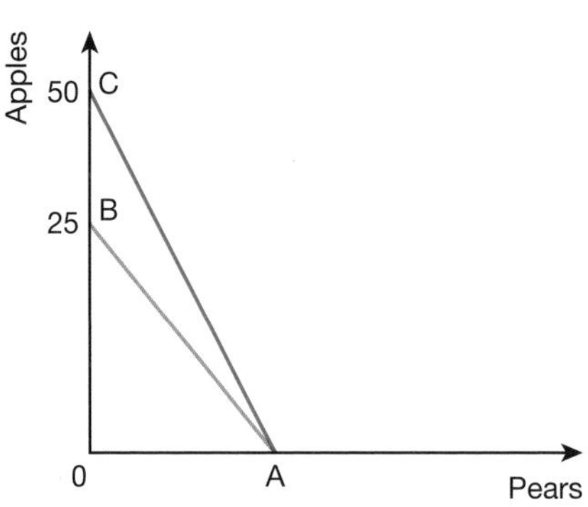

Figure 7.8 Effect on the budget line of a change in price ▲

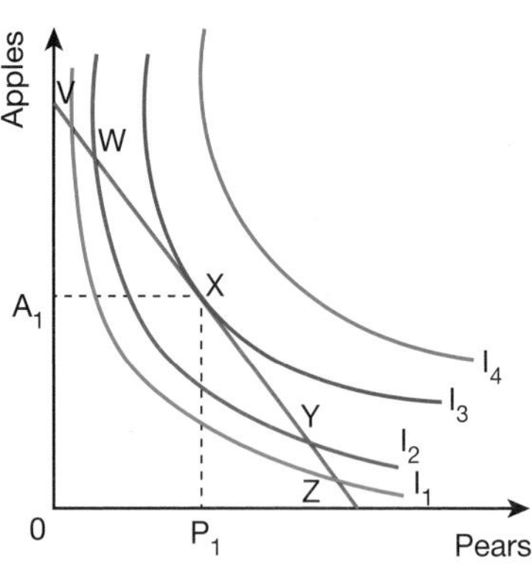

Figure 7.9 Optimum consumption point for an individual ▲

Activities

Budget lines

1 Draw a diagram to illustrate the original budget line with a consumer income of \$100 and the price of apples and pears \$4 and \$2 respectively.
2 Show what happens to the budget line if the price of pears (a) rises to \$5 (b) falls to \$1.

Getting it right

Make sure that you remember that the optimum consumption point for a rational consumer is at the point where their budget line is tangential to the highest attainable indifference curve.

Budget line and changes in price

If the price of one of the products changes, the slope of the budget line will alter. If we assume that the price of apples now falls to \$2 per kilo with the price of pears remaining the same, then it will now be possible to purchase a maximum of 50 kilos of apples rather than the 25 kilos previously. The maximum possible amount of pears than can be purchased remains the same. The budget line now pivots outwards at point A and becomes AC. If the price of apples rises, the budget line would pivot inwards.

The optimum consumption point

We are now in a position to bring together the analysis of indifference curves and budget lines to explain how much of the two goods, apples and pears, will be consumed by a rational consumer. This is illustrated in Figure 7.9.

Rational individuals will wish to allocate their expenditure between apples and pears so as to maximise their total utility, which means they will wish to achieve the highest indifference curve their income will permit. This is at point X in Figure 7.9 where the individual's budget line is tangential to the highest attainable indifference curve. The individual will consume A_1 apples and P_1 pears. Points V, W, Y and Z are attainable, but they are on lower indifference curves and are, therefore, associated with lower levels of satisfaction.

The impact of changes in income and price on an individual's optimum consumption point

The effect of changes in income

The effect of increases and decreases in income are illustrated in Figure 7.10.

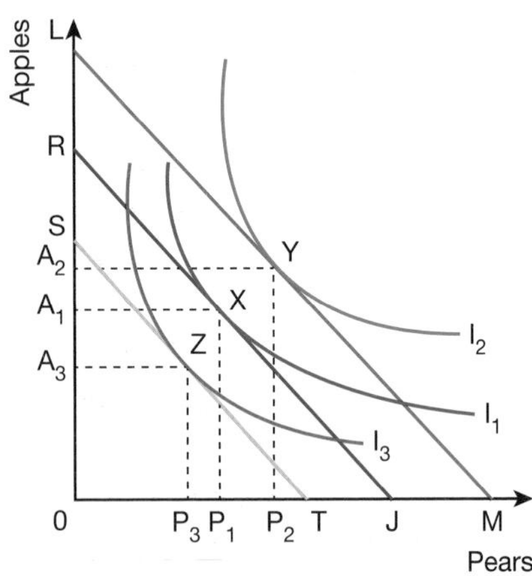

Figure 7.10 The effect of changes in income on the optimum consumption point ▲

The initial indifference curve is I_1 and the initial budget line is RJ. The individual's optimum consumption point is at X with A_1 apples and P_1 pears being consumed. If the consumer's income now increases, the budget line shifts outwards to the right parallel to the original. The new budget line is LM. The individual is now able to consume more of all

T... ...31 December 2015.

Dir...	344 000
Indi... wages	69 000
Purchases of direct materials	287 000
Purchases of indirect materials	43 000
Carriage inwards on direct materials	3 700
Other factory overheads	32 500
Revenue	1 562 000
Administrative expenses	374 000
Provision for unrealised profit at 1 January 2015	27 000
Water and electricity expenses	14 000

Additional information

1 Inventories at 31 December 2015

	$
Raw materials	28 800
Work in progress	72 200
Finished goods at transfer price	186 000

2 Depreciation is to be provided as follows:

Property	5% on cost
Manufacturing plant and machinery	20% reducing balance method
Office equipment	15% on cost

3 Water and electricity expenses owing at 31 December 2015 amounted to $1500.

4 The following expenses are to be allocated as:

	Factory	Administration
Depreciation on property	70%	30%
Water and electricity	80%	20%

REQUIRED

(a) Prepare the manufacturing account for the year ended 31 December 2015.

(b) Prepare the income statement for the year ended 31 December 2015.

(c) Explain why finished goods inventory is not shown at transfer price in the statement of financial position.

Additional information

Sim, the manager of the sales department, says 'It does not make sense for the production department to transfer the goods manufactured to the sales department at a mark-up. As both departments belong to the same company, we should no longer do it.'

REQUIRED

(d) Recommend whether or not they should continue to transfer goods at a mark-up. Justify your answer giving **two** reasons to support your recommendation.

PAPER 3 - 3 HOURS

		15
	...720	1576
	(300)	(180)
...tion	1420	1396
...xation	(317)	(312)
Retained profit for the year	1103	1084

Statements of financial positions at 30 June 2015

	Winterbottom	Ramsey
	$000	$000
Non-current assets	9864	6192
Current assets		
Inventories	782	451
Trade receivables	1362	742
Cash and cash equivalents	135	98
	2279	1291
Total assets	12143	7483
Equity and liabilities		
Equity		
Ordinary share capital ($1 each)	4500	2500
Share premium	200	–
Retained earnings	1447	1244
	6147	3744
Current liabilities		
Trade payables	679	427
Taxation	317	312
	996	739
Non-current liabilities		
6% Debentures (2024)	5000	3000
Total equity and liabilities	12143	7483

Additional information

1 Neither company has paid an interim dividend during the year ended 30 June 2015.

2 The directors of Winterbottom plc propose a dividend of $0.20 per share and those of Ramsey plc $0.35 per share for the year ended 30 June 2015.

3 At 30 June 2015, the market value of an ordinary share in Winterbottom plc is $3.50 and in Ramsey plc $2.75.

REQUIRED

(a) Calculate the following ratios for **both** companies to **two** decimal places.

(i) Income gearing
(ii) Earnings per share
(iii) Price earnings ratio
(iv) Dividend yield
(v) Dividend cover

Additional information

Alfredo is considering investing in one of the companies but is uncertain which will offer the best return.

Recent industry averages were as follows:

Income gearing	20.25%
Earnings per share	$0.33
Price earnings ratio	12.50
Dividend yield	10.45%
Dividend cover	1.20 times

REQUIRED

(b) Analyse the performance of **both** companies compared to the industry averages.

(c) Advise Alfredo which company he should invest in. Justify your answer.

goods. The new optimum consumption point is at Y and the quantities of apples and pears consumed have increased to A_2, P_2. If instead the individual's income falls the budget line will shift inwards to the left of the original to ST. The new optimum consumption point will be at Z with the individual now consuming only A_3 apples and P_3 pears.

Link

For an introduction to normal and inferior goods see Chapter 2 page 41.

The effect of changes in price

The effect of a price change on the quantity of a normal, inferior and Giffen good is shown in Figures 7.11, 7.12 and 7.13 respectively.

Key terms

Giffen good: a good the demand for which increases when its price increases and falls when its price falls.
Substitution effect: the change in the quantity demanded of a good as a result of a change in its relative price.
Income effect: the change in the quantity demanded of a good as a result of the fact that a change in its price has brought about a change in the consumer's real income.

In each case the quantity of good A consumed is indicated on the Y axis and the quantity of good B consumed is shown on the X axis. The initial optimum consumption point is at X where the budget line RJ is tangential to the indifference curve I_1. If we now assume that the price of B falls, an individual is now able to buy more of B but the same quantity of apples and so the budget line pivots about point R and becomes RT. In each of the three Figures the new optimum consumption point is at Y where RT is tangential to the new indifference curve I_2. In the case of both the normal and inferior goods the quantity of B consumed has increased, but in the case of the Giffen good it has fallen. There are two major influences that determine whether individuals increase or decrease their consumption of a good when its price changes – the substitution effect and the income effect – and we need to understand the nature of these in relation to the fall in the price of B.

Income and substitution effects

Key term

Price effect: in indifference curve analysis the sum of the substitution and income effects showing the effect of a change in price on the quantity demanded.

A price effect involves both income and substitution effects. If the price of a product falls it means that it is now cheaper relative to other products and the consumer is likely to purchase more of it. The fact that the consumer is likely to substitute purchases of products whose price has fallen for other more expensive products is known as the substitution effect. The substitution effect always leads to an increase in the consumption of the good whose relative price has fallen.

The fall in price will also mean that the consumer's real income has effectively risen so that more of all products, including the one whose price has fallen, can now be purchased. This is known as the income effect. Whether this leads to more, less or the same amount of the product whose price has fallen being purchased depends upon the nature of the product. If the product is a normal good, then the income effect will operate so as to increase consumption of the product whose price has fallen, but if it is an inferior good then more of perceived superior products will be purchased and the income effect will lead to less of the product being purchased. Nevertheless, in the case of an inferior good the substitution effect will be greater than the income effect and, so, overall the fall in price will lead to an increase in the quantity consumed of the good whose price has fallen. In the case of Giffen goods, however, the income effect will exceed the substitution effect and the fall in the price of the good will lead to less being consumed.

Normal, inferior and Giffen goods

It is possible to illustrate the substitution and income effects of the fall in the price of a good diagrammatically. This is shown in Figures 7.11, 7.12 and 7.13 for normal, inferior and Giffen goods respectively for the fall in the price of good B. As described above, the effect of the fall in price will, in each case, move the consumer from point X (consuming A_1, B_1) to point Y (consuming A_2, B_2). We begin by identifying the substitution effect. In order to do this we need to remove the income effect which is achieved by drawing in a new budget line, SV, parallel to the new budget line (RT), but tangential to the original indifference curve (I_1). This leaves the individual on the original indifference curve and shows how much of B would have been purchased had their real income not been increased. The movement from X to Z represents the substitution effect. The rest of the movement from X to Y is, therefore, the income effect.

It can be seen, therefore, that when the price of B is reduced the change in the quantity demanded resulting from the substitution effect is the movement from B_1 to B_3 and that resulting from the income effect by the movement from B_3 to B_2.

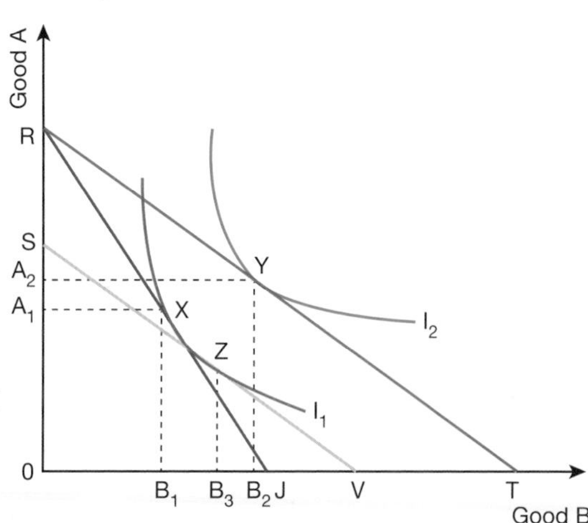

Figure 7.11 Income and substitution effects for a fall in price – normal good ▲

In the case of a normal good (Figure 7.11) the income and substitution effects of the price fall have worked in the same direction in order to bring about an increase in the quantity of B demanded.

Link

To refresh your memory on the distinction between normal and inferior goods see Chapter 2 page 41.

Figure 7.12 illustrates the situation for an inferior good. An inferior good is one for which the quantity demand will fall as consumers' income rises. In this case the substitution and income effects move in opposite directions. The substitution effect increases the demand from B_1 to B_3, but the negative income effect moderates the increase to some extent and will reduce the consumption of B from B_3 to B_2. Notice, however, that

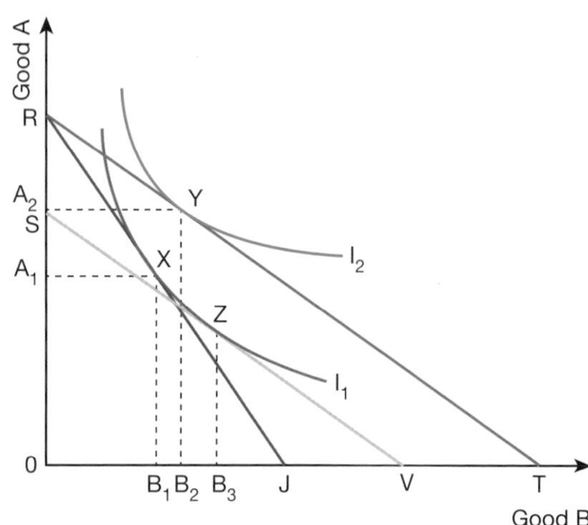

Figure 7.12 Income and substitution effects for a fall in price – inferior good ▲

> **Getting it right**
>
> Make sure you remember that in each of the three diagrams illustrating the income and substitution effects of a price fall, the movement from B_1 to B_3 represents the substitution effect and the movement from B_3 to B_2 represents the income effect.

even though the substitution and income effects move in opposite directions the final effect of the price reduction of good B is to increase the quantity of it, which is demanded.

The final case illustrated in Figure 7.13 is that of a Giffen good. Giffen goods are generally regarded as goods of low quality which are important elements in the expenditure of those on low incomes. A good example is a basic food such as rice, which forms a significant part of the diet of the poor in many countries. The argument, not accepted by all economists, is that when the price of rice falls sufficiently individuals' real income will rise to an extent that they will be able to afford more attractive substitutes such as fresh fruit or vegetables to make up their diet and as a result they will actually purchase less rice even though its price has fallen. In this case, the negative income effect (B_3 to B_2) completely outweighs the substitution effect (B_1 to B_3).

> **Getting it right**
>
> Make sure you have a clear understanding of the substitution and income effects of price changes.

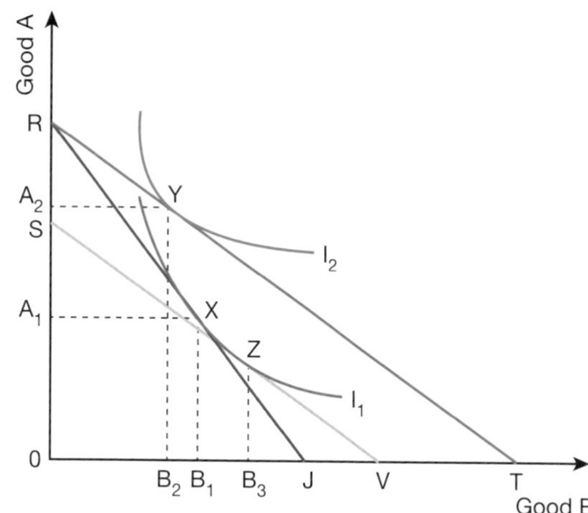

Figure 7.13 Income and substitution effects for a fall in price – Giffen good ▶

> **Activity**
>
> **Income and substitution effects**
>
> Draw diagrams to illustrate the income and substitution effects for a rise in the price of (a) a normal good (b) an inferior good (c) a Giffen good.

Table 7.3 Summary of income and substitution effects of price changes ▼

Price change	Type of good	Substitution and income effect	Change in demand
Fall	Normal	Substitution and income effects both act in the same direction	Rise
Fall	Inferior	Substitution effect increasing demand is greater than the income effect reducing demand	Rise
Fall	Giffen	Income effect reducing demand is greater than the substitution effect increasing demand	Fall
Rise	Normal	Substitution and income effects both act in the same direction	Fall
Rise	Inferior	Substitution effect reducing demand is greater than the income effect increasing demand	Fall
Rise	Giffen	Income effect increasing demand is greater than the substitution effect reducing demand	Rise

Limitations of indifference curve analysis

Although indifference curve analysis gets round the problem of measuring utility, when analysing consumer behaviour it has certain limitations.

To begin with there is the issue of whether individuals can realistically be expected to be able to identify imaginary combinations of two goods which will give equal amounts of satisfaction and then compare them with other combinations of the same two goods which give more or less satisfaction, which is what is necessary to create an indifference map. It is also the case that indifference curves are drawn on the basis of an individual's perception of the amount of utility that will be obtained from commodities, which might differ significantly from the satisfaction that is obtained when they are actually consumed. Moreover, indifference curve analysis is unable to explain purchases of goods such as cars or computers or other consumer durables which are purchased infrequently with no consistent trade off against another product. Such goods may also only be purchased once. Finally, consumers may not act rationally when planning their expenditure. This latter point leads us into a developing branch of economic analysis known as *behavioural economics*.

Behavioural economics

A major assumption underpinning both marginal utility theory and indifference curve analysis is that consumers always act rationally. In the sense that economists use the term, rational behaviour in mainstream economics means that:

> **Key term**
>
> **Rational behaviour:** the assumption made in economics that individuals and firms take into account the marginal costs and benefits in making decisions in order to achieve the optimum outcome (maximisation of total utility).

- individuals act solely to maximise their own personal utility (satisfaction)
- individuals are in possession of or have access to all the information they need at low or zero cost
- consumer decisions are based upon a careful comparison of the costs and benefits in order to achieve the optimum final outcome
- once behaviour has been optimised decision-making is based on changes at the margin
- individuals' preferences and attitude to risk are fixed.

In the real world, however, it is clear that individual behaviour may be irrational from the point of view of traditional economic models. For example, in financial crises and stock market crashes over the past century investors and financial institutions appear to have repeated the mistakes of the past. At the individual level why do individuals keep substantial surplus funds in current accounts or underperforming savings accounts when other accounts paying higher rates of interest are readily available? Why is it that many individuals automatically renew their annual car insurance with their existing company when identical cover can be obtained elsewhere at a lower price?

> **Key term**
>
> **Behavioural economics:** the branch of Economics that attempts to explain the decisions and choices individuals make in practice particularly when they are opposed to those predicted by traditional economic theory.

Behavioural economics is a rapidly developing branch of economics which attempts to explain such apparently "irrational" behaviour. Relying on empirical evidence and experiments, behavioural economics incorporates findings and insights from other disciplines such as sociology, social anthropology and particularly psychology to try to explain how individuals actually behave.

The pioneering study in behavioural economics is "Prospect Theory: An Analysis of Decision Under Risk" (1979) by Daniel Kahneman and Amos Tversky.

Prospect theory attempts to explain how people choose between alternatives involving risk where the probability of each outcome is known. It argues that rather than attempting to achieve optimal outcomes as traditional economic theory suggests, individuals actually make decisions based on the potential gains and losses that may arise.

Kahneman, Tversky and other behavioural economists identify a number of key elements in explaining individuals' apparently irrational behaviour.

Bounded rationality and heuristics

Let us return to our earlier example of irrational behaviour – an individual automatically renewing their annual car insurance with the existing provider. There is obviously an enormous quantity of information available which would enable the individual to make a rational decision as to whether this is in fact the best decision. There are many insurance companies from which to buy, each with their own publicity, website and telephone centres, as well as many comparison sites. However, for a variety of reasons individuals may not be able to effectively use this information to arrive at an optimum outcome. To begin with the timescale may be short and accessing the quantity of available information may take many hours and possibly even involve some financial cost. The individual may feel that the opportunity cost in terms of the time taken in sifting through the information and inputting the same personal information possibly many times may not be worth any potential savings. They might simply find the enormous volume of information overwhelming – too much to absorb within the available timescale. The individual's ability to act in a rational manner is, therefore, restricted; in the language of behavioural economics it is "bounded". In the case of making other decisions it could be the lack of sufficient information or the fact that there may be more than one possible solution that means a consumer may experience what Herbert Simon (1978) termed bounded rationality. As a result individuals may engage in satisficing rather than optimising behaviour in their decision-making.

Link

See page 205 of this chapter for more on satisficing behaviour.

Key term

Bounded rationality: the idea that individuals' ability to make rational decisions is limited by the quantity of information available and their ability to absorb and interpret it within the timescale available.

Heuristics

In such cases behavioural economists argue that individuals resort to heuristics (rules of thumb), which are simplifying strategies or mental shortcuts to arriving at solutions.

Key term

Heuristics: rules of thumb or mental shortcuts made by individuals to speed up the decision-making process.

They argue that empirical evidence and experiment identify many such heuristics including:

- Anchoring – the tendency to rely on the first piece of information obtained (the anchor) when considering a decision.

- Availability – basing decisions on the easiest piece of information to recall. The way and order in which information is presented to an individual will be important here.
- Representativeness – basing decisions on past experience or assumptions. This can lead to stereotyping. An example of the representativeness heuristic would be to argue that simply because we have only met low-income individuals from a particular region that all people from that region must be poor. This particular example illustrates that although the use of these heuristics (rules of thumb) may speed up decisions it can also lead to individuals making mistakes or irrational decisions.

Framing

Another feature of individual decision-making appears to be what behavioural economists refer to as framing. The way in which an issue, question or choice is presented or framed. There is evidence that the same information presented in different ways may lead to a different decision being made. For example, an individual may be more likely to buy an expensive pair of designer shoes if they are advertised as reduced from $400 to $300 rather than simply being priced at $300. Retailers can obviously use this knowledge in advertising and marketing their products.

> **Key term**
>
> **Framing**: the way in which an issue or choice is presented (framed) which may affect the decision made by an individual.

Too much choice? ▲

Other aspects of behavioural economics

In addition to the ideas of bounded rationality, heuristics and framing, the experiments of behavioural economists have identified a range of other insights which challenge the views of traditional economic models of consumer decision-making and may help explain apparently irrational behaviour. These include the following.

The endowment effect

This refers to the fact that individuals appear to be reluctant to give up goods which they own (their endowment) and as a result often demand much more to give up a product (their *willingness to accept*) than they would be prepared to pay for it (their *willingness to pay*). This appears to apply even to relatively mundane goods, e.g. coffee mugs. Some experiments have demonstrated that individuals require twice the amount to part with their endowment that they would have been prepared to pay for it in the first place. This endowment effect appears not to be associated with the value, characteristics or attraction of the product, but more the distress of losing it. Behavioural economists refer to this as loss aversion.

Loss aversion

There is considerable evidence that individuals appear to give much greater weight in their decision-making to the possibility of losses than the possibility of gains even when the probabilities of either occurring are the same.

Reference points

This refers to the apparent tendency for individuals to base decisions on the estimated gains and losses from a particular reference point (their position now) rather than looking at the overall picture. This may lead them to break down or compartmentalise the process of making a decision into a number of individual smaller decisions.

Certainty versus uncertainty

This appears to be linked with loss aversion. Experiments suggest that individuals prefer outcomes that are certain, or perceived to be certain, to those which are uncertain even where the probability was high that the uncertain event would generate a significantly greater gain or benefit. This might explain why individuals might prefer the guarantee of a low return on an investment to a much larger gain from an alternative if there was even a low probability of this leading to a loss.

Over-confidence and over-optimism

It seems from empirical studies by behavioural economists that individuals when looking to the future tend to be over-confident and over-optimistic about potential gains. This might be a factor in explaining speculative bubbles.

Too much choice?

Traditional economic theory argues that competition-creating choice is always a good thing. However, there is evidence that given too much choice individuals fail to make any decision at all.

Conspicuous consumption ▲

Herd instinct and competition

In making consumption decisions individuals are often swayed by the desire to keep up with their peers or friends and as a result purchase products simply because others are doing so. It is also possible that individuals might exhibit competitive behaviour purchasing goods which are perceived to be luxuries, superior to those purchased by friends and peers and, therefore, conferring social status.

Behavioural economists argue that all this research indicates that – counter to traditional economics – individuals' preferences and attitudes to possible gains or losses are not fixed. They may vary over time and according to the perceived uncertainty, risk and amount of money involved. This clearly undermines the assumptions underpinning traditional indifference curve analysis. Indeed one empirical study made in 1990 indicated the possibility of indifference curves intersecting.

Implications for policy

Link

Nudge theory is also discussed on page 216 in Chapter 8.

Behavioural economists argue that their findings can have important implications for government policy. Richard Thaler and Cass Sunstein in *Nudge: Improving Decisions About Health, Wealth and Welfare* (2008) suggest that insights from behavioural economics can be used by governments and others to persuade or "nudge" people into making decisions which are beneficial for them or in their best interests. For example, they suggest that individuals will be more likely to adopt energy conservation methods in their homes if the government advertises them as leading to a saving of $X per year rather than stating that they will lose (the same) $X per year if they do not adopt them – an example of "framing".

Another example is to make "opting in" rather than "opting out" the default position for schemes regarded as beneficial for individuals. For example, there is evidence that workers in a company are more likely to participate in a pension scheme if they are automatically enrolled and required to "opt out" if they do not wish to be a member than if they need to make a conscious decision to join or "opt in".

Overview of behavioural economics

Through experiments, empirical analysis and taking insights from psychology, behavioural economics attempts to find patterns and common themes in apparently irrational behaviour which can be incorporated into economic models of consumer behaviour and decision-making. Supporters argue that behavioural economics improves economists' ability to deal with actual economic life and the way individuals behave in reality. Ignoring behavioural aspects of decision-making they believe may lead to errors in prediction in traditional economic models. In particular it is important to take into account, for example, endowment effects and the fact that some choices involve one or more goods or services with which individuals may be unfamiliar with the consequence that meaningful preferences will only be established after choices have been made.

Criticisms of behavioural economics

Not all economists, however, agree. They argue that the conclusions of behavioural economists tend to be based on experiments involving college students who may not be representative of actual consumers, investors, business owners or entrepreneurs and, therefore, raises the issue of whether they will respond in the same way.

These experiments also, in the main, involve hypothetical options often requiring decisions about preferences which have not yet been made. In some cases the experiments require individuals to make choices or decisions in relation to very large issues which may be well outside their experience. For example, one influential experiment by Kahneman and Tversky involved participants making decisions on alternative treatments for 600 individuals affected by a deadly disease. It is argued that individuals' preferences might alter if the choices or decisions were not hypothetical and were more closely linked to their own experience. The same applies to experiments requiring decisions to be made where there is a risk of financial loss. Would individuals make the same decision if an actual loss was possible rather than a hypothetical one?

Another criticism centres on the fact that behavioural economists tend to ignore the fact that if an experiment was repeated or individuals came up against a particular set of circumstances, they might learn from past errors and, therefore, not repeat past mistakes. This is important in the light of the fact that irrational behaviour seems more prevalent in the short run and disappears as individuals obtain more information.

Finally, with a few possible exceptions, e.g. the endowment effect and loss aversion, heuristics or rules of thumb for decision-making seem to be specific to particular choices or decisions, which makes it difficult to generalise about them and also makes it more difficult to make predictions based on them.

Activities

Behavioural economics and decision-making

In groups of four or five:

1 identify four individual decisions or purchases made in the last week which might be regarded as irrational
2 produce a presentation to the rest of the group explaining the extent to which theses irrational decisions or purchases might be explained by behavioural economics.

Activities

Rational or irrational behaviour

In groups of four or five, discuss the extent to which the following decisions represent rational behaviour and whether they can be explained in terms of traditional economic models or behavioural economics.

1 Clive gives $1000 to charity.
2 Terry continues to pay an extended warranty to cover repairs to his washing machine even though a brand new one could be purchased for $250.
3 Richard continues to hold on to shares even though their price is falling and unlikely to rise in the foreseeable future.
4 Lizzie makes a 30 kilometre round trip to fill her car with fuel at a garage which is selling fuel for 2 cents a litre less than the garage 100 metres from her house.
5 A trade union takes its members out on strike in a dispute over a company's decision to remove a range of workers' perks because it can no longer afford them, even though the industrial action threatens the very survival of the company.

Key terms

Survival: an overarching objective of firms.

Profit maximisation: a possible objective for a firm. In the traditional theory of the firm this is assumed to be the sole objective and is at the output at which MC = MR.

Link

Alternative possible objectives that firms may pursue are considered later in this chapter – see page 202.

Types of cost, revenue and profit

Having looked at the basis of demand it is now necessary to look at the background to supply. The theory of the firm is concerned with the way in which firms in different market structures determine their price, output and competitive strategies.

The way in which firms go about making decisions on these issues depends upon the objectives of the firm and the market structure in which they operate. Although as we shall see later this may not always be the case, the traditional theory of the firm assumes that firms have one sole objective which is profit maximisation.

Profit

For the economist profit is the difference between total revenue (TR) and total cost (TC).

As we saw in Chapter 2, total revenue is the amount received by producers from the sale of their products.

Total cost is made up of all the payments made to the factors of production, i.e.:

- rent, which is the payment for land
- wages, which are the payment for labour
- interest, which is the payment for capital
- profit, which is the reward to the entrepreneur for organising and taking the risks associated with production.

Link

For more on returns to factors of production see Chapter 1 page 16.

This immediately poses an issue. Clearly profit cannot, at the same time, be the difference between total revenue and total cost and an element of total costs, unless we are referring to two different types of profit. This is, in fact, the case. Economists distinguish between two types of profit – normal profit and supernormal or abnormal profit.

Key terms

Normal profit: the amount of profit that can be made in the next most profitable enterprise.
Supernormal or abnormal profit: any profit in excess of normal profit.

Normal profit refers to the minimum payment required to keep an entrepreneur in a particular line of business. If this amount is not made the entrepreneur will leave the industry for the next most profitable business venture, and so in this sense normal profit represents the opportunity cost of a particular line of business – the amount that can be earned in the next most profitable enterprise. Normal profit is regarded as a cost of production because, if this is not earned, the entrepreneur will leave the industry. Normal profit is not a specific sum of money; it will differ from entrepreneur to entrepreneur and may vary over time as market conditions change.

Getting it right

Make sure you have a clear understanding of the difference between normal and supernormal (abnormal profit).

Supernormal profit is any profit in excess of normal profit.

Table 7.4 Summary of profit ▼

Total revenue > Total cost	Firm is making supernormal profit
Total revenue = Total cost	Firm is making normal profit
Total revenue < Total cost	Firm is making less than normal profit

Getting it right

Make sure you have a clear understanding of the difference between economists' and accountants' views of profit.

The economists' definitions of profit differ from that of accountants. Accountants' definition of profit is the difference between revenue and expenses, costs and taxes. Accountants also have a different definition of revenue from economists in that they include not only income from the sale of goods and services, but also any earnings from interest, dividends and rents.

Key term

Equilibrium position for firm: that price and output from which there will be no tendency for change.

Given that profit is the difference between total revenue and total cost, in order to find the profit-maximising equilibrium position for a firm, i.e. that price and output from which once achieved there will be no tendency for change for a firm, we need to analyse how costs and revenue vary as price and output change.

We will begin by looking at costs.

Short-run and long-run production

In analysing costs we need to see how production increases as factor inputs increase and make a distinction between the short run and the long run.

For example, if a supermarket receives a sudden increase in demand it will be able to respond quickly, by perhaps increasing the number of staff or opening for more hours each day, but it will not, immediately, be able to build a new store. Hence, for a period of time, the supermarket will only be able to increase output by making use of additional variable factors. This period is known as the short run. Over a sufficiently long period, however, the supermarket will, if it believes the increase in demand to be permanent, be able to build a new store. This is the long run when all factors are variable and output can be increased by using any of them.

The relationship between the factor inputs required in producing a product and the final output is known the production function.

Link

For more on factors of production/factor inputs see Chapter 1 page 16.

Key term

Production function: the relationship between the quantity of inputs of factors of production and the resulting output.

Production and costs in the short run

Law of diminishing returns

The way output and hence costs vary in the short run is governed by the law of diminishing returns (also sometimes referred to as the law of variable proportions) which states that as increasing quantities of a variable factor are added to fixed quantities of other factors, the return to the variable factor will eventually diminish. This is illustrated by Table 7.5 and Figure 7.14.

Link

For more on law of diminishing returns see Chapter 1 page 12.

Key term

Law of diminishing returns or law of variable proportions: as increasing quantities of a variable factor are added to fixed quantities of other factors, the return to the variable factor will eventually diminish.

Table 7.5: The law of diminishing returns ▼

Number of workers	Total physical product of rice (TPP)	Average physical product (APP) of rice TPP/No. of workers	Marginal physical product (MPP) of rice ΔTPP/ΔNo. of workers
			8
1	8	8	
			20
2	28	14	
			23
3	51	17	
			29
4	80	20	
			40
5	120	24	
			24
6	144	24	
			10
7	154	22	

Continued . . .

Key terms

Total physical product (TPP): the total output produced from a combination of fixed and variable factors.
Average physical product (APP): total physical product divided by the quantity of the variable factor (TPP/quantity of the variable factor).
Marginal physical product (MPP): the addition to total physical product resulting from the employment of an additional unit of the variable factor (ΔTPP/Δ quantity of the variable factor).

Number of workers	Total physical product of rice (TPP)	Average physical product (APP) of rice TPP/No. of workers	Marginal physical product (MPP) of rice ΔTPP/ΔNo. of workers
			6
8	160	20	
			2
9	162	16	
			−12
10	150	15	

The table shows how the production of rice varies as the number of workers employed increases. We assume that:

- the supply of other factors – land and capital – are fixed
- the state of technology is constant
- all workers are homogeneous – no worker is more or less efficient than any other.

As we can see from Table 7.5, as the number of workers increases, the total physical product (TPP) or total output increases until the ninth worker is employed. When the tenth is employed TPP falls because there are too many workers being employed for the quantity of land and capital. The other two columns show the average physical product (APP) and the marginal physical product (MPP).

APP is the output per worker. APP = TP/Quantity of labour

MPP is the increase in TPP as a result of employing one more worker. MPP = ΔTPP/Δ Quantity of labour.

Getting it right

When drawing the APP and MPP curves make sure the MPP and APP curves intersect at the maximum point of the APP curve.

Table 7.5 shows that APP increases up to the employment of the sixth worker and then declines, while MPP increases up to the fifth worker and then declines. It can be seen, therefore, that both the APP and MPP eventually decline as more workers are employed with all other factors of production fixed. This is the law of diminishing returns.

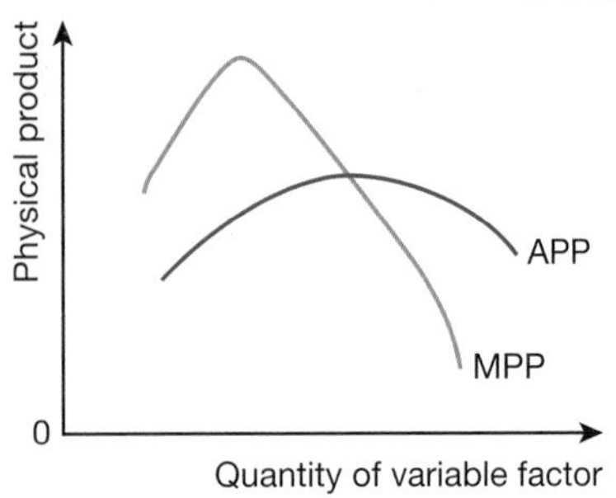

Figure 7.14 Average and marginal physical product ▲

The reason for this is that beyond a certain number of workers employed they will begin to get in each other's way.

The relationship between average and marginal physical product is illustrated in Figure 7.14.

Short-run costs

We can now use the analysis of the short-run production function to show how a firm's costs will vary in the short run. The main cost concepts involved are illustrated in Table 7.5. In the short run some factors are fixed in supply. These will therefore be fixed costs that do not vary with output. The costs of the variable factor, labour in the example above will, however rise with output; these are known as variable costs.

Key terms

Fixed cost: costs which do not vary with output.
Variable cost: costs which increase with output.

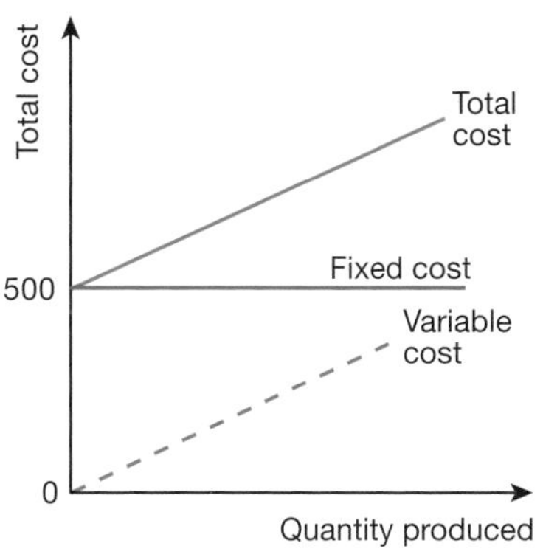

Figure 7.15 ▲

Key terms

Average fixed costs (AFC): Fixed costs per unit – AFC = FC/Q

Average variable costs (AVC): Variable costs per unit – AVC = VC/Q

Links

See Chapter 6 page 137 for more on the optimum resource allocation.

See Chapter 1 page 11 for diminishing returns.

Key terms

Average costs: Costs per unit of production – AC = TC/Q or AFC + AVC

Marginal costs: the addition to total cost when output is increased by one additional unit – MC = ΔTC/ΔQ

Getting it right

When drawing the average variable cost, average cost and MC curves make sure the marginal cost curve intersects with the average variable and average cost curves at their minimum points.

We assume that the fixed costs are $500 and the variable costs are $100 per worker. The TPP figures for column one are taken from Table 7.5.

Fixed costs are the costs of the fixed factor which do not vary with output. Interest on any loans a firm has taken out are an example of a fixed cost in that it will have to be paid whether or not anything is produced.

Variable costs are the costs of the variable factor, in this case labour, which will rise and fall with output. If there is no production there will be no variable costs.

Total costs are equal to fixed costs + variable costs. This is shown in Figure 7.15.

Average fixed costs (AFC) are the fixed costs per unit of output. AFC fall rapidly to begin with and then very slowly as the fixed costs are spread over a larger output. The shape of the curve is a rectangular hyperbola.

AFC = FC/Q

Average variable costs (AVC) are variable costs per unit of output. AVC fall to begin with as the optimum combination of factors of production is approached and then rise rapidly as diminishing returns set in giving a U-shaped curve.

AVC = VC/Q

Average costs are the cost per unit of production.

AC = TC/Q or AFC + AVC

Average costs decline quickly over low ranges of output as AFC are falling rapidly and AVC are falling or rising only slowly, as diminishing returns set in. Over higher ranges of output AVC are rising rapidly and although AFC are still falling they are doing so very slowly and the fall is insufficient to offset the rising AVC. The result is that AC rise rapidly.

Marginal cost is the increase in total cost when output increases by a single unit. If output is increasing by more than one unit then

$MC = \Delta TC/\Delta Q$

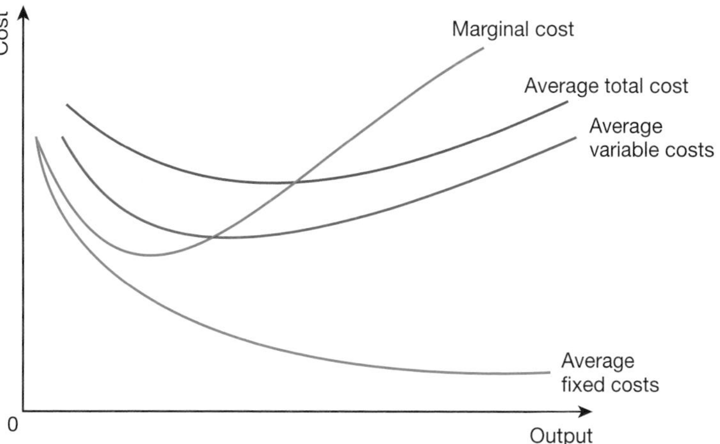

Figure 7.16 A firm's cost curves ▶

Table 7.6 summarises these costs for a typical firm.

Table 7.6 A firm's costs ▼

Column 1 (Q)	**Column 2**	**Column 3**	**Column 4 (FC + VC)**	**Column 5 (FC/Q)**	**Column 6 (VC/Q)**	**Column 7 (TC/Q) or AFC + AVC**	**Column 8 ΔTC/ΔQ**
TPP (Q)	Fixed costs (FC)	Variable costs (VC)	Total cost (TC)	Average fixed costs (AFC)	Average variable costs (AVC)	Average costs (AC)	Marginal cost (MC)
8	500	100	600	62.5	12.5	75	
							5
28	500	200	700	17.9	7.1	25	
							7.7
51	500	300	800	9.8	5.9	15.7	
							3.4
80	500	400	900	6.25	5	11.25	
							2.5
120	500	500	1000	4.2	4.1	8.3	
							4.2
144	500	600	1100	3.8	4.2	7.6	
							10
154	500	700	1200	3.2	4.5	7.7	
							16.7
160	500	800	1300	3.1	5	8.1	
							50
162	500	900	1400	3	5.6	8.6	

Progress question

2 Complete the table below.

Output	**TC**	**FC**	**VC**	**AFC**	**AVC**	**AC**	**MC**
0	110						
1	170						
2	220						
3	260						
4						80	
5						84	
6	560						
7							220
8	1020						
9	1320						
10							300

Long-run production function

The short-run production function and corresponding short-run costs are based on the fact that there is at least one fixed factor. In the long run all factors are variable and so it is possible for the firm to increase output by increasing all factors by the same amount or in proportion. This means that the firm is able to increase the *scale* of production.

In the long run, when all factors are variable firms will be able to produce a given output with any combination of factors. Given the assumption that firms' only objective is to maximise profits, they will try to produce their chosen output by employing factors of production in the combination that minimises their costs of production.

If, as a firm increases its scale of production by increasing all factors of production by the same percentage, output increases by a greater percentage, e.g. if factor inputs increase by 10 per cent and output increases by 15 per cents then the firm is said to be experiencing increasing returns to scale. If on the other hand output increases by a smaller percentage then the firm is said to be experiencing decreasing returns to scale. Finally if output increases by the same percentage as the increase in factor inputs then the firm will be experiencing constant returns to scale.

> **Key terms**
>
> **Increasing returns to scale:** a situation in which a given increase in the quantity of factor inputs leads to a greater proportionate increase in output.
>
> **Decreasing returns to scale:** a situation in which a given increase in the quantity of factor inputs leads to a smaller proportionate increase in output.
>
> **Constant returns to scale:** a situation in which a given increase in the quantity of factor inputs leads to an equal proportionate increase in output.

Long-run costs

SRAC and LRAC

We can now move on to look at costs in the long run. As we have seen, in the long run all factors are variable and, as a consequence, as a firm expands it is able to increase the quantity of factors that were previously fixed in supply. This means that the long run average cost (LRAC) curve will be a combination of a series of short run average cost (SRAC) curves as shown in Figure 7.17.

> **Key terms**
>
> **Short run average cost (SRAC):** a curve which shows how costs per unit (average costs) change as output changes in the period when at least one factor of production is fixed in supply.
>
> **Long run average cost (LRAC):** a curve which shows how costs per unit (average costs) change as output changes in the period when the supply of all factors of production can be increased.

If we take the case of a car assembly plant operating with just one production line (the fixed factor) it will be producing on $SRAC_1$. As it expands its output by introducing new production lines in the long run it will move to a new SRAC curve. With two production lines it will be operating on $SRAC_2$, with three production lines $SRAC_3$ and so on. The long run average cost (LRAC) curve joins all the points, giving the lowest cost of producing a given output. As there are, in the long run, a potentially infinite number of SRAC curves close together, the LRAC is drawn as a smooth *envelope* curve.

What determines the shape of the LRAC curve

As Figures 7.18 to 7.20 show, the LRAC curve could take a number of shapes. Declining long run average costs are the result of economies of scale and increasing long run average costs result from diseconomies of scale.

Economies of scale

Economies of scale can be internal economies of scale, resulting from an increase in the scale of production of an individual firm leading to a movement down along its LRAC curve as output

> **Key terms**
>
> **Economies of scale:** reductions in LRAC as the scale of production increases.
>
> **Diseconomies of scale:** increases in LRAC as the scale of production increases.
>
> **Internal economies of scale:** reductions in LRAC as a result of the firm itself increasing the scale of production.

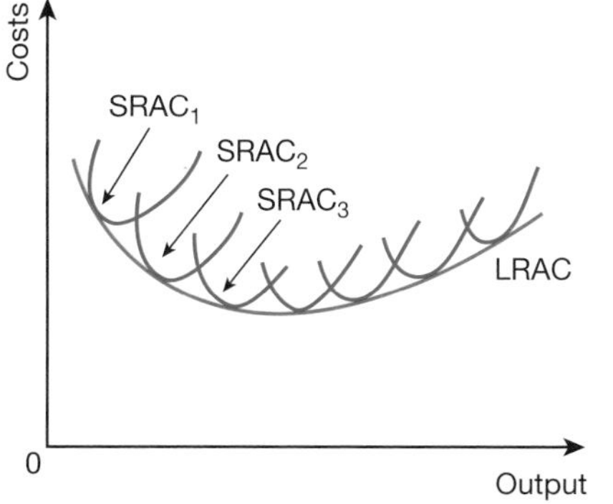

Figure 7.17 LRAC envelope curve ▲

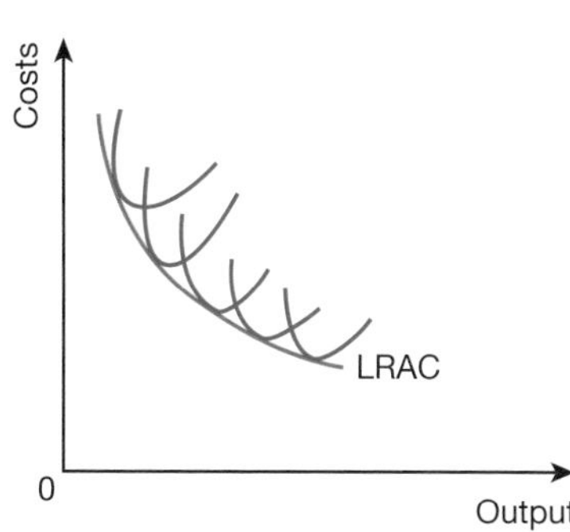

Figure 7.18 Falling LRAC ▲

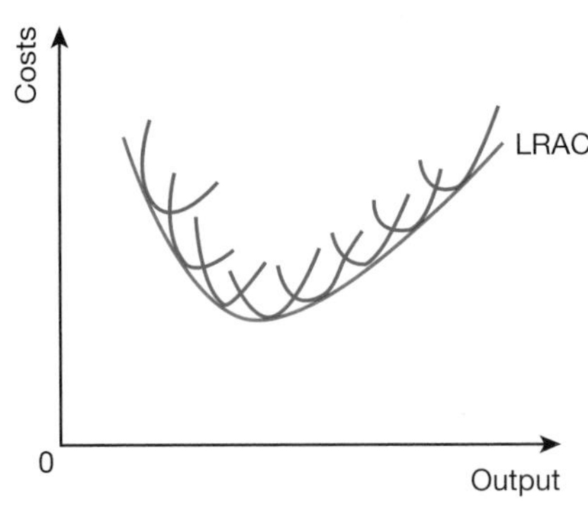

Figure 7.19 U-shaped LRAC curve ▲

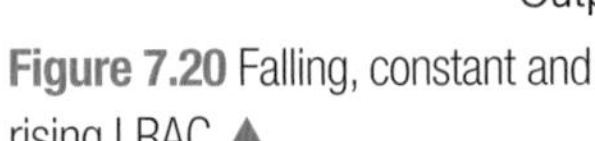

Figure 7.20 Falling, constant and rising LRAC ▲

> **Key term**
>
> **External economies of scale:** reductions in LRAC from a firm as a result of the industry growing in size.

increases, or external economies of scale resulting from the growth and interrelationship of all firms in the industry. External economies of scale are available to all firms in the industry, large or small, and therefore bring about a lowering of the entire LRAC curve of the firm.

Internal economies of scale

The following are a number of possible economies of scale that might be available to a firm.

> **Key term**
>
> **Technical economies:** reductions in LRAC as a result of the improvements and innovations in the production process as the firm increases the scale of production.

Technical economies

Technical economies can take a number of forms.

Economies of increased dimensions

Economies of increased dimensions are linked to the mathematical relationship between the surface area of a container and its volume. The cost of producing a container is normally linked to its surface area. Doubling the length of each of the sides of a cubic container will increase its surface area, and therefore the costs by four times. However, the volume of the container has increased by eight times, thus halving the unit costs of carrying say, oil, compared to the original container. This is the reason for shipping firms building larger and larger super tankers.

> **Key terms**
>
> **Economies of increased dimensions:** reductions in LRAC which arise as a result of increasing the size of a container. Increasing the surface area will lead to a greater increase in volume, thereby reducing unit costs.
>
> **Financial economies of scale:** reductions in LRAC resulting from the fact that large firms have access to a wider range of sources of finance and on more preferential terms than small firms because they are seen as a lower risk.

Division of labour

Large organisations are able to practise division of labour and mass production which small firms cannot. As we saw in Chapter 1, dividing the production process into a number of smaller tasks, each performed by a single individual, will increase the output from a given number of workers, thereby reducing average costs.

Large capital equipment

Large-scale companies producing very high output can afford to buy large specialist equipment to reduce unit costs which would be uneconomic for a small firm because the high cost involved would be spread over too low an output.

Research and development

Large organisations may be able to fund their own research and development departments to develop cost-saving processes and innovations. This is particularly important in industries such as pharmaceuticals.

Key term

Shares: a unit of ownership in a private or public limited company.

Financial economies

Financial economies of scale result from the fact that larger organisations are able to access greater amounts of funds from a wider range of sources and on better terms than small firms. Plcs have access to the stock market and can raise finance through the issue of shares. Large firms are often seen by banks as less risky than small ones and as a result they are able to borrow money at lower rates of interest.

Getting it right

Remember that all firms are able to gain economies of scale and not just large ones.

Marketing economies

Large organisations are often able to obtain discounts on products as a result of buying in large bulk. Large supermarket chains, such as Tesco and Walmart, are able to obtain goods from suppliers at significantly lower prices per unit than a small local store. In addition, such organisations can spread their marketing budget over a larger output and range of products. Large firms may even have their own distribution channels and transport.

Managerial economies

Large organisations, particularly private and public limited companies, are likely to be able to afford to employ highly qualified specialist staff. They may even be able to afford their own departments in areas such as exporting, marketing, human resources and administration. Although these may be expensive they are likely to increase productivity and output significantly and so bring down unit costs.

Key terms

Risk-bearing economies of scale: as a firm grows in size it is able to move into other product areas and markets which reduces the risks associated with a decline in any one of them.

Diversification: the process in which a firm moves into a number of different product areas usually to reduce risk or as a mechanism for growth.

Risk-bearing economies

As a firm grows in size, it may be able to obtain risk-bearing economies of scale by diversifying into other related or non-related areas to reduce the risks associated in operating in a single market. Large supermarket chains such as Tesco not only provide groceries and food, which was their original market, but have now diversified significantly into areas such as clothing, banking, insurance and the sale of fuel. This means that should one market collapse they will be able to fall back on others. Large tobacco producers are another example of diversification to reduce risk.

Economies of scope

This refers to reductions in average costs as a result of a firm producing two or more products. They derive from the fact that advertising and distribution costs can be spread across a range of products. It may be possible to reduce unit costs by transporting a range of products to a given destination rather than just one product. Common raw materials can be used across brands as with Volkswagen using common parts across its VW, Audi and Skoda ranges. It may also be that synergies are created in that a range of products may be seen as more desirable than a single product by consumers.

External economies of scale

External economies of scale are available to all firms in an industry regardless of their size as the industry as a whole grows and develops.

If an industry becomes concentrated in a particular area it may benefit from improved transport links and infrastructure. Ancillary industries may develop to provide supplies of components. Specialist labour with specific skills may become available and colleges and universities in the area may develop courses specifically linked to the industry. All of these developments are likely to increase the productivity of all firms and reduce their average costs.

Diseconomies of scale

Diseconomies of scale refer to increases in LRAC as a firm increases its scale of production. They can be internal, affecting a single firm as it grows, or external affecting all firms in the industry irrespective of their size. Examples of internal diseconomies of scale include managerial diseconomies and alienation of workers. As the firm increases in size, the complexity of the organisation may increase and managers may find it more difficult to effectively co-ordinate production and monitor performance. Communication may become more difficult, time-consuming and costly.

In extremely large organisations workers may experience alienation, feeling that they are merely "a small cog in a large wheel". Their tasks are likely to be repetitive and they may regard them as boring. They may feel unimportant and distanced from management and any involvement in decision-making. As a result they may lack motivation and consequently productivity suffers, leading to falling productivity and rising unit costs. There is also some evidence that larger organisations suffer more from labour disputes. It is also the fact that in large complex organisations labour disputes amongst a few key workers can cause all production to be disrupted.

Getting it right

It is important to remember that in the short run the way in which average costs vary with output is determined by the law of diminishing returns, but in the long run by economies and diseconomies of scale.

Case Study

Increasing size of supertankers

Maersk Lines, the world's largest container shipping line, has ordered 20 supertankers from South Korean shipyards to add to its existing fleet of eight. It already owns the largest container ship in the world, the *Eleonora Maersk*, which is longer than four rugby pitches and is over eight storeys high.

These ships are designed to operate on the world's most important and lucrative sea route from Asia to Europe, bringing low-cost goods from South Korea, Malaysia and China to European shops.

Given that these supertankers cost a colossal $200 million each, why are shipping companies building such gigantic ships?

The answer is economies of scale. To make it viable for shippers and retailers to transport goods halfway round the world huge numbers of containers must be transported at one time enabling European retailers to buy in bulk from low-cost suppliers. Fully laden these ships are capable of carrying 7 500 containers or 100 000 tonnes of merchandise.

Another factor is the price of oil. Oil makes up a large percentage of the cost of operating these ships and its rising cost means that shipping lines need to find ways of reducing the unit costs of carrying each container.

These supertankers incorporate the latest technology so not only are the engines incredibly fuel efficient, but the sophisticated computer technology means that they are capable of operating with a crew of just 13.

All this makes it possible for TVs made in China to be sold at a competitive price in the UK.

1. Explain the economies of scale available to shipping lines and retailers identified in the extract.
2. Explain any other economies of scale that might be available to large shipping lines and retailers.
3. Are there any diseconomies of scale that might result from using such huge supertankers?

Revenue

In order to find a firm's profit maximising price and output, we need to look at both costs and revenue. There are three revenue concepts that are important.

- Total revenue is the revenue received from the sale of a product. As we have seen TR = P × Q
- Average revenue is the revenue per unit. This is calculated by AR = TR/Q

  As TR = P × Q, then AR = P × Q/Q. Therefore, at any given output AR = Price.

Because AR = P, it follows that the demand curve facing a firm, which shows how much will be purchased, must be the same as its average revenue curve which shows the relationship between average revenue and sales.

- Marginal revenue is the addition to total revenue when sales increase by an additional unit and is calculated by MR = ΔTR/ΔQ

Link

See more on total revenue in Chapter 2 page 56.

Key terms

Average revenue: revenue per unit sold. AR = TR/Q = P × Q/Q = P

Marginal revenue: the addition to total revenue when output/sales are increased by an additional unit. MR = ΔTR/ΔQ

Total, average and marginal revenue curves

The shape of the firm's revenue curves depends on whether it is a price taker that charges the same price for all units sold or a price maker that has to reduce the price in order to sell more units. As we shall see later, whether a firm is a price taker or price maker depends upon the market structure in which it operates.

Revenue curves for a price taking firm

Total, average and marginal revenue for a price taking firm are given in Table 7.7 below. We assume all units are sold for $10. It can be clearly seen that in these circumstances AR = MR.

Table 7.7 Total, average and marginal revenue for a price taker ▼

Output	Price	Total revenue	Average revenue	Marginal revenue
1	10	10	10	10
2	10	20	10	10
3	10	30	10	10
4	10	40	10	10
5	10	50	10	10

Table 7.8 shows the total, average and marginal revenue for a price making firm on the assumption that the price of all units is reduced by $1 each time the firm wishes to sell additional units.

Table 7.8 Total, average and marginal revenue for a price maker ▼

Output	Price	Total revenue	Average revenue	Marginal revenue
1	10	10	10	10
2	9	18	9	8
3	8	24	8	6
4	7	28	7	4

Continued . . .

Output	Price	Total revenue	Average revenue	Marginal revenue
5	6	30	6	2
6	5	30	5	0
7	4	28	4	−2

Here, both average revenue and marginal revenue fall continuously and, because in order to sell an additional unit the price of all units has to be reduced, marginal revenue is always below average revenue and falls at twice the rate of average revenue.

Total, average and marginal revenue curves for price taking and price making firms are illustrated in Figures 7.21 and 7.22.

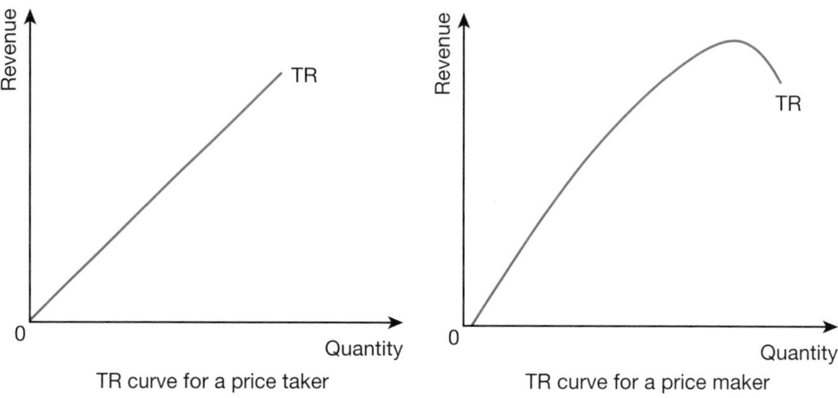

Figure 7.21 Total revenue curves for a price taker and price maker ▲

Figure 7.22 Average and marginal revenue curves for a price taker and price maker ▲

Relationship between price elasticity of demand, average, marginal and total revenue for a downward-sloping demand curve

The relationship between price elasticity of demand, average, marginal and total revenue for a downward-sloping demand curve is shown in Figure 7.23.

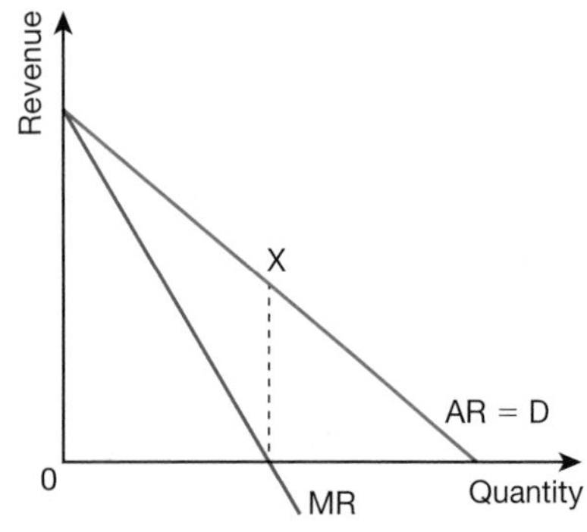

Figure 7.23 Relationship between price elasticity of demand, average, marginal and total revenue for a downward-sloping demand curve ▲

As the graph shows, the marginal revenue curve falls at twice the rate of the demand (average revenue) curve. The point where the MR curve crosses the horizontal axis corresponds to the midpoint of the D (AR) curve, designated X. As we saw from our study of point elasticity of

Link

See more on point elasticity of demand in Chapter 2 page 53.

demand in Chapter 4, at the midpoint of a straight-line demand curve the price elasticity of demand is unity (PED = −1). Total revenue for a firm is maximised at the point where the price elasticity of demand is unity. It follows, therefore, that:

Where MR = 0, the PED = −1 and total revenue is at a maximum.

Profit maximisation

If we now bring the cost and revenue concepts together we are in a position to find a firm's profit maximising output and go on to establish the price charged and the amount of profit obtained. As we have seen, Profit is TR − TC and so the profit maximising output is at the point where there is the greatest difference between TR and TC. This is illustrated in Figure 7.24.

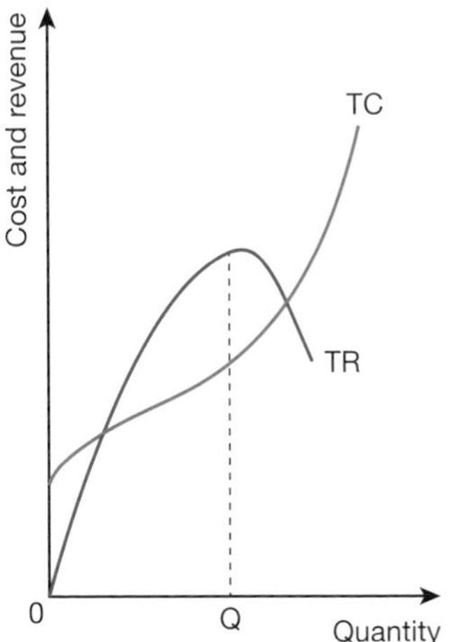

Figure 7.24 Profit maximisation using total revenue and total cost curves ▲

Profit maximisation using total cost and revenue curves

The disadvantage of using total cost and total revenue curves is that it is not straightforward to identify the profit maximising price. As a result it is more common to analyse profit maximisation by looking at average and marginal cost and revenue.

Profit maximisation using marginal and average cost and revenue curves

Profit maximising output

The profit maximising output is found at the point where marginal cost = marginal revenue (MC = MR). This is shown in Figure 7.25.

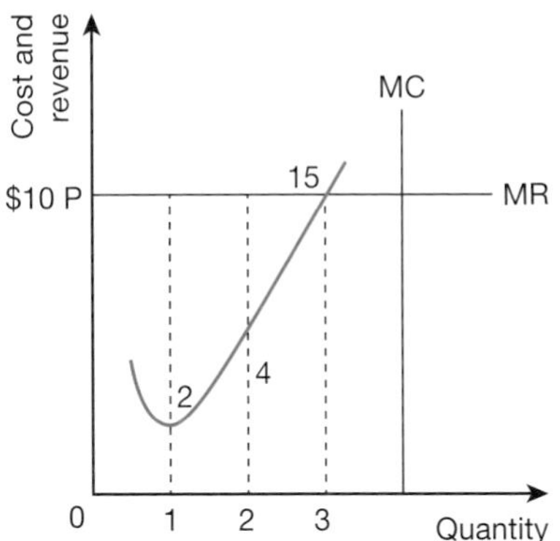

Figure 7.25 Profit maximising output (MC = MR) ▲

When MR > MC it is advantageous for the firm to increase output as each unit produced and sold brings in more revenue than it costs to produce and hence adds to overall profit. In Figure 7.25 the first unit adds $10 to revenue, but only $2 to costs, adding $8 to profits. Producing the second unit adds another $10 to revenue and only $4 to costs and so total profits are increased by a further $6. The third unit adds the same amount to revenue as costs, but if the firm produces a fourth unit costs increase by $15 and revenue by only $10, therefore reducing profits by $5. Clearly it will not pay the profit maximising firm to produce this unit or any other where MR < MC. Consequently the firm will maximise profit at the output where MR = MC.

Profit maximising price and profit level

To obtain the price charged by the firm and the level of profit made at the profit maximising output we need to look at the firm's average revenue and average cost curves. These are shown in Figure 7.26.

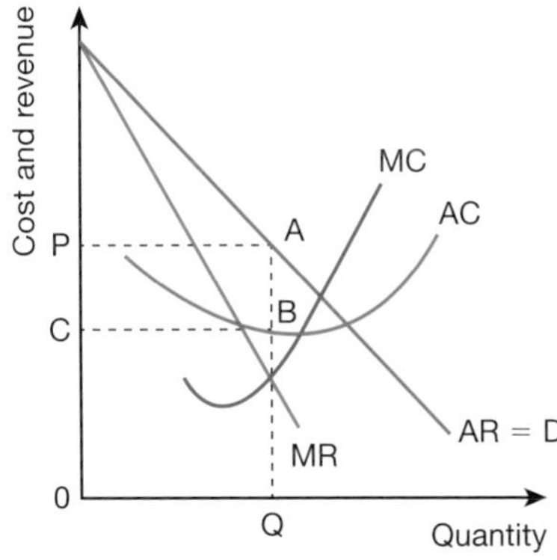

Figure 7.26 Profit maximising price and level of profit ▲

If the profit maximising output is at Q then the price will be given by the AR curve, i.e. P (remember that price = AR at any given level of output). Profit is given by TR − TC at this output. We can calculate the total revenue by multiplying the price by the quantity sold, which gives the area OPAQ. The total cost at this output is given by multiplying the average cost per unit by the output, which gives the area OCBQ. The difference, the area CPAB is the level of profit. Since TR > TC, the firm in this case is making supernormal profit.

Different market structures

We are now in a position to apply the analysis of profit maximisation to the operation and performance of firms in different market structures experiencing markedly different competitive environments. You need to have a good understanding and knowledge of the four market structures:

- perfect competition
- monopoly
- monopolistic competition
- oligopoly.

Perfect competition

In their purist form perfectly competitive markets exist nowhere in the world although there are markets which approximate to them, particularly those for agricultural products produced worldwide as well as the Forex market and the market for stocks and shares.

The benefit to economists of studying perfect markets is that they provide us with an "ideal type" model which can be compared with actual real-world firms in terms of their behaviour and performance.

Characteristics of perfect competition

- Infinite numbers of small producers
- All firms produce a homogeneous (identical product) product
- Infinite numbers of consumers
- Consumers are indifferent as to which firm they buy from – no brand or company loyalty
- Perfect knowledge throughout the market; all decisions made by producers or consumers are instantaneously known to all in the market
- Freedom (zero) cost entry to and exit from the market
- Perfectly elastic supply of all factors of production.

The implication of these characteristics is that all firms in the industry are price takers. The price will be determined in the market through the interaction of demand and supply for the product and each individual firm will have to charge this price. No individual firm by its own actions is able to influence the price.

Take the example of a firm that attempted to increase its profits by raising its price. Instantaneously all consumers in the market would know about it because of the assumption of perfect knowledge, and because consumers are indifferent as to the producer they will shift their demand to other suppliers. These suppliers will be able to obtain the factors of production to meet this increase in demand. The consequence is that the firm which raised its price will go out of business.

Figure 7.27 shows the relationship between the setting of the market price for a product and that charged by an individual firm.

The diagram for the industry indicates that both consumer and producer surplus are at a maximum which means the industry is allocatively efficient.

Getting it right

The profit maximising firm will always produce the output at which MC = MR.

Price at this output is given by AR.

Profit per unit at this output is given by AR – AC.

Total profit at this output is given by TR (the area of the rectangle under the AR curve) – TC (the area of the rectangle under the AC curve).

Key term

Perfect competition: an 'ideal type' market structure in which there are infinite numbers of producers each producing a homogeneous product, freedom of entry to and exit from the market by firms, an infinite number of consumers each of whom are indifferent between suppliers and perfect knowledge within the market, all of which means that all firms within the market are price takers, unable to influence the price of the product by their own actions.

Activity

Market structure

Identify an example of each of the four forms of market structure in your country.

Key terms

Long-run equilibrium for the firm in perfect competition: MC = MR = AC = AR. Firms are both productively efficient, P = minimum AC, and allocatively efficient, P = MC.

Long-run equilibrium for the industry in perfect competition: there is no tendency for the number of firms in the industry to change.

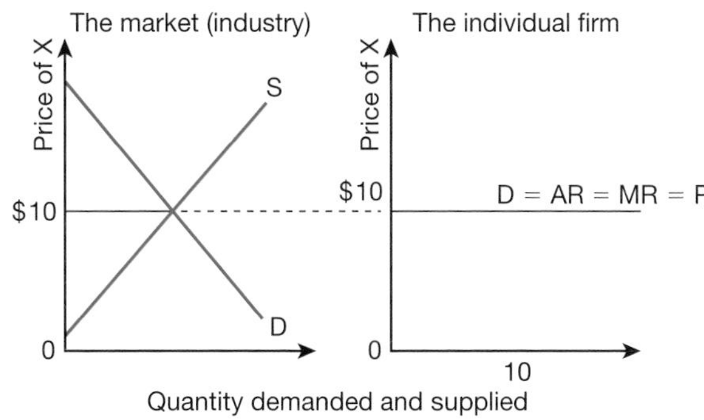

Figure 7.27 Industry and firm in perfect competition ▲

Short- and long-run equilibrium for a firm in perfect competition

Based on the analysis above we can now establish the short- and long-run equilibrium positions for a firm in perfect competition.

In the short run it is possible for a firm to experience supernormal profits or less than normal profits.

Progress question

3 Given the characteristics of a perfectly competitive market listed above, explain why an individual firm would not reduce its price in a perfectly competitive market.

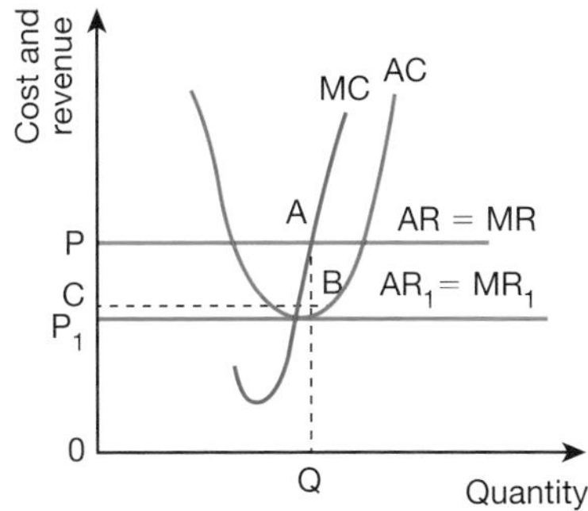

Figure 7.28 Short-run supernormal profits and market adjustment ▲

Figure 7.28 illustrates a firm in perfect competition making supernormal profits in the short run. The market price has been established at P, which means that firms are making supernormal profit equal to CPAB. As a result new firms will be attracted into the industry, shifting the industry supply curve to the right and reducing the market price. This shifts the horizontal D (AR) = MR curve for the individual firm downwards. This process continues until there are no longer any supernormal profits to be earned to attract new firms. This will occur at the point when price has fallen to P_1 with the new D $(AR)_1$ = MR_1 curve tangential to the minimum point of the AC curve and firms making normal profits.

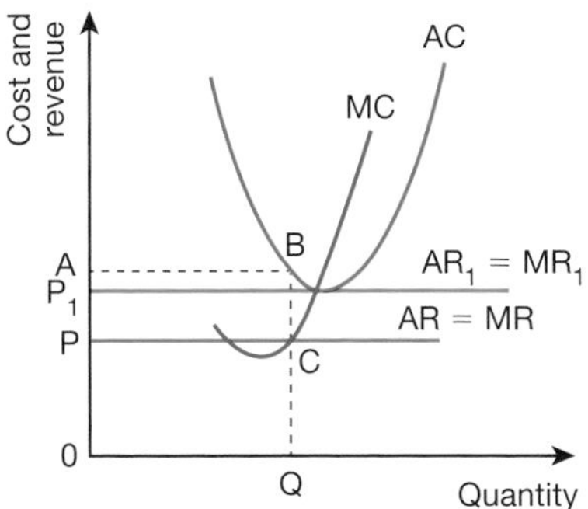

Figure 7.29 Less than normal profits in the short run and market adjustment ▲

Figure 7.29 shows a firm in the opposite situation making a loss equal to PABC because at the point where MC = MR, AC > AR. Firms in this position will ultimately leave the industry and the industry supply curve will shift to the left driving up the market price. This process will continue until the price has risen to a level where AR is just equal to AC and the firm is making normal profits.

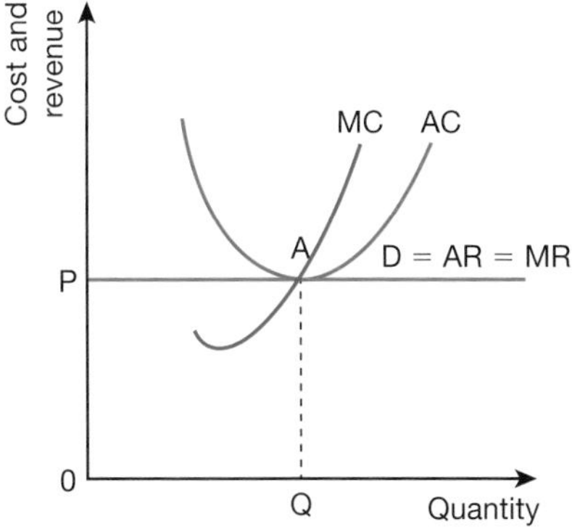

Figure 7.30 Long-run equilibrium for a firm in perfect competition ▲

It is clear therefore that while it is possible for firms in perfect competition to earn supernormal profits or make losses in the short run, the only long-run equilibrium for the firm and industry occurs at the point where all firms are making normal profits as illustrated in Figure 7.30.

As we can see, at the profit maximising equilibrium MC = MR = AR (P) = AC

The fact that P = MC and P = Minimum AC means that the firm is both allocatively and productively efficient.

Supply curve for the firm in perfect competition

It is possible to derive a unique supply curve for a firm in perfect competition. As we saw in Chapter 2, a supply curve shows how much a producer is prepared to offer for sale over a range of prices over a period of time. Figure 7.31 derives the supply curve for the firm in perfect competition. If the price is P the firm will maximise profits where MC = MR at point X and supply output Q. If the price rises to P_1 the firm will again produce where MC = MR, point Y and supply output Q. If price rises to P_2 the firm will produce at point Z and supply Q_2.

Because the profit maximising firm will always produce the output at which MC = MR and all firms in perfect competition are price takers so that Price = MR all the points X, Y and Z lie on the firms MC curve.

In perfect competition, therefore, the firm's supply curve is its MC curve.

Shut down points for the firm

There are certain prices, however, at which the firm will not produce at all. As we saw above, if a firm is making losses it will eventually have to leave the industry and consequently it will be supplying nothing. The question is, how quickly will the firm leave the industry?

The following numerical example will illustrate this.

Take a firm currently producing 100 units.

At this output TR = \$1000 and TC = \$1200 made up of \$800 in FC and \$400 VC. AR = TR/Q = \$1000/10 = \$10 and AC = TC/Q = \$1200/100 = 12. AFC = \$8 and AVC = \$4.

In the long run, this firm must cover all its costs and since it is making an overall loss of \$200, in the long run it must close down. In order to cover its TC the firm must set a price (AR) which at least covers AC. Hence, in the long run, a firm can only stay in business and supply a product if price is at least equal to its AC. This means that the firm will have to shut down in the long run if price falls below minimum AC.

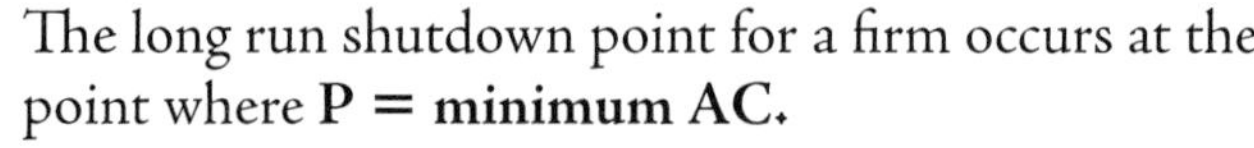

The long run shutdown point for a firm occurs at the point where **P = minimum AC.**

This means that the long run supply curve for the perfectly competitive firm is only that part of the MC curve above minimum AC. This is shown by LY in Figure 7.31.

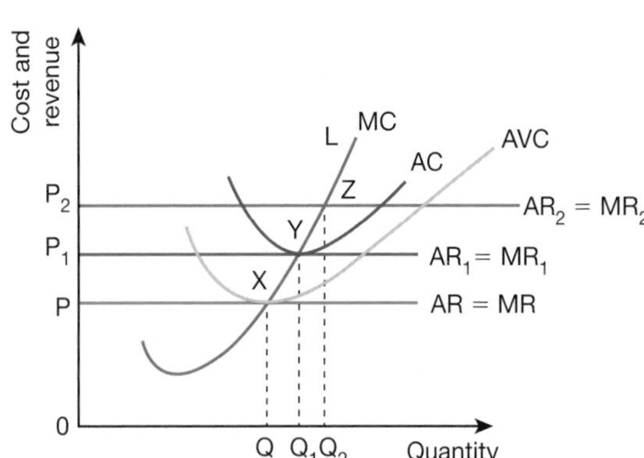

Figure 7.31 Supply curve for a firm in perfect competition ▲

Should this firm close down immediately?

If it does, its TR will clearly be 0. However, in the short run the firm will still have to cover its FC of \$800. This means that it will have TR = 0 and TC = \$800. It will make a greater loss by shutting down immediately – \$800 – than by staying in business until it can exit the industry with no

FC to pay. However, if in this case the TC of $1200 was made up of FC of $1100 and VC of $100 the firm should close down immediately because by staying in business losses are increased to $900. As long as the firm is covering its VC it should stay in business because it will have a surplus of TR over VC which can contribute to the payment of the FC and, therefore, reduce losses. Clearly the shutdown point in the short run occurs where the firm is just covering its VC and the loss is the same whether it continues to produce or leaves the industry immediately. The lowest price at which a firm can produce in the short run is that equal to minimum AVC.

The short run shutdown point for a firm occurs at the point where **P = minimum AVC.**

This means that the short run supply curve for the perfectly competitive firm is only that part of the MC curve above minimum AVC. This is shown by LX in Figure 7.31.

Key terms

Monopoly: sole supplier of a product.

Imperfect competition: market structures in which individual firms have the ability to influence price – monopoly, monopolistic competition and oligopoly.

Barriers to entry: obstacles which prevent new firms entering a particular industry.

Monopoly

The opposite extreme to perfect competition in terms of competitiveness is monopoly which is a situation in which one firm dominates the market. This market structure is an example of imperfect competition.

Monopolies are able to exist because of barriers to entry which prevent new firms from entering an industry to compete.

Sources of monopoly power

There are a number of barriers to entry including the following.

High start-up costs

If a great deal of capital investment is required to enter a particular market in order to achieve the minimum efficient level of scale, then it will be very difficult for new firms to enter the industry. The problem will be compounded if these costs are likely to be sunk costs in the future. This would mean that the initial high costs could not be recouped if the firm was forced to exit the market. These potentially high exit costs would make new firms even less likely to enter the market.

Control of sources of supply

Control of a substantial proportion of the supply of a raw material can enable a firm to acquire monopoly power in a market. For example, the Potash Corporation of Saskatchewan controls some 20 per cent of the world's potash supplies. OPEC is another example in the oil industry.

Copyright and patents

Copyrights guarantee sole rights to producers over new inventions, processes, music and intellectual property rights for a period of time preventing others from exploiting them. An example is Microsoft in the area of computer operating systems and software.

Economies of scale

Firms already in a market may be experiencing significant economies of scale which enable them to produce at low unit costs. New firms will not immediately be able to benefit from these economies of scale and so existing firms may be able to charge low prices with which new entrants could not compete.

Brand loyalty

Brand loyalty may sustain a monopoly if not create one. If a brand becomes identified with a product, such as Coca-Cola with cola drinks and Kellogg's with cornflakes, then this may create a loyalty to the product which creates some monopoly power.

Legal protection

Legal monopolies protect an organisation by law. In many countries, public utilities such as water, postal services and nationalised industries are given monopoly status by the government.

Mergers and takeovers

A firm can obtain a monopoly in an area by taking over other companies in the industry.

Location

Small shops and post offices can have a localised monopoly in a small village.

Equilibrium price and output in monopoly

As the monopolist is a price maker it will face downward-sloping demand (AR) and MR curves. These combined with the AC and MC curves give the profit maximising position shown in Figure 7.32.

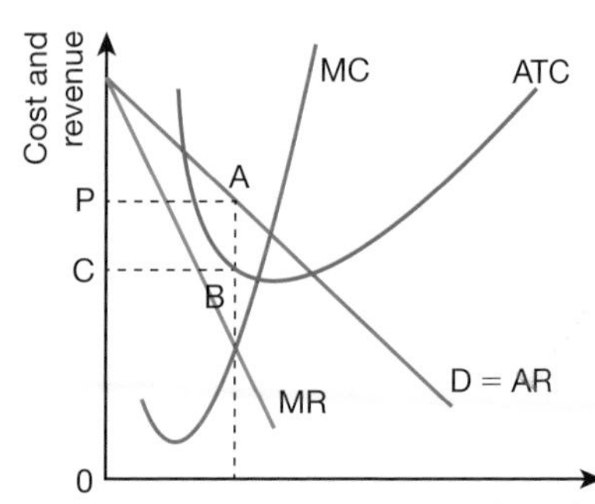

Figure 7.32 Equilibrium price and quantity for a profit maximising firm in monopoly ▲

The profit maximising output is at Q where MC = MR, the price at this output is given by the AR curve and the firm is making supernormal profit. Unlike perfect competition, new firms cannot enter the industry to take advantage of these supernormal profits and thus the monopoly is able to make supernormal profits in the long run.

Natural monopoly

The role of economies of scale in the creation of monopolies has already been indicated. Economies of scale are particularly important in the analysis of natural monopolies. A natural monopoly exists in situations where it would be inefficient and a wasteful duplication of resources for there to be more than one firm operating in the market. Examples include: public utilities such as water, gas and electricity, or railways where having different firms duplicating the required infrastructure to the same area or over the same routes would clearly be wasting scarce resources. Natural monopolies typically have very high start-up costs and because they experience economies of scale over most of their production, the minimum efficient scale of production is only achieved at an extremely high level of output.

The LRAC curve for a natural monopolist is, therefore, downward sloping throughout its length which means that the associated LRMC

Key terms

Natural monopoly: an industry or service which is most efficient when run as a monopoly because the average costs would be higher if the market was shared between more than one supplier.

Minimum efficient scale of production: the level of output at which lowest LRAC begin.

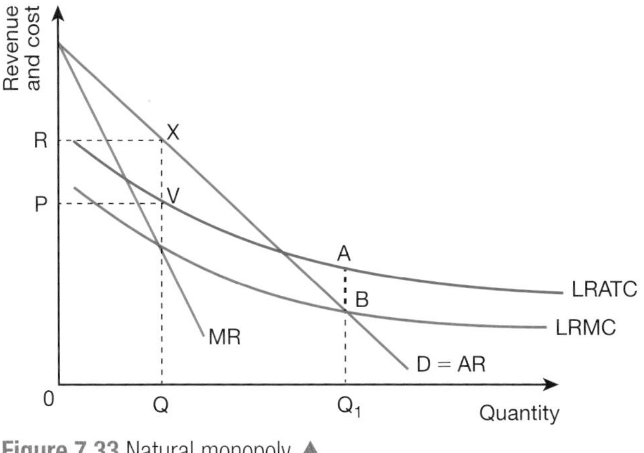

Figure 7.33 Natural monopoly ▲

curve is always below it as shown in Figure 7.33. The profit maximising monopolist will wish to produce at Q where MC = MR, but this output will not enable the full benefits of the economies of scale to be obtained.

The allocatively efficient position occurs where Price = MC which occurs at an output of Q_1 with a price equal to B. However, at this point price is below LRAC and so the firm would be operating at a loss. Therefore, if the government deems the service to be sufficiently important to be provided at this price it must take it into state ownership or provide a subsidy.

Price discrimination

Link

For more on consumer surplus, see Chapter 2 page 70.

Key term

Price discrimination: the practice of selling the same product in different markets at different prices.

Figure 7.34 shows the market for a monopolist's product. If all units of the product are sold at the same price this will be $10 where demand equals supply. However, the demand curve indicates that a number of consumers would be prepared to pay a higher price. As we saw in Chapter 2, the differences between the price individuals are prepared to pay and that which they actually pay represents consumer surplus.

If a monopoly can separate out some or all of these individuals and charge them the price they are prepared to pay it will clearly increase profits. Charging individuals different prices in different markets, when this is not based on cost differences, is known as price discrimination. Most firms with some form of market power are able to exercise price discrimination provided certain conditions are met. These conditions together with an example of their application to the railway industry are summarised in Table 7.9.

Table 7.9 Conditions for price discrimination ▼

Condition	Application
Firm must exercise some monopoly power in the market.	In the UK, train operating companies are granted franchises for a period of time during which they have a monopoly over particular routes.
It must be possible to separate the markets.	Markets are separated in a number of ways according to: • age of customer – cheaper tickets for children • status – student discounts • time of travel – fares lower at weekends, middle of the day.
It must not be possible to buy in one market and resell in another. This is called arbitrage.	Ticket barriers/guards ensure individuals only travel with the correct ticket.
Price elasticities of demand must be different in the markets.	Peak-time business travellers have a more inelastic demand than off-peak leisure travellers, enabling them to be charged a higher price.

Types of price discrimination

Economists identify three types of price discrimination.

First-degree price discrimination occurs when the monopolist is able to charge each individual consumer the maximum amount they are prepared to pay for a product. Individuals with spare tickets for major sell-out concerts and sports events will try to bargain with potential buyers to try and estimate the maximum they are prepared to pay. If first-degree price discrimination is successful the whole consumer surplus will be eliminated. First-degree price discrimination is illustrated in Figure 7.34. If all four units of the product are sold at the same price the firm's TR = \$40. If each unit is sold at the maximum possible price the TR = \$70.

Second-degree price discrimination is common in markets for public utilities such as electricity where different prices are charged for successive blocks of consumption. Electricity companies typically charge higher prices for the first block of units sold and then lower prices for the rest.

Second-degree price discrimination is shown in Figure 7.35.

Third-degree price discrimination refers to the selling of the same product in different markets to different consumers at different prices. Examples include: different fares on public transport for individuals of different ages or different prices for products in domestic and foreign markets.

Figure 7.36 illustrates the way in which output and price are determined under third-degree price discrimination. If there is no price discrimination the price charged will be P in the combined market and the profit is shown by the shaded area. If price discrimination takes place, the firm will equate the overall MC with the MR in the individual markets and charge a price of P_1 in the foreign market and P_2 in the domestic market. The price will be highest in the domestic market as demand is more inelastic because there are likely to be fewer substitutes. The combined total of the profits made in the domestic and foreign markets will exceed the profit made if the same price had been charged for all sales.

Key terms

First-degree price discrimination: the practice of charging each consumer the maximum they are prepared to pay.

Second-degree price discrimination: the practice of charging consumers different prices for successive blocks of consumption.

Third-degree price discrimination: the practice of charging different consumers different prices for the same product.

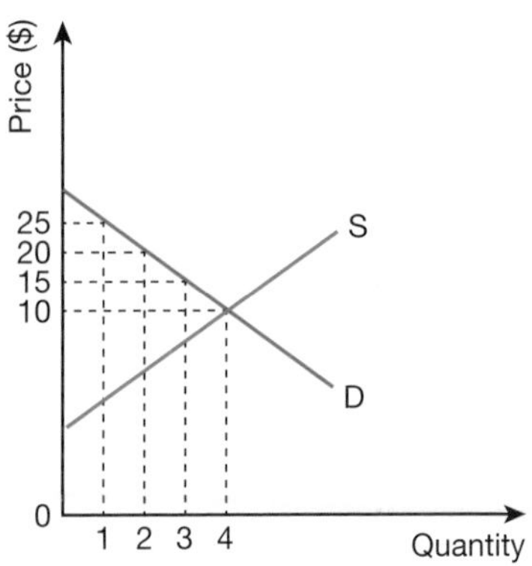

Figure 7.34 First-degree price discrimination ▲

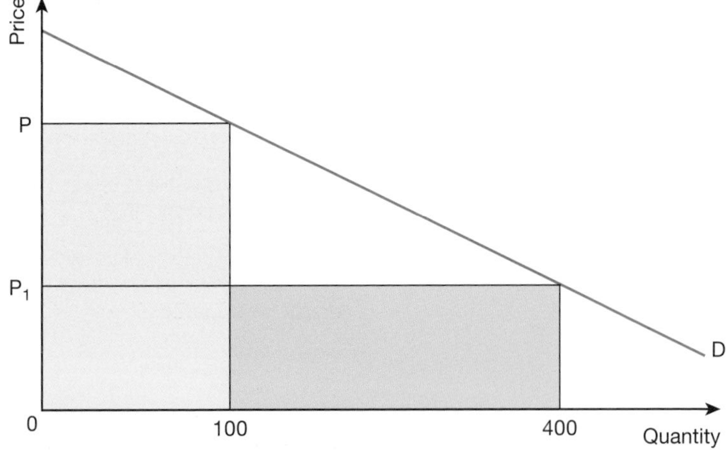

Figure 7.35 Second-degree price discrimination ▲

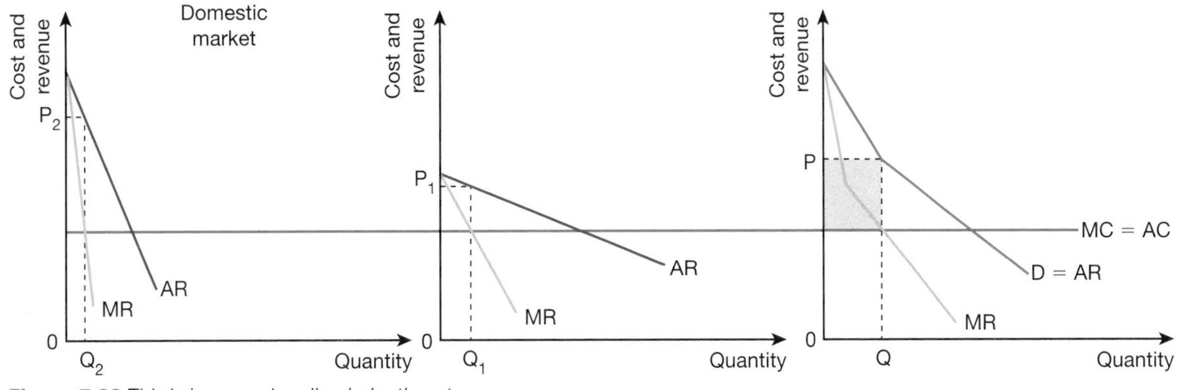

Figure 7.36 Third-degree price discrimination ▲

Issues surrounding price discrimination

It is not possible to make a definitive judgement as to whether price discrimination is in the public interest. Table 7.10 identifies some of the issues.

Table 7.10 Price discrimination ▼

Producers benefit from higher revenue and profits ✓
Welfare loss for individuals as consumer surplus is removed ✓
Some individuals now paying a higher price for the product ✓
Some individuals pay a lower price than previously ✓
Some low income earners may now be able to afford a product that was previously out of their reach ✓
Profits earned by companies may be used to finance R&D which may ultimately benefit consumers in terms of new or better-quality products ✓
Charging some individuals higher prices might enable organisations to provide equipment which benefits all consumers. For example, charging high fees to private patients for operations may enable hospitals to purchase equipment which will benefit non-paying patients

Activity

Price discrimination

Identify two examples of firms operating each of the types of price discrimination in your own country. Are these examples in the public interest?

Case Study

Price discrimination and the internet

The development of the internet has made it easier for individuals to compare prices in order to search for the best deal and so, in line with economic theory, as more perfect information becomes available, price discrimination by firms should become more difficult.

But is this actually the case? There is evidence that the internet actually makes it easier for firms to engage in price discrimination. For example, airline websites can now differentiate fares by date of booking and times of flights. It is not possible to buy such a ticket in one market and resell in another because government security measures mean that a passenger's name must match that on the ticket.

Currently a number of retail outlets, including booksellers, charge different prices for the same product depending on whether it is purchased in one of their stores or via the internet.

1. Explain the conditions necessary for firms to successfully practise price discrimination.
2. Using the information in the case study and your own research evaluate the extent to which the development of the internet might make price discrimination by firms more likely.

Monopoly and perfect competition compared

Price and output

It is often argued that a monopoly will charge a higher price and produce a lower output than is the case under perfect competition. Figure 7.37 analyses the issues.

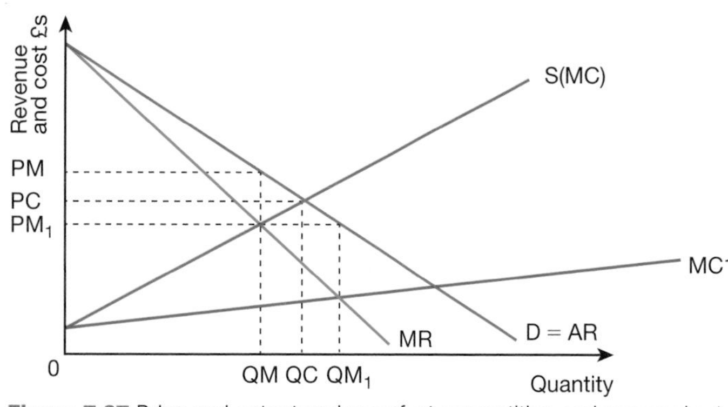

Figure 7.37 Price and output under perfect competition and monopoly ▲

The perfectly competitive industry will produce QC at price PC, which is the point where price equals marginal cost. If the industry is now taken over by a single firm so as to become a monopoly then AR is no longer equal to MR and we need to draw in a new MR curve below the AR curve. The monopolist will now equate MR with MC to give an output of QM and a price PM. This has resulted in a reduction in output and an increase in price.

> **Key term**
>
> **Efficiency**: the use of resources in the most economical or optimal way possible.

However, this assumes that when the perfectly competitive industry becomes a monopoly the cost curves remain the same. It is probable, though, that the monopoly will now be able to enjoy economies of scale, which will reduce costs. If this is the case it is possible that the MC curve will fall sufficiently (shown by MC_1) to intersect with the MR curve to give a higher output and lower price than in the perfectly competitive situation. This is shown by output QM_1 and price PM_1.

> **Link**
>
> See Chapter 6 page 137 for more on the various types of efficiency.

Efficiency

At this point it is useful to remind ourselves of the various types of efficiency.

Static efficiency is concerned with efficiency at a moment in time and incorporates productive and allocative efficiency.

Productive efficiency is achieved when Price = minimum AC.

Allocative efficiency is achieved when Price = MC. At this point consumer and producer surplus are at a maximum.

> **Key term**
>
> **X-inefficiency**: the inefficiency that can occur in a monopoly when production is not at the lowest point on the average total cost curve. It is where production takes place at a cost above the average and marginal cost curve due to a lack of strong competition in an industry and to organisational slack in a firm.

Technical efficiency and X-inefficiency

Technical efficiency is achieved when a firm produces the maximum possible output with given resources utilising the best available technology. Economists use the term X-inefficiency to describe the situation where technical efficiency is not present within a firm. This is often linked to the concept of organisational slack.

Dynamic efficiency refers to efficiency over time resulting from innovation and the development of new products.

> **Link**
>
> For further analysis of the concept of organisational slack see page 212 of this chapter.

Looking back at Figures 7.30 on page 181 and 7.32 on page 184 showing the long-run equilibrium positions of firms in perfect competition and monopoly, we can see that the perfectly competitive firm is both productively and allocatively efficient, while the monopoly firm is both productively and allocatively inefficient.

The analysis of allocative efficiency in perfect competition and monopoly is developed in Figure 7.38.

Under perfect competition the price will be PC and the output QC. The total consumer surplus is given by the areas 1 + 2 + 3 + 4 + 5 and producer surplus by 6 + 7 + 8. Consumer and producer surplus

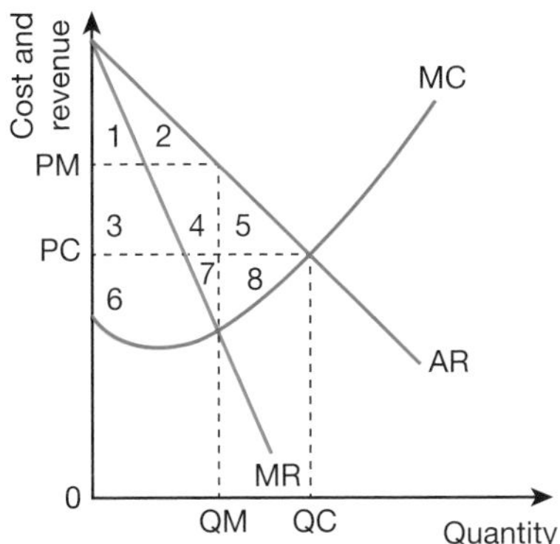

Figure 7.38 Allocative efficiency in perfect competition and monopoly ▲

are both at a maximum and so the industry is allocatively efficient. Consumer welfare is maximised. When the industry becomes a monopoly the output falls to QM and price rises to PM. Consumer surplus has been reduced to areas 1 + 2 and producer surplus has increased to 3 + 4 + 6 + 7. Not only has there been a redistribution of welfare away from consumers to producers, but there has been an overall loss of welfare of 5 (lost consumer surplus) + 8 (lost producer surplus). This is known as a *deadweight* loss in that it is completely lost to society. The area 5 + 8 is known as a *welfare loss triangle.*

Although the monopoly is neither allocatively or productively efficient, as we saw in Figure 7.37, it is possible for the monopoly to be more dynamically efficient than a perfectly competitive industry if it experiences economies of scale and uses its supernormal profits for research and development and the introduction of new products.

It is also the case, as we shall see later in this chapter, that some monopolies operate in markets which are contestable, which means that the behaviour of firms is closer to the competitive than monopoly models discussed.

Link

For an analysis of contestable markets see page 201.

Variety and innovation

It is sometimes argued that because a monopoly is the sole producer of a product with no competition there is no incentive to increase the variety of products, to innovate or undertake investment into the development of new processes and products.

However, an alternative argument is that the security from competition enjoyed by monopolies together with their supernormal profits means that they are prepared to take the risks and incur often massive costs associated with developing new products and innovations, because they know their market will still be there even if they fail. Firms in competitive markets may not be prepared to take the risks associated with such developments because of the risk of losing market share.

The A380 Airbus ▲

Examples of firms with some degree of market power that support this view include: Microsoft which continues to develop new versions of its Windows operating system and Office software; and the European airline corporation Airbus which invested $16 billion in the production of the A380, the world's largest passenger airliner, in an attempt to challenge Boeing's monopoly of the large airline market.

Link

For an analysis of price discrimination see page 184.

Price discrimination

As we have already seen, monopolies are in a position to practise price discrimination. The issues surrounding price discrimination and the public interest have been discussed on pages 185–7 of this chapter.

Monopolistic competition

As the name suggests, this form of competition has elements of both monopoly and perfect competition. Examples of monopolistic competition include hairdressers, solicitors, restaurants and garages.

Key terms

Monopolistic competition: a market with many firms producing similar but differentiated products.

Key term

Product differentiation: the process of creating real or perceived differences between products.

The main characteristics of monopolistic competition are:

- very large numbers of firms
- very large numbers of consumers
- product differentiation
- freedom (zero cost) of entry to and exit from the market.

The crucial difference between monopolistic and perfect competition is the fact that individual firms are producing similar but not identical products. An example would be hairdressers in a particular locality that offer essentially the same service, but may provide a different range or quality of service. Product differentiation may simply be in packaging. Hence an individual firm will have a monopoly of its own product although the product may have a great many similar substitutes. This means that consumers may have some degree of loyalty to a particular firm or brand. For example, a family may always have their cars serviced at a particular garage because it has provided a reliable, quality service over a number of years.

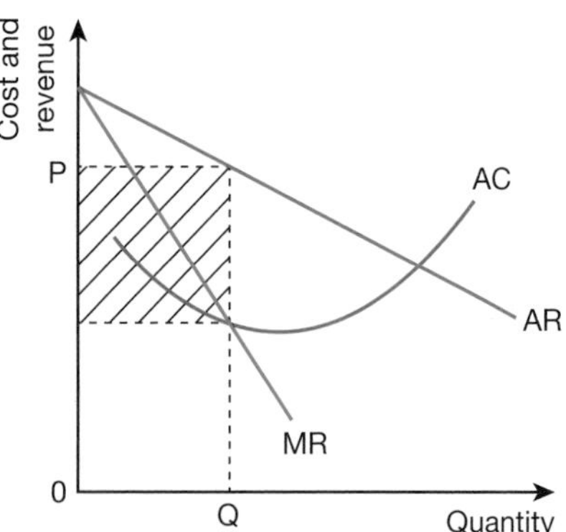

Figure 7.39 Short-run equilibrium for a firm in monopolistic competition ▲

This all means that the demand curve facing an individual firm in an industry will be downward sloping. If the garage mentioned above raises its price it will lose some market share, but not all, as some people remain loyal because of the quality of service. If the garage reduces its price then it is likely to attract more customers, but not the whole market because some consumers will remain loyal to other garages.

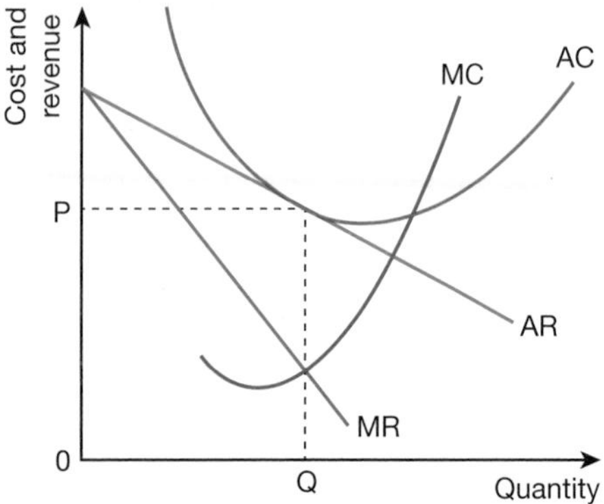

Figure 7.40 Long-run equilibrium for a firm in monopolistic competition ▲

At the same time, however, the demand curve will be relatively elastic because the nature of monopolistic competition is that there are many other firms providing similar substitutes.

Figure 7.39 shows the short-run equilibrium for a firm in monopolistic competition.

The profit maximising output is at Q where MC = MR, the price is P and the shaded area represents the firm's supernormal profit. Apart from the fact that the demand curve is significantly more elastic, the diagram is the same as that for monopoly. The difference, however, is that this is only a short-run equilibrium for the monopolistically competitive firm.

The supernormal profits will attract new firms into the industry. Assuming that the total demand for the product remains the same this increase in the number of firms will mean that the demand for any single firm's product will fall. As a result the individual firm's AR and MR curves will move inwards towards the origin until there are no further supernormal profits to attract new firms into the industry. This will occur when the AC curve is tangential to the downward-sloping AR curve. This is illustrated in Figure 7.40.

The final position has all firms charging the same price and so competition tends to be non-price, for example advertising, promotion, range and quality of service and after-sales service.

Activity

Monopolistic competition

Identify three firms in your area that operate in a monopolistically competitive market and explain the non-price methods they use to compete with their rivals.

Advantages and disadvantages of monopolistic competition

The advantages and disadvantages of monopolistic competition are summarised in Table 7.11.

Table 7.11 Advantages and disadvantages of monopolistic competition ▼

Advantages	Disadvantages
Wide variety of differentiated products	Price higher and output lower than in perfect competition
Prices likely to be lower and output higher than under monopoly	Price > MC – Allocatively inefficient
High levels of competition encourage firms to keep costs down	Price > minimum AC – Productively inefficient This also means firms have excess capacity. Because there are a large number of firms producing very similar products they are not producing at their maximum capacity (the minimum point on the AC curve). Consumers pay for this through higher prices
High levels of competition encourage firms to provide high-quality products	Non-price competition may be wasteful in terms of resources. E.g. advertising campaigns creating minor differences between products

Case Study

Product differentiation in the European low-cost airline market

In an attempt to increase revenue and take market share from its rivals such as Ryanair and Easyjet in the low-cost no-frills airline market, Flybe is introducing a number of proposals to differentiate its services from its competitors. These include:

- removing charges for paying for tickets by debit card
- different classes of tickets to give passengers more choice including one giving access to airport lounges
- increased frequency of flights
- in addition, Flybe hopes to gain a share of European markets by flying more planes under contract for larger airlines.

1. Explain what is meant by product differentiation.
2. Explain the likely effects of these proposals on Flybe itself and the low-cost airline market as a whole.
3. Explain the advantages and disadvantages of Flybe's proposals for consumers.

Key terms

Oligopoly: a market dominated by a few firms which are mutually interdependent.

Mutual interdependence: a characteristic of oligopolistic markets in which each firm is aware that any action it takes will have an impact on other firms and as a consequence will have to take this into account when making any decisions.

Oligopoly

In terms of value of output, oligopolies are the dominant form of market structure worldwide. An oligopoly is a market dominated by a few large firms each producing a large number of brands. Few in this sense is not an absolute number, but is linked to the concept of mutual interdependence. The number of firms in the industry is sufficiently low for each seller to have to take into account the actions and reactions from others in the market to any strategic decisions it might take. A few firms operating in a market will know that their prices and competition strategies are interrelated. If firm A is considering reducing its prices

Link

For more on barriers to entry see page 183 of this chapter.

or increasing its advertising budget in order to increase its market share it will know that other firms in the market are unlikely to take no action in response. Firm A is aware of this and needs to take the likely responses of its competitors into account in formulating its decision.

Oligopolistic markets are also characterised by high barriers to entry similar to those which exist in monopoly discussed earlier in this chapter.

Concentration ratios

Key term

Concentration ratio: the proportion of the output of a market dominated by a given number of firms in the market. For example, a four-firm concentration ratio measures the proportion of the output produced by the four largest firms in the market.

Activity

Concentration ratios

Identify the five markets in your own country that have the highest four-firm concentration ratios.

The extent to which a particular market might be regarded as an oligopoly is often measured through concentration ratios. The most commonly used are the four-, five- or eight-firm concentration ratios which measure the proportion of the market's output provided by the largest four, five or eight firms.

Table 7.12 identifies the ten markets with the largest five-firm concentration ratios in the UK.

Table 7.12 UK Concentration ratios ▼

Industry	Five-firm concentration ratio (%)
Sugar	99
Tobacco products	99
Oils and fats	88
Gas distribution	82
Confectionary	81
Man-made fibres	79
Coal extraction	79
Weapons and ammunitions	77
Soft drinks and mineral waters	75
Pesticides	75

The mutual interdependence and consequent uncertainty caused by having to take into account the possible behaviour of rivals in oligopolistic markets means that, unlike the other types of market structure considered earlier in this chapter (perfect competition, monopoly and monopolistic competition), there is no single model of the equilibrium for a firm in oligopoly.

This will depend upon how firms respond to the actions or anticipated actions of rivals and may change for a particular market over time.

Key term

Collusion: when firms come together to fix prices and output in a market.

Within oligopolistic markets there is a constant tension within an individual firm as to whether to collude with its rivals or compete with them. Collusion brings security and a guarantee of some market share, but is unlikely to enable an individual firm to maximise its profits.

Competition with other firms might bring about increased profits, but there is the risk of retaliation from other firms which might lead to a price war and eventual bankruptcy for the firm.

Analysis of the behaviour of firms in oligopolistic markets, therefore, needs to look at both collusive and non-collusive models.

Collusive oligopolies

Cartels

Collusion can take two forms – formal and informal. Formal collusion involves the creation of a cartel, which is an agreement between firms to fix price and output of a product and may also involve common marketing strategies. The most famous cartel in the world is OPEC in the oil industry.

Key term

Cartel: a formal agreement between firms to collude usually to fix prices and output.

In most countries cartels are illegal. A cartel may either operate as a multi-firm monopoly or set output quotas for individual members.

If it operates as a multi-firm monopoly it will seek to maximise the joint profits of the cartel. This is illustrated in Figure 7.41. The cartel will equate the overall MC of the members with the market MR curve to determine the profit maximising price and output. Competition among the members is then likely to be non-price as in monopolistic competition.

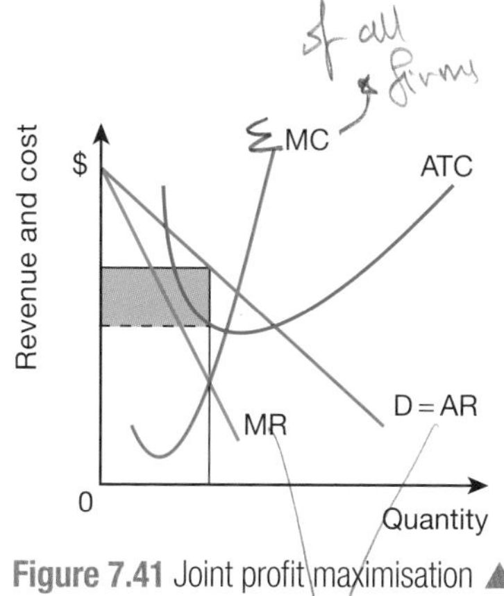

Figure 7.41 Joint profit maximisation ▲

The problem with this is that whilst the overall profit is maximised at this price, individual firms have different cost structures and so not all firms will be maximising their own profits and this can cause constant tension within the cartel. Firms within the cartel, particularly those with low costs relative to the other members, have an incentive to break ranks and increase their own output and sell at a lower price than that which maximises joint profits in order to increase their own profits.

From the point of view of the consumer the price is likely to be high because it will be set at a level which enables all firms, including the least efficient, to make a profit. They may, however, be beneficial if the cartel's supernormal profits are used to provide improved products.

An alternative to joint profit maximisation is for the cartel to set quotas as to the amount each member can produce and sell. The problem for the cartel here is to decide on a "fair" quota for individual companies.

There are a number of conditions necessary for a cartel to operate successfully. These include:

- a limited number of firms in the industry, all of whom are members
- similar cost structures for all firms
- high barriers to entry to prevent new firms entering the industry
- all firms obey the rules of the cartel
- a stable market – cartel agreements are likely to be vulnerable in times of recession when total demand in the economy is falling. This is a particular problem if the product is one with a high-income elasticity of demand
- the firms' produce very similar or identical products which will make agreements on price easier to establish.

Key term

Price leadership: a situation in an oligopoly where one firm sets or changes its prices and others follow.

Informal agreements – price leadership

Informal agreements normally involve some form of price leadership. There are three common models.

Dominant firm model

This normally involves firms following the lead of a firm which has a dominant position in the market in terms of its output and market share. Other firms will be likely to keep to the agreement for fear that if they do not their existence could be threatened by an aggressive pricing strategy by the dominant firm. Saudi Arabia, for example, is a dominant player in OPEC.

Barometric price leadership

This involves leadership by a firm that has consistently been seen to judge market conditions accurately over time and is, therefore, seen as a good "barometer" of market trends.

Parallel pricing

This involves firms in the industry making the same price changes at any given time.

Tacit collusion

A final type of informal agreement is tacit collusion, which occurs when it is recognised in the market that firms will follow certain established guidelines such as average cost plus or average variable cost plus pricing strategies.

Non-collusive oligopolies

In this situation individual firms set their price and output independently, but clearly they have to be aware of the responses of others. The result tends to be long periods of price stability with non-price competition being the norm, although occasional price wars break out as in the UK food retail market in 2011.

Case Study

Supermarket price war

UK grocery market share (February 2011)

Tesco	30.3%
ASDA	16.9%
Sainsbury's	16.5%
Morrisons	12.3%
Co-operative	6.7%
Waitrose	4.4%
Aldi	3.1%
Lidl	2.4%
Iceland	2.0%

In September 2011 Tesco's decision to abandon some of its range of free offers (e.g. "4 for the price of 3") and promotions and instead cut prices, threatened to spark of a price war in the grocery retail market. By marketing this move as providing increased value for money for consumers during the current hard times Tesco was expected by analysts to be the long-term winner in terms of profit and market share. It is anticipated, however, that there will be implications for other players in the market with Sainsbury's and Ocado, the home delivery firm, being hit hardest. Sainsbury's has responded by trialling a similar price reduction scheme in Ireland. Ocado, in an attempt to remove its image as an expensive alternative to traditional supermarkets, has responded by cutting prices on 600 products to make them on average 10 per cent cheaper than Tesco in order to attract more mainstream shoppers.

1 Discuss the likely impact of Tesco's actions on supermarkets in the grocery market and on consumers.

Key term

Kinked demand curve: in a non-collusive oligopoly an individual firm will believe that rivals will not follow any price rise that it makes, but will follow any price reductions meaning that the demand curve it faces will be price elastic for a price rise and price inelastic for a price fall and will, therefore, be kinked at the current price.

The kinked demand curve

One model of the behaviour of oligopolistic firms in non-collusive situations is given by the kinked demand curve developed independently by Paul M Sweezey in America and Hall and Hitch in the UK in 1939.

The kinked demand curve for an individual firm in an oligopoly is shown in Figure 7.42. The firm is initially operating at an output of Q with price equal to P. The firm is contemplating its future pricing strategy.

It would seem reasonable for the firm to assume, based on past experience, that if it reduces its price its rivals will do so also, so that the firm is unlikely to gain significantly from the move. For this reason the firm is likely to perceive its demand (AR) curve to be relatively inelastic. The demand curve D_1 illustrates this.

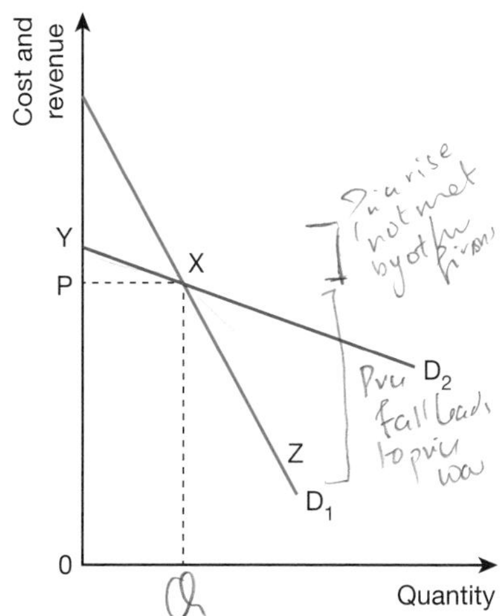

Figure 7.42 Kinked demand curve ▲

However, the firm is likely to believe that if it decides to increase its price its rivals are unlikely to follow suit, hoping by leaving their prices unchanged to increase their market share. Hence for a price rise the firm believes that it is likely to lose a significant amount of sales and in this case is likely to perceive its demand curve to be relatively elastic. This is illustrated by D_2. The overall demand curve that the firm perceives it is facing is a composite of the two demand curves. The overall demand curve is YXZ. The demand curve has a kink in it at point X.

As a result of this the price is likely to remain stable at P because the firm will reason that reducing the price will result in limited gains and might even provoke a price war which it could lose, and raising price will result in a substantial loss of market share.

The kinked demand curve can also be used to explain price stability in oligopolistic markets even in the face of rising costs. This is shown in Figure 7.43.

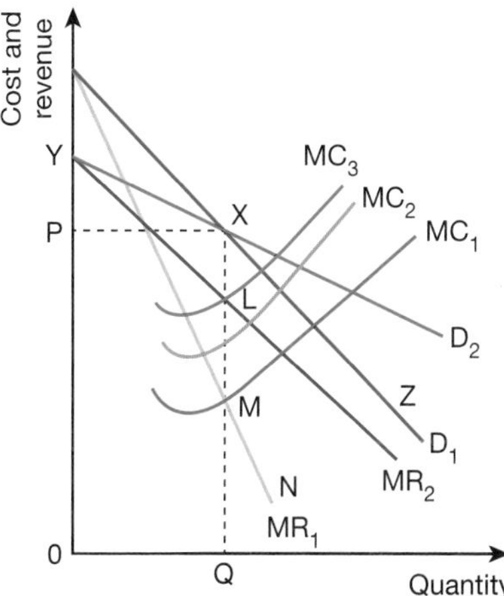

Figure 7.43 Kinked demand curve and rising costs ▲

In order to explain this we need to first of all draw in the MR curve associated with the kinked demand curve. We have established earlier that the MR curve for a price making firm will always be below the AR curve and will fall at twice the rate. Clearly it is not possible for a single continuous MR curve to fall at twice the rate of the kinked AR curve. Hence the MR has a discontinuity in it, LM, at output Q.

Up to output Q the demand (AR) curve is YX and so the MR curve associated with it is YL. Beyond output Q the demand (AR) curve becomes XZ and so the MR curve associated with this is MN. The MR curve, therefore, has a step or discontinuity in it at output Q equal to LM. The overall MR curve is YLMN.

We know that the profit maximising firm will always produce the output at which MC = MR, hence if the MC curve rises within the discontinuity LM, the profit maximising output and associated price will remain unchanged at Q and P respectively. Only if the MC curve rises to intersect with the MR curve at a point above L will the profit maximising price and output change.

Key term

Non-price competition: alternatives to price reductions as methods used by firms to increase market share, e.g. advertising, after-sales service.

Criticisms of the kinked demand curve

Almost immediately the kinked demand curve model attracted criticism, mainly in that it fails to explain how the firm determines the original price and output and also that it assumes firms in oligopolies always operate in the same predictable ways over time. In addition it does not take into account the fact that there is much non-price competition in oligopolistic markets.

Case Study

Oligopoly – the UK petrol market

In 2011 it was estimated that supermarkets such as Tesco, Sainsbury's, ASDA and Morrisons accounted for 45 per cent of UK fuel sales from just 1316 sites, an increase of 8 per cent on the previous year. In 2011 Tesco was the leading fuel retailer with over 15 per cent of the market.

Large oil companies such as BP, Shell, Esso and a number of the small independents argue this is the result of predatory pricing by the supermarkets that have reduced their profit margins on fuel to act as a loss leader to encourage customers into stores to buy high-margin groceries.

Some argue that this shift in the market is reducing choice in that that the number of retail fuel outlets is decreasing markedly. Now there are only 8480; in 1966 there were over 40000. However, many argue that consumers have the right to purchase fuel at the best prices possible.

1 Evaluate the case for and against the trends in the fuel market described.

Activity

Market structures compared

Construct a table comparing the following characteristics of the four market structures in perfect competition, monopolistic competition, oligopoly and monopoly:

- number of firms
- entry to industry
- type of product
- pricing policy
- profit levels
- non-price competition
- productive efficiency
- allocative efficiency
- technical efficiency and X-efficiency and X-inefficiency
- relationship between AR and MR.

Provide an example of each.

Game theory

Developed by John Von Neumann and Oscar Morgenstern in 1944, game theory involves the analysis of the strategies adopted by rational players (individuals, groups, firms or even nations) in situations when each player must make decisions in the knowledge that the final outcome (payoff) will depend on the reactions of other players and where the first player knows the other is thinking in the same way. Game theory has been applied to an enormous range of activities and aspects of human behaviour including wars, chess, driving, choosing a

Key term

Game theory: the analysis of strategies and decision-making by rational players in any activity or situation in which those involved know their decision will have an impact on other players and the way these other players are expected to react will affect the original decision made.

Game theory ▶

marital partner and selling a house. It has applications across a range of disciplines including both the physical and social sciences.

All games, however, have the common features that they are played out in an environment of uncertainty, interdependence and often conflicts of interest amongst the players.

At the highest level, game theory strategy involves some extremely difficult mathematics well beyond the requirements of A Level Economics and so we will concentrate on relatively straightforward two-player zero-sum games where one player's gain must equal the other player's loss.

> **Key terms**
>
> **Zero-sum game**: a game of pure conflict in which one player's gain will equal the other player's loss.
>
> **Prisoner's dilemma**: in game theory a competitive situation in which attempts by two or more firms, individuals or groups to find the best strategy for themselves by acting independently, results in a worse final outcome than if they had colluded or worked co-operatively.

The prisoner's dilemma

The most famous and often quoted example of game theory strategy is the prisoner's dilemma. In this example two individuals Yuchen and Xin have been arrested on suspicion of having committed a very serious crime, which carries a maximum prison sentence of ten years.

Yuchen and Xin are being detained in separate parts of the prison and have no way of communicating with one another.

The chief of police meets with each in turn and speaks to them in the same way:

"I have sufficient evidence to send both of you to prison for three years if neither of you confesses. However, if you alone are prepared to confess to the crime you will receive a light sentence of one year and your partner will receive a prison sentence of ten years.

If both of you confess you will both receive a sentence of five years".

What should Yuchen and Xin do? What is the best strategy for each in these circumstances?

The possible strategies for each are indicated in the two-player pay-off matrix below.

> **Key term**
>
> **Two-player pay-off matrix**: in game theory, a table showing the outcomes (pay-offs) for two players of their respective strategies or decisions.

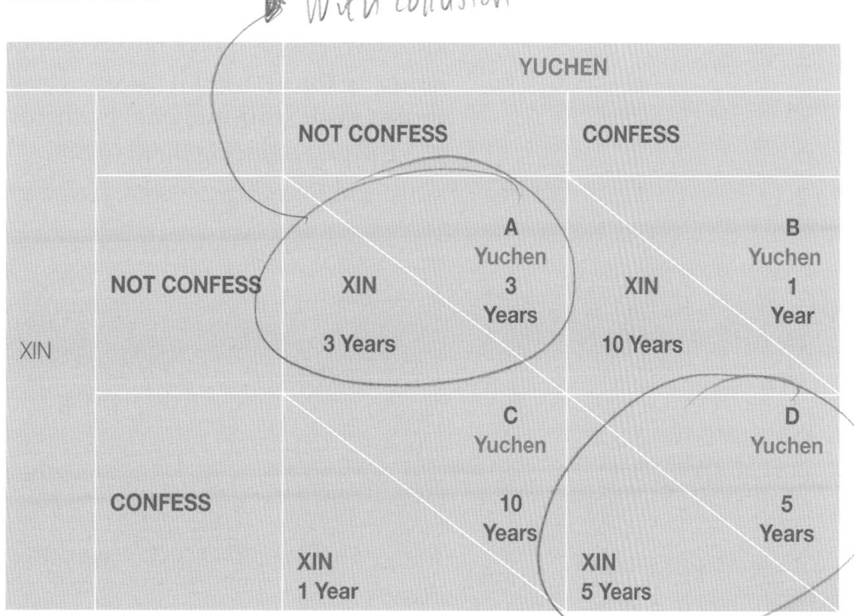

		YUCHEN	
		NOT CONFESS	CONFESS
XIN	NOT CONFESS	A Yuchen 3 Years XIN 3 Years	B Yuchen 1 Year XIN 10 Years
	CONFESS	C Yuchen 10 Years XIN 1 Year	D Yuchen 5 Years XIN 5 Years

Figure 7.44 The prisoner's dilemma

Let us begin with Yuchen. He will reason as follows.

It is best that I confess because in the best case scenario I will receive a light sentence of one year if Xin does not confess and in the worst case scenario I will receive a sentence of five years rather than ten years in prison if Xin also confesses.

Xin will follow the same path of reasoning and also conclude that the best strategy is to confess.

The final result is that both Yuchen and Xin will confess and receive a sentence of five years each as illustrated in quadrant D of the matrix.

Clearly this is not the best outcome (pay-off) for Yuchen and Xin. The best outcome would be for them to co-operate or collude and both agree to not confess as illustrated in quadrant A, which would give them a lighter sentence of three years. However, in the absence of any ability to communicate with one another this is unlikely, and even if they could communicate with one another they would each have to trust in the other's willingness to stick to the deal.

John Nash ▲

Game theory and oligopoly

The application of game theory to the behaviour of firms in oligopolistic markets is most closely associated with the work of the Nobel Prize winner in Economics for 1994, John Nash.

Let us take the example of a duopoly in the low-cost airline market. In this case the two firms, Batflight and Swing Airlines, are the players, the game takes place in the market and the pay-off is the expected final profit for each firm resulting from their respective strategies.

Currently both airlines are charging the same fare, $100 return on a particular route. We assume that they are not prepared to co-operate with one another and are independently considering the impact if they reduce fares on the route to $90 on their profits.

In deciding whether to leave fares at $100 or lower them to $90, each airline will need to take into account the likely response of the other airline to the decision it makes. The pay-off matrix below shows the profits made (in $ millions) by the two firms as a result of leaving fares at $100 and reducing them to $90.

		Batflight	
		Keep fares at $100	Reduce fares to $90
Swing Airlines	Keep fares at $100	A Batflight $30m Swing $30m	B Batflight $35m Swing $15m
	Reduce fares to $90	C Batflight $15m Swing $35m	D Batflight $20m Swing $20m

Figure 7.45 Pay-off matrix for Batflight and Swing ▶

Current profits for each firm are indicated in quadrant A.

If we begin with Batflight and assume that it decides to adopt a conservative approach anticipating that whatever strategy Batflight chooses, Swing will adopt a counter strategy which is best for itself but worst for Batflight, then under these circumstances Batflight should reduce its fares.

Maximin strategy

> **Key terms**
> **Maximin strategy**: in game theory a conservative strategy chosen by a player which provides the best of the worst possible outcomes of a decision.
> **Maximax strategy**: in game theory a strategy chosen by a player which provides the best of the best possible outcomes of a decision.

The reason is this. If Batflight reduces its fares to $90 and Swing leaves its fares unchanged then Batflight's profits will rise to $35 million as shown in quadrant B. If on the other hand Swing responds by reducing its fare to $90 also, then the worst that can happen to Batflight's profits is that they will be reduced to $20 million, which is obviously better than the reduction in profit to $15 million if Batflight had left its fares at $100. This particular conservative strategy is referred to as the maximin strategy.

Maximax strategy

An alternative approach that Batflight might take is a more optimistic, if riskier, strategy known as the maximax strategy which assumes that Swing will respond to any move by Batflight which leads to the most advantageous outcome in terms of profits for Batflight. In this case Batflight would assume that Swing would leave its price unchanged whatever move Batflight made.

However, this maximax strategy would still give the same result. It is still best for Batflight to reduce its fares to $90 as this would result in the position shown in quadrant B with Batflight's profits rising to $35 million.

As with the prisoner's dilemma example, the other player in this game, Swing, is faced with the same choice of strategies as Batflight and so if it plays the game rationally it will come to the same conclusion and will decide its best strategy is to reduce its fares whatever Batflight chooses to do.

> **Key term**
> **Dominant strategy**: in game theory a strategy which leads to the best outcome for a player irrespective of the strategy adopted by other players.

Dominant strategy

Whether the players adopt the maximin or maximax strategies the result is the same – both should reduce their fares and so reducing fares is a dominant strategy in that it is the best one for each player irrespective of that adopted by the other.

Nash equilibrium

> **Key term**
> **Nash equilibrium**: in game theory a solution in a non-co-operative situation in which each firm's best strategy is to maintain its present behaviour given the present behaviour of other firms in the market.

The final position in this game is shown in quadrant D with both airlines reducing their fares and achieving profits of $20 million. This position is known as a Nash equilibrium in that it is the best for each airline given the circumstances in which each finds itself, taking into account the likely decisions of the other, and as such neither airline will have any incentive to change its strategy unless the other does.

It is important to note that while this final position represents equilibrium by acting independently in a non-co-operative fashion, the airlines have failed to achieve the best possible outcome for themselves. This is shown in quadrant A with both firms leaving their fares at $100 and making profits of $30 million.

Collusion

However, if, as is likely in reality, this is not a single-move game but one which is repeated over time, it is likely that the airlines will come to realise that their mutual interests are best served by co-operating or colluding either tacitly or through a formal cartel (although the latter are illegal in most countries).

Link

See page 192 of this chapter for more on collusion.

However, as the pay-off matrix shows, there may still be incentives for one of the players to cheat and undercut the other in order to increase its own profits.

For collusion to be effective, therefore, there must be clear punishments or penalties for cheating that can be imposed for this together with a willingness and ability to implement them. For example, one reason for the OPEC cartel members maintaining their quotas once they have been agreed is that all members are aware that Saudi Arabia is in a position to flood the market with oil thereby significantly reducing its price which would penalise all members. Saudi Arabia actually took this action in the past.

One strategy which may prove effective in ensuring collusion in repetitive games is a "tit for tat" strategy. In this strategy a firm co-operates in the first round of moves, but makes it clear that it will only maintain this stance if all the other firms continue to co-operate. If other firms cheat then in the next round of moves the first firm will mimic the actions of the other firms in the previous round and cheat. This immediately punishes the cheats and ensures there are no long-term gains from cheating. This strategy has the advantage of providing a clear punishment without undermining the collusive agreement because the firm will only cheat if others do.

Game theory in oligopolistic markets conclusion

In this section we have only looked at two-player, single-move (non-repetitive), zero-sum games, but it is clear even from this that game theory provides a useful framework for analysing the behaviour of firms in oligopolistic markets. Not only does game theory provide an insight into the uncertain environment in which firms in oligopolistic markets operate, it highlights their mutual interdependence and the constant dilemma they face as to whether to collude or compete.

In the real world, however, games are far more complicated. Not only do most oligopolistic markets comprise more than two firms, but the firms within the market have more than a single strategy available to them to influence their profits. Within the low-cost airline market in our example the firms do not only have the option of changing their fares. There are also a number of non-price strategies they could adopt in addition or instead of changing prices, such as higher baggage allowances, speedy check-in and on-board services such as free meals, films or extra leg-room.

It is also the case that not all games are zero sum, involving total conflict in that one player's gain is the other player's loss. In reality, games and strategies may involve mutual if not always equally distributed gain. For example, in our airline example it might be that at the same time as Batflight and Swing are planning their price strategies the size of the market is expanding and as a result there may be opportunities for both airlines to benefit. More complex game theory models have the scope to incorporate all of these additional complications.

However, it is important to remember that game theory assumes that all players act rationally in the economic sense when planning their strategies and executing their decisions and as we have seen in our earlier discussion of behavioural economics this may not always be the case.

Contestable markets

Contestable market theory was developed by William Baumol in 1982 to explain why in some monopoly or oligopolistic markets, firms may operate in a competitive manner which will enable consumers to obtain the benefits of economies of scale and lower prices as well as reducing the welfare losses associated with markets dominated by a few firms. The equilibrium position for a firm in a contestable market will be closer to that predicted by perfect competition than monopoly or oligopoly.

Key term

Contestable market: a market or markets in which there is the threat of potential competition in the future, in which case even though an existing firm may currently have a monopoly position it may decide to act more like a perfectly competitive firm (in terms of price and output strategy) in order to deter such competition. The lower the entry and exit costs the more contestable the market.

In the theory of contestable markets, it is not the number of firms in the industry, the actual level of competition, which is important in determining the behaviour of firms within it, but the threat of potential competition from new firms possibly entering the industry.

If an incumbent firm in a monopoly or oligopoly market believes that by fixing high prices and earning supernormal profits there is the possibility that this will attract new firms into the industry who might take over the market, then it might set prices equal to or relatively close to average costs to prevent this from happening. This strategy of setting a price below that which will maximise a firm's profits in order to deter new entrants into the market, is known as limit pricing. In order for it to be successful it is necessary for the incumbent firm to have an accurate knowledge of the cost structure of potential entrants. This will enable it to set a price below the minimum average costs of potential new entrants, which would mean that they would be unable to set a price which would enable them to make a profit. Limit pricing may also have the advantage of making it less likely that a monopoly firm would attract the attention of a country's competition regulator.

Key term

Limit pricing: a strategy adopted by a monopoly or oligopoly of setting prices below that which will maximise profits in order to deter new entrants.

Clearly the extent to which a market is contestable will depend upon how easy it is for new firms to enter the industry and so an absence of barriers to entry or low barriers to entry are crucial in determining this. It is also important for any prospective new entrant that the product is standardised and that they have access to the same technology as established firms.

There must also be no collusion between existing firms.

Key term

Barriers to exit: obstacles which make it difficult or expensive for a firm to leave an industry.

Barrier to exit

However, it is not only the ease of entering the market that is important. Any prospective new entrant needs to plan for the eventuality that its attempt to enter a particular market may fail and that it will be forced out of the industry by the existing firms. The costs for the firm if it has to exit the market, therefore, need to be considered. Sunk costs are those costs which cannot be recovered if a firm goes out of business and may act as a barrier to exit. If entering the market involves the purchase of expensive capital equipment which could not be diverted to other uses or sold if the firm goes bankrupt, then this expenditure represents a sunk cost. If the risk of potential sunk costs is perceived by the firm as great this is likely to deter it from entering the market.

Hence the lower the perceived risk of high sunk costs the more contestable the market is likely to be.

A characteristic of contestable markets is "hit and run" competition. If an incumbent firm in the industry raises its price significantly above AC in order to increase profits to earn supernormal profits, the absence of barriers to entry will attract new firms into the industry who will remain, offering lower prices as long as there are profits to be made. When the incumbent firm reduces its price the new entrants leave. In order to avoid the possibility of hit and run competition the existing firm in the industry will have to keep prices close to AC.

It is important to remember that it is the threat of competition not the actual competition that forces firms to be productively efficient.

Contestable market theory has been used by some governments as an argument for reducing regulatory and legal barriers to entry to some industries in order to increase competition.

Predatory pricing

The extent to which contestable markets can be applied to the real world is questioned by some economists. It is unlikely that a market will be free from sunk costs. Any new firm entering a market is likely to have to undertake extensive advertising and promotion costs at the outset which will be irretrievable. It is also likely that there will be some barriers to entry, either innocent in the form of economies of scale for existing firms, or ones deliberately created by incumbents such as mergers and takeovers, limit and predatory pricing.

Key terms

Merger: the process by which two independent firms come together to form a new company. This will normally involve one company taking over the other through the purchase of shares.

Predatory pricing: a firm setting extremely low prices, often below average costs of production, in order to force competitors out of the market and enable a firm to exploit increased monopoly power in the market by raising prices in the future.

Differing objectives of the firm

Up to now, in considering the traditional theory of the firm, we have assumed that firms have one single objective: profit maximisation. However, with developments such as the growth of modern public limited companies, particularly multinational companies, with large numbers of stakeholders economists have called this assumption into question.

Case Study

Taxis – a contestable market

Is the market for taxis a contestable market?

In theory, yes this should be the case. Costs of entry to the market should be low, all that is needed is a car, and there are rarely any large-scale incumbents in a particular area.

However, completely unregulated markets can cause problems, in terms of congestion, exploitation of consumers, and health and safety issues.

In response to this many countries have introduced licensing systems to regulate quality and ensure fair pricing.

To operate a taxi in Rome or Mumbai drivers are required to live in the geographical area.

London taxi drivers must pass a test to be licensed, but this can take up to four years to complete.

In Tehran any private car can pick up passengers.

In New York a medallion system operates which imposes a cost for a permit for a company to run taxis in the city within certain laid down rules. If a driver breaks these rules he is banned and the medallion is suspended.

However, so lucrative is the market that medallions have been known to sell for $1 million.

1 To what extent can the taxi markets in these examples be regarded as contestable?

It is now recognised that not only may large corporations find it difficult to maximise profits even if they wished to, but they may pursue other goals instead of or in addition to profit maximisation.

We will look at these issues and some of the alternative theories that have been put forward concerning the objectives of firms.

Difficulties in maximising profits

The traditional theory of the firm is that the firm will maximise profit at the output where MC = MR. This presupposes, however, that the firm can actually calculate its MR and MC. In order to calculate the MR curve the firm needs to be able to accurately estimate the position and elasticity of its demand (AR) curve, which is extremely difficult. Calculating MC accurately poses similar difficulties. There is also the issue of whether firms should use short run or long marginal costs. All these difficulties are compounded in extremely large multinational companies producing an extremely wide range of products.

There is some evidence to indicate that rather than using MC and MR to fix price and output firms adopt more simple strategies such as applying a percentage mark up to average costs. This is known as cost plus pricing.

> **Key terms**
>
> **Divorce of ownership and control**: the fact that a public limited company is owned by one group (shareholders) and controlled and run by another (managers).
>
> **Principal–agent problem**: in large public limited companies the divorce of ownership and control may mean that principals (shareholders) may have different objectives from the agents (managers) and principals cannot guarantee that their agents will operate in the principals' best interests.

Alternative objectives of firms

Managerial theories

It is often argued that within large public limited companies there is a divorce of ownership from control, which is a result of what economists refer to as the principal–agent problem. The owners of the company, the principal, are the *shareholders*, but because they do not have the skills, specialist knowledge or expertise to effectively run the organisation they normally appoint *managers* (*agents*) to run the company and exercise day-to-day control. This principal–agent relationship is thus characterised by asymmetric information in that the agent knows more about the business than the principal.

This may lead to a divorce of ownership and control which could produce a situation in which managers/agents pursue their own goals and objectives which may not be entirely consistent with or in some cases opposed to the interests of the shareholders/principal.

Shareholders will wish to make the maximum income possible from their investments and so they will wish the firm to maximise profits.

However, managers may have different objectives. It is assumed that managers will wish to gain the maximum satisfaction or utility from their work. This may be derived in a number of ways, e.g. salary, power, prestige, size of the organisation, growth of the organisation, perks and fringe benefits, discretionary expenditure, etc.

Modern managerial theories attempt to take into account these possible objectives of managers.

Although profit maximisation may not be the primary objective of managers they cannot ignore profit entirely. If profits are too low managers may be replaced at the company's AGM. It is also possible that if profits are too low shareholders may sell their shares, depressing the share price, which might possibly lead to a hostile takeover bid which would also threaten the managers' positions. As a result, purely to ensure their own survival, managers are likely to ensure that a minimum acceptable level of profit for shareholders is achieved before pursuing their own aims. This is known as "profit satisficing".

In addition many firms adopt share and profit sharing schemes for managers, which will increase the incentive for them to pursue profit as one of their objectives.

Key term

Sales revenue maximisation: an alternative theory of the objectives of a firm which assumes that managers aim to maximise sales revenue as opposed to that of the traditional theory which assumes firms aim to maximise profit. Also known as "sales maximisation".

Activity

Sales revenue maximisation

Draw a diagram to demonstrate that if a firm attempts solely to maximise sales revenue it will produce a higher output at a lower price than if it attempts to maximise profits.

Sales revenue maximisation

This theory of the objectives of firms was first developed by William Baumol and argues that managers wish to maximise their salary and perks. There is some evidence to suggest that managers' pay and conditions are linked to the size of the company, which is in turn linked to the sales revenue of the firm rather than profits. If the sole aim of the firm was sales revenue maximisation then the firm would produce the output at which MR = 0. Price would be given by AR at this output. The output will be higher and the price lower than the profit maximising position. In reality the managers are likely to ensure that at least a satisfactory profit is made to please shareholders, which means that the firm is likely to maximise revenue subject to a minimum profit constraint. This would take the price and output closer to the profit maximising position.

The issue for managers in this model is identifying the minimum acceptable level of profit.

Managerial utility maximisation

Oliver Williamson argued that managers attempted to maximise their utility (satisfaction) from their role subject to achieving a minimum level of profit. He argued this utility was derived from factors such as:

- salary
- numbers of staff controlled
- perks such as cars
- freedom to exercise discretionary expenditure on own projects.

One prediction of his theories was the idea of organisational slack or X-inefficiency, which refers to the fact that average costs are likely to be higher as a result, for example, of managers' fringe benefits such as unnecessarily expensive company cars.

Growth maximisation

This theory was put forward by Robin Marris who argued that, subject again to a minimum profit constraint, managers would attempt to maximise their utility, but saw this measured in terms of the size and rate of growth of the organisation.

Organisational or behavioural theories of the firm

Organisational theories were developed in the late 1950s and 1960s as a result particularly of work by Herbert Simon and Cyert and March.

These theories recognise that modern organisations have a range of internal and external stakeholders including managers, workers, trade unions and customers. These stakeholders are likely to have a range of different interests which may differ over time and at times may conflict with one another. For example, customers will wish for quality products at low prices while shareholders may wish for high profits. Managers will thus have to prioritise objectives at any one time. It is likely that the final result will involve bargaining among the stakeholders with the final outcome depending on relative bargaining strengths of those involved.

One feature of these theories is the prediction that firms will practice satisficing behaviour, aiming for a minimum level of attainment of a number of objectives in order to keep as many stakeholders as possible happy. The firm is thus seen to be pursuing multiple goals rather than a single objective as in the traditional theory of the firm. The importance of particular objectives may change over time in the light of market conditions and relative bargaining strengths.

Key term

Satisficing: a situation in which a firm aims for a minimum level of attainment of a number of objectives.

Organisational theories also predict that organisations are likely to experience organisational slack associated with inducements provided to ensure certain stakeholders' agreement, which will raise the firm's costs.

Activities

Stakeholders

1. Identify a large public limited company in your country, identify the main stakeholders it has and explain what their primary interests are likely to be.
2. Explain how these interests might conflict with one another and how this might affect the firm's behaviour.

Other goals of firms

It is also possible that some organisations may have a range of more altruistic goals. Increasingly firms have to consider the environment. Co-operatives may wish to help consumers or producers as in the "fair trade" movement. State run enterprises such as the NHS in the UK, may be concerned with providing a service for the public.

Growth of firms

As we have seen earlier in this chapter there can be considerable advantages growing in size, particularly in terms of economies of scale, and for some managerial theorists this can be regarded as a key objective of managers.

A firm may grow in two ways; internal or organic growth or external growth.

Key term

Internal or organic growth: increase in the size of a company through increasing sales and innovation.

Internal growth

Internal or organic growth is the result of increasing sales which can either be through selling within an expanding market or increasing existing market share through advertising, promotion or price competition.

However sales are increased, it will be necessary for the firm to grow in size, to increase its productive capacity. In order to increase productive capacity investment will be required. It is likely that a mixture of innovation, invention and the introduction of new products will be crucial to internal growth.

Internal growth is usually financed through retained profits, borrowing or the issue of shares.

External growth

External growth is achieved by firms merging or taking over another firm. It is possible to identify four types of merger or integration.

Key terms

External growth: growth through takeovers and mergers.
Integration: the merger of two firms; this can be vertical, horizontal, lateral or conglomerate.
Horizontal integration: mergers of firms at the same stage of production or producing the same product.
Vertical integration: mergers of firms at different stages in the production process.

Horizontal integration involves firms at the same stage in the production process or producing the same product merging together. An example of this is the takeover by Virgin Active, a health club company, of Esporta Gyms for £77.6 million in April 2011. This acquisition meant that Virgin active almost doubled its size, enabling it to increase its market share, increase its range of geographical outlets and reap economies of scale. Lloyds TSB's takeover of HBOS gave it an increased share of the UK mortgage market and a branch network in Scotland.

Vertical integration involves the merger of firms at different stages in the production process. Vertical integration can either be backward towards earlier stages in the supply chain or forward to later stages in the supply chain. A wine merchant buying a vineyard would be an example of backward vertical integration to ensure a source of supply, while the same company purchasing a wine shop or wine bar to ensure an outlet for their product would be an example of forward integration. Vertical integration is common in the oil industry where companies such as Shell and BP are involved in every step in the production, processing and distribution through the process of acquiring oil wells, refineries and outlets for their products. In addition to providing guaranteed sources of supply of raw materials and outlets for their final products which gives a firm some control over both production costs and selling prices, vertical integration is a way for a firm to establish monopoly power in an industry. Of course such monopoly power may have adverse consequences for consumers.

The major disadvantage for the firm is that such mergers may be expensive.

Key terms

Conglomerate integration: mergers of firms producing unrelated products.

Lateral integration: mergers of firms producing similar products.

Conglomerate integration occurs when a firm takes over or merges with other companies in completely unrelated fields. These were common in the US in the 1960s, but are relatively uncommon today. Motives for such mergers include managerial ambition, a desire to expand without contravening any national monopoly legislation, diversification to reduce risk, and the possible benefits that can be derived from shared research and development. Like vertical integration, however, conglomerate mergers can be costly.

Lateral integration occurs when a firm merges with another in a similar field. An example might be a hotel chain taking over a chain of restaurants.

Activities

Integration

1 Identify one example of each type of integration in your own country.
2 Construct a table that summarises the advantages and disadvantages to the firm of the different types of integration.

Survival of small firms

Despite the fact that there are many advantages that accrue to a firm as a result of growth in size, in most countries there are significant numbers of small firms particularly in areas such as farming, car repair, hairdressing and local food stores. The main reasons for the survival of the small firm are summarised below:

- low start-up costs in many areas
- an individual's desire to be their own boss
- the market for the product may be small or highly localised, e.g. a village store
- large-scale production requires the product to be of a standard design. If the market is for a very high-quality product of individual or customised design then a small firm may be better placed to provide, for example, customised jewellery
- small firms may be able to survive by supplying component parts to large organisations
- a small firm may be en route to being very large, e.g. Google started off as a small company
- governments may provide financial support for small firms in some countries.

Activity

Small firms

Identify a small firm operating in your area and explain the factors that enable it to continue its operations.

Key concepts

- **Scarcity and choice** is considered in the sections in this chapter on marginal utility theory and indifference curve analysis which explain how individuals allocate their limited income across all products so as to maximise their satisfaction. In addition the sections on market structures explains how firms in different competitive situations allocate their scarce resources (factors of production) in making price and output decisions which achieve their differing objectives.
- **Margin and change** runs throughout the chapter, but is particularly evident in the sections on consumer decision-making behaviour (marginal utility theory and indifference curve analysis) and the price and output decisions of profit maximising firms in different market structures. The section on behavioural economics explores situations in which consumer behaviour may appear to be irrational and sub-optimal.
- **Equilibrium and efficiency** is particularly evident in the sections on consumer decision-making behaviour and the equilibrium of the firm in different market structures. The different types of efficiency are specifically addressed and the levels of efficiency of firms under different market conditions are compared when looking at the behaviour of firms in these different market structures.
- **Progress and development** is addressed at the microeconomic level when looking at why firms might grow in size, the methods (internal and external) by which they might do so and the economic consequences of such growth for the firm and the economy as a whole.

Summary

After completing this chapter you should be able to:

- understand marginal utility theory and how it can be used to explain the downward-sloping demand curve
- explain indifference curves and budget lines together with the income and substitution effects of price changes for normal, inferior and Giffen goods
- explain the limitations of marginal utility theory and indifference curve analysis as explanations of consumer behaviour
- explain "rational behaviour" as economists use the term
- explain the contribution of behavioural economics to the study of irrational consumer decision-making
- explain how production in the short run is determined by the law of diminishing returns
- explain how production in the long run is affected by economies and diseconomies of scale
- explain the link between production in the short and long run and short- and long-run costs

- explain the concepts of firm and industry
- understand the importance of profit as an objective in the traditional theory of the firm
- explain the main features of the main forms of market structure
- explain the relationship between elasticity of demand, marginal, average and total revenue for a downward-sloping demand curve
- explain, compare and evaluate the conduct of firms in different market structures in terms of pricing and non-price policy, price discrimination, price leadership and in oligopoly mutual interdependence
- explain, compare and evaluate the performance of firms in different market structures in terms of output, profits, efficiency, barriers to entry, price and non-price competition and collusion
- understand why firms may pursue alternative objectives to profit maximisation, including the difficulties involved in maximising profits and the principal–agent problem
- explain why and how firms grow in size and why small firms continue to survive.

Exam-style questions

Data response and essay questions

1 Evaluate the extent to which the law of diminishing marginal utility provides an explanation of the normal downward-sloping demand curve. [25 marks]

2 a Explain the possible implications of the divorce of ownership and control in the modern large corporation. [12 marks]

b Explain ONE theory of the objectives of the firm which has been developed as an alternative to the traditional theory of the firm which assumes a firm's sole objective is profit maximisation. [13 marks]

3 a Define average fixed costs, average variable costs, average costs and marginal costs. [12 marks]

b Explain the factors affecting the shape of a firm's average cost curve in:

i the short run

ii the long run. [13 marks]

4 With the aid of diagrams compare the long-run equilibrium of a firm in perfect competition with one in monopolistic competition. [25 marks]

5 Evaluate the view that monopoly is always against the public interest. [25 marks]

6 a Explain what is meant by the term "rational consumer" as used by economists. [12 marks]

b To what extent does behavioural economics provide an explanation of actual consumer decision-making? [13 marks]

Multiple-choice questions

7 Which of the following is ΔTC/ΔQ? [1 mark]

A Average cost
B Average fixed cost
C Average variable cost
D Marginal cost

8 Which of the following is a characteristic of monopolistic competition? [1 mark]

A In the long run firms produce at the minimum point of their average cost curve
B In the short run firms can make supernormal profits
C There are barriers to entry into the industry
D Firms produce homogeneous products

8 Government microeconomic intervention

In this chapter you will develop your knowledge and understanding of:

- policies to achieve efficient resource allocation and correct market failure
- equity and policies towards income and wealth redistribution
- labour market forces and government intervention
- government failure in microeconomic intervention.

Policies to achieve efficient resource allocation

Application of indirect taxes and subsidies

Indirect taxes and subsidies can be used to achieve efficient resource allocation and to correct market failure. Indirect taxes can be used to discourage the consumption of certain products and subsidies can be used to encourage the consumption of certain products. Chapter 3 dealt with the impact and incidence of taxes and subsidies.

Link

Pages 76–80 of Chapter 3 deal with the application of indirect taxes and subsidies.

Prices and output decisions under nationalisation and privatisation

Nationalisation and privatisation were covered in Chapter 3.

Nationalisation involves the creation of a monopoly. This is a situation where there is just one firm in an industry and this firm can control the supply of the product in the market.

If such a monopoly is in the private sector, the market is likely to be inefficient because there will be a lack of both productive efficiency and allocative efficiency.

Key term

Efficiency: the use of resources in the most economical or optimal way possible.

This inefficiency can be seen in Figure 8.1.

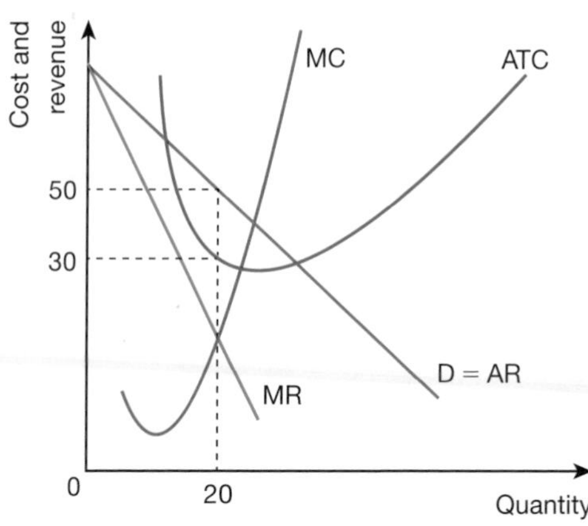

Figure 8.1 Productive and allocative inefficiency in a monopoly ▲

Link

Pages 81–4 of Chapter 3 deal with nationalisation and privatisation.

In a situation of perfect competition, the equilibrium would be where demand and supply intersect, i.e. where the demand or average revenue curve crosses the marginal cost curve. In this situation, the equilibrium quantity would be higher and the equilibrium price would be lower than in a situation of monopoly.

Link

Pages 183–5 of Chapter 7 deal with monopoly.

In a situation of a private sector monopoly, the firm would produce at the profit maximising output where marginal cost and marginal revenue are equal. This can be shown in Figure 8.1 by a price of P and a quantity of Q. The effect of this is that a monopoly firm will therefore make supernormal or abnormal profits.

Link

Pages 137–41 of Chapter 6 deal with productive and allocative efficiency.

In this situation, there is neither productive or allocative efficiency in the market. Productive efficiency would occur at the lowest point of the average total cost curve, but it is clear in the diagram that this is not the case. Allocative efficiency would occur where price was equal to marginal cost, but it is clear in the diagram that this is not the case either. This is why a private sector monopoly is regarded as being inefficient and therefore an example of market failure.

Getting it right

Make sure that you know how to clearly distinguish between productive and allocative inefficiency in a monopoly.

X-inefficiency

There is an additional form of inefficiency that can occur. This is known as X-inefficiency. This can sometimes be referred to as organisational slack resulting from a firm having such a dominant position in a market. There will be a gap between the firm's average cost curve and the lowest possible cost that could be achieved. It results from the lack of competition in the market.

Progress question

1 Explain why a private sector monopoly firm can be regarded as inefficient.

Activity

X-inefficiency

Write down three examples that you can think of where a private sector monopoly could allow costs to be higher than they could be as a result of the lack of competitive pressure.

It is clear from the above that price and output decisions in a private sector monopoly are likely to create market failure because price will be higher, and output lower, than in perfect competition.

However, to avoid such a situation from occurring, a government can decide to run a monopoly firm as a state enterprise. This will enable price to be lower, and output to be higher, than in a private sector monopoly, but the state will need to ensure that this is indeed the case.

Case Study

The Thailand tobacco state monopoly

The Thai government has decided to operate the tobacco industry in the country itself and has established the Thailand Tobacco Monopoly. This state enterprise has a monopoly in Thailand over the manufacture and distribution of cigarettes in the country.

Before the establishment of this state enterprise, there had been a number of rival companies producing cigarettes in the country, but these were no longer allowed to exist. The government's argument was that such a monopoly would bring about a greater degree of efficiency. Many consumers, however, have argued that the lack of competition between producers has led to a situation of higher prices and lower quality than would have been the case if competition had been allowed to continue.

1 Explain why the establishment of TTM could be seen as an example of market failure.

Privatisation

A policy that could be used to try to reduce market failure is to encourage the privatisation of firms or industries. With greater competition in a market, price is likely to be lower, and output higher, than would otherwise be the case. Privatisation broadly means the transfer of the ownership of an economic activity from the public sector to the private sector, but the term can actually be used to refer to a number of different activities.

Table 8.1 indicates the range of activities that can be included as examples of the privatisation process.

Table 8.1 The different forms of privatisation ▼

Economic activity	Meaning of activity
Sale of assets	This is where a nationalised firm or industry is sold to the private sector, a process that is often termed "denationalisation". The firm therefore ceases to be state owned and becomes a private sector company, usually a public limited company, in which shares can be bought.
Deregulation	This process occurs when the regulations, rules, controls and laws that are imposed by the state on a firm or an industry are removed. This allows a much greater degree of competition to take place in the market.
Contracting out	This is where the extent of public sector control is reduced by allowing private sector firms to be involved in certain parts of an operation. There is also the possibility of bringing in private sector firms to provide some of the funding; some countries have specific initiatives to encourage the private sector to provide some of the funding (in the UK, two of these are PFI (Private Finance Initiative) and PPP (public private partnerships).
Franchising	This process occurs where a private sector firm may be allowed to bid for a franchise to operate a particular part of an industry.

Link

The advantages and disadvantages of privatisation are shown in Chapter 3 page 83.

Progress question

2 Explain the differences between the various forms of privatisation that can take place in an economy.

Activity

Privatisation

Find out the extent to which privatisation has taken place in your country or a country of your choice.

Case Study

Privatisation in Pakistan

In recent years a number of industries in Pakistan have been privatised, either completely or to a large extent.

One of these is the telecommunications industry. The Pakistan Telecommunication Company Ltd (PTCL), established in 1947, used to be completely run within the public sector and owned by the government of Pakistan. Since 2006, however, the firm has been partially privatised so that in 2012 a total of 38 per cent of the ownership was in private hands. A total of 26 per cent of the shares are controlled by a company in the United Arab Emirates, Etisalat, and 12 per cent are controlled by the general public in Pakistan.

The consumers in Pakistan have benefited greatly from this partial change in ownership. For example, the cost of a telephone call from Karachi to Lahore in 2012 was 5 per cent of what it was before the change in ownership. The workers in the firm, however, were less pleased. They were concerned that some of them would lose their jobs and that those who kept their jobs would receive a cut in their wages. There were protests and strikes by the firm's workers against the partial privatisation.

Another industry in Pakistan that has been partially privatised is banking. In 2012, 85 per cent of banking was controlled by private banks, compared with only 10 per cent in 1990. The efficiency of the private banks is generally believed to be significantly greater than that of the former public sector banks. The country's central bank, the State Bank of Pakistan (SBP), however, remains under government control.

1 Discuss the possible advantages and disadvantages of privatisation in such industries as telecommunications and banking.

Case Study

Privatisation in Jamaica

The privatisation process began in Jamaica in the 1980s and it has carried on ever since. Over 100 businesses in a variety of industries have been privatised during this period and these have included maintenance of parks, street cleaning and rubbish collection, Trans-Jamaican Airlines, public services and the Jamaica Broadcasting Corporation.

Governments in Jamaica have repeatedly stressed the importance of this process of privatisation to the greater efficiency of economic activity on the island. Creative entrepreneurship has been encouraged and it is believed that this will contribute to a higher rate of economic growth.

Jamaican governments have stressed that the process of privatisation is part of a wider strategy to liberalise the Jamaican economy, creating a more competitive and market-driven economic environment.

1 Explain how privatisation can contribute to more efficient economic activity in Jamaica.

Link

Chapter 3 includes a section on prohibitions and there is a case study in the form of a ban on alcohol advertising in South Africa.

Key terms

Prohibition: a situation where a certain product is banned in a country.

Licence: a situation where permission is given, often by a government, but where the permission is limited or restricted in some way.

Prohibitions and licences

Another policy to achieve efficient resource allocation and to correct market failure is the use of prohibitions and licences.

A prohibition is a ban on certain products being available in an economy, i.e. a particular product is made illegal in an economy.

A licence, on the other hand, gives a government the power to have some control in an economy by granting permission to certain suppliers to produce something, but the licence will limit the freedom of the producers or suppliers in some way. For example, in many countries, it is necessary to obtain a licence before starting a new business. Obtaining a licence will then give an entrepreneur the opportunity to operate a business in a particular city or state. People in certain occupations will need to obtain a licence before they can conduct business.

Property rights

Market failure could arise in an economy because of a lack of clear property rights. If ownership is clear, there is less likely to be a problem because of private property rights. For example, rubbish is unlikely to be dumped on a person's property because that person, in such a situation, would be most likely to take legal action.

> **Key term**
>
> **Property rights**: a situation where owners of economic goods have a right to decide how such assets are used.

However, in certain aspects of an economy, such property rights are not so clear, such as in relation to air, water and certain open spaces. In these situations, there are common, not private, property rights.

In such situations as these, a government could pursue a policy of extending property rights to include the air, rivers and the sea. If voluntary agreements were unsuccessful, a government could decide to introduce a system of pollution permits.

Pollution permits

A pollution permit (or tradeable permit) is an example of a licence that is issued by a government. The licence allows a firm to pollute, but only up to a certain level. The amount of pollution permitted by the licence will be less than what is being emitted at the moment and so in this way a government can reduce the level of pollution in an economy. Over a period of time, it is likely that successive licences will only permit a reduced amount of pollution and so, therefore, pollution will be progressively reduced.

> **Key term**
>
> **Pollution permit**: a licence for a firm to bring about a reduction in the level of pollution over a period of time.

> **Activity**
>
> **Pollution permits**
>
> Find out as much as you can about the different kinds of pollution permits that exist in your country.

Information

A government could try to increase the availability of information to consumers in an attempt to influence their economic behaviour. If consumers are to maximise their satisfaction or utility, then they will need to have the necessary information in order to make appropriate decisions. If consumers do not have perfect information, it is unlikely that they will make the most rational decisions. Information failure is a major cause of market failure and if there is a lack of full and appropriate information in an economy, then the allocation of scarce resources in that economy is likely to be less efficient than it would otherwise be.

A government, therefore, can decide to improve the quality and accuracy of information that is made available to consumers in an economy. For example, information about the advantages of the consumption of merit goods could be improved and be made more readily available. Also, information about the disadvantages of the consumption of demerit goods could be improved and be made more readily available. A particular example of this would be in relation to the application of "nudge" theory.

Behavioural insights and "nudge" theory

Behavioural insights into the achievement of resource allocation and the correction of market failure emphasise the importance of the actual behaviour of people in an economy. This is in contrast to the traditional approach that is based on the idea that a consumer will act in a rational way.

Nudge theory is a particularly good example of this behavioural insight into economic behaviour. The theory is based on the idea that the economic behaviour of people can be "nudged" in a particular direction. An example of this would be in relation to the discouragement of the consumption of demerit goods. Governments in some countries, for example, include a warning about the possible effects of consuming cigarettes. This could be in the form of a relatively mild nudge, such as when a packet of cigarettes includes on it the warning "smoking can damage your health". A stronger nudge could occur, however, if the wording was changed to "smoking can kill".

Key term

Nudge theory: an attempt by a government to alter the economic behaviour of people in some way.

Link

Nudge theory is also discussed on page 166 in Chapter 7.

Similar examples can be found in relation to the consumption of alcohol. A government might decide to nudge consumers in a particular direction by including wording such as "drink sensibly", both on the product and in the advertising of the product. In some countries, the government will support a Drink Aware campaign where consumers of alcohol are informed about the possible dangers to their health of excessive consumption.

Getting it right

It is important that you can clearly recognise that a nudge is an attempt to influence economic behaviour, but it is not the same as a ban.

Progress question

3 To what extent is the behaviour of individuals likely to be "nudged" in a particular direction by government intervention in an economy?

5

Regulatory bodies, deregulation and the direct provision of goods and services

Regulation

Regulation refers to the different laws, rules and controls that can be used by a government to reduce the extent of market failure. There are various examples of such regulation.

Key term

Regulatory bodies: organisations that are set up to enforce particular policies and regulations in an economy.

Regulation of monopolies

A government may decide to introduce a policy on mergers and acquisitions. For example, if a proposed merger was thought to be against the public interest, such as severely restricting the extent of choice for consumers, then the government could use a regulatory body to prevent the merger from taking place.

A government could use a law or a rule to insist that if a monopoly firm did exist, it would need to guarantee that a minimum quality would apply to the good or service being provided by the firm.

A government could insist that there needed to be a certain amount of competition in a particular market. For example, it could instruct a regulatory body to ensure that no one firm should control more than a specified share of a market.

Case Study

Competitive environment in Malaysia

In 2010, two laws were passed in Malaysia, the Competition Act and the Price Control and Anti-Profiteering Act, which were designed to establish a more competitive environment in the country's economy. The aim is to reduce anti competitive practices as much as possible. Consumers should be able to benefit from greater innovation, improved service and more competitive prices.

Neighbouring countries, including Indonesia and Singapore, had already established various regulations and laws to encourage competition in their economies and Malaysia, having taken 15 years to bring these two laws into effect, was keen not to be left behind.

1 Explain the different ways in which countries, such as Malaysia, Indonesia and Singapore, could encourage competition in their economies.

Activity

Competition

Use the Internet to find out as much as you can about the ways in which Malaysia, Indonesia and Singapore have attempted to encourage competition in their economies.

Case Study

Control of monopolies in Argentina

The first anti-monopoly law in Argentina dates back to 1923. The main reason for the introduction of the law was to prevent monopolies operating against the public interest and producing very large profits. The law was further strengthened in 1946 and 1980. Fines can be imposed against firms who are found to be acting in an anti competitive manner.

The law, however, has been criticised for limiting free market initiative in the country. Some of the firms that have been fined have argued that the large profits would be used to fund research and development into new products and into new, and more efficient, methods of production.

1 Discuss the arguments for and against the regulation of monopolies.

Protection of the environment

A government could use taxes to discourage certain forms of production, and subsidies to encourage other forms of production, but it could also use regulation to reduce the level of pollution in an economy. For example, some governments have passed laws giving regulatory bodies the right to fine companies if they are found guilty of polluting the environment.

Case Study

Air quality regulation in the USA

The Environmental Protection Agency, the federal body in the USA responsible for oversight of environmental issues, has introduced a regulation called the Cross-State Air Pollution Rule (CSAPR). The regulation requires states to reduce emissions that contribute to pollution. For example, sulphur dioxide emissions must be no more than 27 per cent and nitrogen oxide levels must be no more than 46 per cent of what they were in 2005.

The Environmental Protection Agency claims that CSAPR will prevent as many as 30 000 pollution-related premature deaths and yielded between $120 billion and $280 billion per year in health and environmental benefits.

The regulation has been criticised by consumers, however, who have pointed out that the cost of implementing the regulation will be higher prices for them. It has been estimated that prices could rise by as much as 20 per cent. There is also a concern that some power plants may be forced to close, leading to a loss of jobs.

1 Discuss the possible advantages and disadvantages of introducing a regulation to limit the amount of pollution in a country, such as the USA.

Consumer protection

In some countries, the government has passed laws which give consumers certain rights. These can cover the description of products being sold, such as ensuring that the descriptions of products are accurate and honest, or the weight of something being consumed.

Case Study

Consumer protection in Sri Lanka

In Sri Lanka, the Consumer Affairs Authority (CAA) is the main government institution with responsibility for protecting consumers against unfair trade practices and safeguarding what might be considered a fair degree of market competition in the country.

The Compliance and Enforcement Division within the CAA investigates complaints made by individual consumers or by consumer organisations. The majority of disputes are usually settled through a process of discussion and negotiation, but if an agreement cannot be reached, the dispute will need to be settled in a court.

Complaints relating to financial products can be referred to the Financial Ombudsman scheme which was established in 2003.

1 Discuss the advantages of consumer protection to consumers, such as those in Sri Lanka.

Transportation

Regulations could be put into operation to control different forms of transportation in a country. This could cover all forms of transportation, including air, rail, road and water.

Activity

Regulation of the market

Find out as much as you can about the different kinds of regulation that exist in your country.

Case Study

Airport regulation in the UK

In the UK, air transport is regulated by an organisation called the Civil Aviation Authority. This body has the power to regulate the take-off and landing charges at UK airports and the number of passengers each year that can use a particular airport.

One airport in the UK, Stansted, experienced a 32 per cent fall in the number of passengers using the airport between 2007 and 2012.

The owners of Stansted airport have argued that if the regulations imposed by the Civil Aviation Authority were to be removed, it would be able to double the number of passengers it can handle from 18 million to 36 million each year. The owners have stated that if the airport was allowed to expand, it would take pressure off other busy airports in the London area, such as Heathrow and Gatwick. The managing director of the airport has stressed that there should be less regulation and more competition, arguing that this would help to keep costs down for both passengers and airlines.

The Civil Aviation Authority, however, has stressed that it has important functions to perform in relation to different forms of regulation, including airspace policy, air traffic control, safety regulation and consumer protection.

1 Discuss the advantages and disadvantages of the regulation of airports, such as Stansted, to consumers.

Progress question

4 To what extent is regulation likely to reduce market failure in an economy?

Deregulation

Deregulation has already been covered in Chapter 3 and the earlier part of this chapter. This is where there is a reduction in the number of rules, regulations and laws that exist in an economy. The aim is to allow a greater degree of competition to take place which should lead to a situation of greater efficiency. An example of this would be the telecommunications industry in the UK. At one point, British Telecom had a near-monopoly in the provision of telephone services, but then deregulation took place, removing many of the existing barriers to entry, and allowing new firms to enter the industry. The greater competition that then occurred led to an increase in efficiency in the industry.

Link

Page 84 of Chapter 3 deals with deregulation.

The direct provision of goods and services

Another way in which a government could attempt to achieve efficient resource allocation and to correct market failure in an economy is through the direct provision of goods and services.

Link

The direct provision of certain goods and services by a government has been discussed on page 81 of Chapter 3.

The extent of market failure could be reduced in an economy if a government decides to directly provide certain goods and services. Examples of such provision, as already discussed in Chapter 6, could include education and health care.

Equity and policies towards income and wealth redistribution

Equity versus efficiency

It is important to stress two particular objectives of government microeconomic policy: efficiency and equity.

Key terms

Efficiency: the use of resources in the most economical or optimal way possible.
Equity: the idea of fairness or justice, such as in terms of the distribution of output.

Efficiency

One reason why a government may intervene in a market to correct market failure is to establish a situation of economic efficiency. This has already been discussed in terms of productive and allocative efficiency.

Equity

Another reason why a government may intervene in a market to correct market failure is because of equity. Equity refers to the idea of fairness or justice. A market may be said to be efficient in terms of the production of a maximum output from a minimum of resources, but the distribution of this output may not be equitable or fair.

Getting it right

It is important that you can clearly distinguish between efficiency and equity.

A government may decide to intervene in a market to bring about a more equal distribution of income and/or wealth, such as through a progressive form of taxation. An alternative approach is through the use of subsidies, such as when these are used to keep down the costs, and ultimately the prices, of essential goods, e.g. certain items of food.

Link

Page 74 of Chapter 3 considers the meaning and effect on the market of maximum and minimum prices.

The problem, however, is that by intervening in a market in these various ways, a government is actually distorting the market. Such government intervention can therefore lead to allocative inefficiency.

Price stabilisation

Chapter 3 discussed maximum and minimum prices and their effect on a market, but price stabilisation could also include a buffer stock scheme.

Price stabilisation refers to a situation where action needs to be taken by a government when there are wide fluctuations in price, largely as a result of unplanned fluctuations in supply. This is a particular feature of agricultural markets where supply is affected by a variety of factors beyond control, such as bad weather, natural disasters and the effects of pests.

Buffer stocks

One way that a government could intervene in such a situation is through the establishment of buffer stocks. A buffer stock is where a reserve of a commodity is kept in order to stabilise prices in a market, so that the prices fluctuate within a given price range. When a surplus of a commodity is produced, the product is bought, adding to the buffer stock. When there is a shortage of the product, stocks can be run down.

Key term

Buffer stock: an amount of a commodity that is held to limit the range of price fluctuations in a market.

The effect of creating a buffer stock in a market can be seen in Figure 8.2.

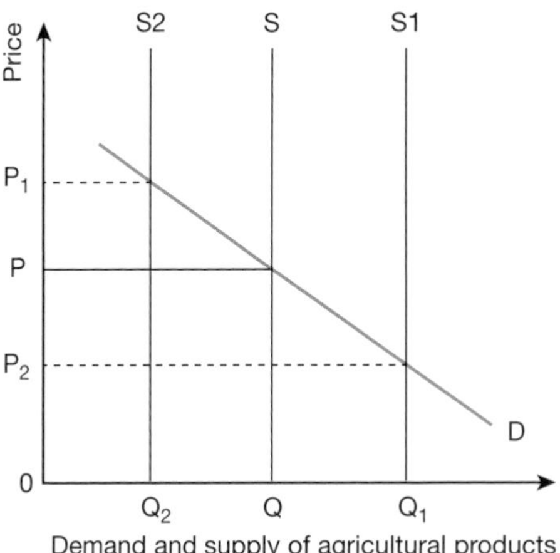

Figure 8.2 The use of a buffer stock in an agricultural market

The supply of an agricultural product in any one year will be perfectly inelastic. The supply in three years is shown by the supply curves S, S_1 and S_2. The government, in operating a buffer stock scheme, will want to maintain a price of P and a quantity of Q in the market.

In the year shown by the supply curve S_1, the equilibrium quantity would have been Q_1 and the equilibrium price would have been P_2. In this situation, the government would buy the extra output shown by the horizontal distance between Q and Q_1 and store it. This would keep the price at P.

In the year shown by the supply curve S_2, the equilibrium quantity would have been Q_2 and the equilibrium price would have been P_1. In this situation, the government would sell the extra output shown by the horizontal distance between Q and Q_2. This would keep the price at P.

Advantages and disadvantages of buffer stocks

There are clearly both advantages and disadvantages of a government operating a buffer stock scheme in a market, as Table 8.2 indicates.

Table 8.2 The advantages and disadvantages of a buffer stock scheme

The advantages of a buffer stock scheme	The disadvantages of a buffer stock scheme
It overcomes the problem of wide fluctuations in prices from one year to another.	It may not be easy for the government to establish what the equilibrium price in the commodity market should be. The producers will want the highest possible price to be maintained in the market whereas the consumers will want the lowest possible price to be maintained.
If prices can be stabilised through a buffer stock scheme, there will also be more stability in the incomes that producers, such as farmers, receive.	The cost of operating the buffer stock scheme will need to be paid by somebody. There may be different views about this. For example, the government may decide to pay for the scheme or it may want the producers to contribute to the cost.
This stability in incomes will encourage producers to make long-term plans.	There may be problems if there is a succession of good harvests. For example, it may be difficult to store all of the stock and there may also be concerns about the perishability of the stock. On the other hand, if there is a succession of poor harvests, it may not be possible to store enough supplies.

Progress question

5 Discuss the advantages and disadvantages of using a buffer stock scheme to bring about greater price stability in a market.

Benefits

Benefits can be paid to people on low incomes in order to increase their disposable income. There are two main types of such benefits: universal benefits and means-tested benefits.

Universal benefits

Universal benefits are paid to every person who is entitled to such a benefit irrespective of their income or wealth. Such benefits have the advantage of providing money to people without having to ask them a lot of questions which could be seen as an invasion of privacy, but they also have the disadvantage of providing money to people who might not really need it. They could therefore be regarded as being somewhat wasteful of public expenditure.

> **Key term**
> Universal benefit: a benefit that is paid to everybody who is entitled to it, irrespective of their income and wealth.

Means-tested benefits

An alternative form of benefit is called a means-tested benefit. This literally means that certain people are tested, by asking them questions, to see if they have sufficient means to pay for certain things; if they can prove that they need additional funds, then they can receive the benefit. Such benefits have the advantage of targeting those people who are most in need of additional funds. As has been indicated above, a disadvantage is that a lot of questions will need to be asked and people might find this very intrusive and embarrassing. Perhaps the most significant disadvantage of means-tested benefits is that they can give rise to what has been called the poverty trap.

> **Key term**
> Means-tested benefit: a benefit that is paid to those people who are entitled to it, taking into account their income and wealth.

> **Link**
> The poverty trap is covered in Chapter 3 page 78.

Transfer payments

A transfer payment is usually paid to an individual by a government. It does not involve any productive effort, i.e. it is not a reward for any output produced. Examples could include a welfare payment or a pension. Transfer payments can be a very useful way to bring about a redistribution of income.

> **Getting it right**
> It is important that you do not confuse transfer payments with transfer earnings.

Progressive income taxes, inheritance and capital taxes

The tax system

The tax system can be used to bring about a redistribution of income and wealth in an economy.

> **Key term**
> Redistribution of income and wealth: government policy which normally involves taking money from the wealthier members of an economy, usually through taxation, and giving it to those on lower incomes often through benefits, pensions, etc.

Progressive income taxes

Certain taxes, such as a tax on income, can be structured to not only take more of a person's income as they earn more, but a higher percentage of that income. This is achieved by having different amounts of income or thresholds; as a person earns more money, the rates of tax can be increasingly higher. For example, a country could have tax thresholds at 10 per cent, 20 per cent, 30 per cent, 40 per cent and 50 per cent (or even higher!).

> **Link**
> See page 307 in Chapter 10.

This system of taxation is known as progressive taxation, i.e. those people earning higher incomes pay not just more tax, but a higher proportion of their income in tax. The average rate of tax that a person pays will increase as they earn more money. It is also the case that with a progressive system of taxation, the marginal rate of tax will be higher than the average rate of tax.

Inheritance taxes

Whereas income tax, as the name suggests, is a tax on the income earned by a person in the form of a wage or salary, an inheritance tax is a tax not on earned money, but on the value of an inheritance. For example, in the UK in 2012, if a person inherited wealth, such as in the form of a property, that person would need to pay inheritance tax of 40 per cent on the value of the property worth over £325,000.

> **Key term**
> Inheritance tax: a tax that is paid on the value of an inheritance, e.g. a property.

Capital taxes

A capital tax is one that is payable on the gain in value when an asset is sold. An example is the capital gains tax in the UK.

> **Key term**
> Capital tax: a tax that is paid on the increase in value of an asset between when it is bought and when it is sold, e.g. a painting.

Tax credits

Another way in which a government could attempt to redistribute income and wealth in an economy is through tax credits. A tax credit is actually a payment from a government to an individual or to a family.

> **Key term**
> Tax credit: a payment from a government to an individual or a family that is dependent on income.

Examples of tax credits could include a child tax credit, if a person is responsible for a child or a young person, and a working tax credit, if a person is employed but receiving a low wage. The actual payments depend on the income; the lower the income, the more tax credits a person can get.

In the USA earned income credit is given to people on low income and the actual amount is dependent on the number of children that they have. Once a person earns above a certain income, the credit is phased out. It is indexed to the rate of inflation. Other examples in the USA include child credit, investment tax credit and work opportunity tax credit.

> **Getting it right**
> Make sure that you can demonstrate that you understand that a progressive system of taxation does not simply mean that a person pays more tax as they earn more, but that they pay an increasing proportion of their income as tax.

Case Study

Income distribution in Bangladesh

All countries in the world have, to varying degrees, an unequal distribution of income and wealth. The table below indicates the distribution of income in Bangladesh.

Division of population into five groups, each showing 20% of the population	Percentage of income held by that group of the population in 2011
Highest 20% of the population	41%
Second-highest 20% of the population	21%
Third-highest 20% of the population	16%
Fourth-highest 20% of the population	12%
Lowest 20% of the population	10%

1 Calculate the percentage of income held by the highest 40 per cent of the population.
2 Calculate the percentage of income held by the lowest 40 per cent of the population.
3 Discuss the measures that could be adopted by the government of Bangladesh to try to bring about a more equitable distribution of income.

Key term

Negative income tax: a system which brings together the payment of tax and the receipt of benefits.

Negative income tax

It will be clear from what has already been said that a government could assist in the redistribution of income and wealth in an economy through a system of benefits and taxes. One proposal, however, has been to combine benefits and taxes in one system.

The idea of a negative income tax involves the combination of the payment of income tax and the receipt of benefits in one system. The government would determine a particular income level and all people earning above that level would pay income tax, while all people earning below that level would not pay any income tax but would receive benefits.

The advantage of this scheme is that it would bring together the income tax and the benefits systems. It would also help make the labour markets more flexible by removing the poverty trap already referred to.

Activity

Average and marginal rates of taxation

A person earns $1000 a month. The person is allowed a personal allowance of $200 a month on which no tax is paid. The person then pays a tax rate of 10 per cent on the next $300 earned, a tax rate of 20 per cent on the next $300 earned and a tax rate of 30 per cent on the last $200 earned.

Calculate (a) the tax that the person pays in the month, (b) the average rate of taxation, and (c) the marginal rate of taxation.

Case Study

Negative income tax in Canada

The government of Canada has been thinking about the possibility of introducing a negative income tax in that country. It was first proposed in 1971.

The idea is that the government would determine a particular level of income. Any person falling below that "income line" would be given benefits in order to reach this "income line".

An advantage of such a scheme is that it would avoid a complicated system of benefit payments and make labour markets more flexible by eliminating the poverty trap. A disadvantage of such a scheme is that it would be difficult for a government to get everybody's agreement as to what the "income line" should be set at.

1 Explain what is meant by a negative income tax.
2 Discuss the advantages of a country, such as Canada, establishing a negative income tax.

Getting it right

Make sure that you understand that a tax credit is something that is given to a person, rather than a tax which involves taking money from a person.

Poverty trap analysis

If a person gains more income, perhaps by working longer hours, the means-tested benefits may be reduced, or even possibly withdrawn, because the person is less in need than was the case before. If this is the case, the person will be less inclined to earn more money; the means-tested benefit therefore operates as a disincentive to work longer hours and earn more money. This disincentive effect is known as the poverty trap.

It comes about because of the combined effects of the marginal rate of taxation paid on any additional income and the rate at which benefits are no longer payable. The tax threshold, at which a person starts to pay tax, may be quite low and the means-tested benefits can rapidly disappear as incomes rise. The overall effect, therefore, is that a person may possibly become worse off as a result of earning more money.

Progress question

6 Explain why a person may not necessarily be any better off as a result of working more hours and gaining a higher wage.

Gini coefficient and the Lorenz curve

The Gini coefficient

Key term

Gini coefficient: a statistical measure of the degree of inequality of income in an economy. The lower the figure, the more equal is the distribution of income.

A Gini coefficient is a way of measuring inequality in the distribution of income in an economy. It is measured by the ratio of the area between the diagonal and the Lorenz curve to the total area under the diagonal. The bigger this area, the more unequal the distribution of income.

It measures the extent to which the distribution of income in an economy diverges from the position of absolute or total equality. The lower the figure, the more even is the distribution of income. In many developed countries, the coefficient is around 0.3, but in developing countries it is likely to be closer to 0.5.

The Lorenz curve

Key term

Lorenz curve: a method of showing the degree of inequality in the distribution of income and wealth in an economy.

This is a graphical representation showing the extent of inequality in the distribution of income in an economy. The more unequal the distribution of income in an economy, the more divergent the Lorenz curve will be from the diagonal line of absolute equality.

Figure 8.3 shows how Lorenz curves can demonstrate the differences in the distribution of income in two countries, country X and country Y. The greater the degree of inequality, the further the Lorenz curve will be below the 45 degree line. It is clear that this is the case with country X, indicating that income is more unevenly distributed in country X than in country Y.

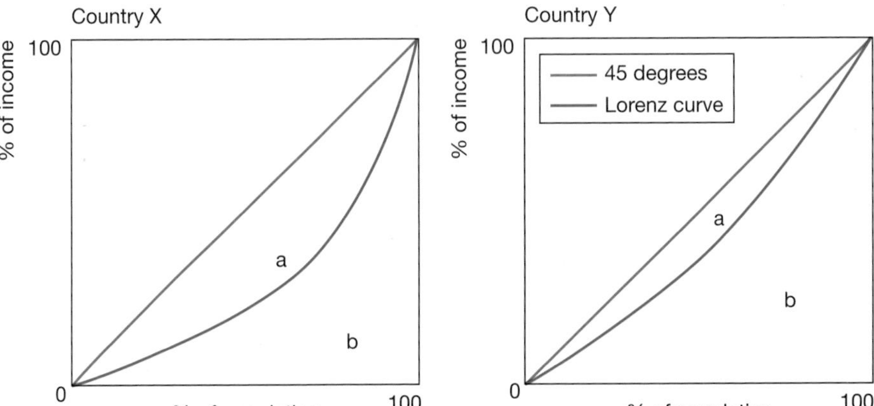

Figure 8.3 A comparison of the income equality in two countries ▲

Key term

Inter-generational equity: the degree to which differences in income in an economy can affect the incomes of people in the future.

Inter-generational equity

The inter-generational equity of income refers to the concept of fairness or justice between the incomes of different people in an economy over a period of time, i.e. the extent to which the distribution of income today can affect future generations. For example, increasing inequality in the distribution of income of relatively high-income countries, such as the USA, is quite likely to limit economic mobility for the next generation of young adults. In many countries, young people are, for the first time, experiencing a lower income than was the case with their parents once the figures have been adjusted for the effects of inflation.

Link

See Chapter 2 page 68 for more on derived demand.

Labour market forces and government intervention

The labour market – the demand for, and the supply of, labour

In this section we shall be concerned with the factors that affect the demand for and supply of labour. This will then enable us to look at the way in which wages are determined in competitive and non-competitive markets and explain the, often significant, differences in the wages paid to different individuals in different occupations and in different countries.

Factors affecting the demand for labour

The demand for labour is a derived demand. The demand for workers in a particular industry is necessarily dependent (derived) from the demand for the product which they help to produce. For example, teachers in a school are demanded because there is a demand from students to study their courses.

We begin by looking at the demand for labour by an individual firm.

The derivation of an individual firm's demand for labour using marginal revenue product theory

We have seen that a profit maximising firm will produce at the output where MC = MR. The principle is the same for a profit maximising employer in deciding on the demand for labour, the number of workers to employ.

The profit maximising employer will employ workers up to the point where the extra cost of employing an additional worker (the MC of labour) is equal to the additional revenue brought in from the worker's output (the MR of labour).

The MC of labour is equal to the wage rate (W)

The MR of labour is known as the marginal revenue product (MRP) and is equal to the extra output produced by the additional worker (the marginal physical product or MPP) multiplied by the additional revenue earned by the firm from this output (the MR).

Hence, MRP = MPP × MR

Key term

Marginal revenue product: the extra output produced by an additional worker (the MPP) multiplied by the additional revenue earned by the firm from this output (the MR).

If we assume that the final product is sold in a perfectly competitive market then as we have seen when looking at perfect competition all units of a product are sold at the same price and so this means that the profit maximising employer will employ workers up to the point where the wage rate equals the marginal revenue product of labour.

W = MRP

The demand curve for labour

> **Link**
>
> See Chapter 7 page 169 for an explanation of the law of diminishing returns.

We are now in a position to derive the demand curve for labour. We assume that the firm is operating in the short run and that labour is the only variable factor with all other factors fixed in supply. In the short run the law of diminishing returns will apply as increasing units of a variable factor are added to fixed quantities of other factors.

Consequently, as the number of workers employed is increased the MPP of labour falls. This is illustrated in Table 8.3 and Figure 8.4.

Figure 8.4 The MPP curve ▲

Table 8.3 Changes in marginal physical product ▼

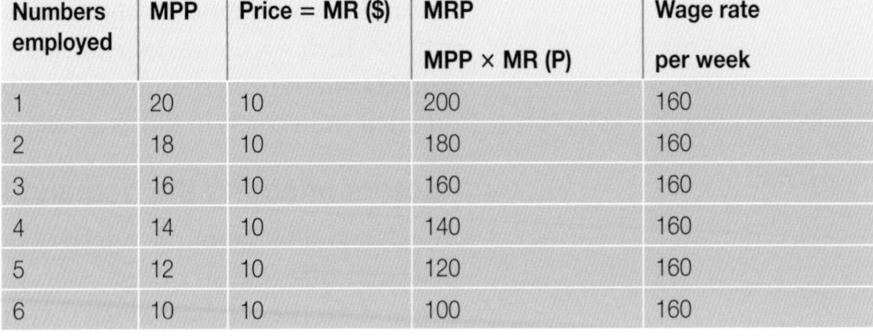

Numbers employed	MPP	Price = MR ($)	MRP MPP × MR (P)	Wage rate per week
1	20	10	200	160
2	18	10	180	160
3	16	10	160	160
4	14	10	140	160
5	12	10	120	160
6	10	10	100	160

If we now assume that all output is sold at $10 per unit, it is possible to calculate the MRP (Table 8.3) and draw the MRP curve which, because all output is sold at the same price, has the same slope as the MPP curve. Figure 8.5 shows the firm's MRP curve.

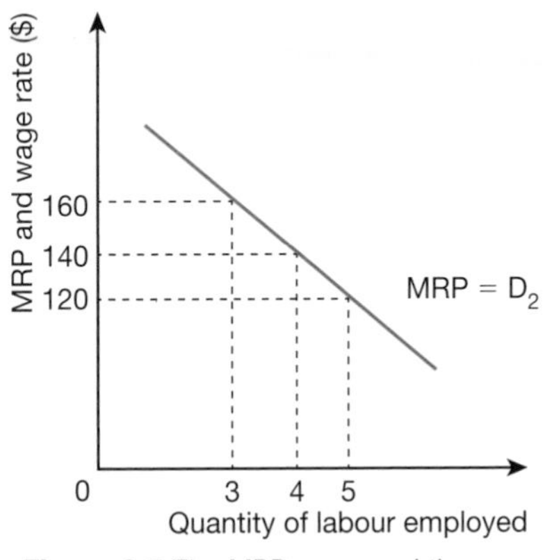

Figure 8.5 The MRP curve and the firm's demand curve for labour ▲

We are now in a position to derive the firm's demand curve for labour. We assume that the current wage rate is $160. The profit maximising employer will employ workers up to the point where W = MRP.

This means that if the weekly wage rate is $160, then three workers will be employed because W = MRP. The fourth worker brings in less in terms of MRP than the wage and so will not be employed.

If the wage falls to $140 this worker now brings in an MRP equal to the wage and so now will be employed. Similarly, if the wage falls to $120 per week then the employer will again fix employment levels where W = MRP and five workers will be employed.

At each wage rate the demand for labour will be at the point where the wage rate = MRP. The MRP curve thus shows the quantity of labour employed at each wage, which is the demand curve for labour.

Therefore **the firm's demand curve for labour is the MRP curve.**

Any change in the wage rate will bring about a movement along the firm's demand curve. A rise in wages will lead to a fall in the quantity of labour demanded and vice versa.

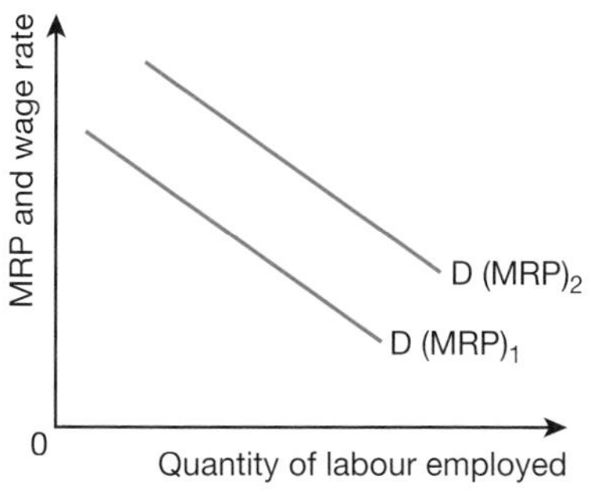

Figure 8.6 Shifts of the demand curve for labour ▲

A shift of the demand curve for labour will be caused by a change in the MPP of labour or a change in the price of the product. For example, if labour productivity increases (increasing MPP) or the price of the final product increases then the demand curve for labour will shift to the right from D $(MRP)_1$ to D $(MRP)_2$ as shown in Figure 8.6.

The industry's demand curve for labour will be the sum of the individual firm's demand for labour at each wage.

The elasticity of demand for labour

The elasticity of demand for labour is a measure of the responsiveness of demand for labour to a change in the wage rate. If demand for labour is elastic then a given change in the wage rate will bring about a greater percentage change in the quantity of labour demanded. If the change in the wage rate leads to a smaller percentage change in the quantity of labour demanded then the demand for labour is inelastic. This is shown in Figure 8.7.

> **Key term**
>
> **Elasticity of demand for labour:** a measure of the responsiveness of the demand for labour to a change in the wage rate.

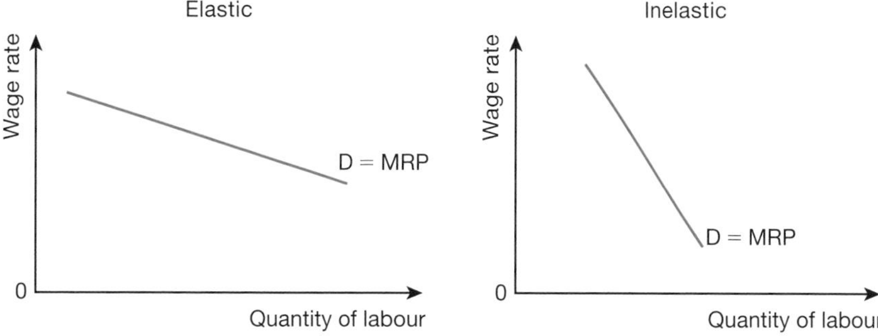

Figure 8.7 Differences in the elasticity of demand for labour ▲

The factors affecting the elasticity of demand for labour are summarised in Table 8.4.

Table 8.4 Factors affecting elasticity of demand for labour ▼

Factor affecting elasticity of demand for labour	Impact
Proportion of labour costs to total costs	If labour costs in a firm are high relative to total costs of production, the elasticity of demand is likely to be high because any given increase in wages will have a significant impact on total costs. For example, if a firm's total costs are \$1 million, of which 90% or \$900,000 are labour costs, then a 10% increase in wages will raise costs substantially by \$90,000. It may prove difficult for the firm to absorb this cost increase by reducing profits or increasing prices. In this case it will have to shed proportionately more labour. However, if labour costs constituted only 10% of total costs then total costs will rise by only \$1000, which the firm might find easier to pass on to consumers or absorb by making savings elsewhere.

Continued . . .

Factor affecting elasticity of demand for labour	Impact
Factor substitution	If labour can easily be replaced by other factors, particularly capital, then demand for labour is like to be elastic. Such factor substitution is more likely if the processes involved require relatively unskilled labour.
Price elasticity of demand for the final product	If the price elasticity of demand for the final product is high then it will not be possible for wage rises to be passed on to consumers through increases in price and so the demand for labour will also be elastic. This is likely to be the case if the firm is operating in a highly competitive product market which means that consumers can easily switch to other substitutes for the firm's products.
Time	The elasticity of demand for labour is likely to increase over time as firms have longer to find substitutes for labour. It is also the case that in some countries government legislation and employment law make it difficult for firms to shed labour in very short periods of time.

Factors affecting the supply of labour

The supply of labour can be viewed from a number of perspectives: an individual's supply of labour to a particular occupation, the supply of labour to a firm and the industry as a whole and the supply of labour to the economy as a whole.

Net advantages and the long run supply of labour

Traditional wage theory argues that an individual deciding upon an occupation will look at the balance of advantages between those available and choose the one which gives the greatest net advantages overall. These advantages will be made up of pecuniary advantages and non-pecuniary advantages. The pecuniary advantages are the monetary rewards associated with the job, mainly the wage rate. The non-pecuniary aspects of a job are any non-wage factors that make it more or less attractive to an individual than other jobs offering the same wage.

> **Key terms**
>
> **Net advantages**: the overall advantages to a worker of choosing one job rather than another. These can consist of both pecuniary and non-pecuniary advantages.
>
> **Pecuniary advantages**: monetary rewards obtained in a particular occupation.
>
> **Non-pecuniary advantages**: non-monetary rewards obtained in a particular occupation.

Wages and the supply of labour

An increase in wages will have a substitution effect and an income effect for an individual, which taken together determine the effect on a particular individual's willingness to supply their labour.

Substitution effect

The substitute for work is leisure. If an individual decides to work an additional hour then the opportunity cost is one hour of leisure foregone. If the wage rate in an occupation is increased then the opportunity cost of leisure increases as more income is given up when not working. The substitution effect, therefore, will lead to individuals working more hours.

Income effect

The income effect tends to work in the opposite direction to the substitution effect, discouraging work. As a result of a pay rise an individual can now achieve a given target income by working fewer hours and may therefore decide to take more leisure.

> **Key terms**
>
> **Substitution effect**: if wages rise, individuals will increase the number of hours worked because leisure has now become more expensive.
>
> **Income effect**: if wages rise, the individual will work fewer hours because a given income can now be achieved through less work.

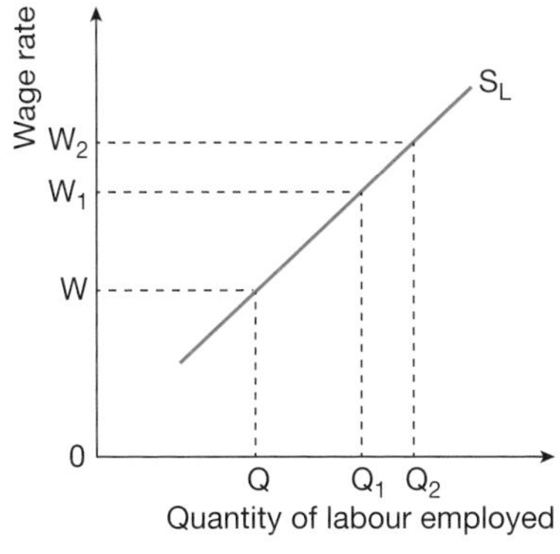

Figure 8.8 Individual's supply curve to a particular occupation ▲

The overall effect of an increase in the wage rate on an individual's supply of labour will clearly depend on the relative magnitudes of the substitution and income effects as shown in Table 8.5.

Table 8.5 Substitution and income effects of a wage increase ▼

Substitution and income effects of a wage increase	Effect on individual's labour supply
Substitution effect > Income effect	Increase
Substitution effect < Income effect	Decrease

For most individuals, particularly over lower levels of income, the substitution effect of a wage increase outweighs the income effect with the result that the supply curve for labour is upward sloping as shown in Figure 8.8 with the supply increasing as the wage rate increases and vice versa.

However, it has been argued that for some individuals, at high levels of income, the income effect may outweigh the substitution effect with the result that fewer hours are worked with each increase in the wage rate. This results in a backward sloping supply curve beyond a wage rate of W_3 in Figure 8.9.

This, of course, can only occur if the individual is in a position to vary the number of hours worked.

The market or industry supply curve for a particular occupation is the sum of the individual supply curve for all the workers in this particular labour market and is shown in Figure 8.10.

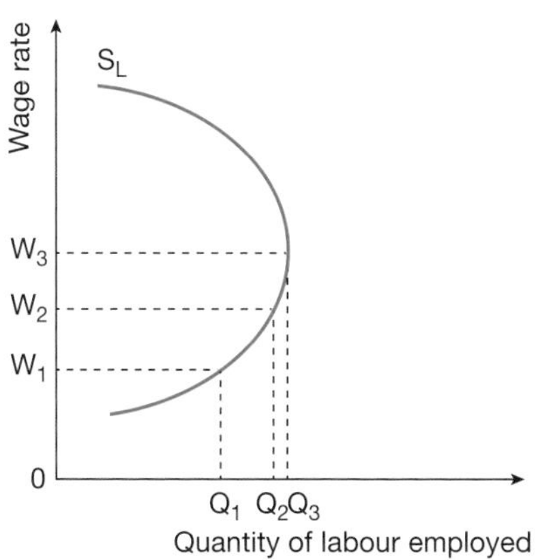

Figure 8.9 Backward sloping supply curve for labour ▲

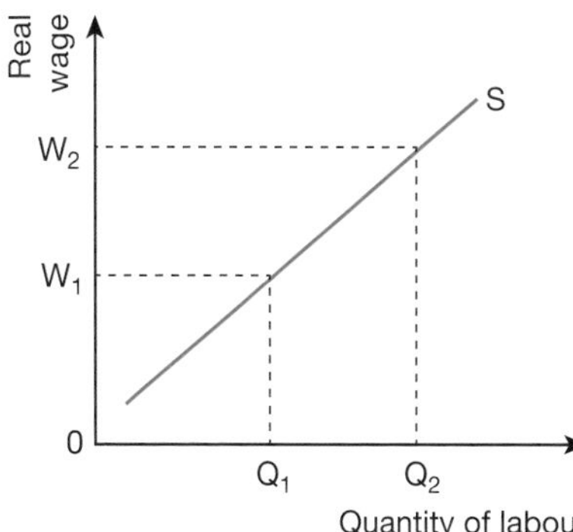

Figure 8.10 Non-pecuniary rewards and the supply of labour ▲

Non-pecuniary rewards and the supply of labour

Changes in the wage rate will bring about movements along the supply curve for labour. Non-pecuniary rewards will determine the position of the curve and changes in these rewards will thus bring about shifts of the individual and market supply curve.

If the non-pecuniary rewards to a particular occupation increase then the supply curve will shift to the right at each and every wage, and if the non-pecuniary rewards are reduced it will shift to the left.

Examples of non-pecuniary rewards include the following features:

- Fringe benefits, such as company cars and free health insurance may add to the attraction of a particular position.
- Status. A barrister may be prepared to take a reduced income for the status and prestige of becoming a High Court judge.
- Working conditions. If the work is unpleasant, dirty or dangerous such as mining, a higher wage may be paid than in other jobs requiring similar skills to compensate for this.
- Individuals may be prepared to accept lower wages for the benefit of being able to work flexible hours.
- Length of holidays may be important for some individuals.
- Sense of vocation. Some individuals may enter professions such as medicine and education because they gain job satisfaction from helping people.

Elasticity of supply of labour

The ease with which the supply of labour can be increased or decreased following a rise or fall in wages is determined by the elasticity of supply of labour. This is illustrated in Figure 8.11.

Key term

Elasticity of supply of labour: a measure of the responsiveness of the supply of labour to a change in the wage rate.

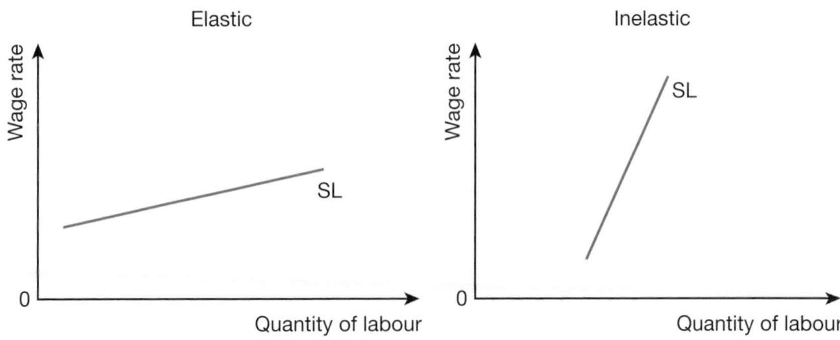

Figure 8.11 The elasticity of supply of labour ▲

A major factor influencing the elasticity of supply of labour to a particular firm or industry is the extent of the occupational and geographical mobility or immobility of labour.

Key terms

Occupational mobility/immobility of labour: the ease or otherwise with which individuals can move between occupations.

Geographical mobility/immobility of labour: the ease or otherwise with which individuals can move between geographical areas.

If labour is highly mobile both occupationally and geographically then the elasticity of supply is likely to be high.

The occupational mobility of labour depends on such factors as the level of education, training and skills required by the post, together with the length of training. It requires a great deal of education and skill as well as many years of training to become a barrister or cardiac surgeon and so the supply of labour can be inelastic for quite long periods of time. If the job requires little skill or training such as stacking shelves in a supermarket then the supply can be increased relatively quickly and is hence elastic.

Geographical mobility is influenced by factors such as family ties and the nature of the housing market. In the UK, for example, the fact that house prices are generally much higher in the south of the country than the north acts as a disincentive for individuals to take up posts in the south even if they are available. This tends to reduce the elasticity of supply.

One important recent development in relation to geographical mobility in Europe has been the enlargement of the EU, which has had a significant impact on immigration and emigration for certain countries. For example, there has been a significant influx of Polish dentists into the UK, thereby increasing the elasticity of supply.

Other factors which might affect the elasticity of supply to a particular occupation or industry include:

- The availability of suitable workers in other industries. It may be possible for labour to be recruited from other industries, particularly if the workers required are unskilled.
- Unemployment in the economy. If there are high levels of unemployment in an economy then there will be a large pool of available labour and supply should be more elastic, but again mainly for industries requiring unskilled labour.

Finally, as with all elasticity concepts, the time period is important. The longer the time period undertaken the more elastic the labour supply is likely to become. Even in fields such as law and medicine, given a sufficiently long period of time more barristers and cardiac surgeons can be trained to the required level.

Wage determination in perfect markets

Activity

Wage differentials

Identify the five highest-earning occupations in your country and explain why incomes in these occupations are so high.

We have now developed the key concepts in relation to the demand for and supply of labour which will enable us to show how wages are determined and explain the significant differences in wages that exist between individuals and occupations in society. This will enable us to explain why barristers and surgeons earn more than cleaners and why some very talented sports stars, actors and musicians receive extremely high incomes.

We will begin by looking at wage determination in perfect markets.

Competitive product and factor market forces determining wage differentials

The conditions here are similar to those in perfectly competitive product markets. The characteristics of a perfect labour market are:

- very large numbers of firms employing labour
- very large numbers of homogeneous workers who are perfectly mobile within the industry
- perfect knowledge in the market for both workers and employers.

Under these circumstances firms and workers in the industry are unable to affect the prevailing wage rate by their own actions. They are effectively price takers in a labour market.

As a result, the wage rate will be determined by the demand for and supply of labour in the particular market as a whole and then each individual firm will employ all the workers it requires at this wage. This effectively means that the supply curve of labour for the firm is perfectly elastic and the equilibrium employment level for the firm will be given by the intersection of this supply curve with the downward-sloping demand (MRP) curve. This is illustrated in Figure 8.12.

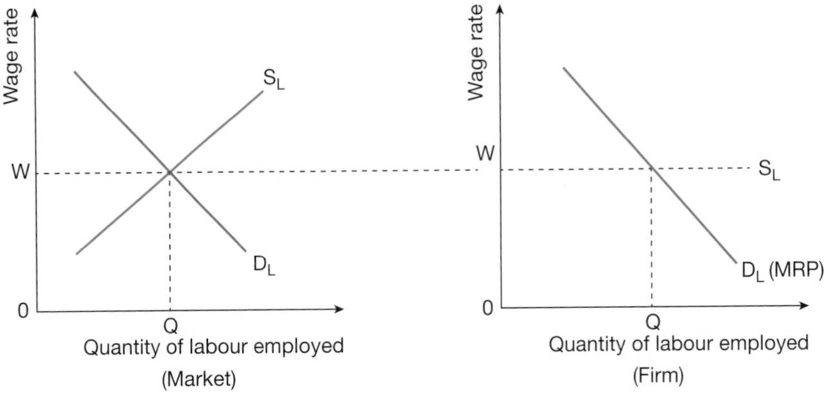

Figure 8.12 Wage determination in perfectly competitive markets ▲

Clearly any factor which brings about a shift of the demand or supply curves for labour will bring about a change in the equilibrium wage and employment levels. This is illustrated in Figure 8.13 and the results summarised in Table 8.6.

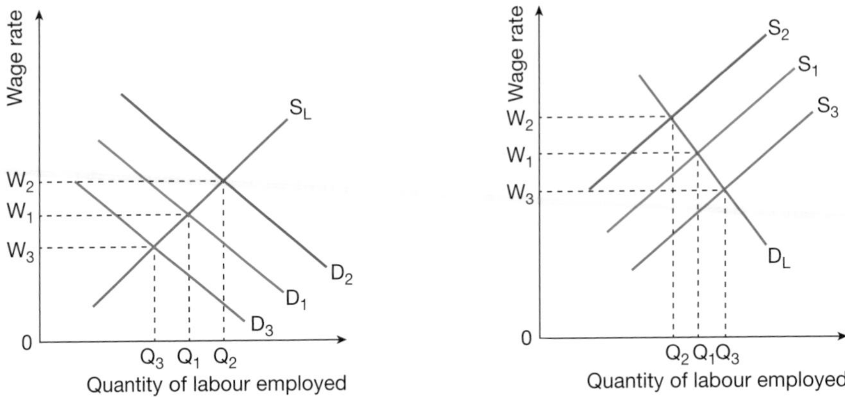

Figure 8.13 The effects of changes in the demand and supply curves for labour on wages and employment ▲

Table 8.6 The impact on the equilibrium wage and employment of changes in demand and supply ▼

Change	Impact
Increase in demand – demand curve for labour shifts to the right	Increase in wages, increase in employment
Decrease in demand – demand curve for labour shifts to the left	Decrease in wages, decrease in employment
Increase in supply – supply curve for labour shifts to the right	Decrease in wages, increase in employment
Decrease in supply – supply curve for labour shifts to the right	Increase in wages, decrease in employment

Wage determination in imperfect markets

In reality, labour markets are not always highly competitive. There are often situations where either the employer is a monopoly buyer of labour or the employer is faced with a monopoly supplier of labour, usually a trade union.

Monopsony

A sole buyer of labour is called a monopsonist.

> **Key terms**
>
> Monopsonist: a sole buyer, in this case of labour.
>
> Trade union: an organisation of workers which is active on behalf of its members in many ways, such as in relation to increasing wages and salaries and improving working conditions.

We will now look at three cases where:

- the labour supply is under the monopoly control of a trade union, but it is purchased competitively by a number of firms
- labour is supplied competitively but employed by a monopsonist buyer of labour
- labour is supplied by a monopoly supplier and employed by a monopsonist buyer of labour.

The influence of trade unions on wage determination

Labour supplied by a trade union, but employed competitively

Under these circumstances the trade union may be in a position to raise wages in a number of ways.

Increase the MPP of labour

Remember that the MRP of labour = MPP × MR (Price). If the trade union can raise either the MPP or the price of the final product then it will shift the demand (MRP) curve for labour to the right increasing both the wage rate and the numbers employed as shown in Figure 8.14. It is unlikely that the trade union will have much direct influence over the price of the final product, but it might be able to increase the level of productivity and hence the MPP of the workers by agreeing to more flexible working practices or the introduction of new technology.

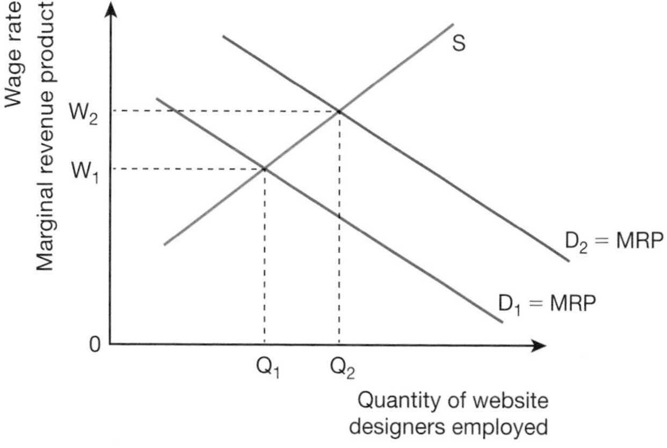

Figure 8.14 The effect of increasing the MRP of labour ▲

Restrict the supply of labour

If the trade union can somehow restrict or limit entry to a particular occupation the supply curve for labour in the industry will shift to the left. Professional associations such as those in law and accounting can achieve this by requiring a certain minimum level of qualifications or period of training in order to work in the profession. As Figure 8.15 shows, this will lead to an increase in wages for those in the industry, but the numbers employed will be reduced.

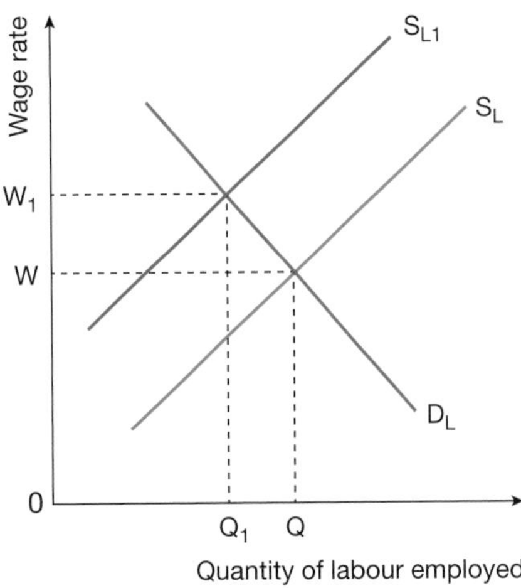

Figure 8.15 The effect of restricting the supply of labour ▲

Collective bargaining or industrial action

Finally, a trade may be able to push the wage rate above the equilibrium by exercising its bargaining strength or threatening or taking industrial action to disrupt production. Some trade unions' ability to do this is enhanced by the fact that they operate a closed shop and, therefore, have the backing of the entire workforce in that industry. This is illustrated in Figure 8.16. Through collective bargaining the trade union has pushed the wage rate up to W2. In this case those workers who retain their jobs in the industry will receive a higher wage, but Q_1–Q_2 workers are made unemployed. In addition Q_3–Q_1 workers who now wish to work at the higher wage are excluded from doing so.

> **Key terms**
>
> **Closed shop**: this occurs when workers are only able to work in a particular industry if they are members of a trade union.
>
> **Collective bargaining**: a process of negotiation over pay and conditions between a trade union, representing a group of workers, and employers.

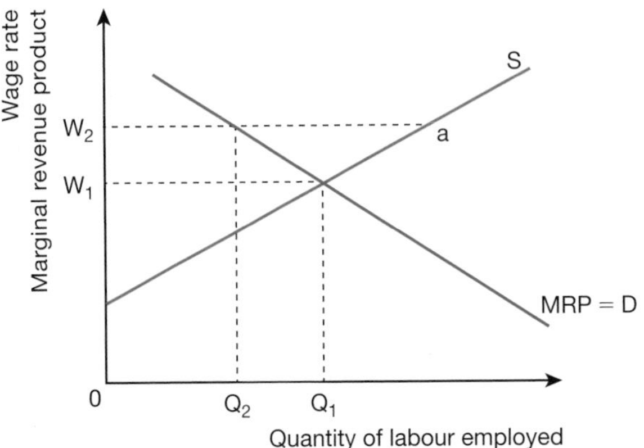

Figure 8.16 The effect of collective bargaining or industrial action ▲

Labour is employed by a monopsonist, but supplied competitively

Table 8.7 and Figure 8.17 illustrate the situation in a labour market where there is a single buyer of labour (monopsonist), but labour is supplied competitively rather than through a trade union.

Table 8.7 Monopsonist buyer and competitive supply of labour ▼

Number of workers	Wage rate ($)	Total cost ($)	Average cost ($)	Marginal cost ($)
1	50	50	50	50
2	55	110	55	60
3	60	180	60	70
4	65	260	65	80
5	70	350	70	90
6	75	450	75	100

Here, in order to attract additional labour, the monopsonist has to increase the wage rate and so the supply curve of labour is upward sloping. It is clear from the table also that the supply curve for labour is the same as the average cost of labour (ACL) curve. In order to attract additional labour the monopsonist will have to increase the wage rate, but this higher wage will also have to be paid to all existing employees. This means that the marginal cost of labour curve (MCL) is above the ACL curve. This is shown in Figure 8.17.

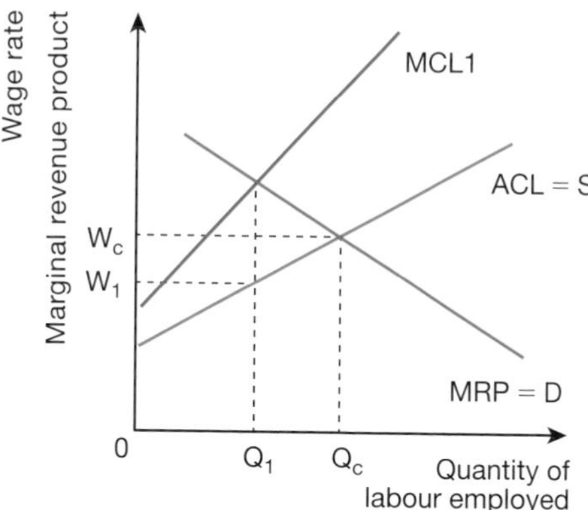

Figure 8.17 Equilibrium in a monopsonist labour market ▲

If we now add the demand (MRP) curve for labour then the profit maximising monopsonist will employ workers up to the point where the (MCL) = MRP giving an employment level of QM. The wage rate will be determined by the ACL = S curve giving a wage rate of WM.

Bilateral monopoly

This is a labour market in which there is a monopoly supplier, a trade union, and a monopsonistic buyer of labour. In order to illustrate the market we again refer to Figure 8.17. The trade union will wish to achieve the competitive equilibrium position with a wage of WC and an employment level QC. The monopsonist, however, will wish to be at the profit maximising position, with a wage rate of WM and an employment level of QM. The wage rate and employment levels eventually agreed will depend upon the relative bargaining strengths of the trade union and the employer at the time, but there is clearly scope within this range for the trade union to achieve an increase in both the wage rate and the level of employment for its members.

Wage differentials

As indicated earlier, there are significant differences in the earnings of individuals within countries and between countries. Table 8.8 shows the ten occupations with the highest and lowest salaries in the UK.

Table 8.8 Highest- and lowest-paid occupations in the UK ▼

Highest-paid occupations	Median full-time weekly pay	Lowest-paid occupations	Median full-time weekly pay
Chief executives and senior officials	1594.40	Hairdressers and barbers	257.00
Aircraft pilots and flight engineers	1528.10	Waiters and waitresses	257.30
Air traffic controllers	1328.20	Bar staff	258.00
Marketing and sales directors	1289.20	Kitchen and catering assistants	262.20
Legal profession	1257.60	Retail cashiers and check-out operators	269.30
Advertising and public relations directors	1221.70	Launderers, dry cleaners and pressers	270.20
Information technology and telecommunications directors	1194.20	Other elementary services occupations	272.20
Medical practitioners	1159.60	Leisure and theme park attendants	277.20
Senior police officers	1107.10	Cleaners and domestics	281.70
Financial managers and directors	1094.20	Nursery nurses and assistants	286.00

In addition, there are individuals who earn truly huge sums of money. In sport, soccer players such as Wayne Rooney, Lionel Messi and Christiano Ronaldo, all earn in excess of £24 million per annum. Roger Federer's earnings from tennis in 2013 exceeded $71 million, and in Formula 1 motor racing Fernando Alonso's earnings of $30 million put him in pole position for 2013. The highest-paid athlete is Tiger Woods, the golfer, who earned $78 million in 2013. Kobi Bryant is the highest-paid basketball player with reported earnings of nearly $63 million. Actors and musicians can also earn vast sums. The ten highest-paid actors earned a combined $464 million in 2013 with Robert Downey Jr topping the list with earnings for the year of $75 million. In music, Madonna earned $125 million and Lady Gaga earned $80 million in 2013.

Activity

Highest and lowest paid

Table 8.8 identifies the highest- and lowest-paid occupations in the UK.

Explain the main factors that might account for the significant difference in the median weekly wage of those in the ten highest-paid occupations and those in the ten lowest-paid occupations

Two examples of highly paid stars: Lady Gaga and Cristiano Ronaldo ▲

What are the reasons for these wage differences?

We have already looked at some of the reasons indirectly when looking at the factors demand for and supply of labour in perfect and imperfect markets.

Reasons for wage differentials

Demand and supply and elasticity of demand and supply

Generally speaking if the demand for labour is high and inelastic and the supply of labour is low and inelastic as in the case of a corporate manager, then the salary will be higher than if the demand for labour is low and elastic and the supply is high and elastic as in the case of a cleaner. This is illustrated in Figure 8.18.

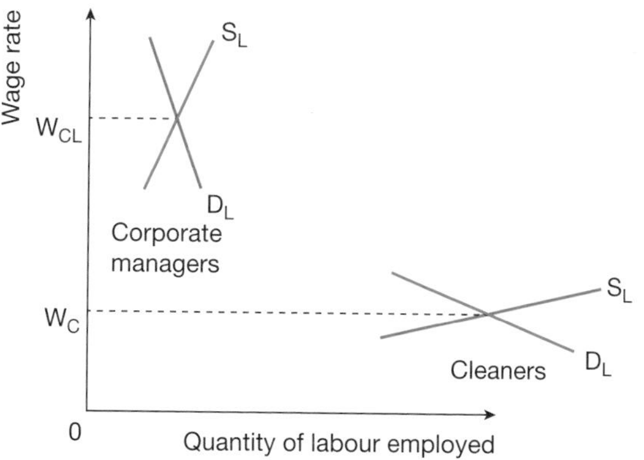

Figure 8.18 Market for corporate managers and cleaners ▲

The factors affecting the levels and elasticity of demand and supply of labour have already been considered earlier in this chapter.

From the demand side, high wages and salaries are likely to be paid if labour has a high MRP and if the demand for the final product of the organisation is high and inelastic. High demand for the final product is clearly a major factor in the very high earnings of professional athletes, actors and musicians.

From the supply side, higher wages and salaries are likely to be paid if high levels of skill, expertise and qualifications are required, long periods of training are necessary or the geographical and occupational mobility of labour is low.

Hence, corporate managers are paid 17 times more than cleaners in the UK because they are perceived to have a higher MRP and they require significantly higher levels of qualifications as well as extensive periods of training compared to cleaners.

Market power

We have already seen that the market for most occupations is imperfect, with workers or employers or both having some power to influence wages. The agreed wage rate is, therefore, likely to be the result of negotiation between the two. The final result will depend on their relative bargaining strength at the time.

Gender

Even though most countries have passed equal pay legislation to ensure that men and women in the same occupation earn the same for performing the same job, it is still the case that women earn on average less than men. There are a number of reasons for this. Women may take time out to have children in their 20s and 30s and may thus miss out on promotion. They are also disproportionately represented in low-wage occupations and part-time work. They are also less likely to be members of a trade union.

Age

In many professional occupations such as teaching, employees will obtain an annual increment to their salary. Hence, older workers will earn more than those new to the profession. Age may also bring with it seniority and, therefore, higher wages.

Non-pecuniary rewards

As discussed earlier in this chapter some workers may be prepared to accept lower wages in return for non-monetary rewards such as holidays, perks or status, or they may demand higher wages to compensate them for dangerous or dirty and unpleasant work.

National minimum wage

Many countries have a national minimum wage which sets the lowest wage that can be paid to workers in particular age ranges. This is normally designed to ensure that all workers have enough to live on. Increases in the national minimum wage may have an impact on other wages as workers seek to re-establish pay differentials.

Link

See page 242 for a more detailed analysis of a minimum wage.

Part-time and full-time work

Generally wages paid to part-time workers are less than those paid to permanent full-time staff.

Discrimination

Although legislation exists in most countries to counter discrimination on grounds, for example, of gender, race, disability or age, there are unfortunately complaints each year that these groups of workers are experiencing prejudice in the workplace, particularly in terms of promotion and salaries. Such discrimination normally acts on the demand side reducing the demand for certain types of labour.

A number of countries around the world are now attempting to counter aspects of negative discrimination by taking measures to actively promote positive discrimination. For example, the EU, India and Malaysia have introduced legislation setting minimum quotas for the number of women to be on the boards of companies in excess of a certain size.

Transfer earnings and economic rent

> **Key terms**
>
> **Transfer earnings**: the earnings an individual can obtain in the next best-paid occupation.
>
> **Economic rent**: earnings in excess of transfer earnings.

An individual's earnings can be divided into transfer earnings and economic rent. Transfer earnings are essentially the opportunity cost of working a particular job. If at least this amount is not earned, the individual will move into the next best-paid alternative occupation. This assumes, of course that the individual is only concerned with the pecuniary rewards of a particular occupation. Economic rent is any earnings above transfer earnings. Hence if an individual is paid $2000 per month and they would have been prepared to work for $500 per week, then the transfer earnings are $500 and the economic rent $1500 per month.

Figure 8.19 illustrates transfer earnings and economic rent. In this case all workers are paid a wage equal to W and Q is employed. However, the upward-sloping supply indicates that all workers except the last employed would have been prepared to work for less than the wage W. The area under the supply curve OBAQ represents the workers' transfer earnings. The difference between the actual wage paid W and the amount the workers would have been prepared to accept is, therefore, their economic rent and is given by the area BWA.

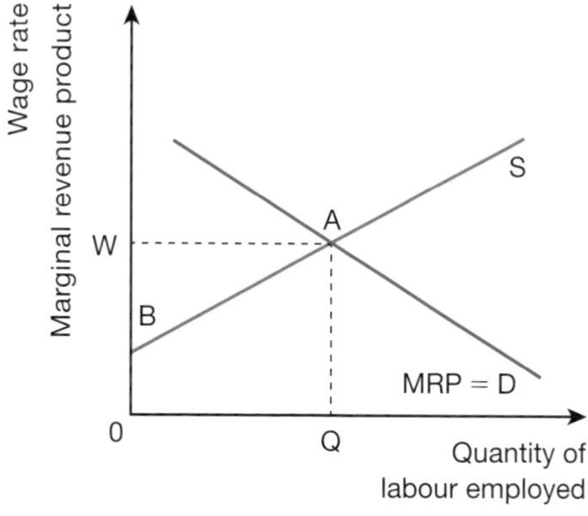

Figure 8.19 Transfer earnings and economic rent ▲

Clearly, the proportion of any given wage that represents economic rent and transfer earnings depends upon the elasticity of supply. The more inelastic the supply, the greater is the proportion of any given earnings that constitute economic rent relative to transfer earnings.

> **Getting it right**
>
> Make sure you are able to explain the transfer earnings and economic rent components of an individual's wage and can illustrate this on a diagram.

The majority of the very high earnings of the athletes, musicians and actors mentioned earlier in this section thus constitutes economic rent because they all have an extremely inelastic supply. In the extreme case of an individual having a unique talent, the supply curve would be vertical or perfectly inelastic and the whole of the individual's earnings would constitute economic rent. In this case the individual's wage would be entirely determined by the demand for their services.

Progress question

7 An individual is currently earning \$500 per week as a builder. They could earn \$400 per week as a taxi driver, \$450 per week as a librarian or \$490 per week working in a supermarket.
Explain the worker's transfer earnings and economic rent in the current occupation as a builder.

The influence of government on wage determination

National minimum wage

The most obvious way in which a government may influence wages is through the setting of a national minimum wage. The effect of this is illustrated in Figure 8.20.

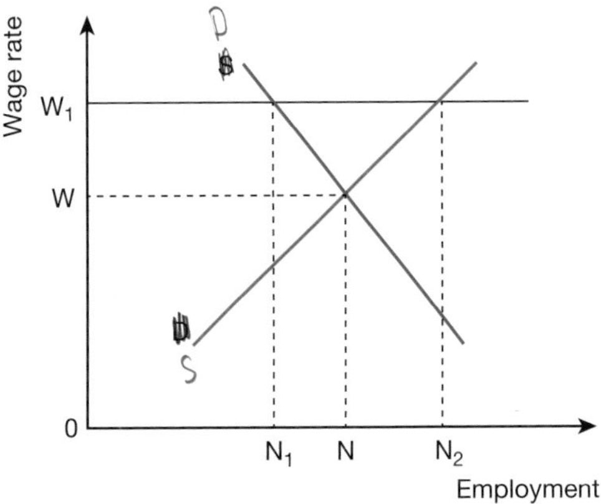

Figure 8.20 National minimum wage ▲

The equilibrium wage is W where the demand and supply curves for a particular occupation intersect. The equilibrium level of employment is ON. If the government imposes a minimum wage above the equilibrium this will increase firms' costs of production and reduce the demand for labour to ON_1. The effect of this is to make NN_1 workers who are currently in work unemployed. At the same time, at the higher wage more individuals in the labour force are prepared to offer themselves for work; the supply of labour increases to N_2. However, as the demand for labour is only N_1, the additional NN_2 workers will be unable to find employment. Overall at the minimum wage there will be an excess supply of labour equal to N_1N_2. Clearly the extent of these effects will depend on the level at which the minimum wage is set and the elasticity of demand for and supply of labour to a particular occupation.

Links

See Chapter 4 page 93 for a more detailed discussion of cost push inflation and Chapter 4 page 94 for more on the balance of payments.

Advantages of the national minimum wage

Economists are divided on the merits of a national minimum wage. Opponents argue that it creates unemployment and by raising costs causes cost-push inflation, which may render the industry uncompetitive and impact negatively on the balance of payments.

Supporters of a national minimum wage argue that it is important in terms of fairness and social justice to reduce income inequality and ensure that all workers are able to afford a minimum standard of living. They also argue that far from creating unemployment it actually creates employment because those on the lowest incomes tend to spend a higher proportion of what they earn. Moreover, they assert that a minimum wage may increase productivity. Workers may feel more valued and therefore work harder and at the same time, because they are paying more, employers may have the incentive to increase expenditure on training and developing their employees. All this may also reduce labour turnover, which will mean that firms can save money on the process of attracting, employing and training new workers.

Progress question

8 From October 2014 the UK minimum wage for workers over the age of 21 increased from £6.31 to £6.50 per hour.

- **a** Draw a diagram to explain this increase.
- **b** Evaluate the case for and against this increase.

Empirical evidence is mixed, but it seems to reinforce the view that the level at which the minimum wage is fixed is crucial in determining the effect on employment. In the USA, the minimum wage is 38 per cent of the median income, in the UK it is 40 per cent with a lower rate for younger workers, and in France it is 60 per cent. In the UK, where the minimum wage is regularly reviewed and increased, and in the USA, the minimum wage appears not to have had a negative effect on employment. In France, however, rates of youth unemployment were very high at 26 per cent for 15–24-year-olds in 2013.

Case Study

A living wage

Many countries now have a minimum hourly wage although the level in relation to the average hourly wage differs significantly between countries. In the UK, however, economists and politicians are increasingly turning their attention to the notion of a "living wage", which is the hourly rate estimated to enable individuals to have a reasonable standard of living. Currently it is estimated that to achieve this in the UK the living wage would have to be at least 15 per cent higher than the current minimum wage for most of the country and probably at least 30 per cent higher in London.

1 Evaluate the likely economic effects of compelling all firms in the UK to pay the "living wage".

Other government influences on wages

There are a number of other ways that a government can influence wages either directly or indirectly. Government equal pay and anti-discrimination legislation will obviously have an impact as will direct action on pay. For example, in 2010 the UK government imposed a two-year pay freeze on all public sector workers earning more than £21 000 per annum and limited annual pay rises for those earning less than this to £250. This was followed by a cap on pay rises for the majority of public sector workers to 1 per cent per annum, which has been extended to 2015–2016.

Progress question

9 Evaluate the likely economic effects of the UK government's decision to cap public sector pay increases to a maximum of 1 per cent per annum for a three-year period.

Government failure in microeconomic intervention

The effectiveness of government policies

Key term

Government failure: the failure of a government to achieve desired objectives as a result of intervention in a market.

The advantages of government intervention to reduce market failure have already been discussed. As well as market failure, there is also the possibility of government failure. This could come about as a result of problems of information, incentives or distribution.

Problems of information

It has already been argued that there are potential advantages of a government intervening in a market to reduce or eliminate failures, but this is only likely to be successful if the government has the necessary up-to-date information to make an informed decision. The concept of information failure was discussed in relation to the decisions of consumers, such as when consumers over-consume demerit goods and under-consume merit goods. The concept can also be applied to decision-making by a government.

For example, a firm may be involved in the creation of a negative externality, such as air or noise pollution, and a government decides, as has already been suggested in Chapter 6, to intervene in the market by imposing an indirect tax on the firm. This would have the effect of increasing the cost of production to the firm, leading to a fall in the output being produced. This will have the effect of reducing the extent of the pollution. The problem with such an approach, however, is that the government may not have all the necessary information that is required in order to decide on the exact amount of tax that is required.

Problems of incentives

Another type of problem that could arise as a result of government intervention in a market is that of incentives. These can be distorted when a government decides to intervene in a market.

For example, a government may decide to reduce, or even withdraw, the benefits paid to a person if that person works longer hours and, as a result, earns a higher wage. The government could defend such a decision on the basis that the person is less in need of the benefit, but the possibility of a lowering or termination of the benefit may act as a disincentive for the person to work longer hours. This is why such a situation has been described as a poverty trap, i.e. it is often not worth working longer hours and gaining a higher income if a person receives less benefits from the state because they are no better off as a result of the extra work carried out.

Problems of distribution

It has already been stated in this chapter that one of the reasons why a government might decide to intervene in a market is to create a greater degree of equity in an economy. It is possible that as a result of such intervention in a market, however, a government may actually increase the degree of inequality, creating a less equitable outcome.

For example, a government may decide to impose a tax on energy producers because of the pollution they have caused. The effect of such a tax, however, may be to increase the prices charged to consumers. The increase in price is likely to be the same for all the consumers of the energy, but the effect of such a price rise will not be equal because some consumers will be better able to afford the price increase. The distributional effect of the tax, therefore, will be a greater degree of inequality than was the case before the tax was imposed.

Progress question

10 Discuss to what extent a government is likely to be successful in its attempt to correct market failure in an economy.

Key concepts

- **Scarcity and choice** can be seen in relation to the decision whether to allow scarce resources in an economy to be allocated through a nationalised industry, where one firm controls the market, or through a process of privatisation, allowing a number of firms in an industry to compete with each other.
- **Margin and change** can be seen in terms of the profit maximisation position where marginal cost is equal to marginal revenue. Allocative efficiency is defined as that position where price is equal to marginal cost. In taxation, it is important to distinguish between marginal and average rates of taxation. In wage determination, marginal revenue product is very important.
- **Equilibrium and efficiency** can be seen in terms of different types of efficiency, such as productive and allocative efficiency. One of the arguments in favour of privatisation is that by allowing for more competition in an industry, it is likely that there will be greater efficiency.
- **Regulation and equity** are both covered in this chapter. There are various types of regulation referred to, such as prohibitions, licences, property rights and pollution permits. Equity is covered in terms of the attempts by governments in many countries to bring about a fairer distribution of income, such as through a progressive income tax system.
- **Progress and development** can be seen in a number of ways. For example, some economists would argue that the privatisation of an industry would enable the greater competition to bring about progress and development by allowing for competition between different

firms. Nudge theory can be seen as an example of government intervention to allow for the progress and development of individuals by encouraging them to limit their consumption of alcohol and tobacco to more moderate levels. Regulation to reduce the extent of pollution in a country could be seen as a clear example of progress and development in terms of healthier living conditions.

Progress check

After completing this chapter you should be able to:

- understand the policies to achieve efficient resource allocation and to correct market failure
- understand equity and the policies towards income and wealth redistribution
- understand labour market forces and government intervention
- appreciate the meaning of government failure in microeconomic intervention.

Exam-style questions

Essay questions

1 Discuss to what extent the privatisation of an industry is likely to improve efficiency in the allocation of resources. [25 marks]

2 Explain why a government might want to exercise greater control over private firms in an economy. [10 marks]

3 Discuss to what extent the removal of imperfections in a market leads to an increase in efficiency in the allocation of resources. [25 marks]

4 Discuss to what extent a government can bring about a more equal distribution of income and wealth in an economy. [25 marks]

5 Explain how wages are determined in a competitive market. [15 marks]

6 To what extent is it possible for a trade union to increase both wages and the level of employment for its members? [25 marks]

Multiple-choice questions

7 An indirect tax imposed on a product will: [1 mark]

- **A** shift the demand curve to the left
- **B** lead to an increase in price
- **C** lead to an increase in quantity
- **D** shift the supply curve to the right

8 A benefit which people are entitled to, irrespective of their income and wealth, is known as a: [1 mark]

- **A** means-tested benefit
- **B** universal benefit
- **C** monopsonist benefit
- **D** Lorenz benefit

9 The macro economy

In this chapter you will develop your knowledge and understanding of:

- economic growth, economic development and sustainability
- national income statistics
- classification of countries
- employment and unemployment
- the circular flow of income
- theory of money supply
- Keynesian and monetarist schools
- the demand for money and interest rate determination
- policies towards developing countries; policies of trade and aid.

Economic growth and development

Economic growth is an increase in the real output of an economy. For real growth to occur it needs to be greater than the increase in inflation. Economic growth can be measured either in terms of GDP or GNP, but is usually referred to as a change in real GDP. It was originally assumed that economic growth would lead to economic development. This assumed that growth would lead to more jobs, higher incomes and less poverty. In practice, although this has happened in some countries in others the standard of living of the poor has hardly improved.

Economic growth and development are linked. While growth is possible without development because growth is just an increase in real GDP, meaningful economic development is difficult if there is no growth.

Economic development is a far more comprehensive idea than economic growth. In addition to a rise in real output it involves changes in the composition of this output and a consequent shift in the allocation of resources as well as the reduction of poverty, inequalities and unemployment. In addition development can refer to the availability of education and literacy rates, see Table 9.1, as well as health and life expectancy.

Key term

Economic development: an increase in the economic wealth of a country, so as to benefit all of its people.

Table 9.1 Male and female literacy rates ▼

Country	Male literacy rate (%)	Female literacy rate (%)	Total literacy rate (%)
Barbados	100	100	100
Singapore	97	89	93
Chile	96	96	96
Maldives	93	95	94
Saudi Arabia	85	71	79
Uganda	77	58	67
Pakistan	63	36	50
Sierra Leone	47	24	35

Activity

Growth and development

Organise a debate or discussion on the topic: Growth can take place without development, but development cannot take place without growth.

Case Study

Health improvements for longer life expectancy in China

The Chinese Health Minister announced in April 2012 that life expectancy would reach 74.5 years by 2015. In 2009 it was 73 years. In addition, China will reduce infant mortality to below 12 per 1000.

All of this will be done by increased spending on health care and reducing the cost of medical care for individuals to below 30 per cent of the actual cost. The government will expand the coverage for basic medical insurance and provide better insurance programmes for the treatment of serious diseases, while ensuring that 10 000 urban residents have at least two general practitioners and that every township clinic has at least one.

In addition, free public health services will be provided to urban and rural residents, including vaccination, maternal and elderly care and the management of chronic diseases.

Links

The following are examined in more detail on the pages indicated:

For GDP and GNP see page 254.

For poverty see Chapter 8 page 225.

For unemployment see page 270.

Activities

Indicators of development

1. What indicators do you think would be most helpful to use for your country?
2. Make a list and then share them with others in your class.
3. Try to draw up a top eight of indicators.
4. What information can you find about these for your country?

1. Explain how the measures outlined above are likely to increase life expectancy in China.
2. Explain two other measures, other than health, that China could take to try to increase life expectancy still further in the future.

Sustainability

Sustainability in terms of both economic growth and development is when present needs are met without imposing costs on future generations. In 1987, the World Commission on Environment and Development defined sustainable development as that which meets "the needs of the present generation without compromising the needs of future generations". Economic growth today must not, therefore, use up raw materials and destroy the environment so as to reduce the quality of life available in the future. This means that there is pressure on countries to ensure that growth does not needlessly waste resources and that it improves not only living standards, but also the quality of life. There are many ways to try to do this including recycling of used materials and reduction of pollution.

Key term

Sustainability: where the needs of the present population can be met without imposing costs on future generations.

Climate change is another aspect of sustainability. Peru launched its own climate change initiative following the melting of glaciers in the Andes, record rainfall in the Amazon basin and high levels of solar radiation. Peru has followed the plans originated by South Africa and being followed by other South American countries such as Argentina, Brazil, Chile and Columbia.

A solar array ▲

The Royal Society of London, in its report "People and the Planet", April 2012, argued that population control together with better education for women were essential, together with taking people out of absolute poverty, reducing material consumption, accelerating the search for alternative measures of development beyond GDP and tackling the environmental impact of urbanisation, if sustainable development is to be achieved.

Activity

Sustainable development

Find out what your country is doing about adopting measures for sustainable development. How do these measures relate to those mentioned in the text?

Case Study

Development in Nigeria

Real GDP per person employed has risen steeply in Nigeria since 2000 to $17,980, but over the same period unemployment has also sharply increased. Poverty levels have remained at around 50 per cent of the population. This is reflected in Life expectancy at birth figures which have only risen very slowly.

On the other hand, there has been some improvement in education with adult literacy for the same period rising from 55 per cent to 61 per cent. A recent project in Lagos state between the government and the World Bank has seen more students passing core subjects and college entrance exams than ever before.

Although growth continues to be broadly based, constraints such as inadequate infrastructure, lack of a real positive climate for investment and the quality of tertiary education, continues to impede development.

1 Discuss the extent to which Nigeria has been successful in achieving economic development.

Key terms

Actual economic growth: the rate of growth in national output or the increase in output when all resources are fully employed.

Production: total output of the goods and services produced by an industry.

Potential economic growth: the rate at which the economy could increase.

Links

The following are examined in more detail on the pages indicated:

Production possibility curve see Chapter 1 page 10.

AD/AS see Chapter 4 page 87.

Actual versus potential growth in national output

Actual economic growth occurs when existing factors of production are utilised in a more efficient manner so as to achieve a higher level of output.

This can be shown using a production possibility curve as seen in Figure 9.1. Originally the economy is producing X amount of goods and services. If, for example, the economy was in recession but the government used fiscal and monetary policies to increase aggregate demand, then output of both could rise to Y on the current production possibility curve AB. This represents an actual increase in growth or GDP. It can also be shown by an increase in aggregate demand, see Figure 9.2. Potential growth can be shown by an increase in aggregate supply, see Figure 9.3.

Further increases in output are only possible if there is an increase in the potential economic growth shown by the outward shift from AB to CD. The output of goods and services could then increase to Z. In the long run, the focus of economic growth needs to be on expanding the potential capacity (potential output) of an economy.

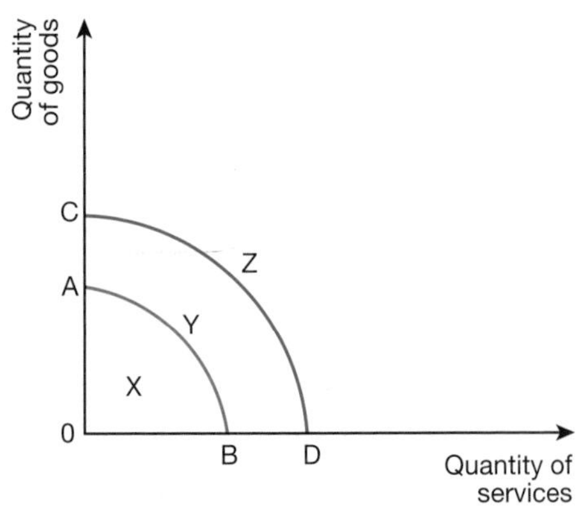

Figure 9.1 Actual and potential growth of an economy ▲

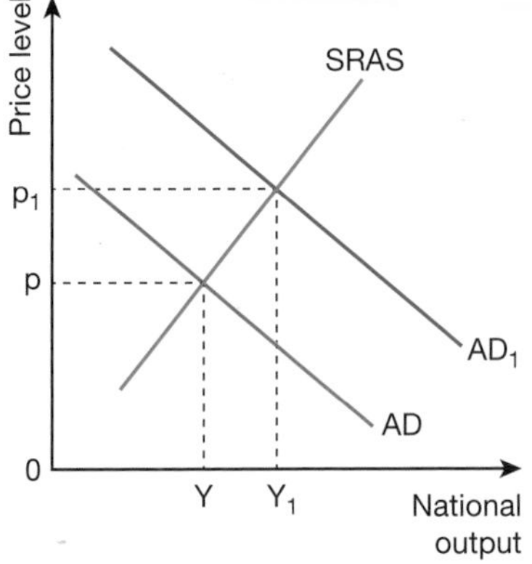

Figure 9.2 Actual economic growth ▲

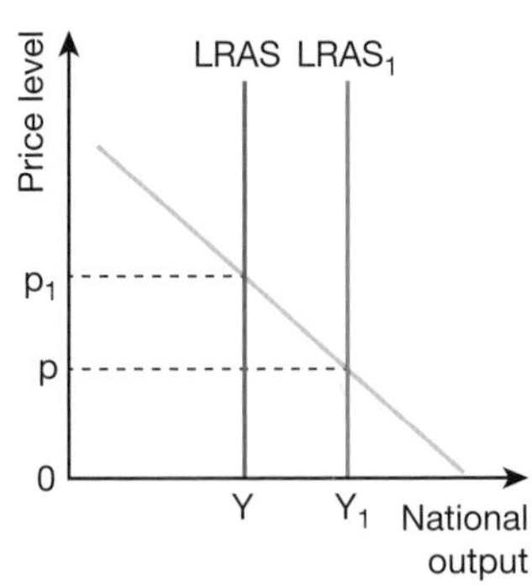

Figure 9.3 Potential economic growth ▲

Key term

Output gap: the difference between actual output and potential output.

Output gap

The output gap measures how close current output is to an economy's long-term potential output, i.e. the difference between the two.

If actual output is less than potential output there is a negative output gap. Some factor resources are underutilised. There is likely to be downward pressure on inflation and higher unemployment. A positive output gap occurs when actual output is more than full-capacity output due to high-aggregate demand resulting in, for example, factories and workers operating above their most efficient capacity. This will result in higher rates of inflation. In both cases the economy is performing inefficiently.

Activity

Output gap

Find out whether your country has a negative or a positive output gap. You must state what evidence you are using for your conclusion.

Progress question

1 Discuss the extent to which potential growth is more important for an economy than actual growth.

Business cycle

Key term

Business (or trade) cycle: the way in which economic growth fluctuates over a period of time.

Business (or trade) cycles consist of boom, slump, recession and recovery as part of short-term changes in GDP – see Figure 9.4. The duration of the cycle varies due to different political and external events, but is often considered to be about ten years.

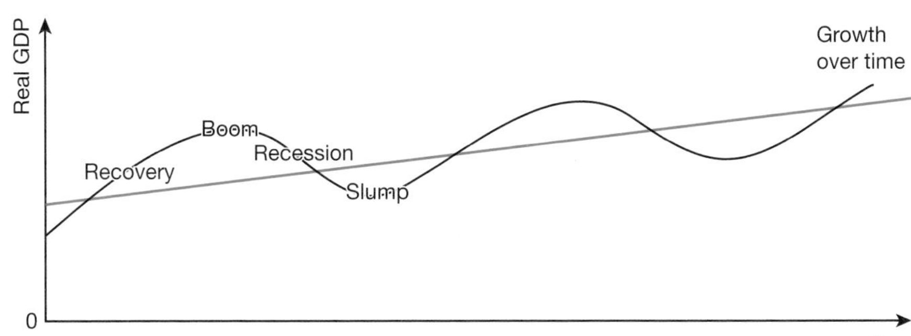

Figure 9.4 Trade cycle ▲

Trade cycles can apply to individual countries or groups of countries or can be on a global scale. The last such was in 2008–2009.

Keynes in the 1930s maintained that it was the role of governments to smooth out these cycles so as to prevent the great differences between a boom and a slump. This would involve governments increasing their expenditure to create jobs and growth.

Link

For more on Keynes see page 289.

Activity

Business cycle

Try to draw a business cycle for your country for the past 50 years.

Discuss as a group what has caused these cycles.

Factors contributing to economic growth

While actual economic growth is determined by how effectively the factors of production are combined and developed, potential growth is mainly determined by what factors of production the country has available.

The main factors contributing to economic growth are explained below.

Link

For more on factors of production and fixed capital formation see Chapter 1 pages 12 and 16.

Natural resources

The existence of natural resources is a potential factor in growth, but not a necessary one. Countries such as Japan and Singapore have achieved growth with few or no natural resources. Equally, countries with large natural resources may fail to fully exploit them for the benefit of their economy. This has been the case in some African countries.

Investment

This means the accumulation of capital (see gross fixed capital formation Table 9.2). This is a statement about the quantity, but not the quality. Quality refers to using the best technology available. Even so, more capital would normally translate into more machines leading to greater output and, therefore, growth. Investment can also be used to increase research and development.

Table 9.2 Gross fixed capital formation and economic growth ▼

Country	Gross fixed capital formation percentage of GDP $ (2012)	Economic growth rate (%) (2012)
China	47	7.8
Tanzania	39	6.9
Indonesia	34	6.2
India	30	4.7
Chile	24	5.6
Mauritius	22	3.2
Germany	18	0.7
Pakistan	13	4.0
Swaziland	10	−1.5
Guinea-Bissau	7	−6.7

Sources: http://data.worldbank.org/indicator/NE.GDI.FTOT.ZS and http://data.worldbank.org/indicator/NY.GDP.MKTP.KD.ZG

As can be seen in Table 9.2 there appears to be a direct relationship between capital formation and growth with countries such as China and Tanzania having high rates for both. However, some countries – such as Germany in the Table – do not have any obvious relationship, which is often to do with either political factors or with the use made of the capital.

Activities

Gross fixed capital formation

1 Find out what your country's GFCF was for the last reported year. How does it compare with that of similar countries?
2 Over a number of years does your country's GFCF have a clear relation to growth in GDP? Explain the relationship you have found.
3 Discuss why some countries have either high GFCF but low growth or low GFCF and relatively high growth.

Links

For more on labour productivity see page 253.

Rate of savings

If Savings = Investment (S = I) then a high level of savings should lead to a potentially high level of investment as firms access the savings in order to purchase capital equipment. The household savings ratio in three of the countries in Table 9.2 are:

- China 24 per cent
- Germany 12 per cent
- Pakistan 11 per cent.

Overall many developing countries, especially China and in East Asia, have a higher savings ratio than developed countries. The World Bank expects that by 2030 developing countries will dominate global saving.

Activities

Economic growth

1 Find out the figures for your country concerning:
   a household savings ratio
   b labour participation rates.
2 How does your country compare to other similar countries?
3 Discuss the extent to which these figures are good indicators of economic growth in your country.

Education and training

An educated and skilled workforce is likely to be more productive and thus generate higher growth. It is also more likely to produce new ideas leading to innovation and inventions. In 2010, eight of the top ten countries for registering patents were developed, the exceptions being China and Russia.

> **Key term**
> **Productivity**: the quantity of goods and services produced per unit of input.

Labour productivity and labour participation

The productivity of labour is closely linked to better capital equipment. Labour participation is about making productive use of a high percentage of working-age people in order to make the best use of their knowledge and skills. High participation, however, such as in Zambia with 80 per cent does not necessarily mean high growth although low participation such as in Jordan, 41 per cent, may indicate growth below its potential.

> **Progress question**
> 2 Investment is the most important factor leading to economic growth. Discuss whether or not you agree with this statement.

Pollution from factories and cars can be a cost of economic growth ▲

Costs and benefits of growth, including using and conserving resources

Traditionally economic growth has been looked on as an "economic good", but it is clear that this overlooks the considerable costs involved both in terms of human lives, culture and the environment. Table 9.3 shows some of the main benefits and costs.

Table 9.3 Benefits and costs of economic growth ▼

Benefits	Costs
Rise in the standard of living – leading to reduction of absolute poverty. In addition, there should be more consumer goods.	Environmental damage – resulting from more pollution from factories, cars etc. Damage to the landscape by extracting mineral resources and in terms of the depletion of non-renewable resources. Global warming is another factor here.
Improved education and health – literacy rates should rise while infant mortality and death rates should fall together with the number of people dying from disease.	Opportunity cost – if a country is on its production possibility frontier then more investment in capital goods can only happen if there are less consumer goods, i.e. current consumption will fall.
Increased tax revenue – to fund better infrastructure, schools, hospitals and to provide benefits for the poor etc. This increase in revenue will come from more output/higher incomes and profits rather than from higher taxes.	Unequal benefits – growth is likely to mean changes in economic structure and ways of production, leading to some people becoming unemployed while others gain from more work opportunities. Equally, growth may mean some workers suffer more stress in terms of both having to learn new skills, but also having to work longer hours etc.
Increase in business and consumer confidence – growth should encourage business to take a positive view of the economy and to want to invest, innovate and use new technology. Consumers will be more willing to spend and thus increase aggregate demand if they feel that the economy is doing well.	Lower quality of life – due to rapid urbanisation leading to poor housing and overcrowding together with greater stress, breakdown of family networks and inferior air quality. This may also involve an opportunity cost, e.g. more income, but a poorer quality of life.

Sustainable economic growth requires that resources are both used and conserved for future use.

Demand for natural resources is greater than the potential supply so if nothing is done they will no longer exist. This has led governments all over the world to think about how to manage use so as to support growth while, at the same time, conserving resources.

Links

The following are examined in more detail on the pages indicated:

Living standards see page 255.

Infant mortality and death rates see page 260.

Opportunity cost see Chapter 1 page 8.

Economic structure see Chapter 1 page 25.

Getting it right

Opportunity cost is a useful concept when discussing costs and benefits of growth.

Activity

Costs and benefits of growth

As a group make a list of the costs and benefits for your country. If you have a large group it could be split into pairs or threes and then each group shares its information to enable a whole group list to be made.

Case Study

Benefits and costs of growth in China

Between 1992 and 2013 China's economy grew on average by just under 10 per cent per annum transforming China into one of the world's major producers. This resulted in considerable increases in the standard of living of many millions of Chinese, especially in cities such as Shanghai.

In January 2013, however, a foul-smelling smog settled on Beijing for several weeks. The concentration of particles with a diameter of 2.5 microns or less reached 40 times the level that the World Health Organization deems safe.

On a wider scale, China's greenhouse gas emissions were about 10 per cent of the world's total in 1990 and are now near 30 per cent.

China has always faced water problems, but these have been made worse by pollution. The Yellow River Conservancy Commission, a government body, found that for a third of its length the water was too polluted for use in agriculture. The housing ministry's chief engineer for water safety says only half the water sources in urban areas are fit to drink.

1. Briefly explain the benefits of growth to China.
2. Why would "a foul-smelling smog" be of concern to the Chinese economy?
3. Discuss the effects of water pollution for the Chinese economy.

Progress question

3. To what extent do the benefits of growth outweigh the costs of growth for your country?

National income statistics

GDP, GNP and GNI

National income can be measured using expenditure, income or output data. As these should all give the same figure the data is usually stated in terms of gross domestic product (GDP), gross national product (GNP) and (net) national income (NI). The difference between these is:

GDP + Net property income from abroad = GNP

GNP – Depreciation = NI

Key terms

Gross national product (GNP): the total value added in the production of goods and services in a country plus net property income from abroad in a year.

National income: the total value added in the production of goods and services within a country plus net property income from abroad minus depreciation in a year.

Net property income from abroad: consists of the inflow of interest, profits and dividends into a country minus the outflow.

Depreciation: a figure used to measure the fall in value of the capital stock of a country. It is sometimes referred to as capital consumption.

Activity
Double counting

In pairs, discuss why it would be wrong when producing a good such as a car to count the value of the; car; tyres, seats; engine; etc., separately.

Link
For constant and current prices see also money and real data in Chapter 4 page 92.

Getting it right
Be very careful when handling data to make certain whether it is at constant or current prices. Constant prices will be indicated, for example, by "2007 = 100" or "in 2007 prices".

Getting it right
Remember that real GNP per person is an average and not what everybody gets. This may disguise great wealth and poverty.

Key terms
Living standards: measures the material welfare of the residents of a country.

Deficit in the public finances: a situation in which government revenue is less than government expenditure.

Link
See page 248 for a definition of economic growth.

GDP can be measured either in terms of value of all final goods and services produced or in terms of the value added in the production process. The key point is that both of these prevent double counting from taking place, i.e. counting the same output twice.

GDP and GNP figures can be shown as either current or constant prices. The difference between the two is that constant prices take out the effect of inflation on the value whereas current prices are the money value. In addition, both can be expressed in terms of expenditure (GDE, GNE) and income (GDI and GNI), e.g. GNP = GNE = GNI. GNI or gross national income is the total value of goods and services produced within a country (i.e. its gross domestic product), together with its income received from other countries (notably interest and dividends), minus similar payments made to other countries.

All of these measurements can be referred to as economic indicators.

Key terms
Constant prices: a measure of value expressed in terms of real purchasing power using a base year as the standard for comparison. It takes into account, therefore, the rate of inflation.

Current prices: a measure of value expressed in terms of actual market prices at which the goods are sold.

Gross national income (GNI): the total value added in the production of goods and services in a country plus income received from abroad minus income paid abroad.

Net domestic product: GDP – depreciation

Net national product: GNP – depreciation

National income statistics as measures of economic growth and living standards

The usual measure of economic growth is real GDP per annum, although GNP is sometimes used.

Equally, real GNP per annum per person (or per capita) is the usual measure of living standards (or standard of living) as net property income is included, but real GDP is often used. The standard of living includes many aspects such as: income; housing; employment; hours of work required to purchase necessities; education; environmental quality.

National debt

If a government has a budget deficit then it needs to raise extra finance. A budget deficit in the public finances arises when government revenue, largely from taxes, is less than government expenditure, e.g. on education, health, defence, etc. It can raise finance either by printing more money or by borrowing. Printing money will reduce its value, leading to inflation.

Borrowing can be either short term or long term, and can be from domestic or foreign sources. The most common method is for the government to issue government bills (short term) or stock (long term).

> **Key term**
>
> **National debt**: the amount of money that a government, or public sector owes both domestically and abroad which has accumulated over a number of years.

Either of these, however, will result in an increase in the national debt. The size of the national debt only becomes important when a large proportion is owed abroad or if it looks as if it can not be repaid, e.g. Greece's borrowing in 2013 was 175 per cent of GDP.

Activity

Government debt and GNI

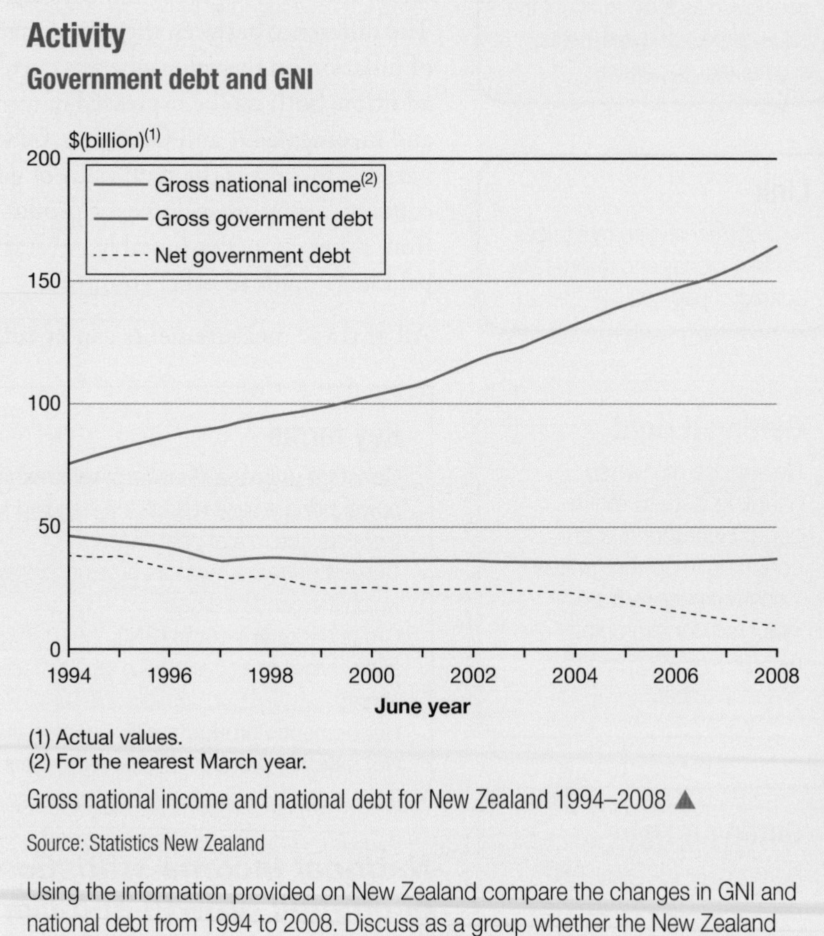

Gross national income and national debt for New Zealand 1994–2008 ▲

Source: Statistics New Zealand

Using the information provided on New Zealand compare the changes in GNI and national debt from 1994 to 2008. Discuss as a group whether the New Zealand government should be concerned by its national debt.

> **Getting it right**
>
> A common error is to confuse the national debt, which is related to the internal government budget, and the deficit on the balance of payments, which is external.

> **Links**
>
> Inflation is covered in Chapter 4 page 90.
>
> For more on the quantity theory of money see page 285.
>
> For more on taxation see Chapter 3 page 75 and Chapter 8 page 223.

Indicators of living standards and economic development

Human Development Index

The problems of using GDP/GNP to compare living standards and economic development between countries and over time has led to the development of other measures, the best known being the Human Development Index (HDI). This measures changes in development levels over time and compares development levels in different countries. As from the 2011 report this includes:

- a long and healthy life: life expectancy at birth
- education index: mean years of schooling and expected years of schooling
- a decent standard of living: GNP per capita (PPP $).

> **Key term**
>
> **Human Development Index (HDI)**: a means of measuring countries' economic and social development using life expectancy, years of schooling and GNI per capita.

Activity

HDI

National wealth has the potential to expand people's choices. However, it may not. The manner in which countries spend their wealth, not the wealth itself, is decisive. Moreover, an excessive obsession with the creation of material wealth can obscure the ultimate objective of enriching human lives. In many instances, countries with higher average incomes have higher average life expectancies, lower rates of infant and child mortality and higher educational attainment and school enrolment, and consequently a higher human development index (HDI). But these associations are far from perfect. In inter-country comparisons, income variations tend to explain not much more than half the variation in life expectancy, or in infant and child mortality. And they explain an even smaller part of the differences in adult educational attainment.

Source: http://hdr.undp.org/en/statistics/hdi/. See http://hdr.undp.org/en/content/copyright-and-terms-use

Discuss this statement from the HDI Report 2011 as a class.

Countries are placed in four categories of human development: very high; high; medium; and low. In the 2013 report these represented the following proportions of the world's population:

- very high and high 30 per cent
- medium 52 per cent
- low 18 per cent.

Table 9.4 The top ten and bottom twelve countries on the HDI ▼

HDI rank	Human Development Index (HDI) Value 2012	Life expectancy at birth (years) 2012	Mean years of schooling (years) 2010[a]	Expected years of schooling (years) 2011[b]	Gross national income (GNI) per capita (2005 PPP $) 2012	GNI per capita rank minus HDI rank 2012	Non-income HDI Value 2012
Very high human development							
1 Norway	0.955	81.3	12.6	17.5	48,688	4	0.977
2 Australia	0.938	82.0	12.0[c]	19.6[d]	34,340	15	0.978
3 USA	0.937	78.7	13.3	16.8	43,480	6	0.958
4 Netherlands	0.921	80.8	11.6[c]	16.9	37,282	8	0.945
5 Germany	0.920	80.6	12.2	16.4[e]	35,431	10	0.948
6 New Zealand	0.919	80.8	12.5	19.7[d]	24,358	26	0.978
7 Ireland	0.916	80.7	11.6	18.3[d]	28,671	19	0.960
7 Sweden	0.916	81.6	11.7[c]	16.0	36,143	6	0.940
9 Switzerland	0.913	82.5	11.0[c]	15.7	40,527	2	0.926
10 Japan	0.912	83.6	11.6[c]	15.3	32,545	11	0.942
176 Guinea-Bissau	0.364	48.6	2.3[a]	9.5	1,042	−6	0.373
177 Sierra Leone	0.359	48.1	3.3	7.3[e]	881	0	0.380
178 Burundi	0.355	50.9	2.7	11.3	544	4	0.423
178 Guinea	0.355	54.5	1.6[s]	8.8	941	−4	0.368

Continued . . .

HDI rank	Human Development Index (HDI) Value 2012	Life expectancy at birth (years) 2012	Mean years of schooling (years) 2010[a]	Expected years of schooling (years) 2011[b]	Gross national income (GNI) per capita (2005 PPP $) 2012	GNI per capita rank minus HDI rank 2012	Non-income HDI Value 2012
180 Central African Republic	0.352	49.1	3.5	6.8	722	1	0.386
181 Eritrea	0.351	62.0	3.4[e]	4.6	531	3	0.418
182 Mali	0.344	51.9	2.0[c]	7.5	853	−4	0.359
183 Burkina Faso	0.343	55.9	1.3[a]	6.9	1,202	−18	0.332
184 Chad	0.340	49.9	1.5[p]	7.4	1,258	−20	0.324
185 Mozambique	0.327	50.7	1.2	9.2	906	−9	0.327
186 Congo, Democratic Republic of the	0.304	48.7	3.5	8.5	319	0	0.404
186 Niger	0.304	55.1	1.4	4.9	701	−4	0.313

Source: http://hdr.undp.org/sites/default/files/reports/14/hdr2013_en_complete.pdf

Measure of Economic Welfare

The Measure of Economic Welfare (MEW) was the work of Nordhaus and Tobin as an alternative to just using GDP. MEW took national output as a starting point, but adjusted it to include an assessment of the value of leisure time and the amount of unpaid work in an economy. This increased the welfare value of GDP. On the other hand, the value of the environmental damage caused by industrial production and consumption was also included which reduced the welfare value of GDP.

Multidimensional Poverty Index

Another measure introduced in 2010 is the Multidimensional Poverty Index (MPI), see Table 9.5. This has three dimensions of poverty: health; education; and living standards, which are divided into ten indicators. This replaced the Human Poverty Index which was based on four aspects of human life: longevity; knowledge; economic provisioning; and social conclusion.

Table 9.5 Multidimensional Poverty Index 2011 ▼

Dimension of poverty	Indicators
Health	Nutrition
	Child mortality
Education	Years of schooling
	School attendance
Living standards	Cooking fuel
	Sanitation
	Water
	Electricity
	Flooring
	Assets

Source: www.ophi.org.uk/policy/multidimensional-poverty-index/

Key terms

Measure of Economic Welfare (MEW): starts with GDP but adds the value of leisure time and the amount of unpaid work in an economy and subtracts the value of the environment damage caused by industrial production and consumption.

Multidimensional Poverty Index (MPI): a measurement of poverty based on health, education and living standards.

Case Study

Multidimensional Poverty Index (MPI)

Income classifications hide wide disparities in MPI poverty. In low-income countries, the percentage of poor people ranges from 5 per cent in Kyrgyzstan to 92 per cent in Niger. In middle-income countries it ranges from 0 per cent in Belarus to 77 per cent in Angola.

Multidimensional poverty within countries varies greatly. Nepal is poorer according to the MPI than Cambodia, but Cambodia's poorest region is poorer than the poorest region of Nepal.

Poverty reduction over time varies by dimension. Bangladesh reduced poverty across all dimensions; Kenya reduced its MPI mainly through improvements in living standards; and Bolivia made great strides in improving school attendance and sanitation but less progress in decreasing under nutrition.

Source: www.ophi.org.uk/wp-content/uploads/OPHI-MPI-Brief-2011.pdf?cda6c1

Measures such as HDI and MPI are often used when comparing the quality of life in countries. Quality of life includes not just income and employment, but also wealth and employment, but also education, the environment, health, political security, and recreation and leisure time. The problem is that there is no agreed definition and the various indexes are all based on different criteria.

1 Compare poverty reduction in Bangladesh, Kenya and Bolivia.
2 Discuss whether indexes such as the MPI are more useful when comparing development in low- and middle-developing countries such as Nepal than measures such as real GNP per capita.

Key term

Quality of life: refers to the general well-being of individuals and societies.

Getting it right

Be careful not to confuse standard of living and quality of life when answering questions.

Link

For more on Gini coefficient see Chapter 8 page 226.

Key term

Kuznets curve: an inverted U-shaped curve with inequality or the Gini coefficient on the *y*-axis and economic development, time or per-capita income on the *x*-axis.

Activity

Kuznets curve

As a group discuss whether your country's development can be shown using the Kuznets curve. What evidence have you used to support your conclusion?

Kuznets curve

The Kuznets curve is an inverted U-curve, although variables along the axes are often mixed and matched, with inequality or the Gini coefficient on the Y axis and economic development, time or per-capita incomes on the X axis.

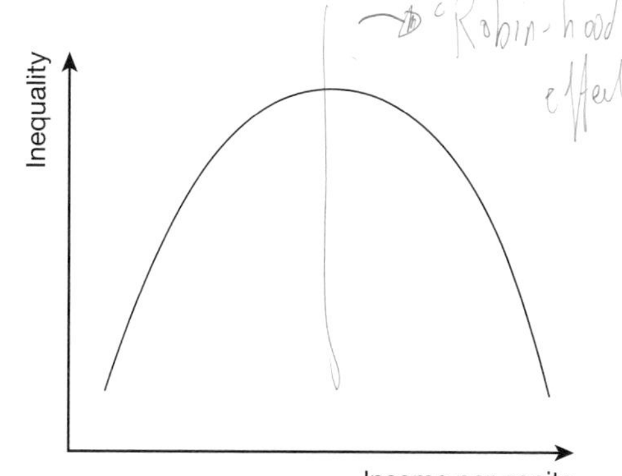

Figure 9.5 Kuznets curve

The curve claims to show that as an economy develops initially inequality increases, but, that after a certain average income is reached, inequality then decreases. This assumes that a country which is industrialising (and mechanising agricultural production) will draw people into urban areas improving their standards of living, but causing greater inequality with those still in rural areas. Only at a later stage will the benefits of growth reach these people and start to close the gap.

Although this was based on historical evidence, the "East Asian miracle" showed low inequality and high output, while in some more autocratic countries there has been high inequality and low output.

Characteristics of developed, developing and emerging (BRICS) economies

Population growth and structure

Birth rates and death rates are two key factors in population growth. As countries develop, health and education services improve, leading to lower birth and death rates. Also important is the infant mortality rate: again improved health care will lead to a decline. It is 4.825 in Denmark, but 66.93 in Tanzania. The greater the difference between the birth and death rates the higher is the population growth. This difference is called the natural increase. This can be seen in Table 9.6.

Key terms

Birth rate: number of live births per thousand population per year.
Death rate: number of deaths per thousand population per year.
Infant mortality rate: the number of deaths of infants under one year old in a given year per thousand live births in the same year.
Natural increase: the difference between birth rate and death rate.

Table 9.6 Birth and death rates in 2011 ▼

Status	Country	Birth rate	Death rate	Difference
Developed	Canada	10.28	7.98	2.30
Developed	New Zealand	13.68	7.15	6.53
BRIC	Brazil	17.79	6.36	11.43
BRIC	India	20.97	7.48	13.49
MINT	Mexico	19.13	4.86	14.27
MINT	Turkey	17.93	6.10	11.83
Developing	Bangladesh	22.98	5.75	17.23
Developing	Zambia	44.08	12.61	31.47

As can be seen in Table 9.6, the developed countries have low birth and death rates with only a small increase shown, whereas the developing countries have very high birth rates, higher death rates and large increases. More recently two groups of countries have been identified as having gone beyond the developing stage. These are the BRIC countries (identified 2001): Brazil, Russia, India and China and the MINT countries: Mexico, Indonesia, Nigeria and Turkey (widely identified 2014). Their birth rates are higher than the developed countries, while their differences are more than the developed, but less than the developing.

Key terms

BRIC: consists of Brazil, Russia, India and China.
MINT: consists of Mexico, Indonesia, Nigeria and Turkey.
Migration: the movement of people between countries.
Emigration: where people leave one country to go to others.
Immigration: where people come into a country from other countries.
Population structure: shows the population of a country by male and female and different ages.

In addition, migration plays a part in determining population growth. In many developing countries there is often a net outflow, emigration, of people seeking employment and higher standards of living in other countries, whereas in countries such as the UK there is a net inflow, or immigration.

Population structure shows the population of a country by male and female and different ages. It is commonly shown as a population pyramid. Developing countries have a wide base indicating a large, young population, while developed countries have more people 65 years and over. Population projections indicate, however, that all countries, except those of sub-Saharan Africa, will have considerable increases in the over-65 age group in the future.

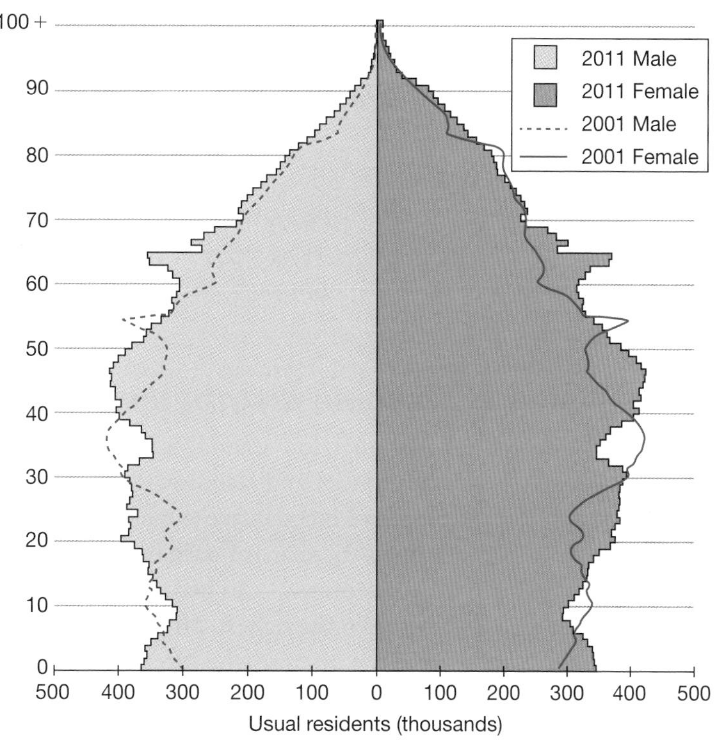

1. Comparison with 2001 is based on mid-year population estimates, comparison with 2011 is based on census results.
2. For the 2001 comparison lines, the 2001 mid-year population estimate of the number of people in the 90+ age category was distributed across single years of age for 91 to 99-year-olds using proportions as estimated in the 2001 Census. 100+-year-olds are shown as a group.

Figure 9.6 Age population pyramid for England and Wales ▲
Source: ONS

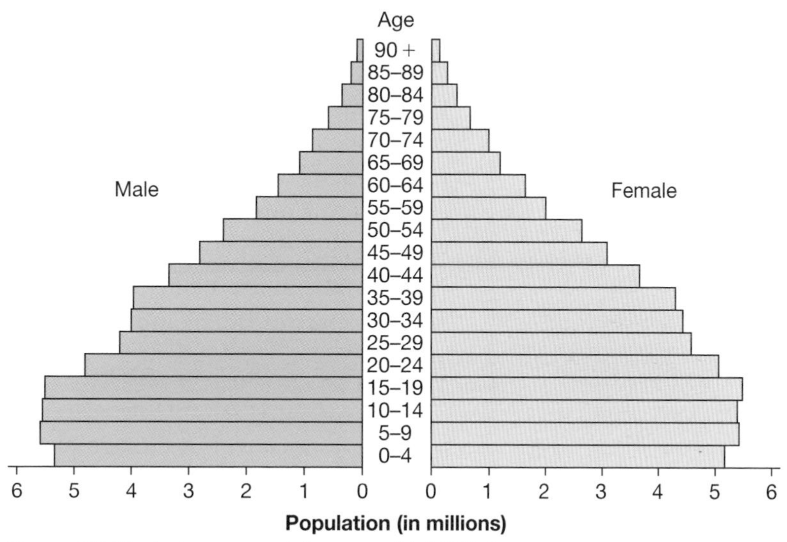

Figure 9.7 Mexico's age population pyramid, 2010 ▲
Source: geo-mexico.com. Copyright Sombrero Books, Canada, 2011

The age pyramids clearly show the difference in structure between England and Wales with its greater proportion of middle-aged and elderly and Mexico with its large, young population. This is typical of developing countries and of some of the BRIC and MINT countries. Uganda, for example, has over 50 per cent of its population under the age of 15. In some cases, high population growth is associated with increased urbanisation often leading to poor living conditions. Seven of the world's largest cities are located in developing countries.

Progress question

4 Explain the economic implications for a country with (a) an aging population, and (b) a largely young population.

Links

For more on Gini coefficient and the Lorenz curve see Chapter 8 page 226.

For more on poverty see Chapter 8 page 225.

Income distribution

Although low standards of living are due to a range of factors such as poor health care and facilities, inadequate education, malnutrition and high levels of inequality, the major factor is often income inequality. Table 9.7 shows the share of national income going to the richest and poorest 20 per cent. As can be seen, many developing countries have a wide gap between the richest, often commanding 40 per cent or more of the income, and the poorest who often have less than 10 per cent of the income.

Table 9.7 Income distribution by highest and lowest quintiles ▼

Country	Top 20% share of income	Bottom 20% share of income
Brazil	58.57	2.85
Egypt	40.34	9.24
Fiji	49.59	6.20
Malaysia	51.54	4.54
Nepal	41.46	8.27
Poland	42.11	7.68
Slovakia	36.23	10.12
Uganda	50.73	5.84

Activities

Income distribution

Using Table 9.7:

1. Discuss which country has (a) the greatest difference, and (b) the smallest difference in income distribution.
2. Compare income distribution between Malaysia and Nepal.
3. Discuss the extent to which the information is helpful when explaining levels of development.
4. Explain two other pieces of information that would be useful in deciding on the level of development of countries.

One way of comparing inequality between countries is to use the Gini coefficient. Table 9.8 shows that developed countries have lower levels of inequality than the other groups. As countries develop rapidly this often results in more unequal income distributions as shown by the BRIC countries Brazil and China.

Table 9.8 Gini coefficients for selected groups of countries ▼

Status	Country	Gini coefficient
Developed	France	32.7
Developed	Norway	25.8
BRIC	Brazil	54.7
BRIC	China	47.0
MINT	Indonesia	34.0

Activity

Income distribution

Find out how your country's income is distributed especially in terms of the top and bottom quintiles.

Compare your findings with those of other similar countries using both the quintile figures and Gini coefficients.

Discuss the findings between members of your group.

Link

For more on primary, secondary and tertiary sectors see Chapter 1 page 25.

Status	Country	Gini coefficient
MINT	Nigeria	48.8
Developing	Botswana	61.0
Developing	Yemen	37.7

Economic structure

The basic rule is that as countries develop, the primary sector becomes less important in terms of contribution to GNP and employment while the secondary and tertiary sectors become more important. In many Western industrial economies the tertiary sector has continued to grow while the secondary sector has declined. Table 9.9 shows the contrasts between a developed, BRIC, MINT and developing countries.

Table 9.9 Economic sector and employment contributions ▼

Country		Primary %	Secondary %	Tertiary %
UK	GNP	1.0	21.0	77.0
	Employment	1.4	18.2	80.4
India	GNP	17.0	17.0	66.0
	Employment	49.0	30.0	31.0
Mexico	GNP	4.0	33.0	63.0
	Employment	11.0	33.0	56.0
Kenya	GNP	24.0	15.0	61.0
	Employment	75.0	11.0	14.0

Employment composition

As can be seen in Table 9.9, developing countries such as Kenya have a high proportion of their population employed in the primary sector. As they develop their industry, employment in the secondary sector increases, as seen in the case of Mexico. Further economic development not only leads to greater demand for services such as education and health, but also greater mechanisation and automation of manufacturing thus leading to greater employment in the tertiary sector and a decline in both primary and secondary, as can be seen for the UK.

The three pie charts Figures 9.9, 9.10 and 9.11 illustrate the employment structure for a developed country (UK) a BRIC (Brazil) and a developing country (Kenya).

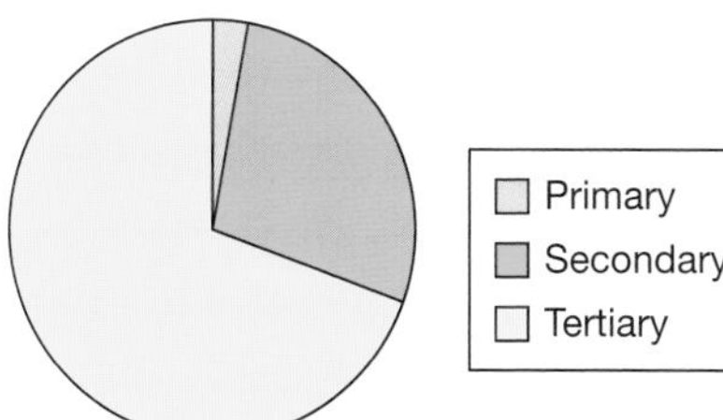

Figure 9.8 Employment structure for the UK ▲

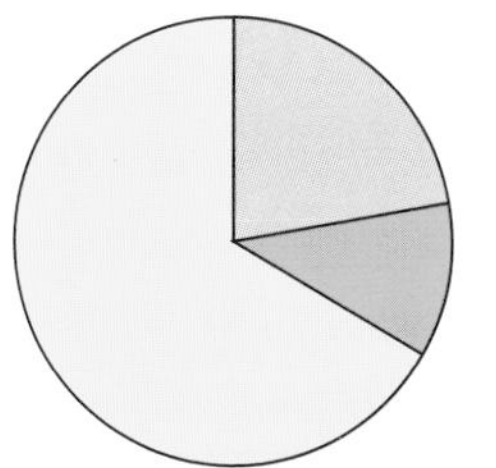

Figure 9.9 Employment structure for Brazil ▲

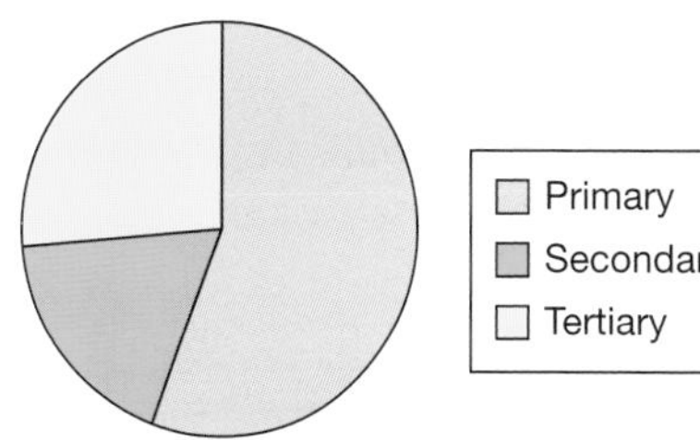

Figure 9.10 Employment structure for Ghana ▲

Activity

Primary, secondary and tertiary

Find out the importance of the three sectors to your country in terms of contribution to GNP and employment rates.

How have these changed over the last 20 years?

Link

For more on trade and absolute and comparative advantage see Chapter 4 page 105.

External trade

Originally developing countries relied heavily on exports of primary products, but in recent years countries such as China have specialised in manufactured goods. This is because the terms of trade of primary goods tend to worsen as against manufactured goods so that these countries receive a lower price for exports and pay a higher price for imports, while the supply and demand for primary products are generally price inelastic, i.e. they earn less for exports and pay more for imports. Differences in trade between developing countries can be seen in Table 9.10. While China, India and Brazil's exports contain a high proportion of manufactured goods, China being over 90 per cent, others are wholly primary with some countries being heavily dependent on one product, e.g. Saint Lucia 41 per cent bananas or Nigeria 95 per cent petroleum and petroleum products.

While developing countries, e.g. Nigeria, often export primary products and import manufactured ones, developed countries such as Italy often export and import similar products.

Table 9.10 Major exports and imports by commodities ▼

Country	Exports	Imports
Italy	Engineering products, textiles and clothing, production machinery, motor vehicles, transport equipment, chemicals; food, beverages and tobacco; minerals, non-ferrous metals	Engineering products, chemicals, transport equipment, energy products, minerals and non-ferrous metals, textiles and clothing; food, beverages and tobacco
Brazil	Transport equipment, iron ore, soybeans, footwear, coffee, vehicles	Machinery, electrical and transport equipment, chemical products, oil, automotive parts, electronics
China	Electrical and other machinery, including data processing equipment, clothing, textiles, iron and steel, optical and medical equipment	Electrical and other machinery, oil and mineral fuels; nuclear reactor, boiler and machinery components; optical and medical equipment, metal ores, motor vehicles; soybeans
India	Petroleum products, precious stones, machinery, iron and steel, chemicals, vehicles, apparel	Crude oil, precious stones, machinery, fertiliser, iron and steel, chemicals
Indonesia	Coal briquettes, petroleum gas, palm oil, rubber and crude petroleum	Refined petroleum, crude petroleum, planes, helicopters, computers and delivery trucks
Nigeria	Petroleum and petroleum products, cocoa, rubber	Machinery, chemicals, transport equipment, manufactured goods, food and live animals
Turkey	Apparel, foodstuffs, textiles, metal manufactures, transport equipment	Machinery, chemicals, semi-finished goods, fuels, transport equipment
Saint Lucia	Bananas clothing, cocoa, vegetables, fruits, coconut oil	Food, manufactured goods, machinery and transportation equipment, chemicals, fuels
Uruguay	Beef, soybeans, cellulose, rice, wheat, wood, dairy products, wool	Refined oil, crude oil, passenger and other transportation vehicles, vehicle parts, cellular phones
Zambia	Copper, cobalt, electricity, tobacco, flowers, cotton	Machinery, transportation equipment, petroleum products, electricity, fertiliser, foodstuffs, clothing

Urbanisation

> **Key term**
>
> **Urbanisation**: the increase in people living in towns and cities.

Urbanisation is the increase in the proportion of people living in towns and cities. This has become very important in developing countries. In Asia, Dhaka, Karachi, Jakarta, Mumbai, Delhi, Manila, Seoul and Beijing each have populations of over 20 million people and this is being replicated in other countries such as Nigeria (Lagos), Brazil (São Paulo), and Egypt (Cairo).

Vila Estrutural, Brasilia ▲

While the growth of cities and towns can lead to economic growth and increased prosperity it is also true that these large urban areas can result in poverty and crime. This is often hidden away as in Brasilia where the poor are hidden away in peripheral areas such as Vila Estrutural.

These problems are starting to lead governments to take action to improve the urban environment. The Chinese government set out its first urbanisation plan in March 2014 with the aim of repairing social exclusion and embracing sustainable city management as an explicit means of sustaining property and growth.

> **Case Study**
>
> ### Urbanisation
>
> Are cities good for us? Badly managed urbanisation will result in fragmentation, social exclusion and inequity. Lack of access to water, sanitation, secure tenure and good housing, exposure to pollution and violence, together with unemployment, will place an intolerable burden of ill health and early death on the poor. This, in turn, will undermine national development.
>
> In Bhutan, while young people are flocking to Thimphu, many have difficulty finding jobs and adapting to being away from their traditional family lives. This can lead to growing feelings of isolation and a worrying rise in everything from suicide and drug addiction to divorce rates.
>
> 1 State three problems mentioned in the passage on urbanisation.
> 2 For each explain why they are a problem for a developing economy.
> 3 Discuss how these problems of urbanisation could be overcome.

> **Link**
>
> For more on purchasing power parity see Chapter 4 page 100.

Comparison of economic growth rates and living standards over time and between countries

> **Key terms**
>
> **Informal economy**: that part of an economy which is untraceable and thus untaxable. It is sometimes called the underground or black economy.
>
> **Distribution of income**: the way in which income is shared out among the population. This can be seen using the Lorenz curve and the Gini coefficient.

It is important to use Real GDP/GNP (or GDP/GNP at constant prices) as this allows for comparisons both within a country and across countries. In order to compare between countries GDP is often transposed into US dollars or adjusted for purchasing power parity (PPP). There are difficulties, however, in using GDP to compare living standards. These include:

- non-traded goods and services or activities in the informal economy (black economy) are not counted
- distribution of income is not considered
- leisure can be lost as people work longer hours to increase GDP

- it ignores what is produced, e.g. large defence expenditure increases GDP, but not living standards
- exchange rate variations, which is why PPP is used
- quality of goods may vary.

> **Progress question**
>
> **5** Explain the problems involved in comparing living standards between countries.

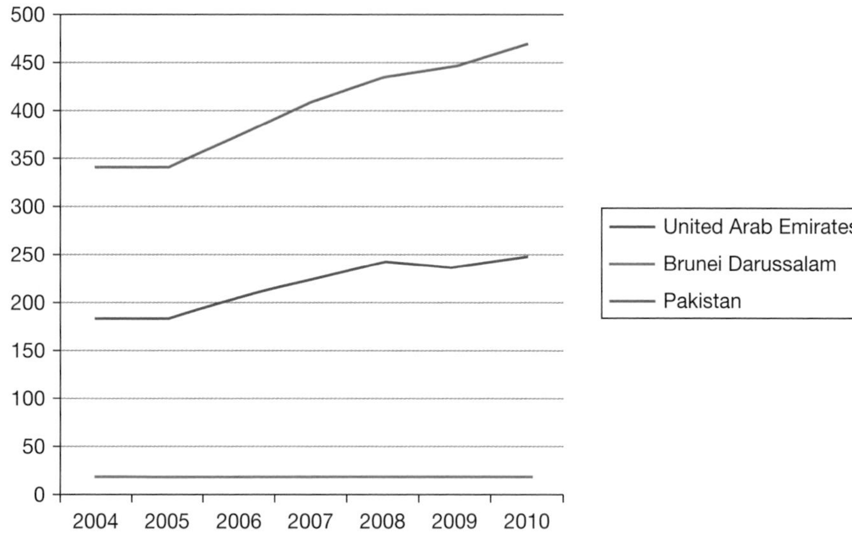

Figure 9.11 Gross domestic product based on PPP ▲
Source: *World Economic Outlook*, September 2011

> ## Activities
> ### Using GDP
>
> Using Figure 9.11:
>
> **1** Compare the growth in GDP of the three countries.
>
> **2** Decide whether you can use the data to compare economic growth rates or living standards. Why have you made this decision?
>
> **3** Identify what other information you would need in order to use the information for both economic growth and living standards comparisons.

In any comparison of living standards between countries it is important to remember that real GNP per capita is an average figure. It ignores the fact that, as shown in Tables 9.7 and 9.8, income may be very unequally distributed so that only some people have a higher standard of living than those in the other country.

Comparing growth rates can be equally problematical. Many of the problems mentioned above apply again, e.g. the black economy leading to understating of real GDP. In addition, in countries where literacy levels (for example the literacy level is only 35 per cent in Sierra Leone) are low information provided by individuals may not exist or may be unreliable. Another issue is how countries value government services which are provided free. These methods not only vary between countries, but individual countries sometimes change how they are estimated.

> ## Activity
> ### Standard of living
>
> Find out as a group what has happened to the standard of living and then, individually, try the Progress question.

> **Progress question**
>
> **6** To what extent has the standard of living in your country increased over the last 50 years?

Getting it right

Do not forget that many of the issues involved in comparing economic growth and living standards between countries and over time are the same for both concepts.

Activities

Comparing growth rates

Using Table 9.11 answer the following questions:

1. To what extent is it possible to compare the developed countries with the BRIC, MINT and developing countries?
2. What other information would be helpful in making the comparisons?
3. Find out the growth rates for your country, or for another country, for the period shown. How well is your country doing?
4. Find out what the growth rate was 20 years ago. Discuss the extent to which you can compare the rates.

Table 9.11 Economic growth rates for developed, BRIC, MINT and developing countries 2009–2012 ▼

Country	2009	2010	2011	2012
Austria	−3.8	1.8	2.8	0.9
Netherlands	−3.7	1.5	0.9	−1.2
Norway	−1.6	0.5	1.3	2.9
USA	−2.8	2.5	1.8	2.8
Brazil	−0.3	7.5	2.7	0.9
Russia	−7.8	4.5	4.3	3.4
India	8.5	10.3	6.6	4.7
China	9.2	10.4	9.3	7.8
Mexico	−4.7	5.1	4.0	3.8
Indonesia	4.6	6.2	6.5	6.2
Nigeria	6.9	7.8	6.8	6.5
Turkey	−4.8	9.2	8.8	2.2
Chile	−1.0	5.8	5.9	5.6
Mauritius	3.0	4.1	3.9	3.2
Tanzania	6.0	7.0	6.4	6.9
Vietnam	5.4	6.4	6.2	5.2

Source: http://data.worldbank.org/indicator/NY.GDP.MKTP.KD.ZG

Table 9.11 shows how difficult it can be to compare economic growth rates not only over time or between very different countries, but also between designated groups of countries.

Case Study

Indonesian development

In the period 2000 to 2010, using PPP, GNP per head rose by 100 per cent while there was a fall in poverty of 50 per cent. This fall could have been greater if more jobs had been available in the secondary sector. As it is, the fall was the result of people moving from the primary to the secondary sector.

The rise in GDP has increased living standards, but this has been accompanied by a rise in the Gini coefficient. As a World Bank report states: overall consumption grew by 4 per cent a year from 2003 to 2010, but while for the richest 20 per cent it rose by 5 per cent, for the poorest 40 per cent it only increased by 1.3 per cent.

This imbalance is further emphasised by government spending as 20 per cent of the budget is spent on energy subsidies, favouring the richer section of the population through cheap petrol. In addition, the majority of internal migrants who move to urban areas work in low-skilled service sector jobs, e.g. roadside food stalls. These jobs are part of the informal economy which accounts for 70 per cent of GDP.

The World Bank claims that the government could benefit not only the poor, but also the economy and the environment by: getting rid of fuel subsidies, reforming taxes and cutting the civil service; and using the money saved on greatly expanding expenditure on infrastructure, health and social welfare.

1 What is the advantage of using purchasing power parity to measure GNP per head?
2 Explain why moving from the primary sector to other sectors of the economy would be likely to reduce poverty.
3 To what extent are the World Bank's findings on consumption growth in line with what often happens in rapidly developing countries?
4 Discuss whether greatly increasing spending on infrastructure, health and social welfare would benefit the economy, the environment and the poor.

Employment and unemployment

Size and components of the labour force

The labour force consists of all those people who are eligible for work and are either employed or unemployed. This will consist of those who are not in full-time education and training and are below the retirement age. In many countries this consists of those over the age of 16 years who are not in full-time education and those under the age of 65 years, although as life expectancy increases this upper age point is increasing.

Key terms

Labour force: all the people in a particular country who are eligible to work, consisting of those employed plus those unemployed.
Dependency ratio: the percentage of the population who are under the working age and over the age of retirement as a ratio of the percentage who are of working age.
Participation rate: the percentage of the population of working age who are in work or are actively seeking work.
Working population: the number of people who are willing and eligible to work.

Dependency ratio refers to how many of those under 16 and over 64 depend on people of working age (16 to 64). Participation rate relates to those in work or seeking work. Slightly different and more wide-reaching is working population which in the UK consists of: the labour force + members of the armed forces + self-employed.

The labour force is usually divided up by:

- the sector of the economy in which they work, e.g. primary, secondary and tertiary
- the degree of economic activity, e.g. employed, unemployed or inactive (those who are not working, but have not registered as unemployed)
- gender participation.

Link

For more on sector of the economy see Chapter 1 page 25.

The size of the workforce depends on:

- birth rate – if this is higher than the death rate then the future workforce should grow
- age of retirement – many developed countries are raising the retirement age, partly to compensate for a declining workforce
- numbers in full-time education – where this increases then less people are entering the workforce.

Labour productivity

Key term

Labour productivity: output per worker per time period.

Labour productivity is measured as output per worker per period of time, usually per week, month or year, although it can be output per hour worked. A fall in the workforce can be compensated by an increase in labour productivity. Equally, a large workforce may not be very efficient and thus have low labour productivity. Labour productivity can be greatly influenced by the type and level of investment as this allows labour to have more and/or better capital equipment and access to modern technology. Whether this results in greater economic growth will depend on how efficiently it is utilised. Another way to increase labour productivity is through improving the education and training of labour. In general, an educated and skilled labour force will be more productive and thus will lead to higher economic growth.

Case Study

Employment in Mauritius

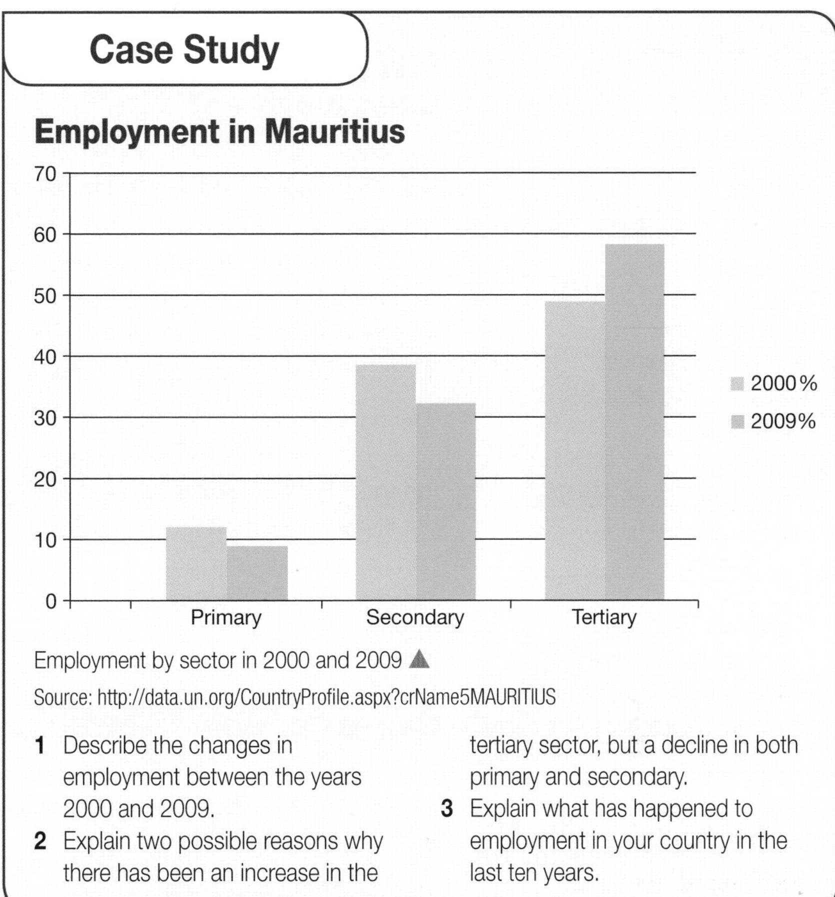

Employment by sector in 2000 and 2009 ▲

Source: http://data.un.org/CountryProfile.aspx?crName5MAURITIUS

1 Describe the changes in employment between the years 2000 and 2009.
2 Explain two possible reasons why there has been an increase in the tertiary sector, but a decline in both primary and secondary.
3 Explain what has happened to employment in your country in the last ten years.

Getting it right

When using percentages be careful what you write. In the chart, secondary employment has fallen by more percentage points than primary. However, within the two sectors the fall is greater for primary than secondary.

Case Study

Mauritius

Labour force participation by gender

Adult female pop. (%)	2009	40.8
Adult female pop. (%)	2000	40.6
Adult male pop. (%)	2009	74.8
Adult male pop. (%)	2000	80.4

Source: http://data.un.org/CountryProfile.aspx?crName5MAURITIUS

1 Give two possible reasons for the changes shown in the table her.
2 Explain what has happened to participation in the workforce by females and males in your country in the last ten years.

Labour productivity is measured by:

$$\text{Labour productivity} = \frac{\text{Total output per time period}}{\text{Number of units of labour employed}}$$

Getting it right

Do not confuse productivity with production. The latter is the total output of the goods or services of an industry, business etc.

Progress question

7 Explain why it is important for a country to try and increase its labour productivity.

Full employment and natural rate of unemployment

Full employment is one of the aims of governments. It does not mean that all those of working age is employed, as some may choose early retirement or to continue with education or to stay at home to look after children. In addition, some people at any time are between jobs. In reality, full employment is usually claimed to have been reached when somewhere between two and four per cent of the working population are not in jobs.

The natural rate of unemployment, sometimes called the non-accelerating rate of unemployment (NAIRU), is where the rate of inflation is unchanging because the aggregate demand for labour equals the aggregate supply of labour leading to no upward pressure on wage rates and thus inflation. It is usually associated with monetarists such as Friedman who argue that the natural rate cannot be reduced as any increase in aggregate demand leads to higher inflation and thus more unemployment. For a diagram please refer to Figures 10.1 and 10.2.

Key terms

Full employment: when all those willing and able to work at the given real wage rate are either in a job or are about to take up a job.

Natural rate of unemployment: the level of unemployment that exists when the aggregate demand for labour equals the aggregate supply of labour at the given real wage rate.

Link

For more on the natural rate of unemployment (NAIRU) see Chapter 10 page 304.

Causes of unemployment

Unemployment means all those people of working age who are actively seeking work at the existing wage rate, but have been unable to do so.

The causes of unemployment are something that different schools of economists have differing views about. Causes are not the same as types, see below, although they clearly overlap.

Classical economists maintain that unemployment is due to trade, or business, cycles which the market is capable of putting right. Monetarists maintain that external interference in the labour market causes supply to not equal demand. They would argue that factors such as minimum wage laws, restrictive union practices, taxes on companies, unemployment and other benefits, and regulations and red tape which detract from production and employment all prevent the market from clearing. Occupational or geographical immobility will have the same effect.

Keynesians emphasise the cyclical nature of unemployment and that lack of aggregate demand for goods and services reduces the demand for workers. This can best be corrected by government intervention to increase demand.

Key terms

Unemployment: means all those people of working age who are actively seeking work at the current wage rate.

Trade, or business, cycles: the fluctuations in GDP in the sequence of boom, recession, depression and recovery.

Getting it right

Note that unemployment consists of those "willing and able" not just out of work.

Karl Marx ▲

Marxists claim that it is in the interest of owners to have unemployment, the "reserve army of labour", as this keeps wages low thus reducing costs. Their solution is to abolish capitalism and replace it with socialism.

Progress question

8 Explain what is the main cause of unemployment in your economy. Justify your choice.

Consequences of unemployment

Unemployment leads both to a wastage of resources and to the opportunity cost of lost potential output. This can be seen in Figure 9.1 at the beginning of this chapter, where the economy is operating at point X. It has both economic consequences for the economy and the individual as well as social consequences.

Economic consequences include:

- Labour resources are wasted not only because output is below what it could be, but also because the resources invested in education and training are not being utilised.
- Fall in living standards as unemployment means less income leading to lower consumption.
- Lower aggregate demand not only from those made unemployed, but also from those in employment deciding to save more, and consume less, in case they are made unemployed. This fall in consumption then leads to further unemployment and the development of a deflationary gap. The rise in savings can lead to a reverse multiplier effect.
- Rise in NAIRU as those made unemployed find that their skills become outdated so that it is harder to find work, leading to a lack of confidence and motivation and higher long run unemployment. This is sometimes called the hysteresis effect.
- In many countries governments provide unemployment benefits, so a rise in unemployment means more money is spent on these benefits. This increases the cost to the taxpayer of having to support these people when governments are receiving less revenue from both incomes and consumer expenditure. This can lead to a budget deficit.
- Regional problems, as unemployment is often concentrated in certain areas of a country. This can lead the younger and the more enterprising people in the area to move away, making it even more depressed and unlikely to attract new jobs.
- Income inequality can be widened as more people go into relative poverty.

Key term

Hysteresis: the tendency for unemployment to lead to longer-term unemployment.

Social consequences include:

- Health: in some countries the loss of income can make it more difficult to provide medical care, while in others financial worries can cause both mental and physical health problems and even higher suicide rates.
- Education: where education has to be paid for, families may be tempted to save money by withdrawing children from schools while at the same time sending them out to work to bring in more income.
- Family: the stress of unemployment can cause divorce and family break-ups if homelessness occurs. It can lead to higher crime rates as people are desperate to survive.

Case Study

Youth unemployment in Tanzania

Although Tanzania has been congratulated for its economic growth which averaged between 6 per cent and 7 per cent in the first decade of this century, it has had an unemployment rate for those under the age of 24 between 9 per cent and 24 per cent depending on the source of information and the ways in which unemployment is defined. Undoubtedly, if disguised unemployment was added the rate would be far higher as a very large proportion of the population is employed in agriculture. This employment often provides only irregular and poorly paid work.

Many young people find getting work difficult due to lack of:

- sufficient education and/or jobs for them once they graduate especially in urban areas
- skills needed for self-employment
- start-up credit facilities
- adequate information, while that which is available is often gender insensitive
- technological progress in agriculture which leads to migration to urban areas.

The consequences include emigration, crime, a rise in HIV and family break-ups.

To counter this Tanzania has plans to create over one million jobs in the next five years.

1 Explain why a large agricultural sector could lead to a high level of disguised unemployment.
2 Using any two of the causes of unemployment mentioned in the passage, explain why these could cause youth unemployment to be high in Tanzania.
3 Discuss whether young people seeking employment abroad would be good for the Tanzanian economy.

Types of unemployment

Table 9.12 shows the different types of unemployment.

Table 9.12 Different types of unemployment ▼

Type of unemployment	Explanation
Casual	Workers are made unemployed on a short-term basis because in jobs such as acting work finishes once the play or film is completed.
Classical or real wage	If real wages are above the market clearing wage there will be excess supply.

Continued . . .

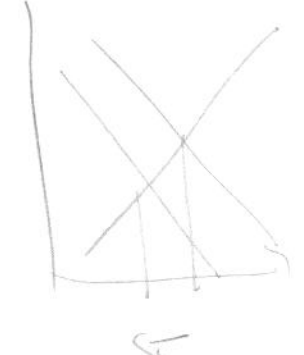

Type of unemployment	Explanation
Cyclical or demand deficient or general	Caused by the trade cycle and occurs during the downswing of the cycle becoming severe during the recession. This is the classic Keynesian unemployment due to lack of aggregate demand in the economy as a whole.
Disguised (under-employment)	Workers may be in jobs, but there is insufficient work for them to do. For often political reasons they are not made unemployed. This hides the real rate of unemployment.
Frictional	This is unemployment that cannot be removed. It consists of those who are moving from one job to another, but have not yet started this new work.
Involuntary	Exists when a worker is willing to take a job at the current wage rate, but cannot find one. This will include those who are cyclically or structurally unemployed.
Regional	A form of structural unemployment where an industry which is located in one or more regions of a country closes down.
Seasonal	In some industries the demand for workers depends on the time of the year. This is especially the case in industries such as agriculture, building and tourism.
Structural	This is caused by a permanent fall in demand for the products of an industry. It is caused by either resources being exhausted or by a country losing its comparative advantage. It is often associated with rising labour costs causing labour-intensive industries to move to low-cost countries.
Technological	This is a form of structural unemployment caused by technology replacing labour.
Voluntary	Some people may decide not to work at the current wage level thus making themselves unemployed.

Getting it right

Be careful that you really know the differences between the various types of unemployment. It is easy to confuse cyclical, frictional and structural.

Link

For more on the trade (business) cycle see page 270.

Activity

Types of unemployment

Discuss as a group what you consider to be the main types of unemployment in your country. Place these in rank order of importance.

Key term

Unemployment rate: the percentage of the working population who are unemployed.

Unemployment rate and patterns and trends

$$\text{Unemployment rate} = \frac{\text{Number of people out of work} \times 100}{\text{Working population}}$$

Patterns and trends in employment/unemployment can be both within individual countries and between different countries. Among the different ways of looking at this are: total, gender, age, economic sector, ethnic group etc.

Looking at Table 9.13, it can be seen that the four countries each have different trends. Unemployment in Angola has remained stable; in Greece it has risen, almost trebling over the four years; in Haiti it has fluctuated (risen then fallen and then gone back to about the same figure); and in Namibia it has fallen. One overall trend is that Haiti's unemployment rate was the lowest at the start and at the end. Another is that Greece and Namibia have switched places as far as having the highest unemployment.

It is also possible to talk in terms of consistently high or low unemployment as seen in Table 9.14.

Getting it right

If you are asked about trends, *do not* describe but try to comment on the overall pattern.

Activities

Unemployment trends

1 Find out what has happened to unemployment rates in your country over the last ten tears. If possible do so by: total unemployment; gender; age groups; etc.

2 Plot the information on a graph (s) and discover the trend.

You may find it useful to split these activities between you and then to compare your findings.

3 If any interesting patterns occur you should discuss why these are happening. You could compare your overall trend with that of another country.

Key terms

Labour force survey: a survey of a sample of households, counting people as unemployed if they are actively seeking work but do not have a job.

Claimant count: measures unemployment according to the number of people claiming unemployment benefits.

Sampling: when a proportion of the population is taken as representative of the whole. The figure for the total is based on this sample being accurate.

Table 9.13 Unemployment rates (%) in selected countries ▼

Country	2009	2010	2011	2012
Angola	7.6	7.6	7.6	7.5
Greece	9.5	12.5	17.7	24.2
Haiti	7.1	8.3	6.7	7.0
Namibia	29.7	22.1	19.8	16.7

Source: http://data.worldbank.org/indicator/SL.UEM.TOTL.ZS

Table 9.14 Unemployment rates (%) ▼

Country	2009	2010	2011	2012
South Africa	23.7	24.7	24.7	25.0
Thailand	1.5	1.0	0.7	0.7

Source: http://data.worldbank.org/indicator/SL.UEM.TOTL.ZS

Difficulties involved in measuring unemployment

Measuring unemployment seems at first easy: just count up all those who are unemployed. It is not, however, that simple. Firstly, there are different ways of measuring unemployment and these can vary between countries.

The International Labour Organization (ILO) uses the labour force survey and this is used for international comparisons. The UK also uses the claimant count, which relates to those registered as unemployed and claiming the jobseeker's allowance. Those people who are not eligible for this, or who have not registered, are not included. This results in the labour force survey giving a higher figure than the claimant count. The labour force survey, however, is subject to sampling errors and may not be entirely representative.

In addition to the possibility of different measures, there are a number of other problems:

- Inactive workers. Although some of these are genuinely not interested in work, e.g. those who have retired early, many would work if either their situation changed, e.g. mothers or fathers with young children, or if the wage rate was more attractive.
- Discouraged workers are those who are willing and able to work, but because they have had no success finding a job have given up actively seeking employment.
- Part-time workers. Many of these may be working part time because they wish to, e.g. mothers or fathers with children at school may want hours which fit with the school day. Others, however, may want to work full time. These are counted as employed, but could be seen as semi-unemployed.
- Unreported legal employment. Some workers may register as unemployed to collect state benefits, but in fact work, thus defrauding the state.

Activities

Measuring unemployment

1. Find out how your country measures unemployment.
2. Does your country have any other difficulties in measuring unemployment?

Link

For more on AD see Chapter 4 page 87.

Key term

Phillips curve: a curve showing the inverse relationship between the rates of inflation and unemployment. See also expectations-augmented Phillips curve and NAIRU.

Links

The following are examined in more detail on the pages indicated:

For fiscal, monetary policies see Chapter 5 page 123.

For Phillips curve see Chapter 10 page 304.

For conflicts between inflation and unemployment see Chapter 10 page 303.

Link

For more on exchange rates see Chapter 4 page 99.

- Unreported illegal employment. The so-called "underground economy" consists of illegal activities, such as gambling, the sale of drugs and prostitution. People engaged in these illegal activities, however, are in employment but are registered as unemployed.

Progress question

9 Explain the problems involved in the measurement of the unemployment rate.

Policies to correct unemployment

Policies depend both on how the causes of unemployment are viewed and also on the time period.

In the short term both fiscal and monetary policies can be used. Fiscal policy will involve: the cutting of taxes for consumers, both direct and indirect, so as to increase consumption (C); cutting of taxes on companies, such as corporation or profits tax, so as to encourage greater investment (I); and a direct increase in government expenditure (G). As C, I and G are all part of aggregate demand (AD) this will then increase, leading to a rise in output, income and employment, see Figure 9.12.

Figure 9.12 shows that any increase in a component of AD will shift it from AD to AD_1 leading to greater output, income and employment at Y_1. If, however, AD increases by too much to AD_2, then inflation rises from p to p_1. This could lead to the long run Phillips curve

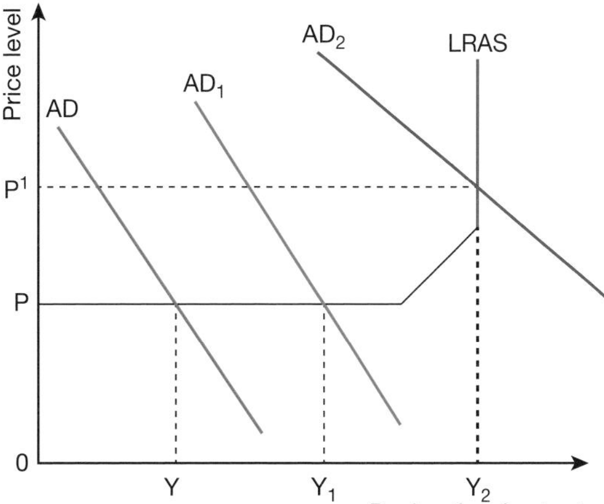

Figure 9.12 An increase in aggregate demand ▲

where attempts to reduce unemployment have no real effect except to increase inflation.

Using monetary policy, the rate of interest can be cut or a policy such as quantitative easing used. Reducing interest rates will: encourage consumers to save less and spend more (as the opportunity cost of doing so has fallen) and to borrow more; encourage firms to invest more as the cost of borrowing has fallen; cause a fall in the exchange rate leading to a rise in exports.

The effect on AD can again be shown by Figure 9.13.

In the long run, supply-side policies would be effective in improving labour productivity by training or retraining and by providing better education and health services. Figure 9.13 shows that shifting AS to AS_1 will overcome any inflationary effects of increasing AD and at the same time increase output, income and employment from Y to Y_1.

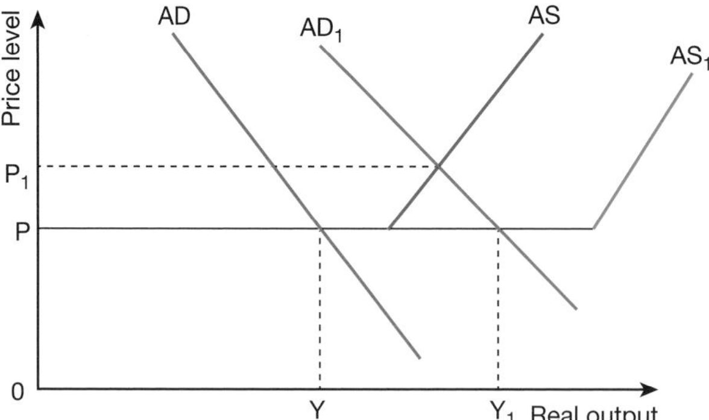

Figure 9.13 Operation of supply-side policy ▲

Key terms

Closed economy: an economy without exports and imports, consisting solely of consumption, investment and government expenditure.

Open economy: an economy in which there are exports and imports.

Progress question

10 Explain the effectiveness of different policies in reducing unemployment.

Link

For more on free market and mixed economies see Chapter 1 page 23.

The circular flow of income

Closed and open economies

The circular flow of income is a way of showing that money flows between households, or individuals, firms and government in an economy. If there is no foreign trade then this is called a closed economy. With foreign trade it becomes an open economy.

Table 9.15 Components of different types of economies ▼

Components	Type of economy
Y = C + S	Simple, closed economy
Y = C + I	Closed free market economy
Y= C + I + G	Closed mixed economy
Y= C + I + G + (X–M)	Open economy

Key terms

Circular flow of income: shows how money circulates in an economy between households, firms and governments.

Consumption: that part of a household's current income which is spent on goods and services.

Saving: that part of a household's current income which is not consumed.

Leakage: income received by households or firms that is not passed on in the circular flow and thus reduces the value of GDP.

The circular flow of income between households, firms, government and the international economy

The circular flow of income refers to the idea that money is provided to the factors of production in exchange for their services. In turn the owners of these factors then spend the money on the goods and services which are provided. In other words, the flow of money is like a circle. In Figure 9.15 households supply labour and in return receive income. They spend this, consumption, and get in return goods and services.

In reality some people save and this is a withdrawal or leakage from the system, reducing the circular flow. This is the same with taxes and imports where the money flows out to other economies. Equally, more

Key term

Injection: money from outside the circular flow that increases the value of GDP.

Link

For more on factors of production see Chapter 1 page 16.

Getting it right

Do not confuse investment, done by firms, which is an injection, and savings, done by individuals, which is a withdrawal.

Activity

Injections and withdrawals

Try to find out the values of the main injections and withdrawals in your country.

Key terms

Average propensity to consume: the proportion of total income that is consumed.

Average propensity to save: the proportion of total income that is saved.

Dissave: a consumer spends more than they earn; where C is greater than Y.

money can be injected into the system through investment by firms, government expenditure and exports where money flows in from other economies.

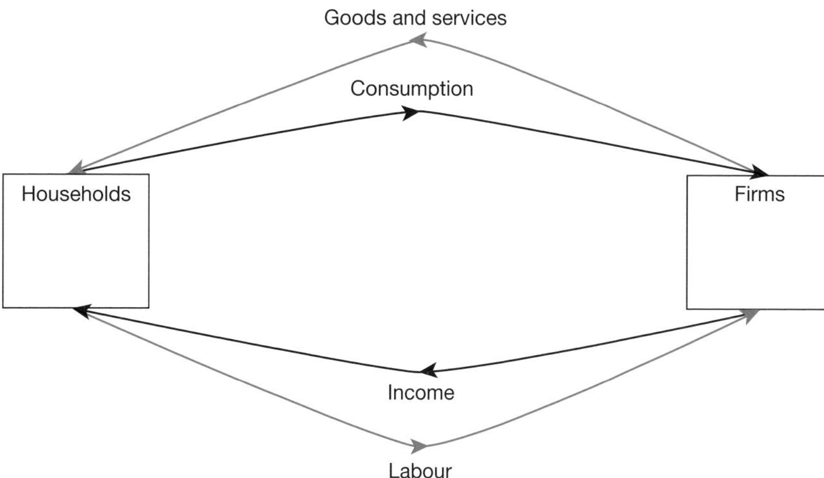

Figure 9.14 The circular flow of income in a closed economy without government ▲

In an open economy we would need to show money from exports coming into the system and money for imports leaving the system.

Progress question

11 Using examples, explain the difference between investment and savings.

Average and marginal propensities to save and consume

The average propensities measure the total of consumption or saving as a proportion of total income. The average propensity to consume (APC) is total consumption as a proportion of total income (Y). It is measured as:

$$APC = \frac{\text{Total consumption}}{\text{Total income}} = \frac{C}{Y}$$

As a person's income rises the APC will fall as that person can now afford to save out of their income and thus consume less of any increase. The opposite will be true of the average propensity to save (APS). Indeed, at low levels of income consumers may dissave by drawing on savings to help their consumption level. APS is measured by:

$$APS = \frac{\text{Total saving}}{\text{Total income}} = \frac{S}{Y}$$

The marginal propensity to consume (MPC) refers to the proportion of any change in income which is consumed, and is measured as:

$$MPC = \frac{\text{Change in consumption}}{\text{Change in income}} = \frac{\Delta C}{\Delta Y}$$

Key terms

Marginal propensity to consume: the proportion of any change in income that is consumed.
Marginal propensity to save: the proportion of any change in income that is saved.
Multiplier: the number of times by which a change in injections is increased, or decreased, to give the final change in national income.

Getting it right

With the circular flow always ask in which direction is the money going. If you do this then you will get X and M correct: X in and M out.

Links

For more on injections and withdrawals see pages 276 and 277.

For more on marginal rate of tax see Chapter 3 page 76.

where Δ stands for change in. Similarly, the marginal propensity to save (MPS) is the proportion of any change in income that is saved:

$$\text{APS} = \frac{\text{Change in saving}}{\text{Change in income}} = \frac{\Delta S}{\Delta Y}$$

As with APC and APS, MPC declines as income rises, while MPS rises.

The multiplier

The multiplier effect happens all the time in an economy. It represents the amount by which any change in injections (J) is increased or decreased to give the final change in national income. If a government, for example, increases its expenditure this results in a greater change in national income.

To explain, this assume that we have a very simple economy with only consumers (C) and investors (I). If investment increases by \$100 and consumers always spend 80 per cent of any increase in the incomes (MPC = 0.8) then they will, in turn, spend \$80 and save (S) \$20. This will continue until there is nothing left to spend as shown below:

$\text{I} = \$100 + \text{C} = (80 + 64 + 51.2 + \ldots\ldots\ldots\ldots) = \$500$

$\text{S} = (20 + 16 + 12.8 + \ldots\ldots\ldots\ldots) = \$100$

There are two different, but related, changes to note:

1. National income has risen by \$500 which is 5× the initial injection. This because the value of the multiplier (k) is 5. This is derived from the following equation: $k = \frac{1}{1-\text{MPC}} = \frac{1}{1-0.8} = \frac{1}{0.2} = 5$
2. Savings have increased to \$100, which equals the amount invested. This is because Injections = Withdrawals.

In a simple economy Y = C + S. In this situation $\text{MPS} = \frac{\Delta S}{\Delta Y}$ which is the same as 1−MPC. In the equation in point 1 above, the MPS is 0.2.

Progress question

12 If a government injects a large sum of money into its economy, explain the difference in its effect if the economy is (a) closed, and (b) open.

Key terms

Marginal rate of tax: the proportion of any change in income that is paid in direct tax.
Marginal propensity to import: the change in imports induced by a change in income.

If all withdrawals (W) are considered then the multiplier will be:

$$k = \frac{1}{\text{MPS} + \text{MRT} + \text{MPM}}$$

Here MRT is the marginal rate of tax and MPM is the marginal propensity to import.

This means that if the marginal propensity to save is 0.2 and of imports is 0.1 while the marginal rate of tax is 0.1 then the value of the multiplier is: $k = \frac{1}{0.2 + 0.1 + 0.1} = \frac{1}{0.4} = 2.5$

Notice that the effect of increasing the withdrawals is to reduce the value of the multiplier because more money leaks out of the circular flow.

If the multiplier is now put together with injections the formula is $\Delta Y = (I + G + X)\,k = \Delta J \times k$.

Keynesian multiplier

There are many different multipliers, but the one used here is the traditional Keynesian multiplier. Many economists now doubt whether there is a real multiplier effect for some injections, but it is clear that the opening of a new factory in an area will not only create jobs directly, but will lead to more demand in shops, increasing their incomes and thus demand for labour, leading to these people having more money, and so on.

Activities

The multiplier

1. If MPC = 0.75, what is the value of k?
2. If MPS = 0.2; MRT = 0.15, MPM = 0.15, what is the value of k?
3. If I = 20, G = 20, X = 10, use the value you got for k in the previous activity to calculate ΔY.

Case Study

The multiplier in different countries

The value of the multiplier will vary between countries depending on factors such as the extent of international trade and people's behaviour regarding saving.

The following values have been calculated for four developing countries:

Iran 2.56

India 3.53

Indonesia 3.20

Malaysia 2.54

1. Calculate the effect of an injection of 10 million rupiah on the Indonesian national income.
2. Explain two different effects on the countries shown of an investment of $10 million from a US company.
3. Explain one other effect that such an investment might have on your country.

Aggregate expenditure (AE)

Using a Keynesian model of income determination, and assuming that aggregate supply is horizontal in the short run, then the equilibrium level of real national income is determined by demand. In the circular flow of income, for it to be in equilibrium planned expenditure must equal planned production.

AE function, meaning, components and their determinants

In a closed economy AE consists of Consumption (C), Investment (I) and Government expenditure (G).

In Figure 9.15, the 45° line is where planned expenditure equals real national income.

In many cases even when $Y = 0$ there will be some consumption. This is called autonomous consumption. The consumption line is shown by the equation $C = a + b(MPC)Y$.

Key term

Equilibrium income: the aggregate demand for goods and services is equal to aggregate supply during a period of time. In this case, the economy is neither growing nor shrinking: J + W.

Y, Y_1 and Y_2 are points of equilibrium. The effect of adding in investment is to increase equilibrium income from Y to Y_1 while the addition of government expenditure shifts it to Y_2.

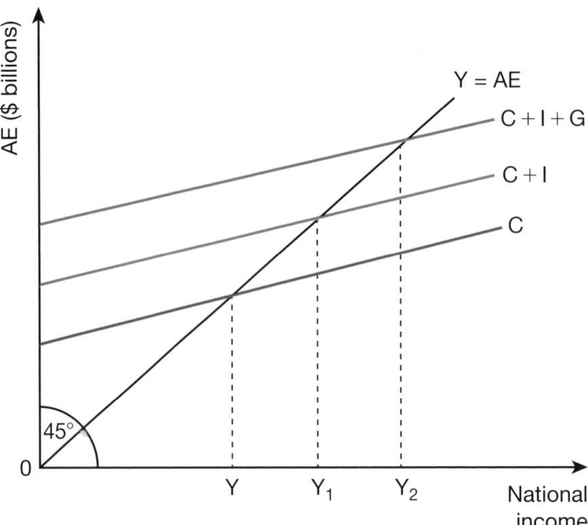

Figure 9.15 Aggregate expenditure equilibrium ▲

An open economy adds net exports (exports (X) – imports (M)) so AE = C + I + G + (X−M).

The slope of the consumption line is determined by the relationship between consumption and income, called the marginal propensity to consume. This is calculated as follows: where C is greater than Y and APS is greater than 1, then households must be using their savings, or borrowing, in order to support their consumption. This is called dissaving. In Figure 9.15 this is anywhere to the left of the 45° line.

The level of consumption is determined by:

- Income, as shown above.
- Wealth, i.e. assets. If a consumers' wealth increases then the consumption function will shift upwards. This could be because house prices rise faster than inflation.
- Rate of interest – if this falls then consumers are likely both to save less and to borrow more, both increasing consumption.
- Expectations – if consumers are optimistic about the future, e.g. they expect their incomes to rise, then they may increase consumption in anticipation of this happening.
- Income distribution – the rich tend to have a lower MPC than the poor so if income is redistributed from the rich to the poor consumption is likely to rise.

The level of investment is determined by:

- The rate of interest: as interest rates fall investment increases because it is cheaper to borrow money.
- Demand: firms will want to invest more if they expect demand to increase as the return on investment will rise.

Link

Merit and public goods are covered in Chapter 1 pages 30 and 32.

- Innovation and technology: innovations and new technology will both lead to more investment as they raise the productivity of capital goods.
- Taxes on company profits: many governments, e.g. Ireland, have lowered corporation tax to encourage greater investment.

The level of government expenditure is determined by:

- Political factors – governments have found it easy to increase expenditure, but politically difficult to reduce it. This can be seen in many European countries in the period 2010 onwards.
- The need to maintain low inflation, full employment and economic growth
- Provision of merit and public goods to help reduce income inequality.
- Ability to borrow money.

The level of net exports is determined by:

- GDP of a country: as this increases so do imports.
- GDP of other countries: if other countries' GDP rises so should exports to them.
- Exchange rates: a fall in a country's exchange rates should assuming the Marshall–Lerner condition improve net exports.
- Competitiveness: if this increases, e.g. higher productivity, then also should net exports.

Link

Marshall–Lerner is explained in Chapter 4 page 101.

Income determination

Equilibrium national income can be determined in two ways: using AE and through injections (J) and withdrawals (W).

Link

For more on injections and withdrawals see pages 276 and 277.

Using AE, as can be seen in Figure 9.15 the level of national income is determined by the point at which the aggregate expenditure line intersects the 45° line. If AE = C + I then this is at Y_1. If AE increases through the introduction of government expenditure then national income rises to Y_2 where C + I + G intersect the 45° line.

Injections and withdrawals

An alternative approach is to use injections and withdrawals:

Injections = Investment + Government expenditure + Exports: J = I + G + X, i.e. money coming into the circular flow from outside the system.

Withdrawals = Savings, Taxes and Imports: W= S + T + M, i.e. money that leaves the system.

Each of the withdrawals is an opposite to one of the injections:

Savings to investment; taxes to government expenditure; and imports to exports.

Activities

Aggregate expenditure and national income

Use the information below to draw an aggregate expenditure diagram similar to Figure 9.15.

Income	Consumption	Investment
300	250	20
250	210	20
200	170	20
150	130	20
100	90	20
50	50	20
0	10	0

1. Calculate the MPC.
2. Calculate APC when Y = 300.
3. When Y = 0 what is the value of dissaving?
4. What is the value of Y when C + I intersect the 45° line?
5. If I increases from 20 to 40 what is the new value of Y?

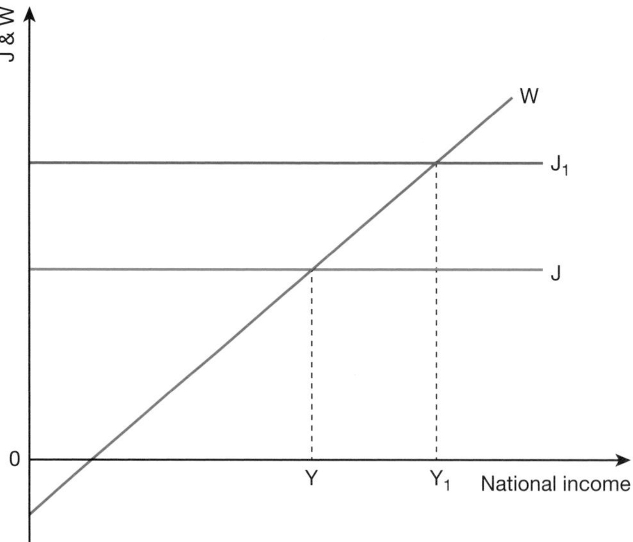

Figure 9.16 Injections and withdrawals ▲

Figure 9.16 shows that national income is determined by the intersection of J and W, i.e. J = W.

The relationship between the two methods can be seen in Figure 9.17. Both methods result in the same level of national income.

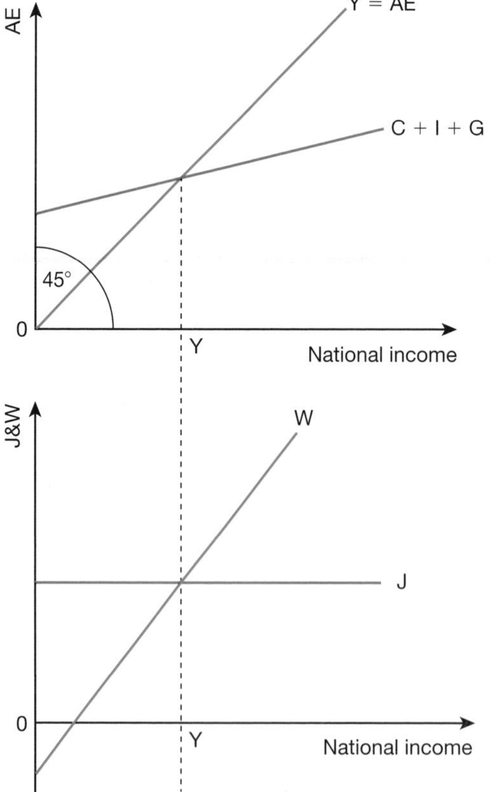

Figure 9.17 Comparison of AE and J/W methods for national income ▲

Paradox of thrift

It is often assumed that increasing savings is good for the economy. This means, however, that planned withdrawals are now higher than

Key term

Paradox of thrift: an increase in savings will eventually lead to a fall in savings.

planned injections. Consumers have reduced expenditure in order to save more. This means that firms need to employ less people. These people will have less income so will save less. This idea that an increase in savings (a to b shown by S to S_1) leads to a fall in savings is called the paradox of thrift.

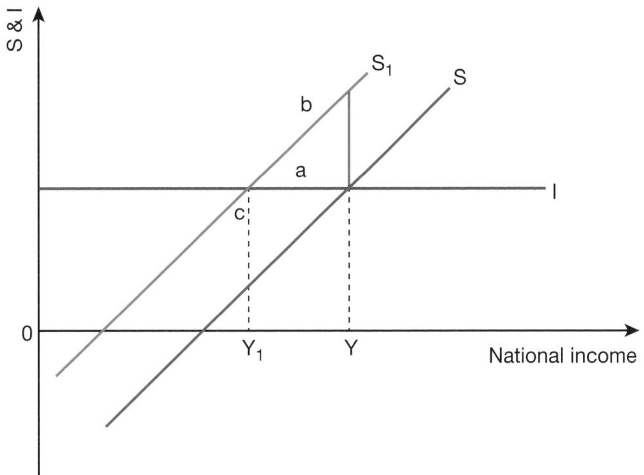

Figure 9.18 The paradox of thrift ▲

Progress question

13 Using diagram(s), explain how an injection leads to an increase in aggregate expenditure.

Key term

Full employment equilibrium: all resources are fully employed. Real GDP = potential GDP.

Full employment level of income and equilibrium level of income

The economy is in equilibrium when J = W or when AE intersects the 45° line. This is not the same as full employment equilibrium which is where resources are fully employed and the price level is not increasing, whereas J = W says nothing about the level of employment or the rate of inflation. The economy can be in equilibrium with millions of people unemployed or, equally, where prices are rapidly rising.

As can be seen below, full employment equilibrium is where all resources are employed.

Getting it right

Be careful not to confuse equilibrium national income and full employment national income. This is a common error made by candidates.

Inflationary and deflationary gaps

Inflationary gaps and deflationary gaps (sometimes called expansionary and output gaps) refer to the relationship between real GDP and potential GDP. This can be shown using AE or AD/AS.

Key terms

Inflationary gap: where aggregate demand is greater than aggregate supply leading to inflation. It is also where real GDP exceeds potential GDP.
Deflationary gap: where aggregate demand is less than aggregate supply or real GDP is less than potential output.

For more on potential growth/ output see page 250.

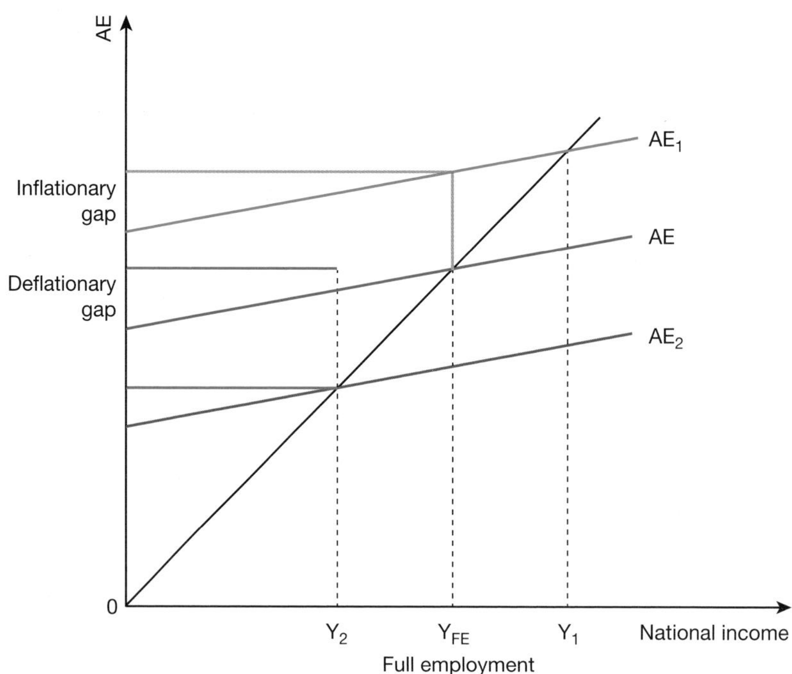

Figure 9.19 Inflationary and deflationary gaps ▲

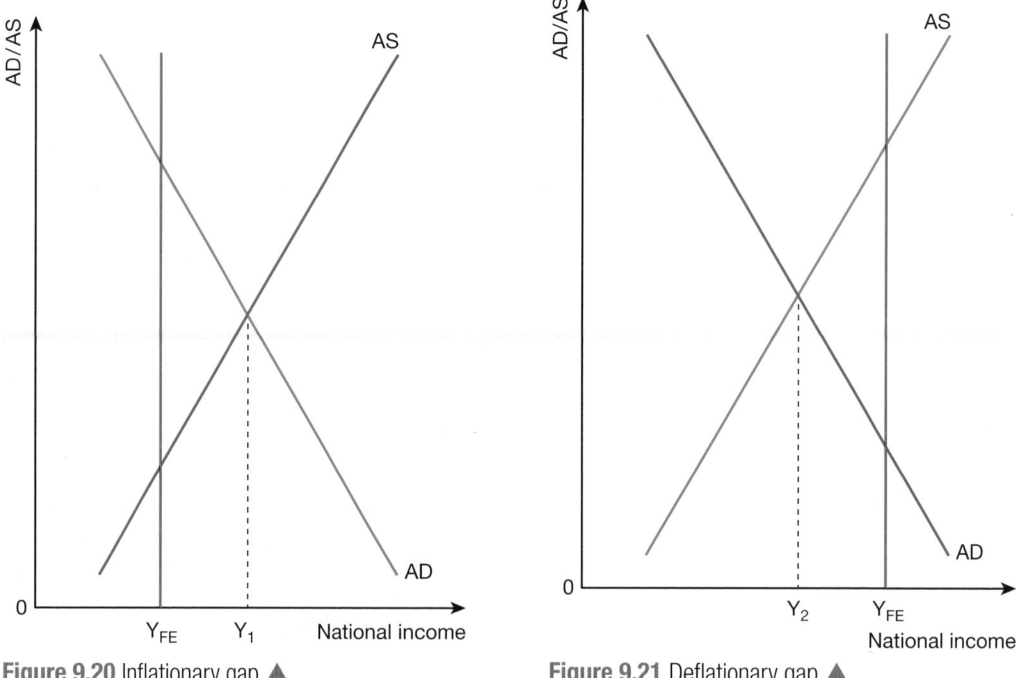

Figure 9.20 Inflationary gap ▲

Figure 9.21 Deflationary gap ▲

In the case of the inflationary gap, as actual demand exceeds that which the economy can supply the gap is filled by the price level rising, i.e. inflation. Equally, in the case of a deflationary gap actual demand is less than the economy can supply so that not all resources are employed.

Progress question

14 Explain what happens to (a) the rate of inflation, and (b) employment when a country has either an inflationary or a deflationary gap.

The accelerator and autonomous and induced investment

> **Key terms**
>
> Accelerator: the level of investment depends on the rate of growth of demand.
>
> Autonomous investment: investment that is not related to the level of national income. It is an injection into the circular flow and interacts with the multiplier.
>
> Induced investment: investment that depends on changes in national income.

The accelerator is based on the idea that the level of aggregate demand generates investment. If national income increases then more investment is needed to meet the higher demand. This investment that responds to changes in national income is called induced investment, whereas the investment as an injection in the multiplier is called autonomous investment.

In Table 9.16 at the start the firm has ten machines, and one of these needs replacing each year to be able to produce 100 units each per year. It shows how investment will respond to a change in demand. In year 4 constant demand means that there is no induced investment, while the fall in demand in year 5 leads to no investment.

Table 9.16 Induced investment and the accelerator ▼

Year	Demand	Number of machines	Machines needed	Replacement investment	Induced investment	Total investment
1	1000	10	10	1	0	1
2	1100	10	11	1	1	2
3	1400	11	14	1	4	5
4	1400	14	14	1	0	1
5	1300	14	13	0	0	0

> **Links**
>
> For more on trade cycles see page 251.
> For more on capital see Chapter 1 page 17.

There are clear links between the accelerator and the multiplier. If income rises then the accelerator predicts that businesses will invest more. Through the multiplier this will, in turn, lead to higher national income. In order to explain the persistence of trade cycles investment is now seen as dependent not only on income, but also on business's productive capacity.

> **Key terms**
>
> Capital-output ratio: the amount of capital required to produce a defined level of output.
>
> Yield: the return, such as interest or dividends, from an asset shown as a percentage of the investment's cost, market price or face value.

An important idea associated with the accelerator is the capital-output ratio. This is the ratio of capital used to produce a unit of output in a given time period. Where capital is cheap relative to other factor inputs, the ratio is likely to be high.

Investment is influenced also by the yield, which is the income return on an investment such as dividends on shares divided by its price. The higher the yield the more attractive is the investment.

Money supply (theory)

Quantity theory of money

> **Key term**
>
> Quantity theory of money: states that any increase in the money supply will lead to an increase in the price level after a time lag.

The quantity theory of money is used by monetarists to help explain the cause of inflation, as they claim it shows a direct link between increases in the money supply and increases in prices.

The quantity theory (sometimes called the Fisher equation) is stated as $MV = PT$ or sometimes as $MV = PY$, where:

- ▶ M is the money supply
- ▶ V is the velocity of circulation or the number of times money changes hands

> **Link**
>
> For more on causes of inflation see Chapter 4 page 93.

- P is the general price level
- T is the number of transactions or output
- Y is real GDP.

The equation itself is true as it says that demand equals supply or that both sides represent total expenditure. To use the equation, V and T are held to be constant over a period of time so that any increase in the money supply must lead to a similar increase in prices given a time lag of around 18 months.

> **Activity**
>
> **Money supply**
>
> Find out how your country's government/central bank measures the money supply.

Broad and narrow money supply

The money supply is the total amount of money in a country. It clearly consists of notes and coins, but today more and more transactions are done using cheques, debit cards, credit cards and electronic bank transfers. It is usual, therefore, to distinguish between narrow money and broad money although there is no completely agreed definition of either between countries or economists. Narrow money is sometimes referred to as M0 or M1 and broad money as M3 or M4.

> **Key terms**
>
> **Narrow money**: consists of notes, coins and usually demand deposits (sometimes called current accounts).
>
> **Broad money**: consists of notes and coins and all bank deposits together with easily available money in other financial institutions.
>
> **Central bank**: controls a country's money supply as the issuer of notes and coins and controls the level of reserves a commercial bank must hold. It also sets the rate of interest.

Sources of money supply in an open economy

The definitions of money supply indicate that there are many sources and not just the currency issued by the central bank in terms of notes and coins.

Commercial banks and credit creation

A major source is the commercial banks through credit creation. This works through the credit multiplier, which is determined by the amount of any deposit that a commercial bank is required to hold in reserves. If, for example, customer A deposits $100 with Bank 1 and the credit ratio is 10 per cent then the bank can lend out $90 to customer B. Customer B then uses this to buy goods from customer C who in turn deposits it with Bank 2 who lends $81 to customer D and so on. This can be seen in Table 9.17. The credit multiplier operates in a similar way to the multiplier with the formula:

$$\text{Change in money supply} = \frac{\text{Initial deposit}}{\text{Credit ratio}} = \frac{100}{0.1\ (10\%)}$$

$$= 100 \times 10 = \$1000$$

> **Key terms**
>
> **Commercial bank**: financial institution in which individuals and firms can save their money and obtain loans.
>
> **Credit creation**: the ability of banks, and other lenders of money, to lend money to borrowers thus increasing the supply of money in circulation.
>
> **Credit multiplier**: the number of times by which a change in bank deposits is increased, or decreased, to give the final change in total bank assets.

Table 9.17 Credit creation ▼

Bank	Liabilities: deposits	Assets: loans	Reserves	Total assets
Bank 1	100.00	90.00	10.00	100.00
Bank 2	90.00	81.00	9.00	90.00
Bank 3	81.00	72.90	8.10	81.00
–	–	–	–	–
–	–	–	–	–
Bank n	0.00	0.00	0.00	0.00
Total	**1000.00**	**900.00**	**100.00**	**1000.00**

Case Study

US housing crisis

The collapse of the US housing market in 2008 seems to have been caused by the over-lending by financial institutions of money to buy houses. This came about because the creditworthiness of borrowers was no longer being checked so money was lent to people who could not afford to pay it back.

Once people started to default on the loans this led to a loss of confidence and banks raised their credit ratios thus reducing the amount of money available to borrow. This meant that people could no longer find the money to buy houses. Thus demand fell and prices collapsed.

1 Explain how raising the credit ratio would lead to a fall in the money available in the economy.
2 Discuss why a loss of confidence could severely affect people's willingness to borrow and lend money.

Activity

Credit creation

Using Table 9.17 recalculate the credit creation process on the basis of (a) a 12.5 per cent ratio, and (b) an 8 per cent ratio.

Link

For more on quantitative easing see Chapter 5 page 125.

Link

For more on national debt see page 255.

Key term

Deficit financing: ways in which the gap between public revenue and public expenditure can be financed.

No single bank can create credit. It is the banking system as a whole which can do this by making loans to individuals or businesses by depositing credit into their accounts. The loans become deposits for other banks. In this way loans make deposits and deposits make loans.

Role of the central bank

The central bank acts as the issuer of notes and coins in an economy and can, therefore, directly determine how many are in circulation. It can also determine the level of deposits that commercial banks must make with it. The larger the deposit the central bank requires, the smaller will be the ability of these banks to create credit. In Table 9.17 a 10 per cent deposit was assumed. If the central bank wanted to reduce the supply of money it could raise this to, for example, 12.5 per cent or if it wanted to increase the money supply it could reduce the level to, say, 8 per cent. In recent years many central banks have used quantitative easing as a way of increasing the supply of money so as to encourage consumption and investment.

Deficit financing

The government can finance a budget deficit, deficit financing, by two methods. Firstly, it can borrow money from the central bank or from commercial banks. If it borrows from the central bank this means that more money finds its way to the commercial banks as deposits so allowing them to expand lending. Equally, if it issues short-term government stock to the commercial banks these act as liquid assets and can be used to back loans. Either way will increase the money supply.

Secondly, a government can sell long-term securities to the non-bank private sector. To purchase these, individuals or firms will draw money from their bank accounts leading to a fall in the money supply.

Key term

Total currency flow: the total inflow and outflow of money as a result of international transactions which are shown in the balance of payments.

Link

For more on the balance of payments see Chapter 5 page 129.

Quantitative easing

Since 2009 central banks have purchased financial assets from banks and businesses resulting in an increase in the money supply.

Total currency flow

Total currency flow refers to the total inflow and outflow of money as a result of international transactions which are shown in the balance of payments. If there is an inflow of money then the money supply will increase.

Progress question

15 Discuss how best a government could try to decrease the supply of money in an economy.

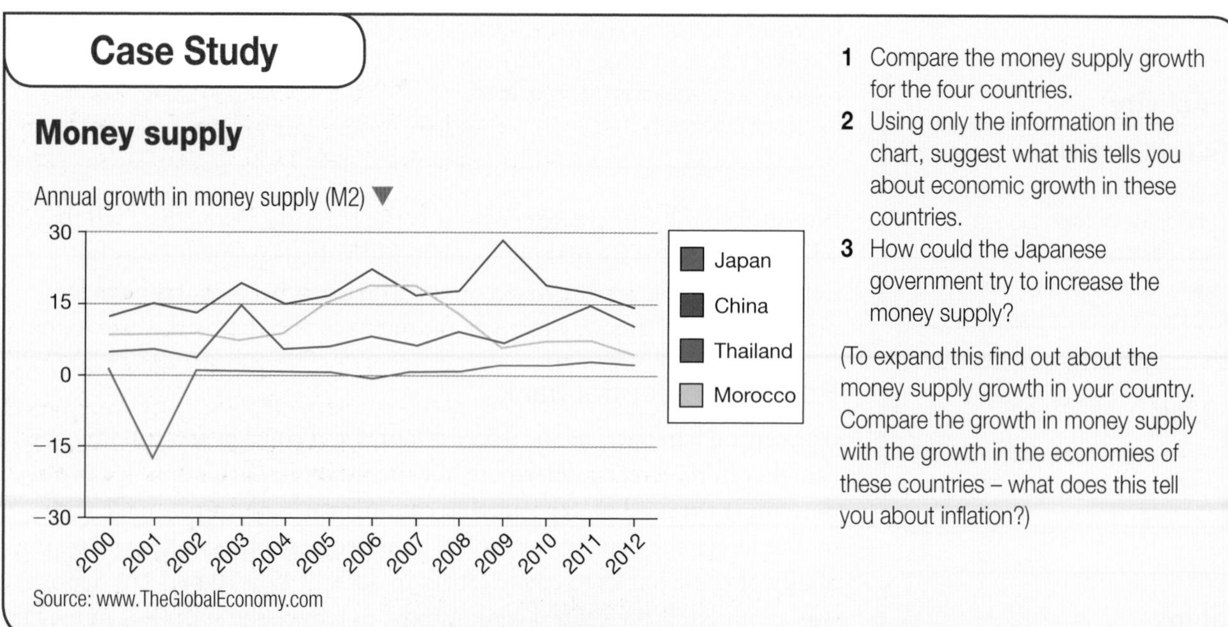

Case Study

Money supply

Source: www.TheGlobalEconomy.com

1. Compare the money supply growth for the four countries.
2. Using only the information in the chart, suggest what this tells you about economic growth in these countries.
3. How could the Japanese government try to increase the money supply?

(To expand this find out about the money supply growth in your country. Compare the growth in money supply with the growth in the economies of these countries – what does this tell you about inflation?)

Transmission mechanism of monetary policy

This is the process through which monetary policy decisions affect economic activity, especially the price level. Due to variable and uncertain time lags it is difficult to predict the precise effect of such decisions. If interest rates are cut, this increases the ability people have to spend and borrow and thus should increase aggregate demand. As has been seen in recent years in many countries, this does not always occur owing to the negative expectations of consumers and investors. Monetary policy also affects other variables, such as asset prices and exchange rates.

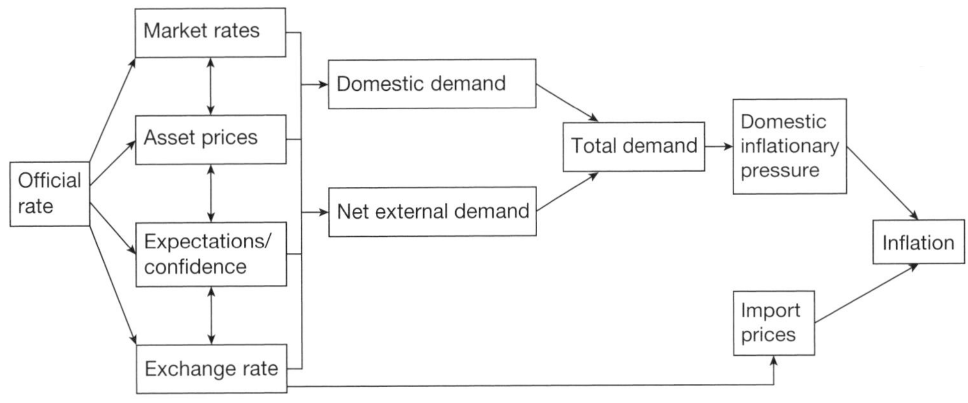

Source: Bank of England, *The transmission mechanism of monetary policy*

Figure 9.22 The transmission mechanism of monetary policy ▲

Links

For more on aggregate demand see Chapter 4 page 87.

For more on full employment and economic growth see pages 270 and 250.

Link

For more on fiscal policy see Chapter 5 page 123.

Keynesian and monetarist schools

There are two main schools of thought on how the macro economy works.

Keynesian

Keynesian economics is based on the work of John Maynard Keynes. His *General Theory of Employment, Interest and Money* was published in 1936. Keynesian economics dominated policy in many countries from 1945 to the 1970s, but then fell out of favour. The global financial crisis of 2007 saw many countries adopt Keynesian policies.

Keynesian economics is based on the idea that governments have an important role to play in helping the economy to achieve full employment and economic growth. It is based on the belief that if aggregate demand is too low then there will be high levels of unemployment, which market forces on their own cannot deal with. Governments, therefore, need to intervene by increasing their expenditure and running a deficit budget in order to boost the amount of money in the circular flow.

In theory, this should be balanced in the long run by surplus budgets so that over a period of time the budget is balanced. In practice governments find that spending money is easy, and popular, but running surpluses is less easy and often unpopular. This use of government revenue and expenditure is called fiscal policy.

Milton Friedman ▲

Monetarist

Monetarism came to replace Keynesian economics in the 1970s and dominated economic policy in the 1980s and 1990s. Monetarism was based on the idea that the money supply greatly influenced aggregate demand in the short term and inflation in the longer term. This meant that any attempt by a government to increase aggregate demand by increasing the money supply would lead to higher prices.

Milton Friedman was the most influential monetarist. He considered that "inflation is always and everywhere a monetary phenomenon". He thought that a central bank should only increase money supply in line with increases in productivity and demand. He thought that this would involve increasing it at a steady rate of between 3 per cent and 5 per cent. He claimed that instead of government intervention, which only made the situation worse, the solution was a more competitive private marketplace.

It proved difficult, however, to control the money supply so it was only a target for government policy for a few years. It was replaced by targeting interest rates. Today, therefore, monetary policy is concerned with targeting inflation by using interest rates, i.e. the price, rather than the supply, of money. As previously noted, with interest rates in the period post 2008 being held very low in most Western industrial countries many of these countries have used quantitative easing, i.e. they have increased the supply of money.

Links

The following are examined in more detail on the pages indicated:

For quantity theory of money see page 285.

For monetary policy see Chapter 5 page 124.

For quantitative easing see Chapter 5 page 125 and above page 288.

Progress question

16 Explain the main differences between a Keynesian and a monetarist's view of controlling an economy.

Activity

Keynes and Friedman

Find out more about both Keynes and Friedman. Which of them is more influential in economic policy today?

The demand for money

There are two determinants of the demand for money:

- Income: the higher is the level of income the greater is the demand for money.
- The rate of interest: the higher is the rate of interest the greater is the opportunity cost of holding money as against interest-paying assets such as government bonds.

Link

Opportunity cost is explained in Chapter 1 page 9.

Keynes argued that people demanded money for three reasons:

- Transactions demand: money held for normal purchases, e.g. food, transport, etc. It is not responsive to changes in the rate of interest, i.e. it is interest inelastic.
- Precautionary demand: money held over and above transactionary demand in case of unexpected needs, e.g. to replace a broken kettle. It is not responsive to changes in the rate of interest, i.e. it is interest inelastic.
- Speculative demand: money held to be used to buy assets in the future. It is inversely related to the rate of interest.

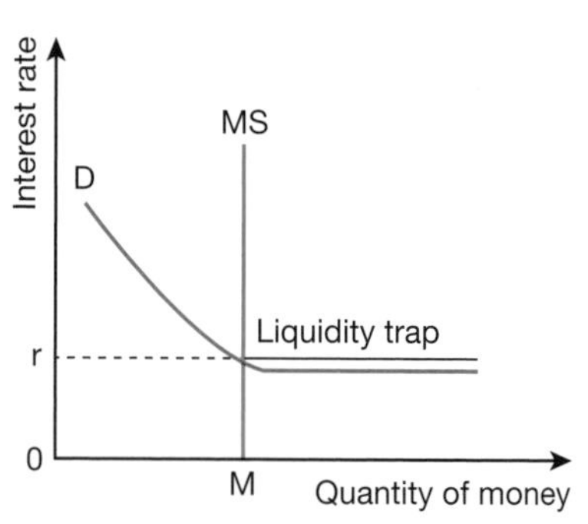

Figure 9.23 Liquidity preference curve ▲

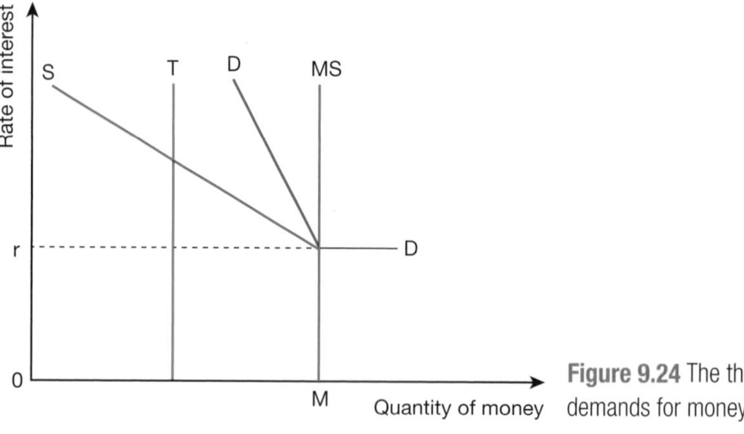

Figure 9.24 The three demands for money ◀

> **Key terms**
>
> **Liquidity preference**: the relationship between the quantity of money people wish to hold and the rate of interest.
>
> **Active balance**: the transactionary and precautionary demands combined. It is not responsive to the rate of interest.
>
> **Idle balance**: the speculative demand, and it is responsive to the rate of interest.
>
> **Liquidity trap**: where any addition to the supply of money results in no change in the rate of interest.
>
> **Loanable funds**: the relationship between those who supply the funds (savers) and those who are demanding funds (borrowers).

In Figure 9.24:

- T is the precautionary and transactionary demands together
- S is the speculative demand
- D = T+S

These three demands added together give the liquidity preference curve as shown in Figure 9.23. The transactionary and speculative demands are used to make purchases and are sometimes called active balances, whereas the speculative demand is sometimes called the idle balance. The curve is completely elastic beyond point M, showing that any addition to the supply of money fails to affect either interest rates or economic growth. This is the liquidity trap.

> **Progress question**
>
> **17** Explain why the rate of interest does not affect the active balances of money, but does affect the idle balances.

Loanable funds

An alternative approach is that of loanable funds. Many monetarists favour this approach which states that the rate of interest is determined by the supply and demand of loanable funds (see figure 9.25). This assumes that there are three major demands for loanable funds:

- households for the purchase of goods and services
- firms for investment
- governments to fund any deficit.

Loanable funds bring together savers who are supplying the funds and borrowers who are demanding funds.

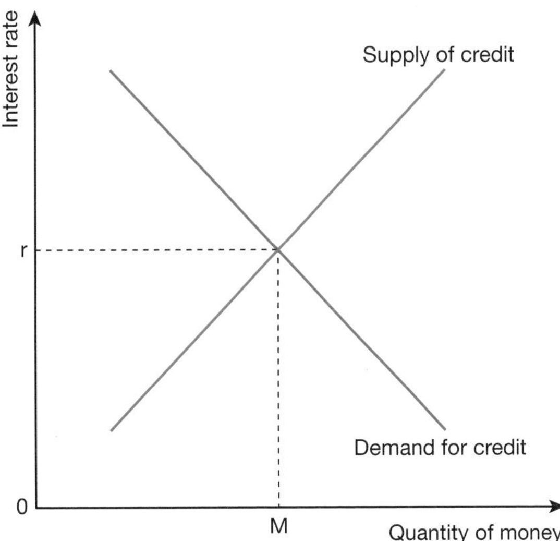

Figure 9.25 Supply and demand of loanable funds ▲

Progress question

18 Explain how liquidity preference theory shows how interest rates are determined.

Case Study

Japan and low interest rates

In the 1990s asset prices in Japan collapsed and economic growth deteriorated. To counter this the Bank of Japan lowered interest rates to almost zero. This did not, however, lead to the expected increase in demand. One reason for this was that the price level was negative leading to a relatively high real rate of interest.

1. What is meant by the real rate of interest?
2. What is meant by a negative price level?
3. How might knowledge of the liquidity trap help explain what happened in Japan?

Activity

Rate of interest

Find out what has happened to interest rates in your country and in either the US or the UK in the last ten years.

Discuss either in small groups or as a class why there are differences and/or similarities. Use your knowledge of economics to try to explain these differences and similarities.

Interest rate determination

Interest rates are determined by the supply of, and demand for, money.

As can be seen in Figure 9.26, the supply of money is fixed so that an increase in the demand will just lead to a rise in the rate of interest. Equally, Figure 9.27 shows that an increase in the supply of money without any corresponding rise in the demand will lead to a fall in the rate of interest.

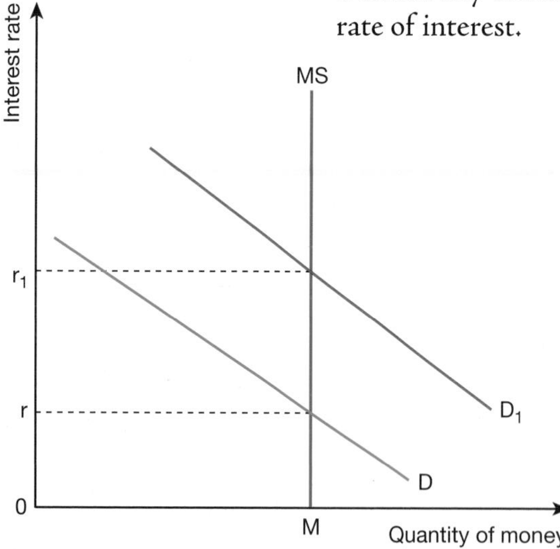

Figure 9.26 Increase in the demand for money ▲

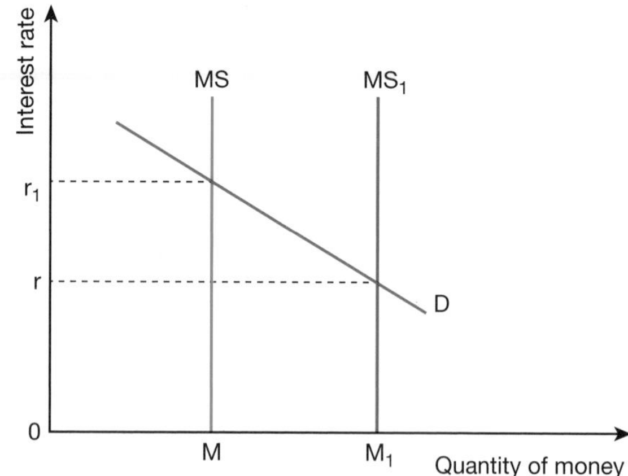

Figure 9.27 Increase in the supply of money ▲

Key term

Transmission mechanism: the way in which changes in the money supply or the interest rate can affect variables such as aggregate output and employment.

Changes in interest rates affect inflation through the monetary transmission mechanism. Any change in the central bank's interest rate will lead to other financial institutions, such as banks, changing their savings and lending rates. The change will affect, also, the price of assets such as shares and houses as well as the expectations of individuals and firms. Externally the change will lead to a movement in the exchange rate.

If the rate of interest was lowered individuals and firms will be more confident about the future. The exchange rate, however, is likely to fall. All of this will affect aggregate demand as, in this example, consumers would be likely to spend more so AD would increase. Exports would be likely to rise and imports to fall, again increasing AD.

Finally, all this would affect GDP and inflation. In this example GDP would rise, and if there was no spare capacity inflation would rise too.

Policies towards developing economies and policies of trade and aid

Types of aid and nature of dependency

There are numerous forms of aid including: humanitarian emergency assistance, food, investment projects and military.

Key term

Aid: the giving of money and/or goods, by one country or by an organisation, to another country.

Link

For more on international trade see Chapter 4 page 113.

Development aid has long been recognised as crucial to help poor developing nations grow out of poverty and, up to the 1990s, aid was often seen by both the donor country and the receiving country as being better than trade. Developing countries largely exported primary products and protected their domestic markets. Donor countries could import the primary goods and export their manufactured ones without competition from developing countries. In addition, there was the moral idea that giving aid was "good" even though few countries achieved the aim of 0.7 per cent of GDI. Overall, both the quantity and the quality of aid has been poor.

Several factors have changed this view. First, aid was seen to have costs for the receiving countries in that:

- aid was often tied so that the receivers had to purchase overpriced and not always suitable goods from the donors
- most aid did not actually go to the poorest who most needed it
- aid amounts were outweighed by the protectionism of the developed countries thus denying access to their markets
- developed countries used aid as a way to open markets in poor countries to their products
- aid was often spent on grand projects for the benefit of leaders rather than on smaller projects to benefit the majority and/or it led to embezzlement.

Second, a number of countries demonstrated that they could develop by using trade. In some cases, e.g. Hong Kong and Singapore, they had no raw materials to export so had to rely on trade. In other cases, such as Brazil, China, India and South Korea, they were able to use their resources, including labour, to drive trade forward as a means of development. These countries have seen large increases in their standards of living.

This has not been possible for all as some developing countries have been held back by lack of productive capacity, difficulties in diversifying their economy, poor infrastructure and export conditions. There is also the fact that aid can contribute to an increase in a developing contry's dependency on developed countries.

Third, under the auspices of the World Trade Organization (WTO) there has been an emphasis on opening up markets leading to increased globalisation. World trade increased rapidly in the period 2000–2008, but then declined only to pick up again in 2010 onwards. Globalisation has meant that India, for example, has become the world's leading exporter of IT services while companies like Toyota move parts and whole cars from country to country.

Key terms

Dependency: a situation in which one country depends on the help of another country either in the form of aid or by being able to export their goods to that country.

World Trade Organization (WTO): the international organisation which establishes, monitors and reinforces the rules of trade between nations.

Link

For more on globalisation see Chapter 4, page 104.

Activities

Globalisation

Find out how globalisation has affected your country.

1 What has happened to exports and imports?
2 Have there been changes in economic structure?
3 Have there been changes in the way the economy works?

Case Study

Competition and growth in Rwanda

Although Rwanda is a poor country with 90 per cent of the population engaged in mainly subsistence farming, it is striving to achieve economic growth and to reduce poverty.

One problem faced in many African countries is a poor business environment. African countries currently constitute 17 of the 20 worst business environments in the world. This is often caused by bureaucratic controls which hinder enterprise.

The president of Rwanda has claimed that "competition in an economy is good for poor people … asking our citizens to compete is the same as asking them to go out there into the world on behalf of Rwanda, and play their part … where some people are shielded from the forces of competition, then it's like saying they are disabled". This approach has allowed Rwanda to become the most business friendly economy in East Africa.

As a result GDP grew in 2011 by about 7 per cent and investment (GFCF) increased to 23 per cent of GDP.

1 Discuss whether competition from engaging in trade is beneficial for development.

Trade and investment, multinationals and foreign direct investment (FDI)

"International trade can play a major role in the promotion of economic development and the alleviation of poverty." (Doha WTO ministerial declaration 2001)

The WTO exists to promote free trade and the reduction of protectionist barriers. Although globalisation has been attacked by many in all types of countries, there is no doubt that it has allowed countries such as China, India and South Korea to develop through export-led growth.

Links

For more on free trade and protection see Chapter 4.

Multinational corporations (MNCs) – sometimes called transnational corporations – are firms that operate in a number of different countries. Among the top 20 firms are Royal Dutch Shell, Sinopec Group, Toyota and Glencore International. Royal Dutch Shell's revenue in 2011 at $484.489 billion is greater than that of the majority of countries.

Key term

Multinational corporations: firms that have their head offices in one country, but have operations in a number of other countries.

MNCs are responsible for foreign direct investment (FDI) into a range of operations. China, next to the US, is the largest receiver of FDI. In Nigeria the oil industry is totally dependent on the FDI received from a number of foreign firms. Over a number of years the total FDI received can amount to many times a country's GDP. While FDI increases growth and employment in a country and, therefore, has a multiplier effect, it may not be entirely beneficial as profits are sent back to the home country of the MNC while they may bring with them their own skilled workforce rather than training people in the developing country. In some cases this can lead to economic dependency where one country exploits the resources of another for the former's benefit.

Getting it right

Do not compartmentalise economics. Remember here that exports are part of aggregate demand.

Key terms

Foreign direct investment: is investment of funds into a business that operates in a different country from that of the investor.

Economic dependency: exists when one country does not control its resources and is dependent on other countries for investment and production in major industries.

Activities

Multinationals

1 In which countries are the head offices of the four firms mentioned in the text?
2 How does your country's GDP in $ compare with that of Royal Dutch Shell?
3 Find out about five other multinationals that operate in your country. What is their policy on employment?
4 Do they have any domestic rivals?

Case Study

Sierra Leone and the UAE: trade and investment

Sierra Leone and the UAE have completed talks on trade and investment between the two countries which included discussions on investment in both the private and public sectors, economic and technical co-operation in the fields of infrastructure developments, and a decision to go ahead with a bauxite mining project in Sierra Leone.

1 Explain two reasons why Sierra Leone might wish to encourage other countries to invest in its industries and infrastructure.
2 Explain two reasons why the UAE might wish to invest in Sierra Leone.
3 Discuss the advantages and disadvantages to Sierra Leone if such investment took place.

External debt, role of the IMF and World Bank

External debt consists of the part of total debt of a country that is owed to people, firms, banks, international financial organisations which are external to the country together with foreign governments. All countries have an external debt, but it can cause problems if a country with a weak economy is not able to repay due to the inability to produce and sell sufficient goods in order to earn the necessary money. The International Monetary Fund (IMF) is one of the agencies that keep track of the country's external debt.

International Monetary Fund (IMF)

It aims to offer:

- policy advice to governments and central banks based on analysis of economic trends and cross-country experiences
- research, statistics, forecasts and analysis based on tracking of global, regional and individual economies and markets
- loans to help countries overcome economic difficulties
- concessional loans to help fight poverty in developing countries
- technical assistance and training to help countries improve the management of their economies.

Key term

International Monetary Fund (IMF): an overarching international organisation which, amongst other tasks, offers advice to governments and central banks and makes loans to countries with severe economic difficulties.

Key term

World Bank: provides loans for developing countries. Its official goal is the reduction of poverty. According to its Articles of Agreement, all its decisions must be guided by a commitment to the promotion of foreign investment and international trade and to the facilitation of capital investment. The World Bank group consists of five agencies.

World Bank

The World Bank Group consists of five agencies:

- The International Bank for Reconstruction and Development (IBRD) lends to governments of middle-income and creditworthy low-income countries.
- The International Development Association (IDA) provides interest-free loans – called credits – and grants to governments of the poorest countries.
- The International Finance Corporation (IFC) provides loans, equity and technical assistance to stimulate private sector investment in developing countries.
- The Multilateral Investment Guarantee Agency (MIGA) provides guarantees against losses caused by non-commercial risks to investors in developing countries.
- The International Centre for Settlement of Investment Disputes (ICSID) provides international facilities for conciliation and arbitration of investment disputes.

Both the IMF and the World Bank aim to try and help countries with debt problems to overcome them through a mixture of advice and aid.

Key terms

Corruption: behaviour which aims to make private gains at public expense.

Legal framework: rules, procedural steps or tests by which judgments can be determined in any given legal case.

Impact of corruption, and importance of the legal framework in an economy

While corruption is present in every country its effects are especially damaging in those which are still developing. The amount of corruption is negatively linked to the level of investment and economic growth, that is to say, the more corruption, the less investment and the less economic growth. Many developing nations, especially in Africa, are endowed with extensive natural resources, yet they continue to struggle to develop. As can be seen in Table 9.18, the ten countries with the lowest GDP per head in 2012 were all African.

Table 9.18 Ten lowest-ranked countries by GDP per head ($) 2012 ▼

Country	GDP per head $
Guinea-Bissau	494
Guinea	492
Central African Republic	483
Ethiopia	455
Madagascar	447
Liberia	414
Niger	395
Malawi	268
Dem. Rep. of the Congo	262
Burundi	251

Source: http://data.worldbank.org/indicator/NY.GDP.PCAP.CD

It is clear that the ability of economies to work efficiently and develop effectively depends on the establishment of an environment in which legal rights, especially property and contractual rights, are enforced and protected, i.e. a proper legal framework is put in place. Christine Lagarde, managing director of the IMF, has said that "countries that have developed strong legal and institutional frameworks have performed better in terms of sustained growth and human development" (www.imf.org/external/np/speeches/2013/060413b.htm).

Further, she identifies two important factors:

- the law must apply equally to all citizens, including those who make the law
- there must be strong institutions that are capable of implementing and enforcing the law in accordance with its terms.

Christine Lagarde ▲

Activities

Corruption and the legal system

1 Find out where your country ranks in terms of GDP per head.
2 Discuss how important corruption is in your country. Do you think it restricts development?
3 If you were to set up your own business. To what extent do you feel the law would enable you to easily grow the business.

Some economists claim that a lack of a system of formal property rights is the main cause of underdevelopment. This can create a large informal economy in which assets are undervalued, unreported and untaxed. This underground economy is estimated to be 30–40 per cent of GDP in developing countries and about 15 per cent in developed ones. As Christine Lagarde said "to think of the lost productive potential in an economy where almost half of activity is unreported and almost half the population is beyond the reach of public services".

Key concepts

- **Scarcity and choice** is covered in economic growth, development and sustainability including the costs and benefits of growth, as well as being important for the characteristics of countries.
- **Equilibrium and efficiency** is covered by reference to aggregate expenditure, policies to correct unemployment, the supply and demand for money and in interest rate determination.
- **Regulation and equity** is covered both in economic development and in terms of corruption and legal framework.
- **Progress and development** is covered throughout the chapter wherever economic growth and development are referred to.

Progress check

After completing this chapter you should be able to:

- understand what is meant by and involved in economic growth, economic development and sustainability
- know what is meant by national income statistics and how to use them
- understand how living standards and economic development can be measured
- explain the characteristics of developed, developing, BRIC and MINT countries
- explain the factors involved in employment and unemployment
- explain and discuss the policies to deal with unemployment
- know what is meant by the circular flow of income; be able to calculate the multiplier and explain aggregate expenditure
- explain what is meant by money supply
- show understanding of Keynesianism and monetarism
- explain the demand for money and how interest rates are determined
- show knowledge of aid, trade, foreign direct investment, external debt, and the role of corruption and the legal framework in development.

Exam-style questions

Essay questions

1 a Explain what is meant by actual as against potential growth in national output. [12 marks]
  b Discuss whether investment is the most important factor in determining economic growth. [13 marks]

2 a Explain how the Multidimensional Poverty Index can be used to measure living standards. [12 marks]
  b Discuss whether real GDP per capita is the best method of comparing living standards between countries. [13 marks]

3 a Explain the causes of unemployment. [12 marks]
  b Discuss how the government of your country should tackle unemployment. [13 marks]

4 a Explain what is meant by inflationary and deflationary gaps. [12 marks]
  b Compare the ways in which Keynesians and monetarists would deal with these gaps. [13 marks]

Multiple-choice questions

5 If the income velocity of circulation of money is constant, the rate of growth of the money supply is 5 per cent and the average price level increases by 3 per cent, what will be the approximate change in real output? [1 mark]

A −2 per cent
B +2 per cent
C +3 per cent
D +8 per cent

6 In an economy from any addition to national income 5 per cent is saved 15 per cent is paid in taxes and 20 per cent is spent on imports with 60 per cent is consumed, what is the value of the multiplier? [1 mark]

A 1.25
B 1.66
C 2.5
D 4

10 Government macro intervention

In this chapter you will develop your knowledge and understanding of:

- government macro policy aims
- the interconnectedness of macroeconomic problems
- effectiveness of policy options to meet all macroeconomic objectives.

Government macro policy aims

This chapter will reflect on economic ideas developed in Chapters 4, 5 and 9. The aims concern:

- inflation
- balance of payments
- exchange rates
- unemployment
- economic growth
- economic development.

Links

See Chapter 4 pages 89, 94 and 99 for inflation, balance of payments and exchange rates.

See Chapter 9 pages 248 and 270 for economic growth, development and unemployment.

Inflation

Although inflation is seen as inevitable, and normal, all governments are concerned to try and achieve stable prices, or at least prices which only rise at a slow rate. If prices are continually rising at high rates then investors are reluctant to invest in new machinery, factories and products because they cannot calculate the outcome of their investments. Rising inflation leads to menu costs, such as sellers having to constantly revise their price lists. Similarly those who are on fixed incomes, usually the economically inactive, such as those relying on state benefits, suffer as any increases lag well behind price rises.

In addition, inflation is likely to lead to other macroeconomic problems as indicated on pages 302 to 305.

Activity

Worst inflation rate in history

In 1946, inflation in Hungary reached a rate of 13 600 000 000 000 000 per cent per month. Prices ended up doubling every 15 hours.

In 2008, prices in Zimbabwe doubled every 24.7 hours.

Discuss as a group what could have been the causes of these very large rises in inflation.

Then, try to find out the actual causes of these inflation rates.

Balance of payments

The ideal situation is for the balance of payments to be in equilibrium, i.e. the inflows of money equal the outflows across the whole account. Countries are usually concerned about their current accounts. If there is a persistent deficit then a country could face severe economic and financial problems such as a depreciating exchange rate, inability to pay its debts and in extreme circumstances bankruptcy.

Equally, a continual positive balance is problematical because it causes difficulties for trading partners especially if they are in a monetary union and cannot depreciate the exchange rate. A number of countries within the Eurozone have faced this with Germany being in credit and, for example, Greece in debt.

This does not mean that a country should balance its account every year with every country it trades with because a country may have a positive balance with some countries and negative balance with others. The aim should be in the long run to achieve an equilibrium level on the balance of payments.

Link

See Chapter 4 page 109 for more on monetary union.

Exchange rates

As far as exchange rates are concerned governments wish to avoid wild fluctuations or changes. This can be achieved for floating exchange rates by managing the float or in the case of a fixed rate by constant intervention in the market to maintain the rate. While in theory governments would like their exchange rate to remain constant this is unlikely if the country has a balance of payments disequilibrium on the current account which is not offset by inflows of capital investment, to meet a deficit, or outflows of aid or investment to other countries in the case of a surplus. In these situations a government would hope for a gradual, managed, depreciation or appreciation.

> **Progress question**
>
> 1 Explain why governments try to avoid fluctuating exchange rates.

Unemployment

Governments aim to achieve full employment. It is difficult to know what this means as not only are there different definitions of full employment, but there is no agreement on what percentage of unemployment would indicate that full employment had been reached. All governments, however, aim for this objective (see the case study below).

Case Study

Full employment in the UK

Speaking at a meeting near London in April 2014, George Osborne, Chancellor of the Exchequer, promised to restore the UK to full employment. He said that there was "no reason why Britain should not aim to have the highest employment rate of any of the world's leading economies". He went on to say "a modern approach to full employment means backing business. It means cutting the tax on jobs and reforming welfare".

The OECD states that Britain's employment rate for those aged 16–64 is 71 per cent, which is more than the USA, France and Italy, but lower than Germany, Canada and Japan. To overtake these three countries would involve creating one million more jobs.

1 What is meant by full employment?
2 Explain how "cutting the tax on jobs and reforming welfare" could lead to full employment.
3 Find out what your current employment rate for 16–64-year-olds is and compare it to two of the seven countries named in the text.
4 Discuss why a government might find it difficult to create a large number of new jobs.

Economic growth

Governments aim to achieve sustainable economic growth. High growth rates may be very good for developing countries, but if they are achieved by depletion and exhaustion of scarce natural resources or by creating too much pollution, leading to climate change, then the high rates will not be sustainable.

Economic development

This is very similar to economic growth in that governments need to achieve sustainable development. Sustainable development ensures that

> **Activities**
>
> **Balance of payments**
>
> Look at the current account of the balance of payments for your country and one other for the last ten years.
>
> 1 Over the ten years have they achieved a surplus, a deficit or nearly equilibrium?
> 2 If it is a surplus have they used this to help trading partners?
> 3 If it is a deficit, how have they financed it? Look at the capital account.

> **Link**
>
> For more on floating and fixed exchange rates see Chapter 4 page 100.

> **Link**
>
> For more on full employment see Chapter 9 page 270.

> **Link**
>
> For more on economic growth and development see Chapter 9 page 248.

> **Activity**
>
> **Government macro policy aims**
>
> Make sure you know what the government of your country, or a country that the group agrees on, has achieved in terms of the six policy aims above.
>
> As a group discuss to what extent you think your government has achieved these.

with economic growth both the standard of living and the quality of life improve now and in the future. All of these should be part of the aim of development for governments.

Interconnectedness of macroeconomic problems

Economic problems such as how to achieve low inflation and full employment do not exist in isolation, but are interconnected. Any action to try and achieve one economic aim, see above, may well result in adverse effects on other aims. In a textbook it is not possible to look at all of the links between macroeconomic objectives, but below a number of the main ones are considered.

Relationship between internal and external value of money

The internal value of money is how much a unit of money can buy, i.e. its internal purchasing power or the real value of money, while the external value of money is the value of a currency as measured in foreign currency. A direct comparison is with purchasing power parity.

A fall in the internal value of money is a result of inflation. A country with an inflation rate higher than that of other countries will find that people lose confidence in holding its currency so its foreign exchange rate depreciates. This means that less can be bought in terms of purchasing power parity. If, however, a country has a lower rate of inflation than its main trading partners then, although the internal value of money is falling, the external value will rise. This is partly because the country's goods will appear cheaper on world markets than those of its competitors and partly because foreign holders of money would prefer to hold that country's currency.

Key terms

Internal value of money: what a unit of money will buy. It is the real value of money in terms of its purchasing power.

External value of money: what a unit of currency will buy when compared to other currencies – see purchasing power parity.

Link

For more on inflation and exchange rates see Chapter 4 page 101.

Relationship between balance of payments and inflation

To some extent, this follows on from the discussion above concerning the internal and external values of money. Inflation will mean that the internal cost of goods and services rises. Assuming that a country's inflation rate is higher than that of its main trading partners, the price of its exports rises while imports now appear to be cheaper. This means that the current account of the balance of payments will deteriorate assuming that the sum of the price elasticities of demand for exports and imports is greater than one, the Marshall–Lerner effect. In addition, higher inflation will deter investors, leading to an outflow of money in the capital account and a worsening of the whole balance of payments account. Once more, if inflation is lower than that of a country's main competitors, or if Marshall–Lerner is less than one, then the opposite effect will be true.

This relationship is complicated because of the exchange rate. If the exchange rate falls then, given the Marshall–Lerner condition, the balance of payments will improve, although this may only happen in the medium term due to the J-curve effect.

Activity

Internal and external values of money

Compare the inflation and exchange rates of your country with that of some of its main trading partners.

What conclusions can you draw from this comparison?

Links

For more on Marshall–Lerner see Chapter 4 page 102.

For more on J-curve effect see Chapter 4 page 102.

A deterioration of the balance of payments is likely to lead to a fall in the value of the exchange rate. This may well increase inflation, making exports more expensive and causing the balance of payments to deteriorate. Elasticities are not always simple. Singapore, for example, has an elastic demand for its exports, but an inelastic one for its imports. In addition, changes in world demand, especially for primary products, can greatly affect the balance of payments from year to year.

On the other hand, any attempt to reduce inflation through a rise in interest rates could lead to an improvement in the balance of payments, assuming a decline in domestic demand, and a rise in the exchange rate. While the improvement in the balance of payments would be a positive effect for a country, the rise in the exchange rate could lead to a fall in exports and a rise in imports, which would be undesirable. This idea that an improvement in one objective can lead to an adverse effect in another objective is called a trade-off.

These trade-offs can often be seen when considering the exchange rate and the balance of payments. A country may not want its exchange rate to appreciate because this would make its exports less competitive. It may, therefore, try to reduce its value by selling its currency. However, if imports are price inelastic then this would raise the amount spent on imports, adversely affecting the balance of payments. In addition, it would lead to higher inflation.

Relationship between balance of payments and economic growth

As an economy grows, import spending is stimulated relative to export revenue. This may result in a balance of payments deficit both because of higher prices, see Figure 10.3 but also because domestic production cannot expand fast enough to meet the extra demand. Where economic growth leads to higher real incomes, consumers may prefer "better" foreign goods, causing higher imports.

Many developing and other countries have used exports to generate economic growth, given that $AD = C + I + G + X - M$. In this case an improvement in the balance of payments can have a positive effect on growth.

Trade-off between inflation and unemployment

One of the best-known trade-offs has traditionally been between inflation and unemployment. If governments try to reduce inflation, for example by using fiscal and monetary policies, then unemployment rises. Equally, any attempt at reducing unemployment by, for example, cutting interest rates or increasing government expenditure, will result in higher inflation.

The ideal situation for an economy would be to have a low and steady rate of inflation together with a low level of unemployment. Generally this has proved to be impossible to achieve. In 1959 Professor Phillips plotted data for the UK for the period 1861 to 1957 to show an inverse relationship between inflation and unemployment; see Figure 10.1.

Activity

Price elasticity of demand for X and M

Are your exports and imports elastic or inelastic? On what have you based your decisions?

If there are several of you this could lead to a debate or a discussion in order to gain a class view.

Key term

Trade-off: when, in order to obtain a desired economic goal, it is necessary to accept an adverse effect on another goal. This idea is closely related to opportunity cost and to production possibility curves.

Activity

Balance of payments and economic growth

Find out your country's balance of payments figures and its economic growth for the last six years.

Can you discover any relationship between them (do not forget there may be time lags).

What conclusions can you draw from your investigation?

Links

For more on fiscal and monetary policies see Chapter 5 pages 123 and 124.

For more on unemployment see Chapter 9 page 270.

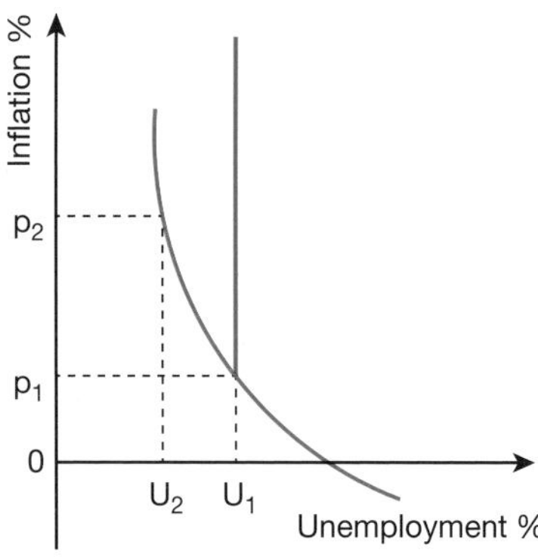

Figure 10.1 Phillips curve ▲

Key terms

Stagflation: this exists where there are high levels of both inflation and unemployment.

Expectations-augmented Phillips curve: this is often called the long-run Phillips curve and is associated with NAIRU. This shows that in the long-run any attempt to reduce unemployment by increasing demand will just lead to inflation.

NAIRU: the non-accelerating inflation rate of unemployment, i.e. the specific level of unemployment that exists in an economy that does not cause inflation to increase.

Getting it right

The long run Phillips curve and the LRAS curves are the same.

Link

For more on Friedman see Chapter 9 page 289.

As can be seen, a fall in unemployment from U_1 to U_2 would lead to a rise in inflation from p_1 to p_2. This is a straightforward trade-off in that a government could choose the levels of inflation and unemployment that they thought correct for their country. This relationship broke down in several countries in the 1970s when stagflation occurred.

Monetarists, however, claimed that although there might be a trade-off in the short run this was not true in the long run. Friedman claimed that people had expectations concerning what would happen to prices and built this in to their demand for wages, while firms had similar expectations for costs so adjusted prices to take this into account. In this way expectations that prices would rise would lead to higher wage demands, thus higher costs and higher prices. As a result he developed the expectations-augmented Phillips curve, often called the long run Phillips curve. This curve is a vertical line based on NAIRU. In the long run any attempt to reduce unemployment by increasing demand will just lead to higher inflation. NAIRU can only be reduced by increasing aggregate supply and reducing inflation through tight monetary policy.

Progress question

2 Discuss the view that the use of fiscal policy to control the economy will only result in higher inflation.

As can be seen in Figure 10.2 an increase in demand to reduce unemployment would take the economy along SRPC from A to B decreasing unemployment, but raising inflation from 0 to p_1. Workers then demand higher wages so that firms' costs rise leading to less employment, B to C, but no reduction in prices. Any further attempt to increase demand moves the economy along $SRPC_1$ from C to D and then E. Friedman argued that continual increases in demand could lead to the relationship changing so that higher inflation would lead to higher unemployment. He felt that the only way, therefore, to reduce unemployment permanently was to reduce inflation first. This has influenced central banks in their targeting of inflation.

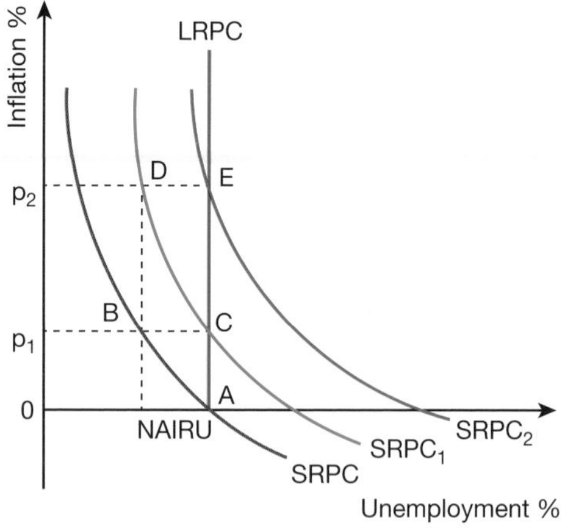

Figure 10.2 Expectations-augmented Phillips curve ▲

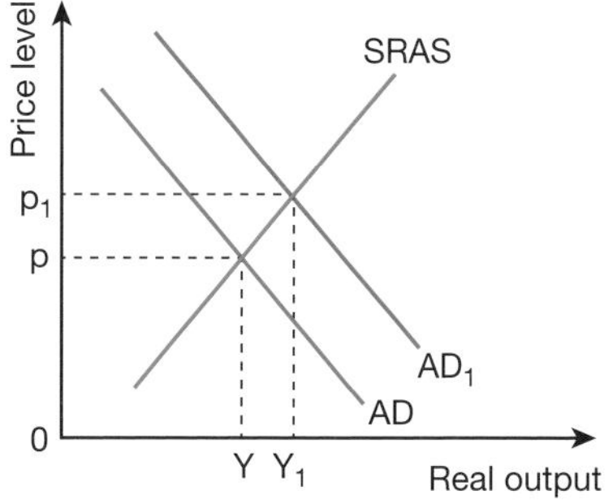

Figure 10.3 Increased economic growth, higher inflation, lower unemployment ▲

Relationship between economic growth, inflation and unemployment

As can be seen in Figure 10.3, an increase in AD, from AD to AD_1, has led, in the short run, to an increase in real output, indicating economic growth and more employment, from Y to Y_1, but inflation has risen from p to p_1.

The relationship, however, is more complex. If the government uses supply-side measures in the long run then as can be seen in Figure 10.4 it is possible to have economic growth, more employment/lower unemployment and a low level of inflation.

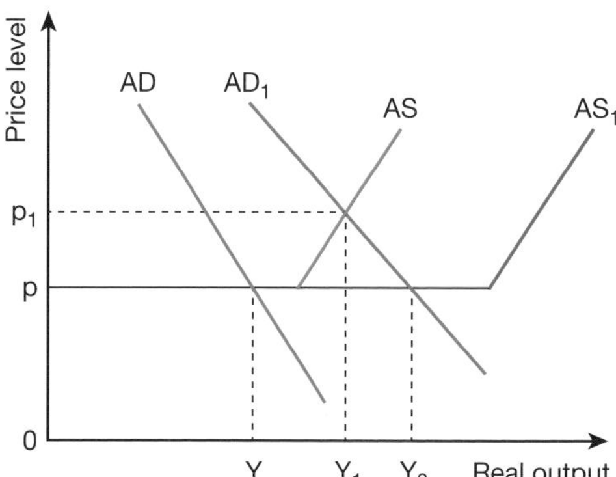

Figure 10.4 Supply-side policy effects on economic growth, unemployment and inflation ▶

Link

For more on economic growth see Chapter 9 page 248.

Link

For more on supply-side policies see Chapter 5 page 127.

In Figure 10.4 the increase in AD has the same effects as in Figure 10.3, but the introduction of supply-side policies shifts the AS curve from AS to AS_1. This results in further economic growth and employment from Y_1 to Y_2, while inflation falls from p_1 to p.

Effectiveness of policy options to meet all macroeconomic objectives

Problems arising from conflicts between policy objectives

Earlier in this chapter it was seen that conflicts could arise between different policy objectives including the trade-off in the short run between inflation and unemployment and the idea that in the long run there is no real effect on unemployment, but only on inflation. To review both this and the problems associated with economic growth, inflation and unemployment see above.

As can be seen in Table 10.1 various policies that could be used to control inflation are likely to have different consequences for both the balance of payments and the exchange rate.

Table 10.1 The effect that policies to control inflation have on the balance of payments and exchange rates ▼

Policy to control inflation	Effect on the balance of payments	Effect on exchange rates
Raise interest rates	Fall in demand for imports improves the current account of the balance of payments. Could lead to a rise in costs, making exports more expensive and worsening the current account.	"Hot money" inflow leading to a rise in the exchange rate. This is reinforced by the fall in imports so less domestic currency is supplied. This could make exports more expensive and imports cheaper.
Increase direct taxes	Fall in consumption and thus imports. The fall in domestic consumption could lead to unemployment and thus fewer domestic goods are produced leading to more imports and/or less exports.	Reduction in people's spending power means they buy less imports and travel abroad less. This means less of the currency is supplied, leading to a rise in the exchange rate which would make exports more expensive and imports cheaper.
Reduce the supply of money	Fall in consumption and thus imports. If imports are cheaper than domestic goods then there will be a fall in demand for domestic goods and more imports.	A reduction in the money supply will lead to a rise in interest rater leading to inflows of "hot money" and a rise in the exchange rate. This would make imports cheaper and exports more expensive.
Cut government expenditure	Government expenditure is part of aggregate demand (AD) so this would lead to a fall in AD. This should lead to a fall in imports. It might lead to a reduction in foreign investment which would lead to a fall in the financial account of the balance of payments.	This would be likely to lead to fewer imports and thus a rise in the value of the currency. If there is less demand for the currency then there would be a fall in its value which would make imports dearer, thus pushing up inflation.

NB: The ultimate effect on the current account of the balance of payments is dependent on the Marshall–Lerner condition.

As can be seen from Table 10.1, policies to deal with inflation will largely assist a balance of payments deficit, but can cause problems for other macroeconomic objectives, not just the exchange rate.

Activity

Effects of deflationary policies

Find out which policies your government has used to prevent inflation and what effect they have had on your country's balance of payments and exchange rates.

Case Study

Argentina in trouble

In 2013 estimates put inflation at 25 per cent, but unofficial forecasts for 2014 were in the region of 40 per cent. Inflation started increasing from 2010, prompting Argentines to spend instead of save, or to send their money abroad. Real wages fell by 10 per cent in the last four months of 2014.

In January 2011, the Argentine peso was devalued nearly 20 per cent, further diminishing purchasing power and making imported items more expensive. It is thought that the governmant may have stopped the exchange crisis with the devaluation and the raising of interest rates with the bank overnight rate rising from 12 per cent to 22 per cent in 2014, although it has since come down to 15 per cent.

1 Explain why Argentines, in recent years, have been spending rather than saving.
2 Explain what is meant by devaluing the currency by nearly 20 per cent.
3 Explain how devaluing the peso and raising interest rates could prevent further falls in the external value of the currency.
4 Discuss the problems that might be caused to the Argentine economy as a result of this devaluation.

Links

For more on taxation, poverty trap, transfer payments and benefits see Chapters 3 and 8.

For more on marginal propensity to consume see Chapter 9 page 277.

Redistribution

One objective so far not considered is the redistribution of income and wealth. Without government intervention it is probable that the rich will get richer and the poor will get poorer. To counteract this governments use fiscal policy such as progressive taxation in which money is taken from the rich and given in the form of public services and benefits to the poor. This can potentially lead to a number of clashes as, for example, increasing taxes may result in businesses being less willing to invest, leading to lower economic growth and higher unemployment. High marginal tax rates reduce income inequality, but may result in lower economic growth.

Redistribution should take from those with a lower marginal propensity to consume (MPC) and give to those with a higher MPC thus resulting in higher consumption and more employment, assuming that the goods bought are domestic and not imports.

Some economists argue, however, that giving more benefits to the poor only encourages unemployment for those whose wages would be only a little bit higher than benefits. These economists would rather see lower taxes and lower benefits to "price people back to work".

The effectiveness of these policies depends on:

- the availability of suitable jobs and their wage rate
- other supply-side policies, such as better education and training
- direct tax cuts not being offset by rises in indirect taxes some of which are regressive
- cultural attitudes to work.

Overall, it is important to remember that both fiscal and monetary policies take time to be fully implemented and effective, while supply-side policies are inevitably long run in their effect.

Links

For more on government failure and the market see Chapter 8 page 244.

For more on national minimum wage see Chapter 8 page 240.

Existence of government failure in macroeconomic policies

In the same way as government failure can cause market failure, it is possible to have government failure in the macro economy. Free market economists argue that attempts by the government to reduce income and wealth inequalities can actually worsen incentives and productivity in the economy. They would argue against the national minimum wage because they believe that it can lead to real-wage unemployment. They would also argue against raising the higher rates of income tax because it is deemed to have a negative effect on the incentives of wealth creators in the economy and generally acts as a disincentive to work longer hours or take a better-paid job. They are critical of the government focusing welfare benefits on the poorest because they might damage the incentive to find work.

Link

For more on Keynesian and monetarist schools see Chapter 9 page 289.

The opposite point of view is that a lack of effective government policies to reduce the scale of income and wealth inequality is also a cause of government failure since inequality can, over the longer term, create many deep-rooted problems for society once social cohesion starts to break down.

Professor Arthur Laffer ▲

In addition, there is once more the problem of information failure. Economic data is constantly revised as more information becomes available. It can mean that policy is being implemented which is wrong for what is actually happening in the economy. This can be compounded by the fact that policies take time to work their way through the economy, e.g. a change in interest rates is estimated to take around 18 months to be fully effective.

Economists cannot agree as to which policies are most effective to meet a certain objective. This, again, may lead to governments not choosing the best policy.

Laffer curve analysis

It is argued that high rates of direct tax act as a disincentive to people to work and firms to make profits. Lower rates would encourage more people to work especially if these were linked to lower unemployment benefits thus providing a real incentive to find jobs. Equally, lower taxes on firms would lead to them trying to be more efficient as they would keep more of their profits and could use these for investment. This idea is associated with Arthur Laffer. Lower income tax will act as an incentive for unemployed workers to join the labour market, or for existing workers to work harder. Lower corporation tax provides an incentive for entrepreneurs to start businesses and so increase national output.

Key term

Laffer curve: a curve indicating that as the income tax rate increases so, at first, does the tax revenue, but after some point higher tax rates will lead to a fall in tax revenue.

As can be seen in Figure 10.5 (the Laffer curve), as the tax rate increases tax revenue at first rises, but then after some point falls.

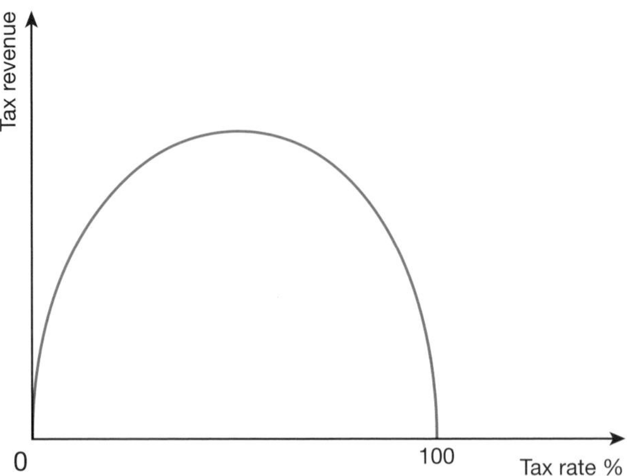

Figure 10.5 The Laffer curve ▲

Laffer first drew his curve in 1974 on a napkin in a Washington DC restaurant. He has pointed out that the idea was not new and goes back as far as Ibn Khaldun in 1377.

Key concepts

- **Scarcity and choice** can be seen in connection with the balance of payments and trade-offs and in policy conflicts where achieving one implies a choice over another.
- **The margin and change** can be seen in relation to decisions which improve one option but make the other worse.
- **Equilibrium and efficiency** can be seen in relation to equilibrium in the Phillips curve/NAIRU and in the section on the relationship between economic growth, inflation and unemployment.
- **Regulation and equity** is addressed in the section on redistribution.
- **Progress and development** can be seen in economic growth and development.

Progress check

After completing this chapter you should be able to:

- have knowledge of, and understand, government macroeconomic policy aims
- understand and explain the links between macroeconomic problems and their interrelatedness
- explain and evaluate the problems arising from conflicts between policy objectives
- understand that government failure can exist in macroeconomics
- explain the Laffer curve.

Exam-style questions

Essay questions

1 **a** Explain two aims of government macroeconomic policy. [12 marks]
b Discuss the problems which can arise if a government tries to achieve both aims. [13 marks]

2 **a** Explain the relationship between the internal and external value of money. [12 marks]
b Discuss the extent to which the control of inflation can cause problems for other macro policy aims. [13 marks]

3 **a** Explain the policy aims of a government with regard to inflation and unemployment. [12 marks]
b Discuss the view that the best way to control unemployment is to control inflation. [13 marks]

4 **a** Explain how government failure can occur in the national economy. [12 marks]
b Discuss whether income redistribution is likely to lead to lower levels of unemployment. [13 marks]

Multiple-choice questions

5 Which of the following is a probable economic effect of an increase in aggregate demand? [1 mark]

- **A** Aggregate supply will rise to meet aggregate demand
- **B** Income inequality will increase and tax rates fall
- **C** Inflation will rise and unemployment fall
- **D** National output will increase and imports fall

6 Which of the following would most likely result in a fall in the exchange rate? [1 mark]

- **A** Direct taxes are increased
- **B** Economic growth increases
- **C** There is an increase in exports
- **D** There is an inflow of capital

Index

N

O

P